RESEARCHING THE TROUBLES

RESEARCHING THE TROUBLES

Social Science Perspectives on the
Northern Ireland Conflict

Edited by Owen Hargie and David Dickson

MAINSTREAM
PUBLISHING

EDINBURGH AND LONDON

ACKNOWLEDGEMENTS

This book would not have been possible without the financial assistance provided by the Office of First Minister and Deputy First Minister (OFMDFM) Equality Unit – Research Branch. We are grateful to them for their support in this respect. We would particularly like to acknowledge Dennis McCoy, who recognised the importance of this text from the outset. Thanks also to the Head of the School of Communication at UUJ, Rosalind Gray. As several projects came together at the same time and our stress levels rose, Rosalind provided both personal understanding and offers of practical assistance that were greatly appreciated. The book could not, of course, have existed without all the contributors who answered our requests and met our deadlines with great goodwill. A special word of thanks is given to the editorial team at Mainstream, for all their help, support and expertise. We also want to give a particular mention to our friend and colleague, Professor David Bamford, who was always there with an ever-listening ear, plus words of encouragement and empathy whenever the going got rough. Finally, we are indebted to our families who provided the necessary motivation and love to sustain us throughout the production of this text.

For:
Our late fathers, Ernest and John. They gave us much, but always in that
understated manner so typical of North Antrim men of their generation.

First published in Great Britain in 2003 by
MAINSTREAM PUBLISHING (EDINBURGH) LTD
7 Albany Street
Edinburgh EH1 3UG

ISBN 1 84018 841 3

A catalogue record for this book is available from the British Library

Typeset in Stone

Printed in Great Britain by
Creative Print and Design Wales

CONTENTS

CONTRIBUTORS

Dr Fiona Bloomer is Senior Research Officer with the Department of Culture, Arts and Leisure, Northern Ireland.

John D. Brewer, FRSA, is Professor of Sociology at The Queen's University of Belfast.

Ed Cairns is Professor in the School of Psychology, University of Ulster.

Dr Paul Connolly is Senior Lecturer in the School of Sociology and Applied Social Studies, University of Ulster.

John Darby is Professor of Comparative Ethnic Studies at the Joan B. Kroc Institute for International Peace Studies, University of Notre Dame, New York.

Dr David Dickson is Senior Lecturer in the School of Communication, University of Ulster.

Karin Eyben is Research Officer in the School of History and International Affairs, University of Ulster.

Tony Gallagher is Professor in the Graduate School of Education at The Queen's University of Belfast.

Cathy Gormley-Heenan is Research Development Officer at the Community Relations Council, Belfast.

Owen Hargie is Professor in the School of Communication, University of Ulster, and Adjunct Professor at the Norwegian University of Science and Technology.

Julie Healy is Policy & Research Officer in Barnardo's Northern Ireland.

Dr Miles Hewstone is Lecturer in the School of Experimental Psychology, University of Oxford.

Gareth I. Higgins has a PhD from The Queen's University of Belfast and is a freelance researcher.

Dr Jennifer Hamilton is Acting Deputy Chief Executive of the Institute for Conflict Research in Belfast.

Neil Jarman is Deputy Chief Executive at the Institute for Conflict Research, Belfast.

Roger MacGinty is Lecturer in Postwar Recovery Studies at the Department of Politics, University of York.

Dr Valerie Morgan is Professor in the School of History and International Affairs, University of Ulster.

Dr Duncan Morrow is Lecturer in Politics in the University of Ulster and Co-Director of the Future Ways Project.

Dr Brendan Murtagh is Reader in the School of Environmental Planning at The Queen's University of Belfast.

Seanenne Nelson is Research Officer in the School of Communication, University of Ulster.

Dr Ulrike Niens is Research & Development Officer with the Peace & Reconciliation Group, Londonderry/Derry.

Dr Gillian Robinson is Senior Lecturer in the School of Policy Studies, University of Ulster.

Dr Marie Smyth, School of Policy Studies University of Ulster, is Chief Executive of the Institute for Conflict Research, Belfast.

Peter Weinreich is Professor in the School of Psychology, University of Ulster.

Dr Derick Wilson is Senior Lecturer in the School of Policy Studies, University of Ulster.

PREFACE

For eight years, beginning in April of 1992, I had the privilege of heading up the research arm of the Central Community Relations Unit (CCRU) (later the Community Relations Unit, CRU). During that period, the Unit funded upwards of 50 research projects, many of which produced outputs that have become seminal works in the fields of community relations and community conflict.

A brief history of CCRU and its research funding would note that the first research budget was established in 1989 to meet research and information needs in community relations. In 1991, CCRU issued its first Research Strategy document, detailing the general framework and priority themes that CCRU wished to set for funding research in community relations. Revised and updated research strategies appeared in 1994 and 1997, each being developed in consultation with policy makers and key members of the research community and each marking a refinement of the link between research and policy need. The overall aim as stated in the 1997 strategy best sums up what we were trying to achieve in research throughout the period of the 1990s: 'to stimulate and promote a wide range of research which will enable policy makers, community relations practitioners, academics and the general public to achieve a better understanding of all aspects of community relations and community conflict in Northern Ireland.'

Initially, the funding for community relations research came entirely from central government in the form of public expenditure grant. From 1994 onwards, however, we were successful in convincing the European Union that research into community relations and community conflict was important enough to establish further grant making capacity and, from that point and until the emergence of the new Structural Funds in 2000, funding under the CCRU Research Strategy was also available from the EU's Physical and Social Environment Programme.

From the outset, we knew that the development of strong links and good working relationships with research and academic institutions in Northern Ireland would be crucial to the success of CCRU's research strategy and to the development of the broader community relations research portfolio. As a result, the Centre for the Study of Conflict, at the University of Ulster in Coleraine, played a key role in much of the research that CCRU funded. Many of the authors in this book have worked there on CCRU-supported projects at some time and, for a period during the 1990s, CCRU also funded a dedicated Research Officer post at the Centre. The

Initiative on Conflict Resolution and Ethnicity (INCORE) has also played a key role in research into community relations and community conflict and CCRU and EU funding were made available to INCORE to help it become established. A continuing relationship with INCORE allowed CCRU to fund a number of significant individual research projects and to support the development of the much used research resource, the CAIN website.

At Queen's University, CCRU put a great deal of effort into developing its links with the Centre for Social Research and funded a number of its research projects including the important early work on the Northern Ireland Social Attitudes surveys. Finally, but by no means least, the Northern Ireland Statistics and Research Agency played a key role in developing the research portfolio and its Chief Executive chaired the CCRU research funding group.

Of course, all this was happening during a decade in which we saw paramilitary ceasefires as well as an unprecedented level of political development that resulted in the Good Friday/Belfast Agreement and subsequent devolution. On the legislative front, we saw new developments on equality and human rights, a greater focus on social inclusion and a relaunching of the government's anti-deprivation policy, (New) Targeting Social Need. Yet, whilst many would agree that these were positive developments, the decade also witnessed the emergence of new stages on which inter-communal conflict was played out. The fields around Drumcree and the streets of North Belfast bear witness to the work that remains to be done if we are ever to establish a truly peaceful and harmonious society in Northern Ireland. And research will need to play its part in that work.

In an environment where there is a greater than ever emphasis on the links between objectives and outcomes, policy and programme development need more than ever to be evidence based and project work needs to be embedded in the very best of good practice. The research challenges for the next decade are, therefore, no less daunting than they were in the period of the 1990s. That we have grown the research capabilities that we have, that we have developed the cadre of researchers that are now working in the field, many of whom are represented in this volume, that we have established unequivocally the value of good and timely research, these are the things that will stand us in good stead in meeting the challenges of the future.

During those eight years as Head of Research at CCRU and then CRU, I was ably supported by a team that was rarely content to take a back seat, that prided itself in being 'hands on' in many of the projects to which we supplied funding and that worked hard to add value to the research with which we were involved. At a professional level, this approach allowed me the opportunity to become more closely involved in the creation, development and outworking of research than I ever had a right to expect. At a personal level, it allowed me to establish valued friendships in a research community for which I have the greatest admiration and regard. This book brings together some of the best of that research and, if the whole is even equal to the sum of the parts, then this volume should, in itself, become an important and influential work.

Dennis McCoy

EDITORIAL INTRODUCTION

The genesis of this book can be traced back to a conference on 'Research and Community Relations in Northern Ireland' organised by the then Central Community Relations Unit (CCRU), which took place in 1999. This was a forum for the presentation of projects funded by CCRU, including one of our own. As we listened to the different presentations, we were struck by the wealth of material that had been produced. After the conference we contacted the then Head of Research at CCRU, Dennis McCoy, with the idea of bringing this material together in book form. Dennis was very enthusiastic about the idea and so it found wings. We reviewed the research projects that had been funded over the past decade, and decided upon the key ones for inclusion in this text. After these decisions had been taken, changes in government and in related departmental structures resulted in responsibility for this area being transferred to the Office of First Minister and Deputy First Minister (OFMDFM) Equality Unit – Research Branch, with whom we then liaised as the fledgling book took off.

At this point it is useful to say a little about why we felt that the project was necessary. A metaphorical fault line crosses Northern Ireland, running through most, if not all, of the major institutions, including, inter alia, sport, education, and work, and separating two communities each with quite distinct politico-religious identities. Indeed, at times the social and psychological barriers transmogrify into actual physical 'peace walls'. On one side is a Nationalist/Catholic community, which seeks unity with the Republic of Ireland and separation from the United Kingdom. On the other is a Unionist/Protestant community, which has the diametrically opposite perspective of supporting the link with the rest of the United Kingdom and opposing unity with the Republic of Ireland.

Northern Ireland has been described as 'one of the most deeply divided countries in the world and one of the most violent' (Greer, 1985: 275). While the violence has decreased considerably over the past few years, the divisions remain, and arguably have worsened. Post-1996, levels of tolerance and respect for diversity have decreased. Segregation of the two main communities continues, with some 70% of publicly owned housing estates comprising 90% mono-religious neighbourhoods. Symbols of division, such as sectarian graffiti and flags, are becoming more rather than less common (OFMDFM, 2001). According to the latter report:

> the evidence reviewed . . . does not suggest that significant progress has been made towards a more tolerant or inclusive society . . . Despite some positive evidence . . . the amount of sharing in our society in education, housing and personal relationships remains limited . . . and measures of crime suggest increasing levels of sectarian violence.

For over 30 years the seemingly irreconcilable divisions between the two groups spawned a great deal of often quite horrific violence and a total of over 3,700 deaths. To put this in perspective, pro rata it would be the equivalent of some 115,000 fatalities in the UK as a whole, or 600,000 in the USA, over the past 3 decades. The toll of injuries is obviously much higher. Given this scale of human suffering, it is imperative that we carry out systematic research to understand how and why such conflict occurs, and attempt to formulate informed ways in which it can be addressed.

The group differences in Northern Ireland have resulted in the Troubles attracting a considerable amount of research. While a great deal of this has been carried out by social scientists it has often been reported in isolation, and frequently in academic journals, which, while prestigious, have a limited and highly specialised target audience. This edited book was therefore designed to bring together for the first time, and make more widely accessible, 14 of the most prestigious research themes into cross-community conflict and reconciliation, funded by the CCRU. These have been conducted from within a range of social science disciplines including Communication, Human Geography, Politics, Psychology, Social Policy, and Sociology. The contributors are all well-known academics from across this broad spectrum of the social sciences. They represent the full gamut of methodologies and paradigms, from broad-brush total landscape scenes of the wider societal picture, to detailed in-depth examination of actual patterns of interpersonal contact across the divide.

Each chapter reflects research, theory and practice within the contributor's field of enquiry; crystallises the core import of their work in illuminating the Northern Ireland situation; and draws wider implications for an understanding of social conflict and conflict resolution processes. The book is therefore based upon the solid bedrock of actual empirical investigation. The lessons learned from each study are applicable across a wide range of contexts where there exists internecine strife and inter-communal conflict. Equally, the results of the research investigations have, in turn, informed a range of social science concepts and theories. The outcomes from the studies provide a breadth and depth of insight into the reasons for, effects of, and possible ways out of, cross-community conflict. As such, we anticipate that this text will be of interest to social scientists per se, to all those who study conflict resolution, to politicians and policy makers, as well as to the interested general reader.

The book is divided into 15 chapters. In Chapter 1, Smith and Hamilton provide stark details of the human costs of the Troubles. They also explore the historical treatment of victims, and discuss the concept of 'victimhood' and all its ramifications. In Chapter 2, we move to the early beginnings of personal awareness of the Troubles. Here, Connolly and Healy investigate the attitudes of children from the age of three years, as they interpret events around them and express their views about the Troubles. Staying with the education theme in Chapter 3, Gallagher then presents an analysis of issues surrounding education and equality. The education system in Northern Ireland is briefly overviewed as a contextual backdrop to providing a detailed examination of comparative attainments of Catholic and Protestant children at school.

Staying with education, in Chapter 4, Hargie et al. move beyond school to an examination of cross-community communication and contact in the university setting. Their study, which is centred in the area of relational communication, includes a comparison of Catholic and Protestant scores on self-report measures, an analysis of actual one-to-one interactions between students, and the findings from focus group interviews. This is followed in Chapter 5 by an analysis of the roots of sectarianism per se. Here, Higgins and Brewer offer a conceptual analysis of sectarianism as occurring at ideational, behavioural and social structural levels. They go on to probe the papal antichrist myth as a basis for Protestant sectarianism. In Chapter 6, Niens et al. present a comprehensive analysis of the impact of contact upon inter-group attitudes, and describe research they have carried out to chart the main variables in this domain, including inter-group anxiety. The issue of contact is pursued by Bloomer and Weinreich in Chapter 7. They report the results of a study designed to assess the impact of cross-community contact projects upon participants. This investigation measures changes in a number of identity indices, and discusses policy implications for this type of work.

In Chapter 8, Morrow et al. also examine issues of the scale and scope of community relations, but from a wider backdrop. They address this from the perspective of first principles by exploring in detail what it actually means to engage in community relations, and whose responsibility it is so to do. One of their conclusions is that organisations must be involved in this type of work, and this theme is further developed in Chapter 9, where Dickson et al. report the results of a study into cross-community contact in the workplace. Using a variety of data-gathering methods they produce an in-depth examination of the state of cross-community organisational communication. Murtagh, in Chapter 10, moves to the wider community context of residential segregation. He explores the nature of such segregation in Northern Ireland, its significance in the construction of identities, and the challenge it poses to those tasked with planning and regional development. The chapter moves on to articulate the salient policy issues around land use planning and the research policy disjunction in addressing ethnic geography.

Also in relation to actual events in the community, Jarman in Chapter 11 gives a fascinating insight into the situation in North Belfast, an area that has been at the fulcrum of conflict and violence throughout the Troubles. Any proposed resolution to the conflict will face its acid test in areas such as this. Jarman highlights key lessons to be learned from the cutting-edge experiences in this part of the city, examining instances of effective and ineffective interventions. In Chapter 12, Morgan reviews the contribution of women to community development over the past 30 years of community conflict and how that contribution has followed trajectories in Catholic and Protestant communities. Political leadership is the central thrust of Chapter 13. Here, Gormley-Heenan and Robinson offer intriguing insights into the processes through which those same party leaders who were implacable opposed in the 1970s and 1980s, came to reach political agreement in the 1990s. The relationship between leaders and those who give them their support is also taken up by Darby and MacGinty in the following chapter. Adopting a comparative perspective, they unpack six key themes seen as common to peace processes in general.

In the final chapter, as editors, we have endeavoured to pull together the main themes emerging from all of the research reported in this book. This was a difficult task, as the breadth and scale of social science perspectives often make comparisons difficult. However, from all of the disparate, yet related, studies we have identified key, recurring themes, which we believe should inform not only any study of the Northern Ireland Troubles, but also other similar conflicts throughout the world. There are central lessons to be learned, which, if taken on board by policy makers, will make a real difference to the lives of those people whom as social scientists it is our professional raison d'être to study.

Owen Hargie and
David Dickson

1. THE HUMAN COSTS OF THE TROUBLES

Marie Smyth and Jennifer Hamilton

INTRODUCTION

When the ceasefires of 1994 occurred, little systematic attention had been given to those who had paid the heaviest price during the course of Northern Ireland's Troubles – those bereaved and/or injured. Media coverage constitutes the most significant source of public information on such issues, and that had been focused on the event itself, its immediate aftermath, the funerals, the condemnations and accusations. Some events where there had been multiple deaths, such as the La Mon House bomb or the Enniskillen bomb, were grievous punctuations in the collective memory of the Troubles. Those bereaved or injured by incidents occurring on the same day as a major event that caused multiple casualties were often ignored, and some such deaths received no media coverage whatsoever. Others, such as the victims of miscarriages of justice, had had sporadic attention in the wake of the Guildford and Birmingham bomb inquiries, where it was revealed that the wrong people had been imprisoned. Typically, attention was given to those affected in the immediate aftermath of an event, but longer-term impacts were largely unexplored.

One of the common responses to the ceasefires of 1994 was a strong sense of the wastage of human lives that the Troubles had entailed. Some public figures and community leaders began to articulate the feeling that the ceasefires were 'too late' for many of those who had lost their lives or family members. This articulation, together with an emerging movement composed of those bereaved and injured led to the political realisation on the part of the government that attending to the wounds of the past was a necessary part of building support for peace. An emerging sense of the moral obligation of society to those who had suffered most underpinned the making of such provision. Yet provision for victims was also essential if the sense of grievance and anger – that clearly held the potential to ultimately derail the peace process itself – was to be defused. It is possible to chart the level of government sensitivity to victims' issues at key moments in the peace process according to other political developments. Concessions to prisoners for example had to be accompanied – or counterbalanced in the eyes of some – by provision for the needs of those who had been bereaved or injured, in order to maintain the moral balance and defuse or pre-empt the grievance and anger of, or on behalf of, victims.

Thus it was in November 1997 that the British government appointed Sir Kenneth Bloomfield as Victims' Commissioner. The Irish government, which had already held two hearings on victims in 1996, as part of their Forum for Peace and Reconciliation, followed the appointment of Sir Kenneth Bloomfield by that of former Tániste John Wilson to an equivalent post in 1998. Both Victims' Commissions published reports. Around this time, the Victims Liaison Unit was established within the Northern Ireland Office, to work specifically on victims' issues, and to provide a direct link between government and victims' groups. The British government subsequently reviewed the Criminal Injuries Compensation provision within Northern Ireland, whereby those bereaved or injured in the Troubles could claim financial compensation. With the establishment of the Northern Ireland Assembly in 2000, the Office of the First Minister and Deputy First Minister was handed responsibility for issues relating to victims within the Assembly remit. The Northern Ireland Office (NIO) Victims' Liaison Unit (VLU) retained overall financial control, and responsibility for all matters within the NIO brief, namely security, policing and compensation.

During this period, when the impact of the Troubles appeared for the first time as an issue within the portfolios of politicians and their civil servants, there was a steep learning curve. The whole-scale policy silence within public policy in Northern Ireland had meant that health, social services, education and other public services operated on policy largely derived from their English equivalents. Much policy had been based on the approach that characterised the political management of the Troubles, namely that the violence was criminal violence, and could be understood and handled within the terms of the criminal justice system suitably amended to take account of 'local' Northern Ireland idiosyncrasies. At the beginning of the peace process, therefore, the Troubles were not factored into public policy, nor was there a policy language or conceptual framework that could facilitate such an incorporation.

In this early phase of the development of victims' policy and provision in Northern Ireland, there had been attempts to learn from the experience of other societies, notably South Africa. Much interest centred on the Truth and Reconciliation Commission in South Africa, in the hunger for new solutions and methods to deal with the effects of the Troubles in Northern Ireland. Politicians, activists, professionals and civil servants travelled to South Africa in an attempt to inform developments at home. However, much of the provision had to be delivered quickly in the interests of demonstrating a humanitarian aspect to the peace process. Circumstances dictated that provision had to be immediate, and this led to a lack of co-ordination and long-term planning in new provision. This, together with a proliferation of short-term funding initiatives, led to a piecemeal set of provisions that were often demand driven, and lacking a systematic and transparent system of targeting need. The public service agencies, subsisting on meagre diets of public funding and ill-equipped by the policy vacuums characteristic of past approaches to the Troubles, had been badly placed to participate in this new development, so much of the new provision was located in the voluntary sector.

POLITICISATION

A further obstacle to a consensual overview of the situation of those who have suffered Troubles-related losses lay in the increasing politicisation of the issue in the public domain. The formation of the early cross-community initiatives for victims, such as WAVE or 'The Cost of the Troubles Study' was overtaken by the proliferation of competing groups. Some, mostly from within the Protestant community claimed the status of 'innocent' victims, implying that others who had suffered were less than innocent. Within the Catholic community, political disquiet on the issue focused on anxiety that victims of state violence should be included in all consideration and provision.

The halting nature of political progress in the peace process was, perhaps, both a product of and a factor in these developments. Unionist frustration about the failure of the Irish Republican Army (IRA) to decommission was matched by Nationalist anger at the perceived failure to implement the terms of the Good Friday Agreement on issues such as policing and the delays in establishing an Assembly. After the resignation of the Deputy First Minister, Seamus Mallon, the Ulster Unionist leader and First Minister of the Assembly, David Trimble, balked at the prospect of further implementation on the grounds that the IRA ceasefire was not secure. Media coverage of continuing paramilitary punishment attacks offered evidence for his scepticism about Sinn Fein's intentions. Families Against Intimidation and Terror (FAIT), a victims' group financed by government victims funding, publicised such paramilitary punishment attacks, thus providing evidence to support Trimble's position.

The tense atmosphere of that time was encapsulated in the campaign for 'Protestant civil rights' in the form of a 'Long March'. This campaign involved some of the newly formed victims groups. FAIR (Families Acting for Innocent Relatives) and Fear, Encourage, Abandon, Roots (FEAR), among others, came together under the umbrella organisation Northern Ireland Victims of Terrorist Violence (NIVTV). NIVTV's demands included: a declaration by the IRA that the war is over; decommissioning including ballistic testing of weapons; destruction of paramilitary weapons; disbandment of terrorist groups; and an international tribunal to investigate the role of the Irish government in the development of the Provisional IRA. Anti-Agreement politicians, the Democratic Unionist Party (DUP) and the anti-Agreement cohort from within Ulster Unionist Party (UUP), marched with the victims' groups. They were joined by one or two unlikely supporters, such as Nell McCafferty, of 1960s' Northern Ireland Civil Rights Association fame. Media coverage on the public expenditure on provision for the resettlement of prisoners ('Outrage shock costs of giving prisoners new lease of life': *Belfast Telegraph*, 4 June 1999) added fuel to the flames of political controversy, and victims' groups were at the centre of such controversy.

However, the groups themselves were not without division and controversy. Subsequently, FAIT was closed down, dogged by allegations of financial irregularities, and one man who had provided some of the controversial evidence on punishment beatings was imprisoned for child sexual abuse. Other groups had similar experiences. Chaos, bitterness, in-fighting and sectarian contest quickly marked the emergence of an organised victims' sector.

Like many aspects of the Northern Ireland conflict, the task of assessing the human damage is performed against a backdrop of political contest and a comprehensive lack of an agreed framework within which to view that damage, and in an atmosphere of ongoing political contest. The subjectivity and loyalties of the researcher place an inevitable gloss on many analyses of the impact of Northern Ireland's Troubles. In the pursuit of a framework that could offer a transparent, comprehensive and graded picture of the human costs of the Troubles, researchers working on the Cost of the Troubles Study chose to chart the patterns of human damage by examining patterns of deaths due to the Troubles. They compiled a detailed database of deaths in the Troubles from 1969 onwards. A more detailed account of the compilation of this database is contained in Fay et al. (1999). Death is a fairly unequivocal concept, and counting and analysing deaths that occurred in the Troubles affords an overview of the pattern of impact. Furthermore, statistical work demonstrates that the distribution of deaths can be used as a fairly reliable indicator of other effects such as injuries in the Troubles.

ANALYSIS OF DEATHS IN THE TROUBLES

TOTALS KILLED AND INJURED

The core analysis for this chapter is derived from a comprehensive database of political deaths between 1969 and September 2001. While death depicts the most extreme consequence of the conflict, it is also a good surrogate for the other effects of the Troubles, such as injury. A comparison of the number of deaths each year and the number of injuries associated with political violence shows a correlation coefficient of 0.93. Injuries outnumber deaths by just over ten to one but have exactly the same cycle. Whilst the combination of deaths and injuries represents the primary human cost of the Troubles, these do not encompass the trauma of grief, imprisonment and intimidation. Nevertheless, the distribution of deaths can illuminate the patterns and distribution of the overall himan costs of the Troubles.

The distribution of political deaths from 1969 until September 2001 in Northern Ireland is shown in Figure 1.1.

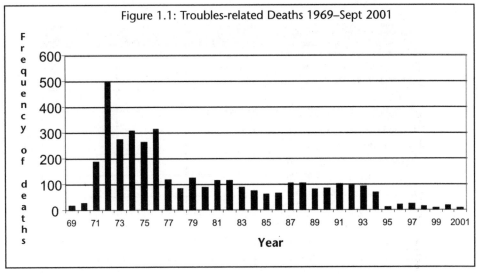

Figure 1.1: Troubles-related Deaths 1969–Sept 2001

Just over half of all the deaths occurred in the period 1971–76. If the frequency of deaths can be regarded as a good indicator of the intensity of the conflict, then these five years stand out as having seen the most intense violence in the entire period of the Troubles. In total over 3,700 people have been killed as a result of Northern Ireland's Troubles, and these deaths have occurred in Northern Ireland, the Republic of Ireland, England, Germany and elsewhere.

In addition to deaths due to the Troubles, it has been estimated that over 40,000 people have been injured throughout the period of the Troubles. However, since this figure is derived from police records, it is likely that the total number of injuries is higher, due to some injuries not being reported or recorded by the police. Table 1.1 depicts the Royal Ulster Constabulary figures for injuries due to the Troubles in the period 1971 to 1996 by the status of the injured person. Civilian injuries account for 68% of all injuries due to the Troubles, illustrating how civilians have borne the largest share of injuries as well as the largest share of deaths.

GENDER

The victims of the Troubles have been overwhelmingly male, with 3,279 males being killed (91.1%) compared to 322 females (8.9%). Thus, men have been the most direct victims of the conflict in terms of the numbers killed. However, it is clear that whilst women may not be killed or injured in equivalent number to men, women's experience of the Troubles has been comprised of absorbing and coping with the consequences in other ways: in visiting the prisons; standing at gravesides; or rearing children alone. Women's and men's suffering have been different and the more indirect effects experienced by women are not revealed in the data on deaths. Men and women both died in substantially greater numbers in the most intensive period of 1971–76. This accounted for 63.3% of all female and 59.9% of all male deaths.

Table 1.1 Injuries due to the Troubles by Status of Injured Person: 1971–96

YEAR	RUC	ARMY	UDR/RIR	CIVILIAN	CIVILIAN %
1971	315	381	9	1887	73
1972	485	542	36	3813	78
1973	291	525	23	1812	68
1974	235	453	30	1680	70
1975	263	151	16	2044	83
1976	303	242	22	2162	79
1977	183	172	15	1017	73
1978	302	127	8	548	56
1979	166	132	21	557	64
1980	194	53	24	530	66
1981	332	112	28	878	65
1982	99	80	18	328	62
1983	142	66	22	280	55
1984	267	64	22	513	59
1985	415	20	13	468	51
1986	622	45	10	773	53
1987	246	92	12	780	69
1988	218	211	18	600	57
1989	163	175	15	606	63
1990	214	190	24	478	53
1991	139	197	56	570	59
1992	148	302	18	598	56
1993	147	146	27	504	61
1994	170	120	6	529	64
1995	370	8	5	554	59
1996	459	53	1	896	64
Total	6888	4659	499	25405	
% of Grand Total	18	12	1	68	

Source: Northern Ireland Office

AGE

In terms of age, the victims are undoubtedly skewed towards the younger age groups as Figure 1.2 illustrates. The highest death rate for any age group is for 20–24-year-olds with this age group accounting for 20.2% of all deaths in the Troubles.

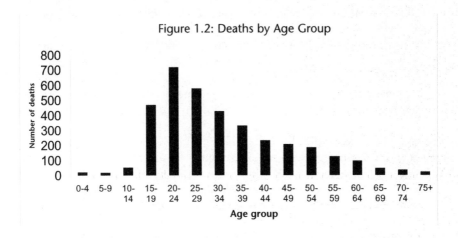

Figure 1.2: Deaths by Age Group

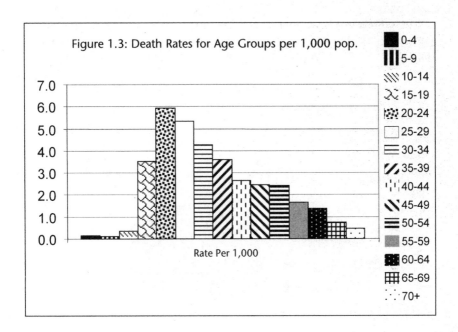

Figure 1.3: Death Rates for Age Groups per 1,000 pop.

Indeed, more than a third of victims were in their twenties. More than half were in their 20s or 30s. Nor were the very young spared – 1 in 6 victims was aged 19 or less. This can be plainly seen if death rates for each age group are calculated by comparing the ages of those in the database with the age distribution of the general population (Figure 1.3). Since the Troubles lasted over 30 years, the population groups were constructed by taking the average figure for each age group from the 1971, 1981 and 1991 censuses. This is a constructed rather than a real population, but this is aimed at overcoming the problem of calculating rates based on a single census, when the Troubles lasted over the period of three censuses.

Even allowing for the differential numbers in the specified age groups among the population, the concentration of deaths remains in the younger age groups – 15–19, 20–24, 25–29, 30–34 and 35–39. Comparatively, the death risk to the 20–24 age group was more than twice as high as any group over 40 and 40% greater than for anyone over 30.

WHO WAS RESPONSIBLE?

Paramilitary organisations in general accounted for just 80% of the deaths and more than half was the responsibility of Republican paramilitaries (2,001 deaths, 55.7%). For each of their own members who died, Republican paramilitaries killed 5.5 other individuals. On the same basis, Loyalist paramilitaries killed 8.5 people for each of their members' deaths with 27.4% (983) of deaths carried out by Loyalists. The security forces in general are responsible for 10.7% of all deaths in the Troubles. Figure 1.4 shows the number of deaths for which each organisation was responsible.

The categories of Republican and Loyalist paramilitaries each subsume a number of distinct paramilitary organisations. Within the Republican grouping, the IRA (formerly the Provisional IRA) was responsible for the greatest number of

Figure 1.4: Responsibility by Numbers of Troubles Deaths

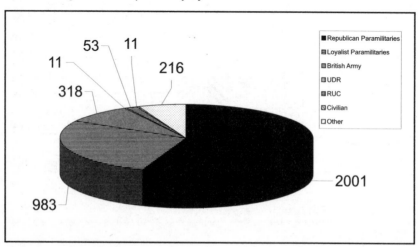

deaths (1,684 or 85% of those attributed to Republican paramilitaries). The numbers killed by other Republican organisations were substantially fewer. For example, the various factions and paramilitary groupings associated with the Irish National Liberation Army (INLA) accounted for 127 deaths. In the construction of the database, it was not possible due to limitations in source material to precisely distribute the deaths caused by Loyalist paramilitaries among the various organisations involved. Thus, 449 deaths were simply attributed to Loyalist organisations in general. Of the cases where the organisation responsible for the death was identifiable, 254 were attributed to the Ulster Volunteer Force (UVF) and 177 to the Ulster Freedom Fighters (UFF). Overall, however, the IRA stands out as having made the largest contribution to the deaths' total.

Since the Troubles in Northern Ireland is composed of contests in defence or opposition to the presence of the British State, religion and identity, we will examine how these variables manifest in the distribution of deaths. Table 1.2 shows the breakdown of deaths in the Troubles by religion and by organisations responsible for the deaths.

Table 1.2: Deaths by Religion and by Organisation Responsible

Organisation Responsible	Don't Know	%	Protestant	%	Catholic	%	NNI	%
Republican Paramilitaries	278	83.5	745	70.0	381	24.7	597	91.4
Loyalist Paramilitaries	25	7.5	207	19.5	735	47.6	16	2.5
British Army	4	1.2	32	3.0	266	17.2	16	2.5
UDR			4	0.4	7	0.5		
RUC	1	0.3	7	0.7	43	2.8	2	0.3
Civilian			9	0.8	2	0.1		
Other	25	7.5	60	5.6	109	7.1	22	3.4
Total	333	100	1064	100	1543	100	653	100

Republican paramilitaries are responsible for 70% of all Protestant deaths and 24.7% of Catholic deaths. The latter figure can be explained by the Republican bombing campaign, particularly in city centres, where casualties are more random than targeted. Loyalist paramilitaries are responsible for 19.5% of all Protestant deaths and 47.6% of all Catholic deaths. If the organisations responsible are cross-tabulated with the political status of victims (Table 1.3), then it would appear that Republican paramilitaries have made a significant contribution (46% or 164 deaths) to the total number of deaths suffered by Republicans.

Thus, the extent to which killings took place *within* communities as well as *between* communities emerges. Feuds and the punishment of informers have led to deaths within communities. Indeed, such deaths seem to account for the largest share of deaths among Republican paramilitaries. Comparatively, the British Army has been responsible for 33% of deaths (117 deaths) among these groups. At the same time, Republican paramilitaries have accounted for almost all the deaths of security forces (1,070). For each organisation responsible, the biggest single category of victim has been civilians.

Table 1.3: Political Status of Victims by Organisations Responsible for Deaths

Organisation Responsible	Repub. Para. deaths	Loyal. Para. deaths	Ex Repub. Para. deaths	Ex Loyal. Para. deaths	Security (NI) deaths	Security (NnI) deaths	Civilian deaths	Other deaths
Republican Paramilitaries	164 46%	31 26%			508 95%	562 95%	713 37%	23 35%
Loyalist Paramilitaries	26 7%	65 56%	3 75%	32 100%	12 2%	3 0.5%	858 45%	14 21.5%
British Army	117 33%	10 8.5%			5 0.9%	14 2%	168 9%	4 6%
UDR	2 33%						9 0.5%	
RUC	16 4.5%	3 2.5%			1 0.2%	2 0.3%	31 1.5%	4 6%
Civilian		1 0.9%					9 0.5%	1 1.5%
Other	30 33%	7 8.5%	1 25%		10 1.9%	12 2%	133 7%	23 35%
Total	355 100%	117 100%	4 100%	2 100%	536 100%	593 100%	1921 100%	65 100%

RELIGION

The religious breakdown of those killed is illustrated in Figure 1.5 and addresses the competing sense of grievance and victimhood between the two communities in Northern Ireland. The absolute numbers show that more Catholics than Protestants have died. The smaller proportion of Catholics in the general population suggests a significantly higher death risk for this religion.

However, the database on which the analysis is based contains a very high proportion of 'not known' religious affiliation among local security deaths. In Table 1.4, this problem is addressed. It is known that the local security forces are 92% Protestant, and this fraction can be used to redistribute the 'not known' deaths between the two religious groups. Secondly, a comparison of death rates

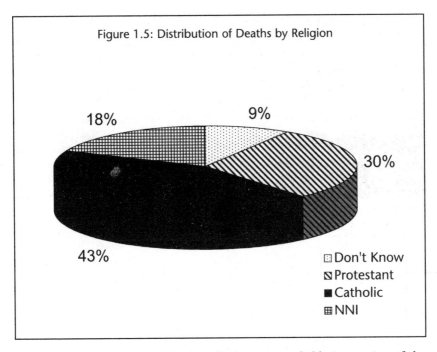

Figure 1.5: Distribution of Deaths by Religion

18%   9%

30%

43%   ▦ Don't Know
       ◩ Protestant
       ■ Catholic
       ▦ NNI

rather than raw numbers of deaths affords a more reliable impression of the relative impact of deaths in the respective Catholic and Protestant communities. However, the deaths occurred over a 30-year period in which the religious composition of the population shifted, and this has to be taken into account in calculating death rates.

Table 1.4: Death Rates per 1,000 between the Main Religions

	PROTESTANT	CATHOLIC
Rate (91 base)	1.49	2.55
Weighted Rate (91 base)	1.92	2.60
Weighted Rate 69–76 (71 Base)	0.69	1.88
Weighted Rate 77–86 (81 Base)	1.35	0.73
Weighted Rate 87–98 (91 Base)	0.42	0.61

Redistributing the 'not known' deaths and taking into account the changes in the relative sizes of the Catholic and Protestant populations over the time period involved led to the production of three death rates for Protestants and Catholics. The first rate, calculated on the 1991 census data, showed a death rate for Protestants of 1.49 per thousand population and 2.55 per thousand for Catholics. This rate was recalculated, with the 92% of the 'not known' deaths redistributed into the 'Protestant' category. This gives a rate of 1.92 per thousand for Protestants and 2.60 per thousand for Catholics. However, the relative proportions of Catholics and Protestants in the population changed over the period of the Troubles, so three other rates were calculated. Deaths in the period 1969–76 were used on the base of the 1971 census, and this gave a Protestant death rate of 0.69 per thousand and a Catholic rate of 1.88 per thousand. A similar exercise for 1977–86 using the 1981 census data produced a rate of 1.35 per thousand for Protestants and 0.73 for Catholics and the calculation for 1987–98 using the 1991 census data showed a Protestant death rate of 0.42 per thousand and a Catholic rate of 0.61 per thousand.

Thus, even when over 90% of the deaths of local security forces are added to the Protestant category, the Catholics' risk overall is higher in both absolute and relative terms, in the total period of the Troubles. It appears that this pattern did not hold in the period 1977–86. However, since the 1981 census figures are generally regarded as unreliable, there may be some doubt about this result.

GEOGRAPHICAL CONCENTRATION
Table 1.5 shows deaths in the Troubles that have taken place in each district council area in Northern Ireland, and compares the number of deaths with the total 1991 populations for each district. Two distinct deaths totals are shown: the first gives the number of violent incidents in which someone died (fatal incidents) within the district; the second records the number of district residents who have been killed (victims). Neither the total of 'fatal incidents' nor the total 'victims' will account for the total of over 3,700 deaths during the Troubles. This is because a number of deaths occurred outside Northern Ireland, a large number of non-Northern Ireland residents were victims and, in some cases, there were difficulties in assigning incomplete addresses to particular districts. In Table 1.5, the number of deaths in each category has been divided by the 1991 figure for the resident population to produce a comparable death rate per thousand population and these have been ranked. Clearly, the death rates are exaggerated by the fact that the accumulated number of deaths is being compared with the population for a single year. True yearly death rates for each district would be considerably lower. Nonetheless, the exercise provides a basis for geographical comparison across district councils.

Belfast, Newry & Mourne, Derry/Londonderry, Armagh, Dungannon and Craigavon stand out as the districts containing the highest number of deaths. In both absolute and relative terms Belfast has experienced the greatest concentration of violent deaths, with the death rates per thousand population almost twice as high as the next district, Armagh. In some districts, the number of incidents and the number of resident deaths are almost the same, whereas in others, the number of incidents is substantially greater than the number of resident deaths, as in Newry and Mourne. This may reflect the distinct pattern of the Troubles manifest in rural areas, where a high proportion of fatal casualties were members of the security forces who did not live in the area. Conversely, in some other areas such as

Table 1.5: Numbers and Death Rates with Northern Ireland District Councils

District Council	Pop. 1991 (000s)	Fatal Incidents	Rate 1,000	Resident Victims	Rate 1,000	Ratio In/HA
BELFAST	294.3	1352	4.59	1216	4.13	0.90
ARMAGH	51.6	129	2.50	128	2.48	0.99
DUNGANNON	45	115	2.56	107	2.38	0.93
COOKSTOWN	30.8	65	2.11	63	2.05	0.97
STRABANE	35.4	58	1.64	67	1.89	1.16
DERRY	97.5	244	2.50	170	1.74	0.70
CRAIGAVON	75.1	110	1.46	121	1.61	1.10
FERMANAGH	54.1	94	1.74	87	1.61	0.93
NEWRY AND MOURNE	82.7	325	3.93	131	1.58	0.40
MAGHERAFELT	35.9	40	1.11	49	1.36	1.23
CASTLEREAGH	61.6	32	0.52	65	1.06	2.03
LISBURN	101	77	0.76	106	1.05	1.38
NEWTOWNABBEY	75.9	39	0.51	75	0.99	1.92
BANBRIDGE	33.4	8	0.24	27	0.81	3.38
DOWN	58.6	46	0.78	42	0.72	0.91
LIMAVADY	29.6	27	0.91	21	0.71	0.78
OMAGH	45.6	41	0.90	31	0.68	0.76
BALLYMONEY	24	13	0.54	14	0.58	1.08
CARRICKFERGUS	33.2	8	0.24	17	0.51	2.13
COLERAINE	52.9	22	0.42	24	0.45	1.09
NORTH DOWN	72.5	12	0.17	32	0.44	2.67
ANTRIM	45.6	15	0.33	20	0.44	1.33
BALLYMENA	56.2	10	0.18	23	0.41	2.30
LARNE	29.4	8	0.27	12	0.41	1.50
ARDS	64.9	8	0.12	26	0.40	3.25
MOYLE	14.6	4	0.27	4	0.27	1.00
TOTAL		2902		2678		

Table 1.6: Deaths by Location in Postal Districts

HOME POSTAL DISTRICT BT	NUMBER OF RESIDENT DEATHS	% OF TOTAL DEATHS	FATAL INCIDENT POSTAL DISTRICT BT	NUMBER OF FATAL INCIDENTS	% OF TOTAL FATAL INCIDENTS
14	248	8.75	12	326	9.88
12	242	8.54	14	272	8.24
13	180	6.35	35	268	8.12
15	164	5.78	13	223	6.76
11	146	5.15	48	197	5.97
48	113	3.99	15	191	5.79
35	91	3.21	11	129	3.91
5	87	3.07	7	104	3.15
71	86	3.03	1	98	2.97
7	79	2.79	71	89	2.70
47	74	2.61	70	78	2.36
60	70	2.47	60	77	2.33
36	66	2.33	5	74	2.24
70	59	2.08	47	71	2.15
6	48	1.69	61	64	1.94
61	46	1.62	34	59	1.79
34	45	1.59	92	54	1.64
66	44	1.55	9	45	1.36
62	43	1.52	66	44	1.33
45	42	1.48	62	43	1.30

Castlereagh and North Down, the number of residents who died was greater than the number of incidents. Although such areas were relatively unscathed by violence, their residents were nonetheless vulnerable to deaths in the Troubles, due perhaps to either membership of the security forces or to random victimisation in the city centre bombing that characterised the earlier phases of the Troubles.

Table 1.6 examines geographical distribution of deaths using postal districts. This ranking points to particular parts of Belfast, Derry/Londonderry, South Armagh and 'Mid Ulster' as the locations that have experienced particularly high intensities of violence. With respect to deaths of residents within each postal district, BT14, BT12, BT13, BT15 and BT11 stand out as having the largest number

Table 1.7: Number of Fatal Incidents and Resident Deaths in Each Belfast Ward

WARDS	FATAL INCIDENTS IN WARDS	RESIDENTS' DEATHS	LOCATION
BALLYMACARRETT	25	38	East
ISLAND	16	7	East
THE MOUNT	8	15	East
RAVENHILL	7	12	East
BALLYHACKAMORE	6	4	East
SYDENHAM	6	3	East
WOODSTOCK	6	14	East
BLOOMFIELD	4	3	East
STORMONT	4	8	East
KNOCK	2	6	East
ORANGEFIELD	2	3	East
BELMONT	1	3	East
CHERRYVALLEY	0	1	East
Ward Average	7	9	
ST ANNES	106	39	North
ARDOYNE	71	67	North
NEW LODGE	58	62	North
DUNCAIRN	56	24	North
CLIFTONVILLE	43	35	North
WATERWORKS	41	42	North
CRUMLIN	40	22	North
HIGHFIELD	35	30	North
LIGIONEL	35	26	North
CHICESTER PARK	34	26	North
BALLYSILLAN	26	29	North
GLENCAIRN	24	24	North
WOODVALE	24	23	North
CASTELVIEW	18	12	North
FORT WILLIAM	6	12	North
BELLVUE	4	4	North
CAVEHILL	3	14	North
Ward Average	37	29	
SHAFTESBURY	55	30	South
BOTANIC	49	33	South
BLACKSTAFF	25	11	South
BALLYNAFEIGH	21	23	South
WINDSOR	11	11	South
STRANMILLIS	9	7	South
ROSETTA	8	5	South
MALONE	5	11	South
UPPER MALONE	3	8	South
Ward Average	21	15	
FALLS	90	57	West
CLONARD	70	56	West

Table 1.7 *contd*: Number of Fatal Incidents and
Resident Deaths in Each Belfast Ward

WARDS	FATAL INCIDENTS IN WARDS	RESIDENTS DEATHS	LOCATION
WHITEROCK	20	55	West
SHANKILL	44	24	West
UPPER SPRINGFIELD	44	46	West
FALLSPARK	30	20	West
ANDERSONTOWN	26	28	West
BEECHNOUNT	25	20	West
GLENCOLIN	24	20	West
GLEN ROAD	14	25	West
LADYBROOK	10	19	West
FINAGHY	4	8	West
Ward Average	36	32	

of local residents killed. All of these districts are in Belfast and together compose the North and West sectors of the city. BT47 and BT48 compose the city and Waterside of Derry/Londonderry. BT34 and BT35 cover Newry and South Armagh while BT60, BT61 and BT71 define 'Mid Ulster'.

Since Belfast has seen the highest concentrations of deaths, a ward analysis (Table 1.7) can reveal further the highly localised nature of the fatal impact of the Troubles. The wards have been assembled under the headings of East, North, South and West of the city to show the spatial concentration of deaths within it. This concentration is manifest in the North and West of Belfast where the highest averages for both incidents and resident deaths occur. In East Belfast, only two wards had scores in double figures and one ward in East Belfast had seen no Troubles-related incidents that resulted in death. It can be seen that some wards were virtually unaffected on this measure whereas some, like Falls, had more than the total for East Belfast. These figures accord with everyday experience that there are parts of Northern Ireland which have only been marginally touched by the conflict. Within Belfast, the intensity of violence has been skewed towards the North and West of the city.

The highest rates of Troubles-related deaths are invariably areas of high deprivation, high unemployment, and report poor health and educational achievement. Those who, by virtue of the fact that they are already suffering the effects of poverty and deprivation and are least equipped to cope with the effects of the Troubles, are those who have suffered most in the Troubles. The interrelationship between poverty and the Troubles is complex. It is not likely that simply targeting poverty will necessarily resolve political conflict, as was argued by the Irish Congress of Trade Unions, who opined at an earlier stage in the Troubles that 50,000 jobs would do more to end the conflict than 50,000 guns (Carlin, 1979).

However, it is possible to look more closely at the relationship between poverty and the Troubles, using the work conducted in the early 1990s undertaken by the Micro Statistics Centre at the University of Manchester (Robson, 1994), which plotted spatial deprivation. Death rates for particular locations can be compared with their deprivation scores. Table 1.8 shows the six district council areas ranked highest for fatal incident per thousand population alongside corresponding ranks for the rates of resident deaths and deprivation rank.

Of the six districts ranked highest on fatal incidents, four were among the six worst deprived, with the exceptions of Armagh and Cookstown. Whilst Strabane ranked highest on deprivation, it ranked eighth on the rate of fatal incidents. Thus, whilst there would appear to be some relationship between deprivation and violence, it is not a simple one. The correlation coefficients of the two violence scores with the deprivation score across all 26 districts were 0.76 and 0.52 respectively. There is a higher level of association between fatal incidents and deprivation than resident deaths and deprivation. It would appear that the rate of fatal incidents occurring in a district is a better measure of the intensity of the violence, although many areas without local experience of Troubles-related violence had residents die elsewhere. It must be concluded, however, that intensity of violence and deprivation do seem to be positively associated. Elsewhere (Fay et al., 1999), we have examined the relationship between deprivation and civilian deaths, which is much stronger. When security forces deaths are removed from the consideration, the correlation between deprivation and death rates increases.

Table 1.8: Violence (1969–98) and Deprivation (1994)
in Selected District Councils

District Council	Rank (fatal incidents)	Rank (residents' deaths)	Deprivation Rank
BELFAST	1	1	2
NEWRY AND MOURNE	2	9	4
DUNGANNON	3	3	5
DERRY	4	6	3
ARMAGH	5	2	13
COOKSTOWN	6	4	8

HELP AND SUPPORT

One of the emerging concerns in the peace process was that people who had suffered as a result of the Troubles had not received help and support with their difficulties. The Cost of the Troubles Study conducted a survey of Northern Ireland, (Fay et al., 1999) which elicited information on this issue. An indicator of symptoms of post-traumatic stress (PTS) was used, and respondents who met the PTS criteria were asked about the help and support they received. Respondents said that they got most of their help from their spouses, immediate family and neighbours. Table 1.9 lists the type of trained help which was received by these respondents. About a quarter of respondents said that they looked for outside help, and those who did were most likely to go to the local doctor or GP (20.5%). Other sources included the chemist/pharmacist (13.4%), lawyer or solicitor (10.4%), local politician (11.3%) and community worker (10.1%). Only 0.8% sought help from child guidance, 1.3% sought help from child welfare, 3.9% sought help from a social worker and 5.9% sought help from a community nurse. The least popular or applicable sources of help were accountants (0.3%), The Samaritans (0.5%) and marriage or relationship counsellors (0.4%).

Table 1.9: 'Have you ever seen a trained helper about the effects of the Troubles on you or on a member of your family?'

	YES (%)	NO (%)	TOTAL (%)
Psychiatrist	63 (4.8)	1238 (95.2)	1301
Clinical psychologist	18 (1.4)	1282 (98.6)	1300
GP & local doctor	268 (20.5)	1042 (79.5)	1310
Community nurse	77 (5.9)	1222 (94.1)	1299
Alternative health practitioner	10 (0.8)	1290 (99.2)	1300
Chemist/pharmacist	174 (13.4)	1129 (86.6)	1303
Social worker	51 (3.9)	1249 (96.1)	1300
Child guidance	10 (0.8)	1287 (99.2)	1297
Support through school welfare	17 (1.3)	1280 (98.7)	1297
Teacher	41 (3.2)	1257 (96.8)	1298
Counsellor	36 (2.8)	1262 (97.2)	1298
Self help group	47 (3.6)	1252 (96.4)	1299
Marriage/Relationship counsellor	5 (0.4)	1294 (99.6)	1299
Social Security Agency	108 (8.3)	1192 (91.7)	1300
Citizen's Advice Bureau	74 (5.7)	1225 (94.3)	1299
The Samaritans	6 (0.5)	1293 (99.5)	1299
Minister or priest	116 (8.9)	1185 (91.1)	1301
Faith healer	8 (0.6)	1285 (99.4)	1293
Lawyer or solicitor	135 (10.4)	1160 (89.6)	1295
Personnel depart. within my employment	16 (1.2)	1278 (98.8)	1294
Accountant	4 (0.3)	1289 (99.7)	1293
Local politician	146 (11.3)	1145 (88.7)	1291
Community worker	130 (10.1)	1163 (89.9)	1293
Other voluntary organisation	100 (7.7)	1193 (92.3)	1293

Table 1.10 gives an indication as to whether the respondents thought the help available was satisfactory. Although the majority of respondents did not seek help, out of those who had sought help, 23.5% thought the help available to them was sympathetic and helpful, while 6.3% thought the help available to them was only adequate. Only 1% of respondents stated that they could not find help, and 0.6% thought the help received was harmful to them. It was also found that 39.5% of the respondents received appropriate help from no-one. When asked to evaluate the help they received, some 17.1% thought the best source of help was from their spouse, followed by 13.8% of respondents who thought their parents provided the best source of help. However, the response rate to this question was generally poor with only 65% of respondents answering. In general, respondents seem to seek help mainly from their families or close friends rather than outside help.

Table 1.10: 'Do you think the help available to you was satisfactory?'

	YES (%)	NO (%)	NOT APPLICABLE (%)	TOTAL (100%)
Yes, it was sympathetic and helpful	298 (23.5)	57 (4.5)	911 (72.0)	1266
It was adequate only	78 (6.3)	133 (10.7)	1037 (83.1)	1248
It was insensitive	14 (1.1)	189 (15.2)	1040 (83.7)	1243
It was harmful	7 (0.6)	196 (15.8)	1040 (83.7)	1243
It was judgemental	18 (1.4)	186 (15.0)	11040 (83.6)	1244
It was critical of me	14 (1.1)	188 (15.1)	1040 (83.7)	1242
I couldn't find help	13 (1.0)	177 (14.2)	1054 (84.7)	1244

COMPENSATION

The issue of financial compensation also emerged during the peace process as a contentious issue for those affected by the Troubles. Although £247.2m was paid by government in Criminal Injuries Compensation in the seven years between 1990 and 1991 and 1997 and 1998, many people who suffered in the Troubles have never received any financial compensation or acknowledgement. Some were disqualified from claiming compensation under the terms of the scheme. Others who were qualified to claim, such as the unemployed, were not entitled to financial compensation, since this was calculated on the basis of loss of earnings, thus disqualifying them. Other inequities in the compensation system were also pointed out by the newly emerging victims' advocates.

In June 1999 a report was submitted to the Secretary of State for Northern Ireland reviewing the Criminal Injuries Compensation. This report reviewed the difficulties with the scheme and made a range of recommendations. First, they recommended that compensation be awarded to families of the disappeared. Second, they recommended that compensation be paid for psychiatric illness resulting from the Troubles, whether or not the person was present at the incident. Third, they recommended that the families of those who had convictions or who were involved in paramilitary activity and were killed could still receive compensation. The review also recommended the adoption of a tariff system for less serious injuries, so that similar injuries attracted similar levels of compensation, irrespective of the earning capacity of the injured party, and that compensation for more serious injuries be determined under common law principles. Most significantly, however, the review recommended that, with the exception of provision for the families of the disappeared, none of their recommendations be enacted retrospectively. Therefore, most people affected by the Troubles who had applied for compensation were dealt with under the old system.

CULTURES OF VICTIMHOOD

One of the most significant aspects of the emergence of 'victims' politics' in Northern Ireland during the peace process was the manner in which this emergence interacted with the wider political atmosphere, and fuelled controversy or elicited new responses from governments. It is a truism to point out that everyone in Northern Ireland has been affected by the Troubles, and the political culture, arguably, is one of universal victimhood, where Unionists/Loyalists, Nationalist/Republicans and State, experience themselves as the victim of one or more of the other parties. Few acknowledge their role in the victimisation of others. What is apparent from the analysis presented here is that the effects of the Troubles are not evenly distributed amongst the population. Whilst some have suffered enormously and repeatedly, others have managed to live through the death and destruction of the Troubles comparatively unscathed. Yet this does not mitigate the widespread and comprehensive identification with the victim position. Victim identity precludes the acknowledgement of the suffering of the 'enemy'. Thus, this political and social culture of victimhood is both cause and effect of the Troubles. The losses and damage of the Troubles creates a consciousness of fear, vulnerability and helplessness, as well as anger. Yet within that very vulnerability and helplessness lies the seed of justification for 'retaliation'. Responsibility for violent acts carried out by victims is commonly allocated – not to the victims carrying out the act, but to the people who victimised them in the first place. Thus victimisation is routinely used to justify violence and the further victimisation of others, and so the cycle continues. This culture of victimhood permeates the political culture of Northern Ireland. Thus, the psychological journey out of victimhood is an important aspect of building a peaceful future in Northern Ireland.

Approaches to date on the part of government and NGOs to the human effects of the Troubles have concentrated on the individual victim, the bereaved mother, the orphaned child, or the injured policeman. Whilst these individuals have needs, they represent more than their individual needs and situations. They become symbols of the grievances of their communities or occupational groups. In the process of peace-building, entire communities or occupational groups that have endured disproportionate damage during the Troubles have determined the dynamics of victims' politics. Yet, with the exception of the situation of disabled police officers, police widows and families of the disappeared, policy makers and service providers continue to see those affected by the Troubles as a series of individuals with individual needs. It seems clear that the street battles that continue between communities in, for example, North Belfast, are driven – at least in part – by a lack of recognition of the situation of continuous embattlement that many communities have lived through *as communities.*

Many people in the communities that have suffered most – and these are also invariably deprived areas – perceive the peace process as not having delivered on the earlier promises of peace and a better life. It is precisely within these most marginalised communities, where the largest number of victims and combatants are to be found, that the prospects for future peace will either founder or prosper. Lessons from South Africa and elsewhere would suggest that unless the most marginalised members of a society gain in the transition to the new political dispensation, their disaffection will threaten the new dispensation itself. Political alienation from the peace process in poor communities will lead to increased social (and political) problems for the new society. The disappointment – or betrayal – felt by those in such communities when seemingly arriving at a long-sought goal, yet gaining nothing, increases the volatility within those communities, which can easily spill over into violence and anarchy. The explosive cocktail of poverty, political marginalisation and disproportionate suffering in the Troubles is not recognised at a policy level, nor is there any acknowledgement within mainstream public policy of the Troubles as a factor in causing and perpetuating marginalisation. The new indicators of deprivation produced for government by the Oxford University team led by Noble examine deprivation without reference to the Troubles, failing to take account of factors such as segregation in relation to access to facilities. It is disappointing, if not entirely surprising that fields of academic study seem to replicate in their disciplines the segregation of the society they study.

CONCLUSIONS

Public acknowledgement in a broad way of the human impact of the Troubles only became possible after the 1994 ceasefires. Prior to that, a culture of silence, and the lack of dedicated service provision, left those affected by the Troubles largely to their own devices when the media attention diminished after the event. Since 1994, much of the development has been driven by the demands of newly formed advocacy groups, and the political need to mitigate concessions to combatants and former combatants. Many of the developments and initiatives to date have been pragmatic, short term, and reactive. Yet it seems clear that the needs amongst those bereaved and injured in the Troubles, and those who have been victims of miscarriages of justice are unlikely to be met within a three- or five-year funding programme or government initiative. Longer-term strategic planning to meet medical, psychological and financial needs is required, alongside public initiatives to provide public acknowledgement and education, justice, and information about events in the past. Such needs should be met in a way that takes account of the culture of victimhood, and should avoid approaches that serve to perpetuate such a culture. Rather, recipients of services should be encouraged to acknowledge the past and put it in its place, to maximise their quality of life in the present and the future, and to transcend a victim identity by recovering their power and control over their lives.

The politicisation of the 'victims issue' in Northern Ireland has left many agencies nervous of intervention, in case their humanitarian work is used to fuel political conflict and ultimately to justify more violence. A clearer differentiation of the limits to the remits of the various agencies offering help, and a restatement of their commitment to making provision according to need and to the principles of equity and transparency, would ease the anxiety surrounding this issue. Alongside this, a comprehensive and transparent system for targeting need would also assist policy makers and service providers. Yet it is the work with aggrieved communities and sub-groups to challenge their perpetuation of victim culture that poses the greatest challenge and offers the greatest potential reward. Only such work can minimise the risk of the creation of more victims in the future, and deliver recovery, healing and peace to those most in need of it.

2. THE DEVELOPMENT OF CHILDREN'S ATTITUDES TOWARDS 'THE TROUBLES' IN NORTHERN IRELAND

Paul Connolly and Julie Healy

INTRODUCTION

Ever since the early 1970s, the plight of children in Northern Ireland has been a central concern for social researchers. At that time, two publications emerged raising concerns about the position of children in the region and the impact that the violence was having on their socialisation and moral and emotional development (Fields, 1973; Fraser, 1974). While they were viewed as rather anecdotal and sensationalist in style, they paved the way for a plethora of research studies that were conducted up until the mid-1980s that explored the impact of 'the Troubles' on children's experiences, attitudes and behaviour.[1]

One of the central concerns underpinning this work has been the question of when children first begin to categorise each other in terms of the Catholic/Protestant divide and in what ways they tend to do this. Overwhelmingly, researchers during this period have attempted to answer this question using a wide variety of indirect, experimental methods. One typical example is provided by Jahoda and Harrison's (1975) pioneering study of sixty boys aged six and ten from Belfast and a further control group of 60 boys from Edinburgh. One technique they employed was to ask the boys to sort a variety of differently coloured geometric shapes. They found that there was no difference between the Belfast and Edinburgh six-year-old boys in relation to whether they chose to sort the items by colour or shape. However, at the age of ten, all of the Belfast boys were found to sort by colour whereas all those from Edinburgh sorted by shape. This, they concluded, suggested that the boys in Belfast were more likely to be aware of the cultural and political significance of certain colours. Another test they gave the boys was to ask them to rank a collection of individuals in terms of those that they 'most' and 'least liked'. These included a soldier, a policeman, a Catholic priest and a Protestant minister. The results indicated that even the attitudes of the younger boys, aged six, appeared to have been influenced by the conflict in that both Catholic and Protestant boys of this age demonstrated a more negative evaluation of the policeman than the control group from Edinburgh. Moreover, both religious groups from Belfast gave a low ranking to the 'outgroup figures', represented by the Protestant minister and Catholic priest respectively. Jahoda and Harrison found that these attitudes developed with age so that the attitudes of the ten-year-old boys towards the two religious figures had become stronger and more polarised.

The many studies that followed Jahoda and Harrison's (1975) work tended to adopt a similar indirect and experimental approach and focused on a variety of issues including children's ability to: recognise the terms 'Catholic' and 'Protestant' (McWhirter and Gamble, 1982); discriminate between stereotypically Protestant and Catholic first names (Cairns, 1980; Houston et al., 1990) and faces (Stringer and Cairns, 1983); and between Belfast, Dublin and standard English accents (Cairns and Duriez, 1976). Overall, as Cairns et al. (1995: 138) concluded in relation to their summary of this work, the findings appear to offer a relatively consistent picture that 'although children have some understanding of the denominational group labels at an early age, it is not until about the age of ten or eleven that the majority of children acquire the specific skills required to discriminate between the two groups'.

The research that provides the focus for this present chapter has been undertaken in response to three principal concerns regarding the methodological approach employed by this work. The first is a concern that such structured and experimental designs may have failed to detect the more complex and varied ways in which children tend to demonstrate their awareness and understanding of the communal divisions that exist. There is a danger that researchers are simply using the most common ways that adults tend to distinguish between Protestants and Catholics and applying these to children. While the majority of children may not have 'learnt' these specific ways of distinguishing between and categorising others until the ages of ten or eleven, it may be that they simply tend to do it using alternative social cues and markers to adults. A need exists, therefore, for more unstructured methods to be used that enable a greater focus on the children's own experiences and perspectives and the particular ways in which they have come to make sense of and articulate these.

Second, one of the inevitable consequences of adopting such structured and experimental research designs is that the attitudes and behaviour of the children are studied without reference to the specific social contexts within which they take place. While a child may demonstrate a tendency to discriminate between Protestant and Catholic first names or to express less favourable attitudes towards the police, such studies can therefore offer little understanding of *why* he or she does this. Without further evidence, researchers are simply left to hypothesise about the possible effects of the violence and communal divisions on that child's attitudes. However, it is only by adopting more qualitative and unstructured methods of investigation that are sensitive to the particular social contexts within which the children are located that an appreciation can be gained of the specific motivations that lie behind their attitudes and the broader social factors and processes that tend to inform these. In other words, while such experimental designs play an important role in identifying patterns of behaviour among children and specific differences and/or relationships that might exist, they can offer little by way of explaining the causes of these.

Finally, there is a danger that such experimental designs tend to reify children's identities and sectarian attitudes. By not studying the children's attitudes and behaviour in relation to specific contexts, such work runs the danger of unproblematically presenting their prejudices as fixed and given. It may well be that some children are aware of differences that exist between Protestants and Catholics, and possibly of their own identity as a Protestant or Catholic. However, this may not be a particularly significant or salient feature of their lives. It is only through the consideration of children's perspectives within the specific contexts within which they occur that an understanding can be gained of when and where they attach importance to such attitudes. Moreover, such an approach with its emphasis on context focuses attention on the social causes of particular attitudes and forms of behaviour and thus avoids the danger of constructing them as fixed and given.

THE PRESENT STUDY

The data upon which this chapter is based is drawn from a much broader study of the attitudes and experiences of children aged three to eleven in Belfast. With the three concerns outlined above in mind, one of the key aims of the study has been to use largely unstructured, qualitative methods to document the nature and extent of the children's awareness of and attitudes towards the conflict and how these develop with age. Before discussing some of the findings to emerge from the research, it is useful to begin with a brief outline of the methodology employed.

The research focused on three age groups of children: three to four, seven to eight and ten to eleven-year-olds from four areas in Belfast: two located in predominantly working-class areas that have had a history of sectarian violence and conflict (one Catholic, the other Protestant) and two located in predominantly middle-class areas that have experienced very little violence directly over the years (again, one Catholic, the other Protestant). In each area, access to the children was gained via a primary school and a local nursery. Each school/nursery was fully informed about the focus and nature of the research and the written consent of parents was gained in relation to all of the children who took part in the study. At the time of writing, the fieldwork has been completed in relation to the two working-class areas and has just begun in the two middle-class areas. The data discussed below is therefore drawn from the interviews with the working-class Protestant and Catholic children.

The two areas from which these children come are neighbouring ones and separated by a peaceline; a fortified brick wall purposely designed to keep the two communities apart. Graffiti, murals and painted kerbstones mark out the areas as

Republican and Loyalist respectively, visibly displaying the very distinct political identities of each community. However, at another level the two areas have much in common. Both experience some of the highest levels of social deprivation within Northern Ireland, as illustrated by such indicators as high levels of long-term unemployment and poverty, poor health and educational performance. The areas also suffer from high levels of anti-social behaviour such as joy-riding and vandalism. These communities have also experienced some of the highest levels of violence during 'the Troubles' and despite the ceasefires there is still a high presence of paramilitary activity, often displayed in response to anti-social behaviour.

There remains a general sense of unease between the two areas. At the margins of each community is an interface area, a shared barren space named 'the field'[2] by the children in the study. It is a venue for sporadic conflict, particularly between children and young people. This type of routine, 'low-level' sectarian violence has been termed 'recreational rioting' (Jarman, 2001). However, during periods of political unrest this conflict can take on a more serious nature and often spills over into more serious violence in the wider area and beyond.

The fieldwork was conducted by the second author, who spent a term with each group of children, visiting them usually for two days per week at their respective schools/nurseries. Her time was spent largely in the classroom with the children, helping the children with their work and using the opportunity to develop a rapport with them. The main method of data collection was largely unstructured small group interviews that had been developed and successfully used by one of the authors elsewhere (see Connolly, 1998; Connolly with Maginn, 1999). Children were usually interviewed in same-sex friendship groups of three, away from the main classroom. During the course of the term, most children were interviewed on at least three occasions. This helped to increase the rapport between the researcher and the children further and also allowed the children to feel more relaxed and comfortable with the interview setting.

For the two older age groups (seven to eight and ten to eleven-year-olds), the interviews themselves were largely unstructured. Beyond asking very general questions about what they liked to do at home and what they liked to play in the playground, the children were left to raise and discuss whatever topics they felt to be important. The role of the interviewer was simply to seek clarification and further information from the children on issues that they had raised which were also deemed to be relevant to the present study. At no time did the interviewer introduce any topic related to the conflict and/or divisions that existed. Such an approach was used for two main reasons. First, it allowed the children's own experiences and perspectives to predominate. Second, the relatively unstructured nature of the conversations meant that the children were free to raise and discuss matters relating to the conflict when they felt it was important to do so. This provided valuable insights into the salience of the conflict in their lives and precisely when and where it became significant to them.

Two particular ethical issues arose from this approach that needed to be addressed. The first related to the danger that the interviews would simply act to increase the children's existing awareness of the conflict and/or encourage them to think in terms of the divisions that exist. This was avoided by the interviewer purposely not introducing any topic relating to the conflict but simply allowing the children to raise and discuss those issues that they were already aware of and concerned about. The second ethical issue related to those occasions where the children chose to express prejudiced and sectarian statements. In such circumstances, it was important that the interviewer did not give the impression that she condoned these attitudes and also made it clear that she did not agree with them. This was done by the interviewer asking the child to explain and justify what they had said and also by responding with statements such as 'that's not a nice thing to say is it?' and/or questions like: 'how would you feel if that was said about you?' A more detailed discussion of the ethical issues involved and also the problems associated with analysing and interpreting the children's conversations is provided elsewhere (*see* Connolly, 1996, 2001).

For the three- to four-year-old children, a slightly different approach was adopted given the fact that their language skills and attention spans were much more limited. Alongside short group discussions, much greater emphasis was placed upon observations of the children at play and the conversations they had during these times. In addition, with the aim of stimulating conversation and assessing the children's cultural awareness more directly, individual interviews were conducted with the children. These typically lasted for about ten minutes. A variety of items were shown to the children in these interviews including small hand-held flags (the British Union Jack and the Irish Tricolour), mini football tops (Rangers and Celtic tops)[3] and photographs of a range of common events in Northern Ireland including an Orange march, a police Land Rover and an Irish dancer. All of the items represented common symbols and/or events in Northern Ireland that most of the children would have already come across at some point.

For each item the children were simply asked whether they had seen these before and, if so, what they knew about them. If the child demonstrated some knowledge of a particular item they were then asked whether there was anything else they wanted to say about it. If they stated that they had not seen it before and/or did not demonstrate any awareness of the item then it was simply removed and the next one was introduced. The interviewer was careful not to offer any information to the children regarding the items shown. For those children who had either no knowledge or just a limited understanding of one or more of the items, this approach meant that their awareness of these would not have been increased.

In outlining and discussing the data below, each of the three age groups of children will be discussed in turn. Given the limited space available, and the fact that the research is still ongoing, the main aim of what follows is simply to offer some indication of how the awareness and attitudes of children can emerge and develop with age. However, it needs to be stressed that the children who form the focus for this chapter do not constitute a representative sample but rather are drawn from areas that have experienced and continue to experience high levels of sectarian tensions and conflict. It would be wrong, therefore, to draw any general conclusions concerning the overall levels of children's awareness and the development of their attitudes from what is, therefore, an atypical group of children. Moreover, it should be noted that, even with the findings from the interviews with the children from the two middle-class areas, the overall aim of this research is not to make generalisations about children's attitudes and awareness as a whole in Northern Ireland. Rather, it is simply to identify the broad range of attitudes and levels of awareness that exist. It is hoped that a much larger study could then follow that would attempt to ascertain how representative these findings are in relation to the population of children as a whole in the region.

CHILDREN AGED THREE TO FOUR YEARS

It was interesting to note that the three- and four-year-old children spent very little time in the nursery focusing on and/or talking about matters relating to the conflict and the communal divisions that exist. However, it became clear when interviewing them on an individual basis that many had some awareness of relevant cultural events and symbols. For these children, their awareness appeared to be centred most commonly on the more visible events and symbols, principally: football shirts, flags and marching bands. As regards football, many of the children were already beginning to show signs that they were developing preferences for the football teams associated with their community – Celtic for Catholics and Rangers for Protestants, as the following two conversations with James[4] and Kyle (both Protestant) illustrate:[5]

> *Interviewer:* Who does he [*his friend*] support?
> *James:* [*points to mini football top*] Rangers!
> *Interviewer:* He supports Rangers or that's Rangers? [*referring to the top*]
> *James:* That's Rangers.
> *Interviewer:* Very good. How did you know that was Rangers?
> *James:* Cos . . . I have a top.

> *Kyle:* [*notices the football top*] What's that . . . [It's] Rangers! [*very excited*]
> *Interviewer:* It is Rangers, you're very clever [. . .] Do you like them?
> *Kyle:* Yes [*lifts jumper and looks at his top*]
> *Interviewer:* Do you have a top like that?
> *Kyle:* Yes.

Moreover, for some of the children, a preference for one team was also matched with a dislike for the other. This can be seen in the following conversations with Adrian and Patrick (both Catholic):

Interviewer: Well, so you know this is Celtic football team [*holding up the Celtic football top*], do you like them?
Adrian: Yeah.
Interviewer: And [you say] this is Rangers [*holding up the Rangers football top*], do you like them?
Adrian: No.
Interviewer: Why not?
Adrian: Cos they're crap!
Interviewer: Are they? But Celtic are good?
Adrian: [*nods*]
Interviewer: Do your friends like Celtic?
Adrian: Yes.
Interviewer: Do you know anybody who likes Rangers?
Adrian: No!

Patrick: [*pointing to the Rangers football top*] They beat me, they beat me!
Interviewer: Rangers beat you?
Patrick: Yeah.
Interviewer: At football . . . or [did] they beat you up?
Patrick: [*angrily*] I'm going to beat them up!
Interviewer: Do you not like them?
Patrick: I'm going to knock them all down [*knocks over Rangers top*]
[. . .]
Interviewer: Which of these two do you like the best?
Patrick: Celtic!

It is not possible to conclude from conversations such as these whether the children were aware that the two football teams and the rivalry that existed between them tended to represent the broader divisions between the Catholic and Protestant communities. These particular children certainly did not demonstrate any such knowledge. However, the important point is the fact that children are already at this young age beginning to learn and assimilate some of the key cultural symbols and cues for distinguishing between Catholics and Protestants in Northern Ireland.

This also appeared to be true in relation to flags. Even at the ages of three and four, the children were beginning to demonstrate a preference for one flag over another and, for some, to regard a certain flag as their own. This can be seen in the two discussions with Roberta (Protestant) and Aileen (Catholic):

Roberta: I seen that one [*Union Jack*] but not that one [*Tricolour*].
Interviewer: But if you had to pick one which one would you pick?
[. . .]
Roberta: [*points to Union Jack*] My one.
Interviewer: That's your one?

Roberta: Cos that's the one that was up on the wall.

Aileen: [*reaching out for flag*] Aye, I've seen that there one, green, white and orange, my granny gave me that one.
Interviewer: Do you like that one?
Aileen: Yes.
Interviewer: Where else have you seen this one?
Aileen: In my street [. . .] and in my school.
Interviewer: Right, so which flag do you like the best [*showing her both flags*]?
[. . .]
Aileen: This one [*the Tricolour*].

The two conversations above again point to the way in which the children in this study are already beginning to assimilate preferences for key cultural symbols and markers that reflect their own community. However, as before, there was generally little evidence that most of the children at this age explicitly understood that either they belonged to a specific community and/or that a particular flag represented their community.

For some of the children, particularly the Protestant children, they were able to associate particular flags with the bands that would often accompany Orange Parades. This can be seen in relation to the discussion with Natalie (Protestant) below. Moreover, as the conversation with Richard (Protestant) that follows demonstrates, the children's awareness sometimes extends beyond the immediate item being discussed:

Interviewer: Now what is this?
Natalie: A flag.
Interviewer: You're waving it about. What flag is that?
Natalie: A band flag.
Interviewer: Does daddy's band have one? [*Prior to this she had been talking about her daddy's band.*]
Natalie: No, but I have one of those at home with my toys.

Interviewer: Have you seen that flag before?
Richard: It's a flag for the bands.
Interviewer: [. . .] Do you get a flag when you go to see the bands?
Richard: Not like that, I get a King Billy one but [*inaudible*] lost it
[. . .]
Interviewer: What was on it?
Richard: King Billy.
Interviewer: A picture of King Billy?
Richard: And his horse.

> *Interviewer:* Really? What colour is his horse?
> *Richard:* It was white on it.
> *Interviewer:* A white horse. And who is King Billy?
> *Richard:* I saw him on TV.
> *Interviewer:* What was he doing on TV?
> *Richard:* He was beside the bands.
> *Interviewer:* Does he like the bands?
> *Richard:* He loves the bands.

Overall, therefore, the general picture that appears to be emerging for young children of this age is that they are actively engaging with the social and cultural events that surround them and are attempting to make sense of them. For the children in this study, it is not surprising that they are developing a limited set of preferences given the fact that they are living in highly segregated areas. While the majority may not be aware at this stage of the existence of the Catholic and Protestant communities and the divisions that exist between them, they are certainly already learning and assimilating the key cultural cues and markers that tend to set the two communities apart.

Finally, besides these common cultural symbols and events a small handful of children were also beginning to pick up and use the language of sectarianism as illustrated in the discussion with Patrick and David (both Catholic) below. Again, it is impossible to state whether Patrick was aware of who the 'Orangies' were and/or who they represented. However, the significant point as with the other symbols and events is that he is already acquiring and assimilating an awareness and set of attitudes that underpin more explicit sectarian beliefs and behaviour among older children and adults:

> *Patrick:* We go up to the field and there's Orangies up there.
> *Interviewer:* There's Orangies up in the field?
> *David:* Yes.
> *Patrick:* And dogs.
> David: Soldier dogs.
> *Interviewer:* Soldier dogs? . . . What are Orangies?
> *Patrick:* They have knives . . . my daddy. They kill you.
> [. . .]
> *Patrick:* [My daddy has a gun and] there's bullets in it.
> *Interviewer:* What does he have a gun for?
> *Patrick:* To shoot the Orangies.
> *Interviewer:* To shoot the Orangies?
> *Patrick:* Aye, we go to the field.
> *Interviewer:* Does he take you with him?
> *Patrick:* Yeah.
> *Interviewer:* Yeah? Why does he do that do you think?

[...]
Patrick: There's Orangies and there's ones who go there [...] They have knives, and guns and bullets [*excitedly*].
Interviewer: My goodness and why do they have those?
Patrick: They have a bomb!
Interviewer: A bomb? Why?
Patrick: Aye, and they shoot the bomb and the blows.
Interviewer: And why do they do that, Patrick?
Patrick: Cos.

CHILDREN AGED SEVEN TO EIGHT YEARS

By the time the children in these areas reach the ages of seven and eight, they are likely to spend much of their time outside playing. This not only increases their general exposure to the various cultural symbols that could be found in their respective areas (including flags, murals and painted kerbstones), but it also means that they are likely to become aware of the peaceline and interface areas and thus of the very real threat posed by those 'on the other side'. The existing cultural cues and markers that they had already learned and assimilated at an earlier age appeared to now provide the ideal language for representing and making sense of this threat. This can be seen in relation to the remarks made by Louise and Aine (both Catholic) during one group interview where the conversation had turned to those living across the peaceline:

> *Louise*: Protestants support Rangers.
> *Interviewer*: Why is that?
> *Louise*: Because Rangers are Protestants.
> *Interviewer*: So what are Protestants, what does that mean?
> *Louise*: It's bad to be a Protestant and/
> [...]
> *Interviewer*: What was that Louise?
> *Louise*: [*quietly*] Protestants come down and shoot ye.
> *Interviewer*: Do they?
> [...]
> *Aine*: They shot a man down our way.
> *Interviewer*: Why did they do that?
> *Aine*: I don't know.

While the children were found to actively draw upon and make use of the knowledge and language they had assimilated in order to make sense of their experiences, it was also clear at times that their actual understanding of what some of the terms meant was limited. This is certainly evident in the above discussion with Louise and Aine. The tendency for some of the children to mix up and confuse terms and issues is evident in the following comments made by Ryan (Protestant) who had, again, been talking about the community across the divide:

> *Ryan:* [*chanting*] IRA! Dirty Orangies! Green, white and orange!
> *Interviewer:* Who is the IRA?
> *Ryan:* Orangies, Peelers [*i.e. the police*] [. . .] Yeah, green, white and orange.
> That's what they wear, Orange. And it's for the IRA.

While some of the children of this age appeared to have direct experience of stone-throwing and fighting at interface areas, the majority were certainly aware of and able to recall incidents and events involving conflict with the other side. This is illustrated in the discussion among Chloe, John and Mandy (all Protestant):

> *Interviewer:* Do you ever go over there [*across the peaceline*] to play?
> *Chloe:* Aye, and get my head bricked in!
> *Interviewer:* Why would that happen?
> *Chloe:* Cos they're bad.
> *Interviewer:* They're bad?
> *John:* They are Catholics.
> *Interviewer:* And does that mean that they're bad?
> *All:* Yes.
> *Chloe:* They throw bricks and all over at us.
> *Interviewer:* Why?
> *Chloe:* I don't know.
> *Mandy:* Ivor got chased by the Fenians [*derogatory term for Catholics*] in three cars.
> *Interviewer:* Who's Ivor?
> *Mandy:* My brother.
> *Interviewer:* Oh dear, who chased him?
> *Mandy:* The Fenians.
> *Interviewer:* Who are they?
> *Mandy:* Catholics. Bad people, throw bricks at all our houses.
> *Chloe:* My wee friend got her windows put in by one of them.
> [. . .]
> *Interviewer:* So why do they throw bricks in at your houses?
> *Mandy:* Cos they're bad and because we don't support Celtic.
> *Interviewer:* Is that the only reason?
> *Mandy:* Yeah.

It is interesting to note in relation to Mandy's final comments about Celtic how the general cultural preferences and awareness that the children have been assimilating for a number of years provides a resource they can then draw upon to explain the conflict they are witness to. More generally, a number of children also tended to claim involvement in the fighting as a way of gaining status among their group and demonstrating bravery and strength as the following discussion among Ryan, Andrew and Matthew (all Catholics) illustrates:

> *Interviewer:* So why do you fight with Orangies?
> *Ryan:* Cos we like to.
> *Andrew:* I booted one in the privates [*very pleased with himself*].
> *Matthew:* Ahhhh!
> *Interviewer:* Why did you do that?
> *Andrew:* Cos, I hate the Orangies.
> *Interviewer:* But why?
> *Andrew:* Cos, before one of them booted me in the privates.

Finally, it was also noticeable how the children by this age had developed a clear and matter-of-fact awareness of local paramilitaries in their areas. The discussion below with Brittany and Karen (both Protestant) illustrates this. Again, it is interesting to note how the children's existing awareness of and preference for certain flags provides the basis upon which further knowledge and understanding is developed as they grow older:

> *Brittany:* There's loads of flags in my street.
> *Interviewer:* What flags are they?
> *Brittany:* Red, white and blue, yeah, red and white and blue.
> [. . .]
> *Interviewer:* Why are they red, white and blue and not a different colour?
> *Karen:* Cos that's our colour, that's our kind of flag.
> *Interviewer:* When you say our colour, who are you talking about?
> *Karen:* Us!
> *Brittany:* The UFF.
> *Karen:* The UFF?
> *Interviewer:* Is that their colour?
> *Karen:* [*to the interviewer*] It isn't the UFF.
> *Brittany:* I was only joking!
> *Interviewer:* But who are they?
> *Karen:* My daddy put some flags up.
> *Brittany:* So did my daddy.
> [. . .]
> *Interviewer:* Why do people put flags up?
> *Davy:* For the bands you see.

The generally matter-of-fact and accepting way in which the children talk of the local paramilitaries is also evident in the following conversation with Rosie and Louise (both Catholic). In what follows, Rosie is describing a street fight involving several adults. She is disappointed that despite trying to reach the IRA only the 'Peelers' arrived in time:

> *Rosie*: No sure we phoned the IRA and everything but they didn't come in time, only the Peelers came in time.
> *Interviewer*: So did you phone both?
> *Rosie*: Yeah, we phoned the IRA and the Peelers were only down the street from us and they came up anyway, and Frances phoned the IRA and thing, they didn't come in time.
> *Interviewer*: What do you think they would have done?
> *Rosie*: They would have stopped it and all cos we had to get the IRA or somebody up, or a/
> *Louise*: /A big strong man to beat them.
> *Rosie*: We get the IRA anytime there's fighting so we phoned the IRA and Frances tried to phone everybody.
> [. . .]
> *Interviewer*: What do you know about the IRA then, what do they do?
> *Rosie*: They always, we tried to phone everyone to come to get the Provos to come around but no one came, only the Peelers. See when the Peelers came everybody throwed big bottles of glass at them, at the Peelers and the Peelers had to stop and talk to Marty in our street cos he was throwing bottles at them.
> *Interviewer*: Why were they throwing bottles at them?
> *Rosie*: I don't know, they always do it.

For some of the boys, especially, such discussions at times developed into fantasies about being members of particular paramilitary organisations as the following discussion involving Phil and George (both Protestant) illustrates:

> *Phil*: The UDA, they're men and they have guns.
> [. . .]
> *George*: I work for the UDA [*laughs*].
> *Phil*: [*singing*] We all work for the UDA! We all work for the UDA!
> *George*: They're good.
> *Phil*: Sometimes they're good and sometimes they're bad.
> *Interviewer*: What good things do they do?
> *George*: Hundred guns in your head!
> *Phil*: I don't know.
> *George*: I know something good they do, they won't blow up this school.
> *Interviewer*: Will they not?
> *George*: Cos we're all Protestants.
> *Phil*: Cos we're all Prods, everyone here in this here whole estate is all Prods.
> *Interviewer*: Why is that?
> *Phil*: Just is, I don't know.

Overall, the picture that is emerging from interviews with the seven and eight year olds is that the majority now appear to be acutely aware of the division that exists between themselves and the neighbouring 'other' community. For some, this extends to direct involvement in stone-throwing and other interface violence while for the majority it involves both the telling and retelling of stories about fighting as well as about the local paramilitaries that most had simply come to recognise and accept. The general repertoire of cultural markers and symbols that the children had learnt and assimilated at a much earlier age was now providing the basic language and knowledge to try to describe and make sense of what was going on.

However, this is still an age of learning where the children's actual understanding of the terms they use and symbols and events they refer to is often limited and, at times, contradictory. Nevertheless, the key point is that the children are actively engaged in drawing upon and attempting to use such cultural and political markers and symbols to help them explain and understand the very real violence and sense of threat that they experience. The sectarian attitudes that can be found to be emerging at this age, therefore, do not simply reflect the influence of parents and older siblings. In other words, the children are not just uncritically repeating what they have been told by others but are actively involved in constructing an understanding that can help them comprehend what is going on around them.

Finally, it is also important to note that such attitudes emerge largely in relation to the children's experiences that are generally limited to playing locally and possibly being involved in (and/or certainly being aware of) the conflict with children from the neighbouring community at 'the field'. As such, their awareness of those from the other community and their attitudes towards them tend to be overshadowed by the local sectarian tensions that exist. Their attitudes are therefore focused mainly on the neighbouring community and are very negative and stereotypical, with little ambiguity or recognition of the complexities that exist.

CHILDREN AGED TEN TO ELEVEN YEARS

By the age of ten or eleven the children had a number of years' experience of living with sectarian tensions and the ever-present threat of attack and conflict. The fear of venturing out beyond their own local area was still as great as was the sense of territory and boundaries that accompanied this. As Christine and Anne Marie (both Catholic) explained:

> *Interviewer:* Christine, can you finish what you were saying about why you never go over to [the neighbouring loyalist estate]?
> Christine: Cos you'd get beaten up!
> Interviewer: Why?

Christine: Cos we're Catholics! [*said as if this was self-evident*].
Interviewer: How do the people there know that, how do they know you're not from there?
Christine: I know, that's what I always say/
Anne Marie: /I know but you're walking from that there direction.
Interviewer: And even if you were alone, would you get into bother?
Anne Marie: Probably . . . yes. My brother got beaten up by Orangies by goin' over.
Interviewer: Was he on his own?
Anne Marie: [*nods*].
Interviewer: And if someone from there came over here would they get beaten up?
All: Yeah [*Christine laughs*].

By this age, however, the children were more likely to have been directly involved in particular clashes with children from the other side. Indeed, this type of stone-throwing and sporadic violence had become a routine and taken for granted part of life for many of the children. This is illustrated in the following discussion with Debbie and Shauna (both Catholic). It is because of the ritualised nature of incidents such as the one they discuss that they tend to also provide a source of humour and a wealth of stories to tell:

Shauna: There's Orangies up there [*at the field*] . . . see the Orangies, there was a big riot and they had bricks and daggers/
Debbie: /The Peelers and all came [. . .] Didn't the peelers chase us and not chase them uns [*the Protestants*]?
Shauna: Aye [*angrily*]. The Peelers drove up and/
Debbie: /And we didn't even start it.
Interviewer: Did they start it?
Debbie: Yeah, and the Peelers had the cheek to chase us and not them uns.
Shauna: The Peelers came up and went WHAA! [*shouts*] like, and we had built a wee road so they couldn't [get] past, so they couldn't chase us and they broke it . . . cos/
Debbie: /They had the cheek to chase us and not them uns.
[. . .]
Shauna: I didn't go up, I'll tell you why, cos I was too scared of getting killed.
Debbie: You do be afraid/
Shauna: /I just stand back and watch them going [*shouting*] 'Go on! Go on!' See one time we went up and they all hid behind trees, all the Catholics hid behind trees and all, and here's me [*shouts very loudly*] 'Peelers!' and they all came running out and there wasn't even any Peelers or nothing! All you could see was all these wee white tops and Celtic tops all running from everywhere.

Discussion of local paramilitaries had also become more in-depth and detailed for the children at this age. The boys in particular spent a significant amount of time discussing the presence and activities of local paramilitaries in their area. As can be seen in the following discussion that took place between James, Paul and Thomas (all Catholics), they were also attempting to gain status by claiming knowledge of individual IRA men in the area:

> *Thomas:* The Provies [*Provisional IRA*] give out these wee lists of people in the park who are like are smoking and drinking, know like teenagers and that. Something about telling their mummies and all, the Provies like to stop you from sniffing [glue] and all, if they see you sniffing and all. It's a wee bit bad on the some ways and a wee bit good on others.
> *Paul:* I like some of the things they do.
> *James:* I like Brian/
> *Paul:* /Aye I like Brian Smyth.
> *James:* Brian Smyth's all right.
> *Paul:* I like Connor.
> *James:* Who's he?
> *Thomas:* Black hair.
> *Paul:* Aye, he thinks he's dead important.

The Protestant children showed an awareness of the diversity of opinion and groups within Loyalist paramilitarism. Many were familiar with the divisions within these groups and the history of the Loyalist feud that reached a head towards the end of the fieldwork (i.e. the summer of 2000). In the following conversation, Robert and Martin (both Protestant) discuss one of the incidents they had witnessed personally on the Shankill Road during the Loyalist feud:

> *Robert:* And then the UVF started shooting in the air, and everybody ran and it was mad, and they were in the Bar blocked the way off and [. . .] we got as far as there [*the chip shop*] and some woman gave us a lift up and see five days after that I was still scared.
> [. . .]
> *Martin:* . . . and then when it all started [*the feud*] we didn't go down again [to the Shankill Road] for about two months, that was the next time you saw us down the Road.

Many of the Protestant children spent a significant amount of time discussing the Loyalist feud and demonstrated some awareness and understanding of its history and nature. In the following, Elaine and Gillian (both Protestant) discuss the implications and complexity of being aligned to one group or the other:

> *Elaine:* Miss, know the way when all the fighting was on the UDA was

fighting with the UVF [. . .] And do you know what I think would be smart, just going altogether, Miss.

Interviewer: Why do you think that?

Gillian: Know who I hate? Johnny Adair and Michael Stone, I hate them uns.

[. . .]

Elaine: Somebody says they're Johnny Adair's cousin . . . who is it?

Gillian: Sonia.

Elaine: Sonia! But Sonia likes the UVF!

Later in the same conversation Gillian tells us how she would like a UVF mural on the side wall of her house:

Interviewer: And what would it [*the mural*] be of?

Gillian: Probably people with a gun, know like my daddy's picture/

Elaine: /Her next door neighbour is in the UDA too!

[. . .]

Interviewer: How do you know they're in the UDA?

Gillian: Cos . . . they have the flag and all in their house and know Mack, he's never out of their house [. . .]

Elaine: So if you get that UVF thing there and about ten UDA people walk past your house and all that fighting starts again you'd get thrown out of your house.

Gillian: I wouldn't/

Elaine: /People told me you were getting thrown out of your house.

Alongside a more detailed awareness and understanding of local paramilitary organisations and their activities, these children also tended to show a growing appreciation of the broader historical and political background to the conflict in comparison with the seven and eight year olds. This appreciation is illustrated in the following separate comments made by Thomas and Michelle (both Catholic) and Martin (Protestant):

Thomas: Because, because years ago like in Bloody Sunday and all they just lifted you and all for nothing. My grandad got lifted for nothing, he was just walking down the street and they lifted him and put him in the back of the van.

Michelle: I remember when we got stuck between the barricades and we had to go and stay in a hostel filled with all people from here and it was away down in the country and we had to stay for a couple of nights until they had stopped you know throwing and shooting and all. It was terrible.

Martin: Beside that wall [. . .] that's where all the Catholics live and so they put that wall there . . . When [my brother] was a wee baby we used to live up here, but I wasn't born up there, and then the war and all started and they didn't have the wall then. So they put that wall there so that people couldn't get over. But people threw petrol bombs over, but I was never alive then and see the army, they were trying to shoot over. And see my old house? They were shooting bullets, the army, and it just missed my wee brother.

Finally, alongside the prejudiced and negative attitudes that these children tended to express about one another, there was also emerging among children of this age an additional strand of thinking that was more positive and constructive. This appeared to reflect the broader knowledge and experiences the children were gaining through such channels as the television and cross-community contact. Inevitably, however, the two sets of opinions did not sit easily against each other and led to a series of contradictions as illustrated in the following conversation between Shauna, Debbie and Natasha (all Catholic) about a past cross-community school trip that they had been on with children from a Protestant school:

> *Interviewer:* So was spending time with [the Protestant School] a good experience?
> *All:* No!
> *Shauna:* No way, I never want to see them again.
> *Debbie:* I don't like them.
> *Shauna:* It wasn't their fault like but you . . . and you get a partner/
> *Debbie:* /Aye, partners/
> *Natasha:* /There was some of them OK.
> *Shauna:* Some partners were all right. My partner was nice.
> *Debbie:* Aye, we bought each other presents. I bought mine a Barbie.

The types of cross-community schemes that these children were more likely to have had experience of by this age appeared to lead to contradictions like the one illustrated above where positive attitudes towards specific individuals co-existed with blanket rejections of the community from which those individuals came from. The tendency for this age group to be able to express more positive and reconciliatory attitudes towards those from the other community is also evident in the following discussion involving Robert and Martin (both Protestant):

> *Robert:* They [*Catholics*] don't like the [Orange] Lodge.
> *Martin:* They just don't like Protestants, it all happened away hundreds of years ago.
> *Robert:* I don't know why, Catholics are just the same as us, although they talk differently from us, but they're just the same.
> [. . .]

Robert: Yeah, there's some good Catholics.
Martin: My mum and dad tell me to try and get on with Catholics.

Given the tensions that exist between the children, however, the potential for conflict between the two groups – even on cross-community trips – is ever-present as the following comments from Liam and David (both Catholic) illustrate:

Interviewer: Why did you not like [the Protestant school]?
David: Cos they're Protestants [*they giggle and look at interviewer in amazement as if it is obvious*].
Liam: Cos they were slabbering [calling names] to us all and all, and we were like messing about.
David: They were slabbering to me so I . . .
Interviewer: Why did they slabber at you?
Liam: Cos they don't like us.
David: See the wee Protestant, ahm, I was beside, he said to me [*whispers*] 'I'm going to knock you out' and I said [*leans forward as though he didn't hear him*] 'Wha?' and he was going to dig me.

More generally, the positive attitudes that some of the children expressed did not appear to be sufficient to counteract the overarching influence of the divisive geography and continuing tensions that existed in the area. Even for those willing to make conciliatory and positive comments, they appeared to be resigned to the reality of segregation and had no burning desire to integrate more. As Elaine (Protestant) commented during one interview:

Elaine: Ach, I'm sure they're [*Catholics*] all right like, but we don't really need them, we've loads of people to hang about with.

These were sentiments echoed by Shauna and Debbie (both Catholic):

Interviewer: Would you like to be on better terms with the Protestants?
Shauna: No, not really.
Debbie: I'm all right.
Interviewer: So you don't think you're missing out by not having them as friends?
Shauna: No, I've got my own friends.

Overall, it would appear that by the age of ten or eleven, the children in these areas are developing a much more in-depth and detailed understanding of the conflict both in terms of the actual incidents and events that are taking place as well as beginning to acquire an appreciation of the broader political and historical background to the conflict. Alongside this greater understanding, the other key difference when comparing them with the seven and eight year olds is the greater tendency for these children to subscribe to more positive and reconciliatory beliefs. While the younger children's experiences were limited and tended to be dominated by the immediate tensions that exist at the interface areas, these older children seem to have acquired slightly broader knowledge and experiences from a range of sources, including television and cross-community activities. Therefore, their attitudes tended to be more contradictory; continuing to reflect the reality of sectarian tensions in the area and the very real sense of threat that accompanies these tensions but also beginning to recognise the limitations of the simple stereotypes that they had developed a few years earlier.

CONCLUSIONS

The purpose of this chapter has been to offer a review and critique of existing research on children and the Troubles in Northern Ireland and to model out an alternative methodological approach using data from a detailed and largely unstructured qualitative study of children aged three to eleven. With this purpose in mind, it is hoped that the case study above has been successful in highlighting the potential that qualitative methods have in helping to identify and explain the nature of sectarian attitudes and behaviour among children. The data discussed above clearly demonstrates the importance of focusing on children's perspectives and locating these within the specific social contexts within which they are formed. Also, while it has not been one of the main aims of the present chapter, it should also illustrate the ability of such an approach to help understand the particular processes and factors that tend to either increase or decrease the salience of sectarianism in the children's lives.

More substantively, the chapter has offered some insights into the key findings that are emerging from our research with regard to the nature and extent of sectarianism in the children's lives and how this emerges and develops with age. It needs to be stressed, however, that these are preliminary findings and also only offer the briefest of sketches of the developmental processes involved. Also, and as outlined at the beginning, these children are a very atypical group and it would be misleading to even attempt to generalise from this one case study to the population of children as a whole in Northern Ireland. The fieldwork that is currently under way with middle-class children at the time of writing will help to provide a more balanced picture of the range of attitudes and behaviours that exist in the region. Even then, however, it would require a separate study with a more quantitative design to be able to assess the extent to which these findings can be generalised to the population as a whole. If nothing else, however, this present chapter should serve as a reminder of the need for any such quantitative study to be informed by the findings of more in-depth qualitative studies such as this one.

ACKNOWLEDGEMENTS

We are grateful to the former Central Community Relations Unit for initially commissioning this work and for the Equality Unit Research Branch within the Office of the First Minister and Deputy First Minister (OFMDFM), who took over the management of the project, for their continued help and support. The views expressed in this chapter are our own and not necessarily those of the OFMDFM. Thanks also to Karen Winter for her comments on an earlier draft of this chapter.

NOTES

[1] For summaries see Cairns (1987); Gough et al. (1992); Trew (1992); Cairns and Cairns (1995); Cairns et al. (1995); Connolly with Maginn (1999).

[2] This is a pseudonym used to maintain the anonymity of the two areas concerned.

[3] These are two Scottish football clubs located in Glasgow. Support for the two teams has traditionally been split along sectarian lines with Catholics tending to support Celtic and Protestants tending to support Rangers. Within Northern Ireland, support for these two teams has become a key marker of difference between Protestants and Catholics.

[4] All names used are pseudonyms to maintain anonymity.

[5] Key to the transcripts can be found below.

KEY TO TRANSCRIPTS

/	Indicates interruption in speech.
[. . .]	Extracts edited out of transcript.
. . .	A natural pause in the conversation.
[*Italic text*]	Descriptive text added to clarify the nature of the discussion.
[normal text]	Text added to help clarify the point the child is making.

3. EDUCATION AND EQUALITY IN NORTHERN IRELAND

Tony Gallagher

INTRODUCTION

The Centre for the Study of Conflict, University of Ulster, had a particular purpose in addressing issues related to conflict in Northern Ireland. One of its programmes, the Majority Minority Report series (Gallagher, 1995), concerned an examination of the comparative positions of the two main communities, Protestant and Catholic, in Northern Ireland. This chapter examines one of the themes in this series, that is, the comparative position of Protestants and Catholics in education. As we shall see below, one of the key characteristics of education in Northern Ireland lies in the existence of two parallel religious school systems. On one level this fact made a comparative examination of the two communities relatively straightforward. However, for years there was an official fiction that this religious segregation did not exist and that there was a system of Catholic schools and a 'State' system. One of the consequences of this was that official data tended not to be published in a way which allowed for the direct comparison of the educational experience of the two communities. This limited the extent to which official data could be used for the Majority Minority comparison, and placed heavy reliance on research studies which included this variable in their analysis. In fact, in a neglected field, for years the most significant and important contribution in this area was provided by researchers associated with the early years of the Centre for the Study of Conflict (including John Darby, Seamus Dunn and Dominic Murray), and the work of Bob Cormack, Bob Osborne and others on aspects of fair employment. One of the key themes of this present chapter is to highlight the extent to which community relations policy in Northern Ireland has had the impact of encouraging more openness in the publication of official data and thereby allowing for more complete analysis of comparative data.

The second main theme of this chapter is to show how the educational differences between the two communities have narrowed over time. Part of the chapter looks at the development of separate schools, a pattern which was closely linked to the broader political climate. Indeed, the 1990s saw not only the clearer development of a community relations policy by government in Northern Ireland (which this book is, after all, about), but also the establishment of more equitable policy and practice towards the separate school systems in Northern Ireland. The analysis in this paper suggests that this also led to the narrowing of differences on key indicators. In fact, one of the more remarkable aspects of preparing this chapter has been the extent to which recent debates in education in Northern Ireland have been more marked by issues of class and gender than by issues of religion. In education, at least, the debates may now be less about the relative treatment of the two communities, and more about the way the education system as a whole can contribute to the development of a more tolerant and integrated society.

Community relations policy in Northern Ireland was driven by three main goals: the provision of more opportunities for cross-community contact, the promotion of greater tolerance of cultural pluralism and a commitment to equality of opportunity. Much policy work in education tended to focus on the first two of these, but the focus of the Majority Minority series tended to be on the issue of equality. It is this that forms the main substance of the present chapter. In addition, the focus of the discussion will be on the schools' system. There was a series of important studies carried out on participation in higher education by Cormack and Osborne (e.g. Cormack et al., 1984; Cormack et al., 1989) (and more recently the present author), but, as yet, official sources have not advanced to the stage where more routine monitoring of the experiences of the two communities can be considered.

EDUCATION IN NORTHERN IRELAND

The two most important legal frameworks for the current structure of education in Northern Ireland are provided by the 1947 Education Act which established free, but academically selective, post-primary education (Wilson, 1987) and the 1989 Education Reform Order which introduced elements of an educational market and competition between schools, but also introduced important aspects of community relations practice into the new statutory curriculum and obligated government to support developments in integrated education.

Whereas the rest of the United Kingdom moved towards non-selective arrangements from the 1960s onwards, selection at 11 years remained the predominant form of transfer from primary to secondary education in Northern Ireland. Between 1981 and 1985, for example, some 90% of pupils were involved with the selective procedure. The remaining 10% of pupils were involved with alternative transfer systems available in Northern Ireland (Wilson, 1986), which included a system of delayed selection operating in the Craigavon area and a number of de facto comprehensive schools which take pupils of all abilities. There had been an attempt to move away from the selective arrangements at the end of the 1970s, but these measures were stopped when the first Thatcher government was elected in 1979. Thereafter the selective system remained fairly secure, despite some critical evidence arising from a series of reports from the Northern Ireland Council for Educational Research. Following the election of the Blair government in 1997 there was a widespread expectation that the issue would be reopened. In fact, the Minister with Responsibility for Education, Tony Worthington, decided to commission some research studies to inform debate on the issue. Two main studies were published on the Craigavon arrangements (Alexander et al., 1998) and on the effects of the selective system (Gallagher and Smith, 2000). Following the latter study, a Review Body was established by Minister of Education, Martin McGuinness, to consult and bring forward recommendations on the future organisation of post-primary education. The Review Body's report, the Burns Report, was published in October 2001 (Burns Report, 2001). At this point Martin McGuinness announced a consultation on its recommendations to conclude in May 2002.

Apart from the selective nature of the system, the other main characteristic of education in Northern Ireland lies in the existence of parallel religious school systems, largely catering for Protestant and Catholic students separately. Prior to partition most schools were owned by Church authorities. After Northern Ireland was established there was an attempt to create a non-denominational, but not secular, school system in the hope that eventually most Churches would transfer their schools to public ownership. In fact, the Catholic Church did not reach a rapprochement with the Northern Ireland government until 1968, while during the 1920s and 1930s legislative amendments created a system of 'State' education that was Protestant in all but name (Akenson, 1973; Buckland, 1979; and Dunn, 1993). The next major changes came in the 1980s with the development of a third Integrated sector, and the creation of the Northern Ireland Council for Integrated Education (NICIE) and the Council for Catholic Maintained Schools (CCMS) to promote the interests of their respective schools. Partly in response, the Transferors' Representative Council (TRC) was established, although on a non-statutory basis, to represent the Protestant interest and legacy in local authority schools.

The effect of these developments can be seen in the religious composition of schools in Northern Ireland in 2000–01. From Table 3.1 we can see that the majority of Catholic pupils attend Catholic schools and the majority of Protestant pupils attend Protestant schools. Although the religious composition of pupils attending Integrated schools is more mixed, the overall proportion attending these schools remains small.

Table 3.1: Percentages of Pupils by Religion and Type of School (Primary, Prep, Secondary and Grammar), 2000–01 (source: calculated from Department of Education statistical press release, 30 April 2001)

SCHOOLS	CATHOLIC	PROTESTANT & OTHER	NOT RECORDED	TOTAL
Protestant schools	4	94	89	49
Catholic schools	92	1	2	47
Integrated schools	3	5	9	4
ALL SCHOOLS	100	100	100	100

PRE-SCHOOL CHILDREN

Pre-school provision in education is not compulsory in Northern Ireland and has been, traditionally, very limited. Thus, for example, a report by the Northern Ireland Council for Educational Research (NICER) estimated that in 1985 nursery places were available for 13% of the three and four year olds in Northern Ireland (Wells and Burke, 1986; see also Foote, 1980). By 1990–91 the situation had changed little: in that year there were only 85 funded nursery schools with a total enrolment of 4,946 (PPRU, 1992).

One of the priorities of the Labour government elected in 1997 was for an expansion in pre-school provision and, in consequence, the availability of places has expanded markedly. By 2000–01 the total number of funded places in pre-school provision had risen to 17,878, with the majority being in nursery schools or classes and the rest mainly in reception classes of primary schools or playgroups. Although there was no data to confirm this provision, it was widely believed that the enrolments of nursery schools were mixed in religious terms, and that this pattern of mixing declined as the total number of places increased. The evidence from current data (see Tables 3.2 and 3.3) does suggest that there is a high level of segregation in nursery schools, and in nursery and reception classes in primary schools, although it should be noted that still as many as a third of the pupils in 'Protestant' nursery schools are, in fact, Catholics.

Table 3.2: Religion of Pupils in Nursery Schools by School Type* and Religion of Pupils (Percentages) (source: calculated from Department of Education statistical press release, 30 April 2001)

NURSERY SCHOOLS	CATHOLIC	PROTESTANT & OTHER	TOTAL (EXCLUDES NOT RECORDED)
Protestant schools	33	67	100
Catholic schools	97	3	100
Integrated schools	–	–	–
All schools	51	49	100

*In this and subsequent tables the 'school type' is taken as referring to the religious tradition of the school as outlined in the section of this paper on segregated schools.

Table 3.3: Religion of Pupils in Nursery and Reception Classes by School Management Type (Percentages) (source: calculated from Department of Education Statistical Release, 30 April 2001)

NURSERY AND RECEPTION CLASSES	CATHOLIC	PROTESTANT & OTHER	TOTAL (EXCLUDES NOT RECORDED)
Protestant schools	13	87	100
Catholic schools	97	3	100
Integrated schools	48	52	100
All schools	55	45	100

PRIMARY EDUCATION

In 2000–01 there were a little over 175,000 pupils aged between four and eleven years in 900 primary schools and a handful of preparatory departments in grammar schools. This is in marked contrast to the situation in the late 1940s, the first years in which pupils could take advantage of the 1947 Education Act and attempt to qualify for a non-fee-paying place in a grammar school. In 1949, for example, a slightly higher number of pupils was taught in over 1,600 primary schools and almost 32,000 were 12 years of age or older (Ministry of Education, 1950).

We have noted above the extent of religious segregation that exists in the school system. Up to the early 1960s, data on the religious composition of schools was published by the Ministry of Education (Akenson, 1973), but after this period no data was published until the 1990s. In the interim there was official reluctance to accept that the schools were divided in this way: the official position was that there were Catholic schools and State schools, with the latter open to all. In strict legal terms, of course, this was accurate, but for all practical purposes this distinction was a fiction. In the absence of official data, commentators had to rely on the limited data on religious segregation that emerged from a range of research studies (*for example*, Darby, 1973, Darby et al., 1977, Murray, 1978 and Greer, 1983). Thus, for instance, in the 'Schools Apart?' study, Darby et al., (1977) found that, of 150 primary and post-primary schools responding to a survey, over 95% of Protestant schools had less than 5% Catholic enrolment and over 98% of Catholic schools had less than 5% Protestant pupils. Similarly, of 750 primary school teachers in the survey, only three were employed in schools of a different religion. The current picture with regard to pupils can be seen on Table 3.4 which shows the high degree of religious homogeneity in the Protestant and Catholic schools, as compared with the balance achieved at an aggregate level by the Integrated schools.

Table 3.4: Percentage of Pupils in Primary Schools by Religion and School Type, 2000–01 (source: calculated from Department of Education statistical press release, 30 April 2001)

PRIMARY SCHOOLS	CATHOLIC	PROTESTANT & OTHER	NOT RECORDED	TOTAL	CATHOLIC	PROTESTANT & OTHER	TOTAL (EXCLUDES NOT RECORDED)
Protestant schools	4	87	9	100	4	96	100
Catholic schools	99	1	0	100	99	1	100
Integrated schools	41	43	16	100	49	51	100
ALL SCHOOLS	51	44	5	100	53	47	100
ALL SCHOOLS	*85,749*	*75,126*	*8,825*	*169,700*			

Under the 1989 Education Reform Order the funding for primary schools was based largely on pupil numbers and a statutory curriculum was established. The research carried out for SACHR (Standing Advisory Commission on Human Rights) (Cormack et al., 1991), referred to above, had suggested that there were differences in the level of recurrent funding available to Catholic schools, but such differences as existed will have largely disappeared due to the new funding arrangements. The other two main issues that had been addressed in regard to primary schools concerned any curricular differences that existed between Protestant and Catholic schools, and the possibility that the selective system had a differential impact on them.

With regard to the curriculum, the expectation would be that the statutory curriculum introduced after 1989 would have reduced any significant differences between Protestant and Catholic schools, although there are no studies that have specifically examined this issue: some differences are likely to remain if only because of the time spent in Catholic primary schools in preparing pupils for religious sacraments. In addition, one might expect that the curriculum offered by Integrated primary schools should offer some distinctive experiences in comparison with either Protestant or Catholic schools.

The evidence on curricular differences between Protestant and Catholic primary schools before 1989 falls into three main areas. The first area concentrates on the relative impact of selection on the curriculum (Sutherland and Gallagher, 1986; Teare and Sutherland, 1988), the second on the teaching of history (Magee, 1970; Darby, 1974) and religious education (for example Greer 1972, 1978, 1979–80, and Greer and Brown, 1981), while the third is derived from comparative information gained in the 'Schools Apart?' study (Darby et al., 1977) and a subsequent detailed follow-up investigation of two schools (Murray, 1985a). A number of main themes emerge from this data, including the higher status accorded to religious education in Catholic schools and the allocation of more time to this subject; the perceived greater impact on the curriculum of Catholic schools as a consequence of preparation for the transfer tests; and differences in some of the sporting activities followed in the schools.

Magee (1970) provided the classic study on the teaching of history in schools and, although the main issues in this area concerned post-primary schools, he did identify problems in primary schools also:

> In primary schools (History) was an optional subject, and in classes preparing for county council scholarships and, later, qualifying examinations, the temptation for teachers was to leave it alone. History teaching in the primary schools of Northern Ireland was – and continues to be – spasmodic, uncoordinated and largely academic, a 'watered-down' version of grammar school history. (p. 19)

Magee's work will be discussed more generally in a later section and it should be noted that one of the early innovations in schools in Northern Ireland following the outbreak of violent conflict was improvements in the history textbooks that are available for schools and the philosophy underlying the teaching of history (see, for example, Austin, 1985; see also Darby, 1974).

In a series of publications Dominic Murray (Murray, 1983; 1985a; 1985b) examined some of the differences in the style and operation of Protestant and

Catholic primary schools in Northern Ireland. Murray expanded upon the original 'Schools Apart?' study by spending six months each in a Protestant and Catholic primary school. He argued that the two separate school systems reflected the two dominant cultural communities in Northern Ireland and demonstrated this with regard to textbooks, ritual, symbols and general ethos. In his direct and detailed comparison of the two primary schools, Murray found that the Protestant school identified much more closely with the policy making and administrative apparatus of the educational system. By contrast, the Catholic school only contacted administrative bodies on occasions of dire necessity. This difference was not confined to educational bodies. Murray noted that pupils in the Protestant school paid more frequent visits to community organisations such as the fire brigade, post office, local government offices or police stations, which probably reflected the different nature of the relationship at the time between the two communities and public authorities or institutions of various kinds.

Perhaps Murray's most significant claim was not in the extent of separation, but rather in the perceptions made of these differences. In an abstract sense, it was not surprising that the Catholic school, for example, displayed numerous religious artifacts. Nor, in an abstract sense, was it surprising that the Protestant school flew a Union flag. Murray pointed out, however, that the perceptions of either side viewed such symbolic gestures as deliberately antagonistic. He observed that the two dominant cultures are so mutually antipathetic that any demonstration of one is perceived as an assault on the other (Murray, 1983). In the first edition of the Majority Minority Report on education (Gallagher, 1995) it was noted that Murray's study stood as just about the only in-depth study of primary schools in Northern Ireland. In 2002 the same gap remains. The one area where a significant new body of evidence has emerged lies in the impact of the selective system and, while most of the recent research was not directly concerned with the relative impact of selection on Protestant and Catholic schools, much of the data does allow for this relative comparison.

THE IMPACT OF SELECTIVE EDUCATION

A variety of selective procedures have been used in Northern Ireland since 1948 (Sutherland and Gallagher, 1986; Wilson, 1987; Gallagher, 1988). From the later 1960s until the end of the 1980s pupils in their final year of primary school sat two verbal reasoning-type tests and a proportion of the top-ranked pupils were then deemed qualified for a non-fee-paying place in a grammar school. In 1988, following a court case supported by the Equal Opportunities Commission, the practice of treating boys and girls as separate groups for the determination of qualified status was discontinued (Gallagher, 1989). For the last decade or so the system was changed in a number of important ways. Firstly, the use of verbal reasoning-type tests was discontinued in favour of attainment tests in mathematics, English and science. Secondly, quotas for school intakes were removed and all schools were given maximum admissions numbers in order to allow for parents to express a preference for a school. And thirdly, the schools then had to declare criteria to be used when selecting pupils in circumstances when they had more applications than places, but only grammar schools were permitted to use an academic criterion.

Until recently the main body of evidence on the operation of selection in Northern Ireland has been provided by a series of studies carried out by the Northern Ireland Council for Educational Research (NICER). Wilson (1986) detailed the transfer status of all pupils entering post-primary education between 1981 and 1985. Wilson's data pointed to a small, but noticeable, attainment gap between pupils in the Protestant and Catholic school systems, with this gap narrowing over the period 1981 to 1985. Despite this, Wilson found a significantly higher proportion of pupils in Protestant grammar schools as compared with Catholic grammar schools, a difference which had been noted in other studies (Osborne, 1985; Livingstone, 1987). In part this was explained by a differential extent of fee-paying in that a higher proportion of pupils entered Protestant grammar schools as fee-payers. Wilson (1986) found that 5% of 'non-qualified' pupils entered Protestant grammar schools as fee-payers, compared with 2% entering Catholic grammar schools. This differentialmay have been related to the tendency for preparatory departments to be based in Protestant, rather than Catholic, grammar schools, although this ceased to be relevant after the 1989 Education Reform Order as fee-paying was abolished.

A more significant issue in Wilson's data, however, was that a higher proportion of qualified pupils entered Protestant, as compared with Catholic, grammar schools. Two explanations were offered to account for this differential pattern of entry. Livingstone (1987) argued for a choice explanation such that more parents of pupils in the Catholic school system opted to send their children to non-grammar schools even though they were eligible for grammar school places. Osborne et al., (1989) argued for a structural explanation such that there was a relative shortage of places available in Catholic grammar schools. The system of open enrolment and the quantification of the capacity of grammar schools provided an opportunity to assess these competing explanations. The analysis was carried out as part of the SACHR investigation (Cormack et al., 1992a) and showed that, in 1990, the Catholic post-primary school system had 34% of pupils in grammar schools, while the Protestant school system had 42% of pupils in grammar schools. Had the grammar schools been operating up to their maximum capacity, the Catholic system would have had 36% in grammar schools while the Protestant system would have had 46% in grammar schools. On the basis of DENI pupil projections to 1995 it was calculated that 33% of pupils in the Catholic system would be in grammar schools in comparison with 46% of pupils in the Protestant system: the shortfall in the Catholic system is explained by the higher rate of growth of that sector. This analysis pointed to a clear structural problem. In July

1992, the DENI announced the creation of two new Catholic grammar schools, in Belfast and Derry, to increase the number of places available in Catholic grammar schools.

More recent data has become available on this issue. In 1996 the Department of Education published two statistical bulletins on the relationship between social background, school performance and transfer test performance (DENI, 1996a, 1996b). A number of themes emerged from the bulletins. First, there was a clear relationship between transfer test performance and social background: in schools where less than 11% of pupils were entitled to free school meals, over half the pupils taking the transfer tests obtained the top grade. By contrast, in schools where more than half the pupils were entitled to free school meals, only 16% achieved the top grade. The second theme to emerge concerned a difference in the transfer grade profile of Protestant and Catholic schools. Thus, for example, in 1995–96 34% of pupils entered for the transfer tests in Catholic primary schools achieved the top grade in comparison with 41% of pupils in Protestant or Integrated schools. In part this was explained by the different social profile of the two communities and, hence, the extent of social disadvantage in Catholic schools. Thus, schools with less than 11% entitlement to free school meals comprised 10% of pupils in Catholic schools, but 43% of pupils in other schools. By contrast, schools with more than half their pupils entitled to free school meals comprised 23% of Catholic schools, but only 7% of other schools (DENI, 1996a, 1996b). In addition, analysis of transfer data for the last few years of the 1990s confirmed the stability of the relationship between social background, as measured by entitlement to free school meals, and transfer test performance (Gallagher, 2000). Despite this, and the continuing pattern whereby there is a higher level of free school meal entitlement in Catholic primary schools, the gap in transfer grade performance had disappeared. Thus, in 1998–99 among all pupils in the final year of primary schools, an average of 25% of pupils in Catholic schools achieved a top grade in comparison with an average of 23% in other primary schools.

As far as participation in grammar schools is concerned, data for Year 12 pupils was available from the Department of Education School Performance Tables (DENI, 2000). The last published Tables, for 1998–99, showed that for grammar schools, 45% were in Catholic schools and 55% were in Protestant schools. By contrast, for the same year group, but for pupils in secondary schools, 51% were in Catholic schools, 44% were in Protestant schools and 5% were in Integrated schools. Looked at another way, this suggests that, within the Catholic sector, 34% of Year 12 pupils were in grammar schools, while within the Protestant sector 43% of pupils were in grammar schools. Thus, there remains something of a shortfall in grammar places in the Catholic sector, although it has narrowed and the effects of the second new grammar school have not been felt at Year 12 level. In addition, there is known to be a proportion of Catholic pupils in 'Protestant' grammar schools (*see below*).

POST-PRIMARY SCHOOLS

Secondary intermediate schools were established alongside grammar schools after the 1947 Act to provide free post-primary education for the majority of pupils in Northern Ireland. In the immediate post-war period it took some time to build the new secondary intermediate schools. The main period of rapid growth in Protestant secondary schools began in 1954 and continued until 1962. By contrast, among Catholic secondary schools the main period of rapid growth did not begin until 1958. The time lag was probably due to the requirement on the Catholic authorities to contribute to the capital cost of new schools. Following the SACHR research on school funding and performance all schools were permitted access to 100% capital grants if they were prepared to make minor adjustments to the composition of the Boards of Governors: by 2000 all but about 20 post-primary schools had opted to take this course. In addition, the introduction of local management of schools (LMS) meant that recurrent funding levels were equalised to the extent that the bulk of a school's funding was based on pupil numbers. Thus, while the funding differential between Catholic and other schools had been a bone of contention for some years, following the policy decisions in the aftermath of the SACHR research (Cormack et al., 1991; Osborne et al., 1989), much of the controversy reduced. To the extent that there are current debates, they tend to focus on the proportion of recurrent funds that should be allocated on the basis of social disadvantage. To use a measure of social disadvantage alone, such as free school meals, would result in transfers to the Catholic sector. The difficulty is that there are only limited direct measures of educational need available and the use of these might introduce negative incentives for increased standards of performance. At the time of writing the Department of Education had proposed a new mechanism for distributing these funds that used both free school meal entitlement and Key Stage results as a basis for allocation decisions, but final decisions had yet to be made.

Tables 3.5 and 3.6 show the religious composition of secondary and grammar schools in 2000–01. As with primary schools, the tables show that the school system remains highly segregated, with a high level of religious homogeneity in Protestant and Catholic schools: the highest degree of mixing is found in Protestant grammar schools, but even here the proportion of Catholic pupils is less than one in ten. Data supplied to the Department of Education TACOT (Towards a Culture of Tolerance) working group indicated that of the 1,100 or so schools in Northern Ireland, about 40 were Integrated and mixed, but only 40 more had a minority enrolment of 10% or more. In other words, 93% of schools in Northern Ireland contained 90% or more pupils from one religious community. Table 3.5 also shows that, at an aggregate level, the Integrated schools have achieved a balanced enrolment.

There exists quite a substantial body of research evidence on the curricular similarities and differences between Protestant and Catholic post-primary schools,

Table 3.5: Percentage of Pupils in Secondary Schools by Religion and School Type, 2000–01 (source: calculated from Department of Education statistical press release, 30 April 2001)

SECONDARY SCHOOLS	CATHOLIC	PROTESTANT & OTHER	NOT RECORDED	TOTAL	CATHOLIC	PROTESTANT & OTHER	TOTAL (EXCLUDES NOT RECORDED)
Protestant schools	3	91	6	100	3	97	100
Catholic schools	99	1	0	100	99	1	100
Integrated schools	41	53	6	100	44	56	100
All schools	54	43	3	100	56	44	100
N	49,958	39,826	3,195	92,979			

Table 3.6: Percentage of Pupils in Grammar Schools by Religion and School Type, 2000–01 (source: calculated from Department of Education statistical press release, 30 April 2001)

GRAMMAR SCHOOLS	CATHOLIC	PROTESTANT & OTHER	NOT RECORDED	TOTAL	CATHOLIC	PROTESTANT & OTHER	TOTAL (EXCLUDES NOT RECORDED)
Protestant schools	8	82	10	100	9	91	100
Catholic schools	99	1	0	100	99	1	100
All schools	48	46	6	100	51	49	100
N	30,339	28,587	3,648	62,574			

although much of it is based on sample data or is inferred from examination profiles. The work of Greer, on religious education, and Magee, on history, have already been mentioned as has the 'Schools Apart?' study (Darby et al., 1977). In addition, there is limited evidence on the timetable allocations of a sample of pupils in Protestant and Catholic grammar and secondary schools (Sutherland and Gallagher, 1987). Prior to this the main evidence in this area concentrated on the public examinations taken by pupils at 16 and 18. The sources of this evidence were a series of studies sponsored by the Fair Employment Agency (e.g. Osborne 1985, 1986; Osborne and Murray, 1978), the NICER Transfer Procedure project (e.g. Gallagher, 1988; Sutherland and Gallagher, 1987), and the work of McEwen and colleagues on sex differences in A-level subject choice (e.g. McEwen et al., 1986) which was to be followed up ten years later (Gallagher et al., 1996). In order to inform the process of establishing the statutory curriculum, the DENI carried out a major investigation of the timetable followed by pupils in Northern Ireland in 1989 (DENI, 1989). Data from that survey was analysed as part of the SACHR research into attainment in Protestant and Catholic schools (Cormack et al., 1992b). As in the primary schools the programme of work carried out by Greer and colleagues suggested that more time was spent on religious education in Catholic schools and that the subject was accorded a higher status (Greer, 1991). This pattern has been confirmed in all the surveys of pupils' timetables. If Magee (1970) had been critical of the teaching of history in primary schools, he was scathing about the quality of teaching in post-primary schools: 'The impression generally was that Ulster children could be educated as if they were living in Chelmsford or Bristol or Haverford West' (p.19). By contrast, pupils in Catholic post-primary schools were taught Irish history using books published in Southern Ireland and 'the emphasis was almost entirely on Irish military heroes' (p.19). In a similar vein, Barritt and Carter (1962) suggested that Catholic schools treated Irish history as the story of heroism in maintaining national feeling under foreign rule.

Throughout the 1970s this situation improved in that better textbooks became available, a wider range of supplementary material was produced (for example, the series of historical documents produced by the Public Records Office of Northern Ireland; *see also* Darby, 1974) and innovative suggestions had come forward on local and environmental history teaching (*for example,* Austin, 1985). Given the importance attached to historical symbols in Northern Ireland generally, it is not surprising that the teaching of history quickly came under critical scrutiny. It is equally unsurprising that this area of the curriculum has undergone marked change in the last 20 years. These changes have continued apace as the Council for the Curriculum, Examinations and Assessment (CCEA) has produced increasingly imaginative history materials and textbooks.

The 'Schools Apart?' survey of curricula in Protestant and Catholic post-primary schools revealed some differences in cultural and sporting activities, but also many similarities in the routine activities of the schools. One area of marked difference in addition to the teaching of religious education was the provision of Irish which was almost always a compulsory subject in the junior years of many Catholic post-primary schools, but absent from the timetable of all Protestant schools. The most extensive survey of the curriculum, carried out by the Department of Education (DENI, 1989) for planning towards the statutory curriculum, highlighted some differences, but as with the earlier Darby et al., (1977) work, many similarities. Indeed, sector differences, between grammar and secondary schools, and sex differences were perhaps more striking. Osborne and Murray (1978) and Osborne (1985) provided a picture of O-level subject passes for all pupils in Northern Ireland for the years 1967, 1971, 1975, 1979 and 1982 (*see also* Osborne and

Cormack, 1989). These studies were published by the Fair Employment Agency and as such are primarily concerned with the qualifications taken into the labour market by pupils from Catholic and Protestant schools. Analysis of this data tended to show that disproportionately higher numbers of boys in Catholic schools passed religious education and languages, while disproportionately higher numbers of boys in Protestant schools passed science and technical subjects. Gallagher (1988) analysed the examination presentations by a sample of pupils drawn from across Northern Ireland and, while there was a core set of subjects which most pupils studied, there were differences in religious education, some languages and science subjects in line with the earlier studies.

Osborne and Murray (1978) and Osborne (1985) also analysed data on A-level passes for boys only for 1967, 1971 and 1975, and for all pupils in 1979 and 1982, and found higher rates of humanities subjects in Catholic schools in comparison with higher rates of science subjects in Protestant schools, a pattern of difference that was confirmed by a survey of some 1,400 sixth-form pupils in 21 grammar schools in Northern Ireland (McEwen et al., 1986). Although this survey found no differences in A-level subject choice for girls in Protestant or Catholic grammar schools, significant differences were found for boys. A ten-year follow-up study found that the most significant changes occurred in the gender patterns, with more girls taking science subjects (McEwen et al., 1997a; 1997b; Gallagher et al., 1996; 1997). The main reason for this appeared to be the girls' perceptions of occupational opportunity and this was taken by Gallagher et al. (1996) to be linked to the equal opportunities environment encouraged by legislation against sex discrimination.

PUPIL PERFORMANCE

Prior to 1989 it was extremely difficult to carry out analyses of school performance in general and to compare the performance of Protestant and Catholic schools in particular. The studies which did offer some data on this (for example, Osborne and Murray, 1978; Wilson, 1985; 1989; Sutherland and Gallagher, 1987; Gallagher, 1988; Osborne, 1985, 1986; Osborne and Cormack, 1989) either had to collect performance data from pupil samples, or accessed official data through special requests. In the latter circumstance access to data was normally couched in terms of extraordinary confidentiality and, in particular, publication of individual school-level data was rarely, if ever, permitted. This was a period of excessive, if not obsessive, secrecy.

After 1989, two important changes occurred. First, under the Education Reform Order, a decision was made to publish annual School Performance Tables showing various enrolment and examinations data on every post-primary school in Northern Ireland. The rationale for this was to provide parents with information on school performance as part of the basis for informed parental choice. Inter alia the publication of individual school level data allowed for the comparison of performance levels of Protestant and Catholic schools. The second change followed from the SACHR (SACHR, 1992) research that had argued that there was a need to recognise the religious divisions within schools and to monitor the impact of policy on the parallel school systems. One of the consequences of this was that Department of Education statistical data on schools started to include disaggregation by management type: the form of disaggregation was between 'schools under Catholic management arrangements' and 'schools under other management arrangements'. Thus, the Department of Education statistical data does not, as yet, permit direct examination of data for Integrated schools and the sole Irish Medium school is categorised in the 'Other' category. In the Majority Minority Report on education it was necessary to rely on a variety of sources in order to carry out an analysis of performance in Protestant and Catholic schools, a comparison which can now be carried out much more straightforwardly, as we will see below. There is one caveat to this: not long after the election of Martin McGuinness as Minister of Education, a consultation was held on the future of School Performance Tables and it was decided that they would not be published after 1998–99. The Department of Education is prepared to provide limited access to aggregate data for 1999–00, but it is no longer possible to obtain data on individual school performance so, once again, detailed public monitoring of comparative patterns of performance has been constrained.

As noted above there are two main sources that can be used to compare school performance: the data from the School Performance Tables (up to 1989–99) and data from Department of Education statistical bulletins on school leavers. The school leavers' data includes information on the qualifications of leavers and their destinations after school. Figure 3.1 shows a comparison of the proportion of leavers from Other and Catholic schools with five or more 'good' GCSEs or equivalent (with a 'good' GCSE defined as an O-level pass, a CSE grade 1 or a GCSE at grade C or above). The datapoints for 1975, 1986 and 1987, and the few years from 1989 onwards, were made available by the Department of Education for specific projects until the data was routinely published in this way. Figure 3.1 shows that up to the mid-1990s there was a slightly higher proportion of leavers from Other schools achieving this criterion as compared with leavers from Catholic schools, with a particularly marked difference in 1975. By the end of the decade the difference had almost completely disappeared.

A pattern of even closer equality can be seen in Figure 3.2 which shows the proportion of leavers who failed to achieve the equivalent of one O-level or one GCSE at grade C or above. In 1975 over half of school leavers achieved this criterion and the proportion of these leavers was higher in Catholic as compared with Other schools. From the mid-1980s onwards, however, the proportion of leavers at this performance criterion steadily fell and was very similar for Other and Catholic schools, although it has stabilised at about 20% over the past five years.

Figure 3.1: % Leavers with 5+ Good GSCEs

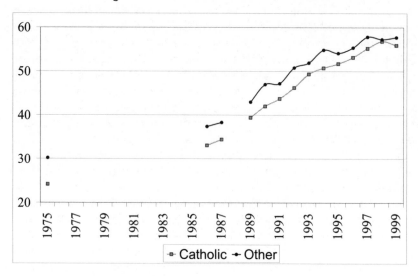

Figure 3.2: % Leavers with <1 Good GSCE

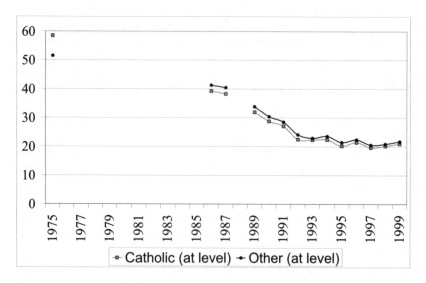

Figure 3.3: % Leavers with 2+ A Levels

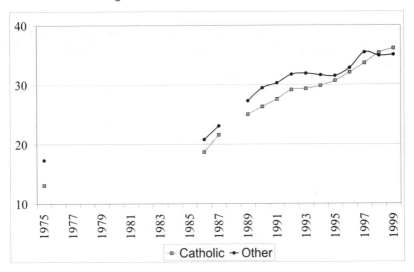

Figure 3.3 reveals another part of the picture by showing the proportion of leavers with two or more A-level passes: this is the group who might normally be expected to seek places in higher education. From Figure 3.3 we can see that the proportion of leavers meeting this criterion was higher for Other schools as compared with Catholic schools up to the latter part of the 1990s at which point virtual parity was achieved. Once again, the difference in 1975 was particularly marked.

Thus, this data suggests that there had been a performance gap between Catholic and Other schools in the past, but that this gap has narrowed virtually to the point of disappearance by the end of the 1990s. This gap had occurred in a context where the overall levels of performance of school leavers had steadily risen over the entire period.

The next issue concerns where the school leavers went. This data is shown in a series of tables below (previous studies which have examined population or sample data on school leaver destinations include Cormack et al., 1980; Cormack and Osborne, 1983; McWhirter et al., 1987; McWhirter, 1989; Murray and Darby, 1978; Murray and Darby, 1983; Osborne, 1985). Table 3.7 shows the destinations of leavers from all schools in 1986–87 and 1999–00 (data on leavers entering employment, unemployment or training were not available for 1986–87). Three features are noteworthy from this table: first, the proportion of leavers entering higher education doubled over the period; second, the proportion of school leavers who left education fell considerably, although it was still the modal category in 1999–00; and third, the pattern for leavers from Catholic and Other schools is very similar in both years, although in 1999–00 a slightly higher proportion of leavers from Catholic schools entered training.

Table 3.7: Destinations of School Leavers in (a) 1986–87 and (b) 1999–00 (in percentages) (source: calculated from Department of Education data)

1986–87 ALL	CATHOLIC	OTHER	ALL
Higher Education	15	16	15
Further Education	28	26	27
Employment			
Unemployment			
Training			
Other not FE/HE	57	58	58
All	100	100	100
N	12,523	14,275	26,798

1999–00 ALL	CATHOLIC	OTHER	ALL
Higher Education	31	30	31
Further Education	28	33	30
Employment	13	13	13
Unemployment	4	4	4
Training	24	18	21
Other	1	1	1
Other not FE/HE	41	37	39
All	100	100	100
N	12,006	13,073	25,079

Of course, there are marked differences in the destinations of leavers from grammar and secondary schools, so the next two sets of tables show data for these leavers separately. Table 3.8 shows the destinations of leavers from grammar schools. In 1986–87 a little under a half of grammar school leavers entered higher education, but by 1999–00 this had increased to two in three. In consequence, the proportion of leavers who left education more than halved over the period. It is noteworthy also that the proportion of leavers entering higher education was higher for Catholic schools in both years.

Table 3.8: Destinations of Grammar School Leavers in (a) 1986–87 and (b) 1999–00 (in percentages) (source: calculated from Department of Education data)

1986–87 GRAMMAR	CATHOLIC	OTHER	ALL
Higher Education	48	44	45
Further Education	31	30	31
Employment			
Unemployment			
Training			
Other not FE/HE	*21*	*26*	*24*
All	100	100	100
N	3,363	4,800	8,163

1999–00 GRAMMAR	CATHOLIC	OTHER	ALL
Higher Education	68	65	66
Further Education	22	26	24
Employment	6	5	5
Unemployment	1	1	1
Training	2	2	2
Other	1	1	1
Other not FE/HE	*10*	*9*	*9*
All	100	100	100
N	4,309	5,376	9,685

Table 3.9 shows the destinations of leavers from secondary schools. Over the period the proportion of leavers entering higher education rose markedly, although still was less than one in ten overall in 1999–00. The proportion that left education fell from almost three in four in 1986–87 to under three in five in 1999–00. It is noteworthy that the proportion of leavers entering higher

Table 3.9: Destinations of Secondary School Leavers in (a) 1986–87 and (b) 1999–00 (in percentages) (source: calculated from Department of Education data)

1986–87 SECONDARY	CATHOLIC	OTHER	ALL
Higher Education	3	1	2
Further Education	26	25	26
Employment			
Unemployment			
Training			
Other not FE/HE	*71*	*74*	*73*
All	100	100	100
N	9,160	9,475	18,635

1999–00 SECONDARY	CATHOLIC	OTHER	ALL
Higher Education	10	6	8
Further Education	31	37	34
Employment	17	19	18
Unemployment	5	6	6
Training	36	30	33
Other	1	1	1
Other not FE/HE	59	57	58
All	100	100	100
N	4,309	5,376	9,685

education was higher in both years for Catholic schools, but so too was the proportion who left education and, in particular, entered training. One further point of note is that among grammar and secondary school leavers, separately, the proportion of leavers entering higher education was higher for Catholic schools.

Nevertheless, this difference was not evident when the data for all school leavers was examined and it is explained by the earlier finding that the proportion of pupils in the Catholic sector who are in grammar schools remains a little less in comparison with the Protestant and Other schools.

The final way we can examine school performance is through the Department of Education School Performance Tables (DENI, 2000). Figure 3.4 shows the level of detail provided by these tables for the last year in which they were published (1998–99). The figure reveals the proportion of Year 12 pupils achieving five or more GCSE passes at grade C or above for Catholic and Other (Protestant and Integrated) schools separately, against the proportion of pupils in the schools who were entitled to free school meals (FSME) (note: the Free School Meals Entitlement data was provided by the Department of Education and was not routinely published on the Performance Tables). In addition, Figure 3.4 shows separate trendlines for the relationship between FSME and performance for Catholic and Other schools separately. A number of features can be seen on Figure 3.4. First, the relatively advantaged position of the grammar schools, which combine low levels of FSME with high performance levels, is evident, particularly within the two categories. Second, the relationship between FSME and performance is clear, again most notably when the two categories of schools are considered separately, although the variation of individual schools around the trend is quite marked. And third, although the general level of social disadvantage (as measured by FSME) is higher in the Catholic schools, for any particular level of FSME the performance of Catholic schools is, on average, higher. Furthermore, the extent of this gap in favour of Catholic schools widens slightly as the FSME level increases. Thus,

Figure 3.4: % Year 12s with 5 Good GSCEs, 1998–99, by School Type (source: calculated from the Department of Education 1998–99 school performance tables)

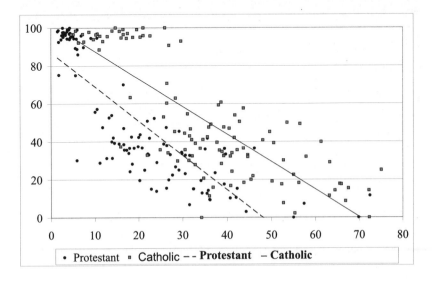

although the comparative performance of Catholic and Other schools on this criterion is about equal (95% each for grammar schools, and 33% for Catholic secondary schools as compared with 30% for Other secondary schools), this implies that Catholic schools are actually performing at a slightly higher level given the higher level of social disadvantage in that community and reflected in the schools.

Since the decision was made to cease publishing School Performance Tables in 1999–00 it is not possible to examine individual school level data. However, the Department of Education has been willing to issue aggregate data for 1999–00 on school performance levels disaggregated by school type and categories of FSME. Previous School Performance Table years for which FSME data was available can be categorised in the same way to provide an additional longitudinal measure of performance.

Table 3.10 shows the pattern for grammar schools for the years 1997–98 to 1999–00 using the criterion of seven GCSE passes at grade C or above that was introduced for grammar schools in 1997–98. Overall, all grammar schools showed an increase in this criterion over the period, with a slightly higher increase for the Catholic schools. However, among the Catholic schools there was actually a decrease in this criterion among the schools with the lowest proportion of FSME, from 96% in 1997–98 to 91% in 1999–00. There was a slight increase in this criterion for Other schools across all FSME categories, although in 1997–98 and 1999–00 none of these schools had 10% or more of their pupils entitled to free school meals.

Table 3.10: % Year 12 Pupils in Grammar Schools with 7 Good GCSEs, 1997–00 by School Type, Year and Free School Meal Entitlement Category (source: calculated from Department of Education data)

FSM CATEGORY	SCHOOL TYPE	1997–98	1998–99	1999–2000
0–4.9	Catholic	96	92	91
	Other	87	90	91
5–9.9	Catholic	86	90	90
	Other	85	82	86
10+	Catholic	84	88	89
	Other	–	86	–
All schools	Catholic	85	88	90
	Other	87	88	90

Table 3.11 shows longitudinal data for secondary schools using the criterion of five GCSEs at grade C or above. For these schools FSME data is available also for

1996–97, and baseline data for 1992–93 is included for comparative purposes. The table shows an overall pattern of improvement in this criterion over time for all three school types. In the case of the Integrated schools, the instability in the pattern in recent years is probably explained by new schools coming into this category both because of transformation schools and the maturity of new Integrated schools opened during the 1990s. The table also shows that the highest rate of increase over the years 1996–97 to 1999–00 occurred for schools in the lower FSME categories and for those in the highest FSME category. In the latter case the

Table 3.11: % Year 12 Pupils in Secondary Schools with 5
Good GCSEs, 1992–93 and 1996–97 to 1999–00 by School Type,
Year and Free School Meal Entitlement Category (source: calculated
from Department of Education data)

FSM CATEGORY	SCHOOL TYPE	1992–93	1996–97	1997–98	1998–99	1999–00
0–19.9	Catholic		25	36	48	44
	Other		38	39	40	41
	Integrated		43	47	32	45
20–29.9	Catholic		42	51	51	48
	Other		27	29	31	30
	Integrated		45	45	33	39
30–39.9	Catholic		39	38	35	35
	Other		22	22	23	24
	Integrated		34	33	37	31
40–49.9	Catholic		32	35	35	33
	Other		14	12	9	13
	Integrated		26	19	36	37
50–59.9	Catholic		27	25	28	26
	Other		7	2	3	6
	Integrated		–	–	–	–
60+	Catholic		19	18	20	24
	Other		4	10	5	9
	Integrated		–	–	–	–
All schools	Catholic	26	32	33	35	34
	Other	24	28	29	31	32
	Integrated	29	39	40	33	39

high relative increase was from a low base in 1996–97. It is perhaps also noteworthy that, for all schools, although Integrated schools have the highest proportion at this criterion in 1999–00 and the difference between Catholic and Other schools is quite small, within each FSME category the Catholic schools tend to have a higher proportion at this criterion, especially in comparison with the Other schools.

CONCLUSIONS

The one area not considered here at any length concerns the role of education in promoting reconciliation, an issue that has been subject to an extensive literature (*see* Boyle, 1976; Darby et al., 1977; Darby, 1978; Darby and Dunn, 1987; Dunn et al., 1984; Dunn, 1986; Dunn and Morgan, 1988; Dunn and Smith, 1989; Smith and Dunn, 1990; Fraser, 1974; Fulton, 1982; Heskin, 1980; Moffatt, 1993; Smith and Robinson, 1992; Spence, 1987; for related research, *see* McKeown, 1973; Russell, 1974–75; McKernan, 1982; Harbison and Harbison, 1980; Harbison, 1983). Put simply, the experience of education in the conflict can be divided into three main phases. In the 1970s, schools were normally cast as 'oases of peace' in which the Troubles were left outside, although there were a couple of notable projects attempted at this period (Skilbeck, 1973; Malone, 1973; O'Connor, 1980). In the 1980s, this strategy of avoidance was replaced when a number of teachers and others began to seek ways in which schools could proactively work towards better community relations. This period included the development of a number of curriculum initiatives and the first stirrings of the Integrated schools movement. In the 1990s, much of this work was put on firmer policy ground when it was incorporated into the 1989 Education Reform Order. In particular, for the first time, schools were required to include elements of community relations in their practice through the statutory educational themes of Education for Mutual Understanding. However, analyses of the experience of these themes (Smith and Robinson, 1992; Leitch and Kilpatrick, 1999) have been critical, despite the existence of strong guidance material (CCEA, 1997). Perhaps the main consequence of this has been to move CCEA towards the idea of some form of citizenship education programme in the new Northern Ireland Curriculum planned for 2003 or 2004. At the time of writing, work on this new programme is well under way by a team based in the UNESCO Centre of the School of Education, University of Ulster, and an emergent programme based on elements of rights, justice and political literacy is under development. The hope is that the explicit content of these programmes will make it harder to avoid dealing with significant controversial issues, while at the same time ensuring there is a cadre of teachers with the required skills and expertise to engage with these topics. The danger is that the goal of an engaged education system which equips young people to deal with the demands and problems of a divided society will remain elusively out of reach.

The main focus of this chapter has been on another body of research that also developed over this period, that is, research dealing with equality and religion in education. Two main conclusions emerge from the analysis presented in this chapter. The first is that debates over equality in education are less fraught at present in comparison with only a short time ago. And second, current education debates, perhaps most notably over selection, have tended not to have a strong religious dimension: if anything, divisions based on social class have played a more potent part in the discussions. These two main themes have emerged in large part because most of the problems of religious inequality in education have been addressed and the evidence on outcomes and qualifications suggests that such differences as exist between Protestants and Catholics are very small. This is not to say that the issue is dead: as long as separate school systems exist then there is always potential for a sectarian debate over the allocation of resources between the sectors. In addition, separate school systems, with a high degree of religious homogeneity, are unlikely to contribute to greater inter-community harmony and understanding unless some proactive measures are taken to encourage more social integration. There is likely to be a slow, but steady, increase in Integrated schools over time, but perhaps greater opportunities for social integration could be provided by the innovative proposals in the Burns Report for a system of interdependent and collaborating schools in a Collegiate system. Decisions on whether this will be established will not, however, be taken until at least mid-2002.

4. A LESSON TOO LATE FOR THE LEARNING? CROSS-COMMUNITY CONTACT AND COMMUNICATION AMONG UNIVERSITY STUDENTS

Owen Hargie, David Dickson and Seanenne Nelson

INTRODUCTION

Many children in Northern Ireland have never experienced life without religious segregation, sectarian prejudice and violence (Toner, 1994). Indeed, some have claimed that fewer than one in four children in Belfast actually know someone from the other religious group (McWhirter and Gamble, 1982). This, no doubt, is in part a legacy of the essentially segregated dual education system, wherein almost all Protestant children go to State-controlled schools while the vast majority of Catholic children attend those in the so-called 'maintained' sector (*see* Chapter 3). While there has been a growth in the number of children attending Integrated schools, the comparative reality is not impressive, so that Integrated schools educate less than 3% of the school population (Smith, 1999). Indeed, DENI has been criticised for failing to fulfil its objectives to facilitate integrated education, and a deceleration of new Integrated schools has taken place (Dunn and Morgan, 1999).

As well as integrated schooling, an increasing number of contact schemes have been designed to promote interaction and foster improved relations between young Protestants and Catholics. In a review of such educational interventions, Gallagher (1992) noted that psychological research has been limited, due to insufficient contexts available in which to examine the impact of contact on inter-group relations. In fact, the stark reality is that for most young people who progress from school to higher education, university offers the first real depth of opportunity to communicate with, and study alongside, those from the other cultural tradition (apart from those who progress via the further education colleges which like universities have always been integrated). Thus, at university the potentially volatile mix of Protestant and Catholic young adults is brought together often for the first time on any permanent basis. For many of these students this shared experience is new and unfamiliar.

Increased contact and possibilities for relational development raise intriguing questions about strategies for managing divisive issues. Stringer and Hvattum (1990) investigated denominational differences between university students in relation to the issues which they were prepared to discuss amongst themselves. Both Catholics and Protestants reported significantly more frequent discussion of the Troubles with in-group rather than out-group members. This trend was significantly greater among Catholics who also reported better outcomes from such discussions. The extent of contact with members of the out-group, and the value of discussion were related, although this was not congruent with an increase in actual discussion between groups. Stringer and Hvattum suggested that these findings may be a display of the minority group's (Catholics in Northern Ireland) reluctance to discuss divisive issues. Alternatively, informal rules may be in place, which are used to regulate the potential for any interpersonal conflict. This could force Catholics to defend characteristics of their group with which they may not even agree, as a result of self-stereotyping.

More generally, research by Kremer et al. (1986) considered perceptions of discrimination in a peaceful area and compared these with patterns in a comparable area of conflict. They reported in-group favouritism and out-group discrimination among Catholics, but not Protestants in traditionally violent towns. In contrast, Stringer and Cairns (1983), using stereotypical pictures of Catholic and Protestant faces, found in-group favouritism in ratings by Protestants. Catholics did not display negative evaluations of Protestants, and recorded in-group devaluation.

This lack of consistency in findings typifies much of the social science research in the area. Failure to bring a single image of the situation into sharp focus is multi-causative and includes differences in methodology employed, location chosen for data collection, and timing of the research. Alternatively, variability may reflect socio-cultural reality and ongoing developments of the political face of Northern Ireland (Trew, 1992). This may be further complicated by changing environmental circumstances affecting the saliency of group identification for individuals (Waddell and Cairns, 1986). In turn, this could impact upon the degree of contact and interaction that occurs between groups (Stringer and Hvattum, 1990). The Troubles have varied over time and location. Incidences of violence, civil disorder, unemployment, emigration, poor housing, and ill-health have not been evenly distributed over time or place (Heskin, 1980). Nevertheless, a corollary of the complexity of the findings to emerge is the need for sophistication in any theorising aimed at advancing a satisfactory explanation of inter-group attitudes and relational inclusivity.

Two main theoretical perspectives in this regard have been put forward, namely Social Identity Theory and The Contact Hypothesis, but both have failed to fully explain the nuances of inter-group differences (see Chapters 6 and 7). Given the inability of these two main conceptual frameworks to adequately account for the inter-group relational discord, it may be more useful to approach the subject from a different angle. At the heart of the problem is the lack of relational communication between the two 'sides'. In other words, there is little relational development between members of the opposing groups. A clearer understanding of the problem may therefore be garnered through exploring the relational milieu.

RELATIONAL COMMUNICATION

There has been growing realisation that in order to fully understand the phenomenon, social scientists must begin to adopt a multi-disciplinary approach, rather than 'psychologising' inter-group conflict (Cairns, 1994). Unlike previous research, which aims to highlight the differences between the two denominations using specific 'group' theories, the study described in this chapter adopted a different perspective, drawing upon a nexus of concepts perceived to be pivotal for relational development. Interest in, and study of, the field of relational communication has increased exponentially in recent years (Duck, 1999), and the concepts studied therein can inform any analysis of interaction and contact between individuals and groups.

A key component examined, which is central to the framework of relational formation and maintenance, is *self-disclosure* (Baxter and Sahlstein, 2000). It can be defined as the process by which one person reveals personal information (including thoughts, feelings, and experiences) to others. Self-disclosure and personal relationships are considered to be mutually transformative (Tardy and Dindia, 1997). Indeed Hargie and Tourish (1997: 364) argued that self-disclosure is 'a cornerstone of the initiation, development and termination of relationships'. While self-disclosure changes the direction, definition and intensity of relationships, the nature of the relationship changes the meaning and impact of self-disclosure (Derlega et al., 1993). Since self-disclosure is held to be essential for relational development, and is perceived to be strongly related to two key components of friendship, namely trust and attraction, it is important to consider the degree to which inter-group members, when placed in a neutral environment which makes such contact possible, feel predisposed to disclose to one another.

Relational research has frequently examined differences in self-disclosure between genders (Hargie and Dickson, in press). Although it is widely held that gender role predisposes females to self-disclose to a greater extent than males, recent studies have shown that gender differences in disclosure are in fact small, and are moderated by the sex of the person being disclosed to (Dindia 2000a,b). As far as cultural differences are concerned, little research has been carried out on self-disclosure between Catholics and Protestants in Northern Ireland. The only study to have centrally considered this question revealed few significant between-group effects (Hargie et al., 1995).

Self-disclosing is dependent on two main factors: the individual's need to be open, and trust in the partner's discretion. This has been explained in terms of the Trust-Attraction Hypothesis (Fisher, 1984), which purports that we like those who disclose more to us. As A discloses, B perceives this as trust, and is consequently more likely to be attracted to A. This increased liking leads B to disclose more to A. Analyses of relationships suggest that reciprocity of disclosure may well be based on reciprocity of trust (Hargie and Dickson, in press).

One pervading feature of cross-community communication has been a consensual unwillingness to discuss the Troubles with those from the other side. This mechanism of polite avoidance permeates both friendship and work relations, and is adopted to 'manage' interaction. Yet in so doing it may also forestall relational development. The tentacles of Troubles-related silence reach into every crevice of (polite) society. One legacy is that more confidence is placed in 'outsiders' than on the out-group. This has resulted in the recent significant contributions made by those like the American George Mitchell who was central to the negotiations between local politicians to achieve a political settlement in the form of the Good Friday Agreement.

The interpersonal attraction of another person is also founded, in part, on perceived similarities of personality, values, attitudes, beliefs, needs or interpersonal skills (Cialdini, 2001). Attraction between Catholics and Protestants is likely to be an important precursor to any relational development, being regarded as a facilitator of interpersonal communication across a wide range of cultures (Hargie and Tourish, 1997). Furthermore, a considerable degree of interpersonal communication exists for the primary purpose of enhancing attraction (Little and Perrett, 2002). The greater the level of attraction, the stronger the influence on interpersonal communication – the key to forming and maintaining relationships. *Attraction, trust* and *self-disclosure* are therefore complexly intertwined in the process of forming and sustaining relationships.

Research into the Northern Ireland situation has often been contentious and inconclusive with studies focusing on only one or two aspects of inter-group relations. Our study set out to be more inclusive in its analysis of relational variables. The main objective was to compare and contrast in-group and out-group contact amongst a cohort of university students at the beginning of their first year and again at the start of their second year. Attitudes towards mixing with members of the out-group were also considered, together with a complex of constructs identified in the literature as being central to friendship development, namely group identification, self-disclosure, attraction and trust.

THE RESEARCH STUDY

Participants constituted an opportunity sample of full-time first year students enrolled in one faculty at the main campus of one of the universities in Northern Ireland (n=270: 161 Catholic, 109 Protestant; 48 males, 222 females; mean age=20 years; modal age=18 years). Students were invited to take part in a study into relational development among first-year students. A triangulation approach was employed, in which three main methods were used to collect data:

- Self-report inventories
- Analyses of video-recorded interactions
- Focus groups

SELF-REPORT INVENTORIES
In this part of the research all students completed five instruments:

Out-group Contact Questionnaire. This questionnaire was specifically designed by the authors to examine attitudes towards, and extent of previous contact with members of the out-group, together with levels of cross-community friendship. Questions related to school, socialising, sport, family, studying and accommodation at university. Choices in accommodation were included to examine the extent to which participants did, or would, consider flatmates' religion when choosing where to stay.

Self-disclosure Scale (Miller et al., 1983). Here, participants rated their willingness to disclose to:a stranger of the same religion; a stranger of the opposite religion; a friend of the same religion; a friend of the opposite religion; and others.

Group Identification Scale (Brown et al., 1986). This was administered to identify participants' strength of feeling of identity as a Protestant or Catholic. Given the pluralistic nature of Protestantism, those who described themselves as such were requested to complete an additional modified version of the Scale to examine their strength of feeling of identity to their particular church denomination (e.g., Presbyterian, Church of Ireland, Methodist, etc.).

Individualised Trust Scale (Wheeless and Grotz, 1977). This measured level of trust towards the 'other religious group'.

Interpersonal Attraction Scale (McCroskey and Richmond, 1979). Thisgauged the degree of attraction towards the 'other religious group'.

Data from the Self-report Study was collected from the Year 1 students within the first two weeks of term when participants were expected to have experienced relatively little contact with classmates. These instruments were then administered to the same cohort twelve months later.

Results showed a clear trend towards increased contact and more positive inter-group friendship occurring between the two communities after a year spent at university. Prior to university, inter-group contact was relatively low, with approximately three-quarters attending segregated schools, and only one-quarter having relatives from the out-group. On commencing their first year of study at university only one-half of students worked, socialised or played sport with, and around one-third did not regularly talk to, members of the other community.

As shown in Table 4.1 some 66% of the participants were either currently living with, or were willing to live with members of the out-group. Almost two-thirds (64%) reported living near to members of their respective out-group, with some 60% claiming to have close cross-religion friendships. However, almost one-third did not regularly engage in conversations with members of the other religious denomination. Some 50% affirmed that they did not regularly work or socialise with members of the 'other' religious group, with close to 20% reporting that they did not anticipate regularly socialising with the other denomination at university, and 10% being 'put off' by living and studying in close proximity to members of the opposite religion.

Table 4.1: Extent of Reported Contact with the 'Other' Community on Entry to University (Year 1) and after One Year (Year 2)

OUT-GROUP CONTACT	YEAR 1	YEAR 2
Live near out-group	64%	60%
Have 'close' friendships	60%	81%
Do not engage in regular conversation	33%	6%
Work together	50%	76%
Intend socialising with	82%	85%
Regularly socialise together	50%	70%
Live (or would¹ live) in co-religion housing	66%	75%
Did (or would¹) consider religion of co-habitants when seeking accommodation	10%	10%
Did (or would¹) attempt to find accommodation with co-religionists	10%	10%
Feel put off living and studying in close proximity	10%	3%
Object to (or would¹ object to) sharing accommodation	10%	8%
Play sport together regularly	48%	43%

Regarding out-group contact in living arrangements at university, in their first year 97% did not share a room and 60% did not share a house with people of the other religion. Of the total sample, 39% had neither been allocated housing by the university nor lived with relatives and therefore had more choice in their selection of flatmates. Of these, the majority (62%) lived with same-religion others. The majority (75%) of students had no relatives from the 'other' religion but the remaining quarter who did have, categorised relationships with them as 'close'. Of the 40% of the sample who played sport, 48% reported playing regularly with members of the other denomination, while 34% stated that they did not do so. In relation to schooling, 72% attended single-religion Catholic or Protestant primary and secondary schools. A further 26% reported either attending an integrated primary and secondary school, or a single-religion primary school followed by a mixed-religion secondary school.

One year later there was an increase in the number of students reporting: close friendships (20% increase); working together (26% rise); and socialising together (20%). A small increase was reported in the numbers living in co-religion housing (9%). Table 4.1 shows a fall in the numbers reporting: not engaging in conversation with the out-group (27% reduction); feeling put off by living or studying close to (7% decline); objecting to sharing accommodation with members of the 'other' community (2% decrease). However, there was a small decline in the numbers playing inter-group sports and living near the out-group. At the beginning of Year 2, some 80% of students claimed that the religious make-up of cohabitants was coincidental, with only 8% reporting that this had been a deliberate choice. Despite almost all students (95%) living at home or with relatives reporting that they would be willing to share a house with members of the 'other' religion, 19% reported that they would still try to obtain accommodation with co-religionists. Table 4.2 shows that the most important factor when seeking accommodation, was moving in with friends.

Table 4.2: Factors Influencing Accommodation Choices

MOST IMPORTANT FACTOR WHEN CHOOSING ACCOMMODATION	YEAR 1	YEAR 2
Moving in with someone I knew	44%	72%
Location to university	29%	11%
Automatically given a place in halls	14%	–
Religion of others in the house	4%	–
Moving into a safe area	9%	17%

A series of statistical tests examined mean rank differences between Protestant and Catholic scores on the measures of Self-disclosure, Group Identification, Attraction and Trust. Catholics were significantly more willing to disclose to a same-religion friend than were Protestants. Catholics and Protestants were significantly more likely to disclose to friends than to strangers, with same-religionists more likely to be disclosed to than opposite religionists. In terms of gender, females were more willing to disclose in each of the categories than were males. Protestants showed significantly lower identification with their own group than Catholics. There were no significant differences between Protestants and Catholics on measures of trust or out-group attraction, and no significant difference between Protestant church affiliation and strength of identity to the Protestant denominational group. Females were significantly more trusting and more socially attracted to the other denomination than males. There were no significant differences between males and females in identification with their group, or in attraction towards their out-group.

Significant results were also found from Year 1 to Year 2. There was a major decrease in trust towards each out-group over the period of a year. Catholics also displayed significantly lower scores on trust towards the out-group than did Protestants, and were less willing than Protestants to disclose to out-group strangers. This year period also affected gender ratings, with females showing a greater decrease in trust than males. However, females were more willing than males to disclose to an opposite religion friend. Identity to one's group increased among both Protestants and Catholics, from first to second year, although Catholics displayed a stronger level of identification with their in-group. On the positive side, scores of attraction for the out-group increased.

ANALYSES OF VIDEO-RECORDED INTERACTIONS

Astratified random sample of 60 students (10 males, 20 females; 30 Catholic; 30 Protestant) was selected from the total sample. They were asked to participate in an experiment early in the first term of first year when it was anticipated they would have experienced little or no inter-group contact. Participants, as strangers to one another, were paired into one of three conditions (Catholic–Catholic; Protestant–Protestant; Catholic–Protestant). A procedure used successfully in other studies (e.g. Reno and Kenny, 1992; Segrin, 1996) was adopted to allow participants to deduce the religion of their dyadic partner. Students were told that they were participating in a study exploring relational development at university, and that this involved them being allocated to either a 'same religious background group' or a 'different religious background group'. Religious affiliation had been established from biographical details surveyed earlier. Students were also asked if they knew one another before the experiment took place, and if they did know a particular student, they were then separated for the dyadic interactions.

Participants were seated in armchairs at a 90° angle and a low coffee table was placed between participants upon which a poster was placed stating in capitals either 'DIFFERENT RELIGIOUS BACKGROUND' or 'SAME RELIGIOUS BACKGROUND'. They were then instructed that they were to spend ten minutes on their own discussing events of the week, i.e. what they had done, or been involved in, seen, watched, experienced, or directed, in the past seven days, but to feel free to discuss any other topics that emerged during conversation. They were told that the interactions, which would be video-recorded, would be strictly confidential. Recording took place, with the students' written consent, in an adjoining room, filmed through a masked window. Immediately following interaction, participants were taken to separate rooms and asked to complete the Interpersonal Attraction Scale.

In relation to the analysis of recorded interactions, these were based upon fine-grained behavioural cues associated with interpersonal constructs of affiliation, intimacy, affection and control. Analysis was conducted using the Noldus Observer 4.0 System. This package provides a link between video-clip and computer, enabling analysis to take place by viewing the clips on the computer monitor where a sophisticated system of defining, coding, analysing and editing takes place.

Results revealed that the saliency of social identity was significantly more evident during communication with in-group than out-group members. Same-religion pairs used significantly more:

- collective in-group reference pronouns (e.g. 'we', 'us', 'our');
- verbal agreement and reinforcement (e.g. 'exactly', 'that's right', 'I agree completely');
- in-group identifiers, such as social club membership, or socialising in segregated locations relating to only one group (e.g. 'Did you go to the hurling final on Sunday?' – in fact reference to GAA sporting and social events occurred exclusively, and frequently, in Catholic–Catholic dyads);
- markers that identified group membership, including reference to, searches for, and discussion of, other in-group members known to both interactors (e.g. 'Do you know Jim Bloggs?');
- additional topics for discussion (mainly to do with girl/boyfriends, transport and financial matters).

These all contributed to what was a clear pattern of convergence and 'we-ness' during in-group dyadic communication. In Catholic–Protestant pairs there was a marked increase in discussion of neutral topics and a corresponding reduction in reference to aspects of own group identity.

At the same time, an important finding was the lack of significant differences in other markers of relational development across conditions, specifically in terms of a lack of significant differences in general self-disclosure, and non-verbal indicators of intimacy. This would suggest that there was openness to relational development across the divide, and that religious affiliation was not the only factor in determining relationships between students. One consideration here is that partners' prototypicality to their social group is an important variable in establishing degree of liking and attraction (Gudykunst and Hammer, 1988; Turner and Onarato, 1999). It is likely that during interactions with those from the out-group, participants shared a salient group identity as *students* per se, particularly given their status as newcomers at university. This shared identity as fellow freshers in the university environment, taking part in an 'experiment' (and a 'tricky' one at that!), is likely to have facilitated a sense of solidarity and attraction.

Another salient feature of identity is of course gender, and, interestingly, higher ratings of interpersonal attraction were given in same-gender pairs, with females in turn giving higher ratings than males. No religious difference occurred in relation to attraction. Thus, and importantly, students were more influenced by gender than religious affiliation when making ratings of the attractiveness of the other person as an interactional partner. Also, in relation to gender, findings supported those of Jones et al. (1999) that females attune and achieve relational harmony to a greater degree than do males. For example, females used significantly more verbal reinforcement than males.

FOCUS GROUPS
In this part of the investigation, the total sample was comprised of 12 groups (6 Catholic; 6 Protestant: n=60) randomly selected by religion. Six of these (3 Catholic; 3 Protestant) were held at the beginning of fresher year, with a further six at the start of second year. Same-religion participants and moderators were selected, in keeping with the principle of maintaining within-group homogeneity (Morgan, 1997). Prior to commencing discussion, the moderator explained the purpose of the study (to examine relational development at university), informed participants of the religious composition of the group, and assured confidentiality. The groups discussed aspects of out-group contact, both pre-entry and post-entry to university; relational development with out-group members; factors which maintained division; and those which fostered integration. Discussion was audio-recorded, transcribed, and submitted to thematic analysis. Three broad themes, each with sub-themes (underlined), emerged.

1. *Out-Group Contact.* The first sub-theme here was that students had no depth of contact with members of the out-group before university. Such contact as did exist tended to have been the result of part-time work or on a cross-community contact scheme. Ongoing friendships were the exception rather than the rule. As one student said:

> Some of the guys have never seen a Catholic in their lives . . . apart from on TV or something. I think before you come to university you have a very sheltered life, you're in one community and you stay on that side, you don't venture. I think university's a time when both come together and start integrating from there. (P, G2, S3)[2]

The most significant factor preventing inter-group contact was felt to be the ongoing geographical segregation, particularly in urban working-class areas. Going beyond the safety of one's own area to visit out-group friends caused unease. As two students reported:

> Where I come from in Belfast, I don't mix with Protestants . . . It is a bother, you have to go out of your way to have Protestant friends. (C, G6, S2)

> I know Catholics that live in quite predominantly Catholic areas . . . and I
> honestly wouldn't feel comfortable going there . . . You get a lot of . . .
> extremely bitter [people] and you're not going to go into that area because
> of your friend but because of who lives there . . . If any of my friends were
> coming down [to my equally segregated area] they would have the same
> feeling as I would . . . so you probably would arrange to meet a person in
> mutual territory. (P, G1, S5)

An overriding concern expressed by many participants was the need to conduct
themselves in such a way as not to be perceived to be narrow-minded or bigoted,
but rather to be seen as broad-minded and liberal. Being overly concerned with
issues of religious difference could attract negative attributions from others. The
most common response therefore was to minimise the personal significance of
politico-religious division. Thus, Catholic and Protestant students in both fresher
and second years consistently claimed to be largely apathetic about the relevance of
other students' religious affiliations. Exemplar comments were:

> It doesn't bother me. (C, G3, S4)

> I never thought about it. (P, G2, S1)

Interestingly, and despite these disclaimers, another sub-theme was that of
automatic labelling of others. First-year students had considered the level of inter-
group mixing that would probably occur. Even at a very early stage, students had
already established the religious affiliation of their classmates and housemates:

> It's really weird . . . the way religion doesn't matter but whenever I did meet
> everyone in my class in the back of my head I was wondering what they are
> . . . which doesn't make a difference. (C, G5, S4)

> It is a Northern Ireland thing that somebody says their name and you are
> immediately working out in your head . . . sorting out who is who
> [identifying religious affiliation]. (C, G2, S4)

By second year some students had formed close friendships across the divide,
showing how contact can foster inter-group friendship. As one student put it:

> I expected them to have a different attitude . . . now I have got experience of
> it, people who have a different religion, it has come up and it has been great
> crack [fun] talking about it . . . which I enjoyed immensely. (C, G6, S1)

On the other hand, consolidating patterns of in-group socialising were also
identified. Catholic students, for example, perceived a tendency for Christian

groups (i.e. devout/fundamental Protestants) to spend free time with friends of similar persuasion, and to have different socialising preferences, for example:

> . . . we don't have much in common with them – they don't go out and get drunk and are up for the crack. They want to go home. (C, G2, S3)

> We don't have that much in common with them, they don't go out. (C, G5, S1)

2. *Perception and Management of Inter-Group Difference.* A variety of interaction management techniques was used to negotiate relationships. These included, avoidance of potentially divisive topics with out-group members and the adoption of silence in uncomfortable situations. For some, there was a degree of discussion of sensitive political issues in second year. However, the overwhelming emphasis was upon not raising contentious issues in the company of the other side. This theme recurred frequently:

> Everyone tries to avoid politics as much as possible . . . people are very unbending as to what they think. (P, G1, S1)

> . . . it is like talking to girls about sex, maybe you wouldn't be as explicit to a girl as you would to a mate. That is it . . . it is all about tactics, being a wee bit sensible. (C, G6, S1)

> If something happens, some atrocity . . . you do get angry and you do think why has this happened and maybe you talk about it to your family or something but other than that [you don't talk about it]. (C, G4, S4)

> I think you wouldn't want people of a different religion to think that you were pushing your [views] onto them. (P, G1, S4)

> We would always be sort of conscious, you know, you don't want to make anyone feel uncomfortable. You don't want to antagonise anyone, so you just sort of be careful and try your best not to put your foot in it. (C, G1, S4)

The divisive influence of sporting preferences was also noted, due to lack of commonality between groups. In Northern Ireland one or other sector of the community plays some sports almost exclusively. Sports organised by the Gaelic Athletic Association (GAA) – Gaelic football, hurling and camogie (for females) – are almost exclusively played and watched by Catholics. Rugby and field hockey, on the other hand, are mainly Protestant, while others such as soccer, golf or tennis are played by both sections of the community. Sport can thereby become a divisive conversation piece. For students, it was felt that by restricting it as a topic exclusive to in-group members, they were able to avoid potential conflicts:

> You just keep your sport and your culture to yourself and get on with enjoying university. (C, G1, S2)

> I would watch Gaelic on TV now and again, but to a certain extent . . . I just wouldn't have that link to talk about . . . we don't have that something in common. (P, G1, S1)

> One of my Protestant friends asked me one day if she could come to Gaelic with me and I said, 'You're not going to feel intimidated?' . . . I wouldn't do it if I was in her shoes. (C, G2, S1)

> I think it comes very strong at times, like this is our sport. You [Protestants] play soccer, you play hockey, you do not play Gaelic and camogie. (C, G2, S3)

Another 'rule' of inter-group communication was the recognition of need for sensitivity in relation to symbols of difference. This was encapsulated in the following comment:

> I wouldn't wear a poppy, because I knew the class [were majority Catholic] and I didn't want to walk in and nobody else wearing one, trying to be divisive or something. (P, G5, P3)

This stands in stark contrast to the common practice, in various regions, of deliberately flaunting symbols of in-group identity in the form of flags and insignia as a means of marking territory or antagonising the other side, especially at times of violence and tension in interface areas. However, despite this universally acknowledged need for sensitivity, the Protestant students reported the existence of Catholic insensitivity in displays of culture. They simultaneously claimed that this did not offend them, although this was negated by their comments. There was a distinct feeling amongst Protestants of being the minority on the campus. This feeling was in fact grounded in reality. At the time of this study, Protestant full-time students comprised 39% of the population within this campus, and 37% in the university as a whole.

As a result of this religious imbalance, many Protestant students felt that there were specific clubs and events that were not welcoming of their tradition. They stated that some Catholic students deliberately flaunted the symbols and ceremonies of their politico-religious affiliation, with a lack of regard for Protestant sensitivities. Specifically, stridency was seen to be exemplified in the use of Irish signs in the Students' Union, the singing of Irish republican songs in the student bar, the wearing of Glasgow Celtic shirts, and the ubiquitous display of GAA sports shirts and sports bags. Protestant students claimed that they would not engage in similar behaviour to conspicuously mark their group identity:

> I never thought there would be as many Celtic bags and if we did the same it wouldn't be welcome . . . you would never see someone . . . in a Rangers shirt, even a Northern Ireland football shirt. (P, G6, S2)

> I don't care whether they put [Irish language] signs up . . . but it's why some people want the signs that's more the problem, not the signs being there . . . some people feel it's there to make the division, it's not there to be a cultural thing. (P, G1, S1)

> I couldn't believe the amount of Gaelic symbols about the place. (P, G5, S6)

There was a desire among Protestants to have a neutral environment, where they would not be constantly reminded of their minority status. Indeed, in the dyadic part of this study described above, one student in a Protestant–Protestant pair who were discussing the number of GAA shirts worn by Catholic students, remarked: 'How would they feel if we walked along the [main university thoroughfare] wearing Orange sashes?' Catholic students confirmed this pattern, agreeing that there was a greater number of visible symbols of difference displayed by their group, which were absent amongst Protestant students. They also agreed that this could cause offence if such a pattern were reversed. As a Catholic student put it:

> Yes, I can see how it could offend people right enough . . . it is fellows that don't even play in football teams are running about with their football jerseys on . . . just for show. (C, G6, S5)

Where difficult issues existed, students described a further rule in managing inter-group difference – the use of the facilitative medium of humour. This was considered to be the only mechanism through which taboo subjects could be raised. A recognition and acknowledgement of differences expressed through the use of humour was described as facilitative of inter-group relations:

> Banter is very important [in helping to develop cross-community relationships]. . . I don't think they ever really had much contact with Protestants before and they weren't too sure how to handle us. And then whenever we started joking or whatever, it was brilliant. It really did help [foster good relations], and we all ended up being quite good friends. (P, G6, S3)

> Well, they would joke and pass it off lightly sort of thing and just go on with other conversation. (C, G5, S1)

> I think most of our age don't really care about it and I think it is genuine when you make fun of it. (P, G5, S3)

The likelihood of discussion of divisive topics was also felt to be related to knowledge of the other person's views. This situation was beginning to change for some, but not all, in second year. It was pointed out by a number of students that disclosure would depend on how well you knew the other person and were in agreement with their opinion:

> I would change my level of discussion depending on . . . how well I knew them or whether I thought they were the same mind as me. (P, G5, S4)

> I think it is the level of friendship and trust you have with the person. (C, G6, S5)

> [You would] Probably avoid [contentious issues] but if you knew them well you could talk about it. (P, G6, S1)

3. *Recommendations for Improving Inter-group Relations.* Students were appreciative of the fact that university provided the opportunity to meet and interact with members of other traditions. One student remarked:

> Your [home] area may be all Catholic or all Protestant and you never leave that area, we have come to university and we have got our eyes open . . . but if you don't get out of it [home area] you are stuck in that generation . . . You can see the difference in friends who have gone to college and those who haven't . . . you don't realise how much you have changed until you go back home. (C, G4, S2)

When asked for their views about levels of contact between the two communities, all students agreed that inter-group contact prior to university should be improved. They expressed unanimous support for integrated education at both elementary and secondary school levels. Some felt that failing this ultimate solution, there ought to be a better availability of cross-community schemes while still at school. In particular, they felt that denominational differences could be greatly reduced through traditionally segregated sports being taught to all pupils. As summarised by one student:

> You would need all types of sports [to be] introduced and it can only really happen in schools too, because at home it is pretty Nationalist and you are not going to get bringing hockey in there, definitely not, so it can really only happen in a . . . more integrated school context. (C, G4, S3)

CONCLUSIONS

This multi-layered study produced a wealth of data and in this chapter we have been able only to present a broad overview of the findings. The interested reader is referred to other reports of specific aspects of this research (Hargie et al., 1999, 2002; Dickson et al., 2000; Rainey et al., in press). However, in general terms we wish to highlight some main findings:

1. *The apparent need for educated people not to be perceived as bigoted.* Students are the neophyte professional class and as such they model their behaviour upon those they wish to emulate. A strong sentiment expressed by both Catholic and Protestant students was that they had a general apathy about religio-political difference. This in part reflected a need to be seen as liberal and enlightened. Intelligent people do not get involved. Thus, students were positive about living, studying and working together and indicated that out-group contact per se had increased over the period of a year. While a few reported in the focus groups having had unfortunate experiences with out-group members, the overwhelming view was that university provided an effective milieu for inter-group relations to foster. How much of this reflects reality and how much is the perceived socially desired response is of course a matter for debate. However, there was a conflict. The minimalist nature of contact prior to university entry, combined with a pattern of in-group socialising during university, remained a large feature of students' lives. The progression from positive expressed attitudes to actual social change was therefore problematic.

2. *The most common method for dealing with difference is through avoidance.* Interpersonal communication is governed by unwritten rules that specify which behaviours members of groups or cultures believe should or should not be carried out (Argyle and Henderson, 1985). Such rules serve the important purpose of reducing uncertainty about appropriate behaviour in social settings (Hargie and Tourish, 1997). One such rule in polite society is not to raise contentious politico-religious issues especially in mixed company – it seems to carry an even stronger opprobrium than discussing bowel movements! In fact, appropriate disclosure avoidance has been shown to be a universal feature of skilled performance in social contexts (Hastings, 2000a,b). In other words, in certain situations, with particular people, and at set times, we decide that it is best not to express our opinions on a specific topic. Afifi and Guerrero (2000) identified the main reasons for avoidance as being:

- social inappropriateness – it is not 'the done thing' to discuss this topic in this setting;
- futility – views are already set and so it is pointless opening up discussion;
- wanting to avoid embarrassment or criticism;
- a desire to avoid conflict;
- protection of the existing relationship – sometimes things are better left unsaid;

● a wish for privacy and to keep one's personal views to oneself. Here the oft-quoted Northern Ireland maxim is 'Whatever you say, say nothing'.

The applicability of all of these reasons to the avoidance of disclosure about one's personal opinions of Troubles-related issues with out-group members can readily be realised. One may be viewed as at best impolite and at worst a bigoted extremist if one expresses a partisan opinion on political issues in mixed company. Others are likely to squirm, be embarrassed, and keep quiet, or even say they do not wish to discuss this. It may lead to heated argument or aggression. Most people know that the other person's opinions are probably fixed and intractable anyway. Last, but not least, it is possible to maintain an amicable relationship (especially a working one) with someone from the opposite community background without travelling down the political road, which could well jeopardise this. Students in this study were very au fait with the avoidance tactic and in fact used it as a template to guide discussion topics with out-group members.

Paradoxically, these efforts to avoid discussion of contentious topics in order not to damage relationships, may in fact stunt their development. There is an interesting contrast in stances between, on the one hand, the unanimous view of students that it is best to avoid raising potentially divisive issues in mixed-religion company, and the nostrum of those social engineers who argue that such latent tensions are best remedied through openly confronting and debating those very issues that cause the division. One of the early stages of relational disintegration is termed 'circumscribing', which is defined in terms of the avoidance of sensitive topics and unresolved issues (Knapp and Vangelisti, 1992). Subsequent stages are 'stagnation', where discussion of the relationship itself is a taboo, and 'avoidance', where interaction and physical proximity are shunned. Thus, in the case of students, the use of circumscribing tactics may well be speeding up the process of relational disintegration.

3. *The tyranny of the majority – if you've got it, flaunt it.* In this study, Protestant students strongly felt (and were made to feel) their minority status, and were offended by what they saw as the strident display of majority (Catholic/Irish) symbols. Thus, although sensitive topics were not being raised in discussions, differences were being flagged through a range of insignia, but only by the majority. Several Protestant students commented on symbols of Catholic culture as being 'in your face' in the university environment, and felt quietly hurt (as one student put it: 'you simmer in silence') by their overt display. Clearly, the freedom of one group of students to display their identity needs to be balanced by the offence this may cause to those from another group. In Northern Ireland, flags, anthems and other paraphernalia play the role of semiotic symbols used to convey clear signals about group control and dominance. They reflect in-group identities, highlight and exacerbate difference, and can be viewed, especially by the minority group, as triumphalist and exclusivist emblems of power.

There is a divergence of views about the extent to which such symbols should be permitted in the workplace. Many organisations have policies that restrict the display of specified divisive emblems, and the student minority in this university expressed the view that this should be introduced. Our research (*see also* Chapter 9) indicates that the majority group in any organisation tends to be more sanguine about embracing diversity in terms of insignia than the minority (Dickson et al., 2002). This is simply because the only symbols likely to be displayed are those of the majority, and so the minority becomes more alienated (and this is usually unspoken).

4. *Inter-group differences can be avoided by greater in-group adherence.* Within the safe houses of the in-group, contentious topics can be discussed, existing attitudes reinforced and worth of identity affirmed, and all without the risk of being labelled as a bigot. The interactive part of our research showed clear behavioural differences between same-religion and mixed-religion dyads. The former were characterised by a more facilitative and relaxed style of interaction. This has implications for self-disclosure, which, as discussed earlier, is a linchpin in the formation of friendships. If people adhere to the sanctuary of their in-group, disclosure about certain topics to and from out-group members will ipso facto be low. But trust is dependent upon openness of self-disclosure and vice-versa. Not surprisingly, therefore, over the period of a year at university, students displayed a decrease in trust towards their respective out-groups. Where students are unable to disclose information and discuss sensitive topics comfortably with those from the other group, there are likely to be serious ramifications for relational development and in turn a reduction in trust. In consideration of the recommendations from the Focus Group Study that there should be greater contact at school, and through sport, perhaps at the time of university it is too late for major changes in trust towards the out-group to occur quickly or easily. This finding also supports the general view that an outfall from the Good Friday Agreement has been a reduction in levels of trust between the two communities. It also fails to support the Trust-Attraction Hypothesis (Fisher, 1984), since while ratings of attraction increased, levels of trust were reduced after a year at university.

5. *Minority and majority are shifting concepts with changing views.* Who constitutes the majority changes depending upon whether one considers Northern Ireland alone, the whole island of Ireland, the UK, a city, a part of a city, a town, a townland, a university campus, a degree cohort, or a year group within that degree. This means that research findings must be interpreted with caution. Interpersonal attraction is also related to degree of communication and hence self-disclosure. In this investigation, Catholics were less attracted towards the out-group at Year 1. This may explain the lack of trust or, alternatively, it may be related to their stronger sense of group identification, which would inevitably encourage them to be more attracted to and seek the company of in-group members. With regard to group identification, it has previously been reported that, in line with Social Identity Theory (Tajfel and Turner, 1986), individuals are more likely to rate their in-group more positively than their out-group. Therefore, stronger identification

with one's in-group is related to greater differentiation from one's out-group. This can help to explain the results described here. While both groups held positive attitudes about one another which may in some way increase self-esteem, a stronger sense of identification among Catholics does appear to be related to lower levels of trust, attraction and self-disclosure towards Protestants, as shown in the self-report part of this study.

It would seem in this case that the minority group in Northern Ireland (Catholics) do not hold the majority group in higher esteem than their own-group, therefore rejecting the minority group concept to explain results. However, this phenomenon may be influenced by the changing political face of Northern Ireland. The Belfast Agreement has been more widely and warmly welcomed by Catholics than Protestants. Both SDLP and Sinn Fein are in government, and the increased cross-border links could be affecting group perceptions of 'minority–majority' status among Catholics. It may also be influenced by the setting in which the study took place, in that at this university and this campus, Catholic students are in the majority and Protestants the minority.

Protestants tended towards a greater degree of trust for their out-group than did Catholics, and were also more attracted towards Catholics than vice-versa. In terms of group identification, they showed a significantly weaker sense of belonging to their in-group. This latter finding confirms the earlier one by Hargie et al. (1995). In combination, these results portray a reasonably coherent picture. Protestants' perceptions of both their in-group and their out-group seem different to comparable perceptions held by Catholics. A weaker sense of in-group identification could reduce the degree of corresponding categorisation and stereotyping amongst Protestants. Finding the out-group more attractive and tending towards being more trusting of them would be anticipated consequences.

Some speculative reasons for differences in group identity can be offered. Catholics have minority status in terms of numbers in Northern Irish society. This, together with a history of perceived discrimination and marginalisation at the hands of the out-group, may have produced a strengthened sense of in-group cohesion and solidarity, commensurate with early findings on the effects of inter-group threat on intra-group dynamics (Sherif and Sherif, 1953). It may also have effected a resolve by Catholics to preserve, protect and express their cultural and religious identity through customs and practices. In focus groups, both religions felt that emblems and symbols identified with the Catholic/Nationalist culture were displayed by Catholics in a very proactive manner. This display of recognisable and culturally significant identifiers may be considered to highlight their allegiance, sense of belonging and identification with their group. As such, they may be much more likely to categorise and stereotype than would members of a group whose identity has not been similarly threatened.

6. *The role of education in facilitating the integration of groups.* This research has shown that while students express support for positive inter-group relations, this is combined with a decrease in trust and a lack of discussion of politico-

religious issues. The pattern of results indicates that although students down-play the importance of religious difference they remain influenced by it, as identified through, inter alia, predominantly co-religion friendships, different levels of disclosure, lower trust, distinct interactive patterns, avoidance of contentious issues, separate sporting preferences and preference for in-group flatmates. Given that it seems that views about core politico-religious issues are rarely openly discussed between members of the two groups, or opinions shared, it can easily be seen that distrust is likely to be fermented. The results suggest that, while university life is functionally desegregated, it is far from being fully integrated. Students attend classes together, use the students' union, canteens, library, etc. side-by-side, but this does not mean they are communicating across the divide at any depth. Indeed, students themselves expressed the view that integration would not just happen, and wanted the university authorities to take steps to actively encourage it.

They also recommended that a greater degree of inter-group contact should occur before the age of university entry, with greater effort to promote cross-community events. In particular, they proposed the removal of segregation in sport, through the teaching of major games and activities to members of all traditions. This would mean that at university, sport would no longer play a divisive role. They also expressed a preference for the introduction of integrated schools. Given the lack of inter-group contact before university, these opportunities, if pursued, could reverse the segregation experienced by members of both communities through geographical location, schooling, and sport. Finally, Protestants clearly wanted to be educated in a neutral environment in which they were not reminded of their status as a minority group on a daily basis.

This research has highlighted problematic relational development between Protestant and Catholic students. Since university for many represents one of the first experiences of integration with members of the out-group, further research is required to chart the patterns of communication between the two groups in their later years in university. It could be that students gradually find that they have indeed more in common with other in-group members, and this then facilitates communication flow and convergence, leading to same-religion friendship formation. The initial differences may then become accentuated and subsequently 'hard-wired'. Alternatively, as students become accustomed to interacting with those from the out-group, barriers may be broken down, and cross-community friendships formed.

In conclusion, we feel that the focus on the core dimensions of relational communication in this study not only provided a conceptual underpinning, it also produced a rich seam of data with which to understand and interpret interpersonal and inter-group dynamics. Given the history of physical segregation within Northern Ireland, disclosure and relational development are more likely to occur with the in-group. As discussed in the introduction to this paper, the insufficiency of existing theories further reifies the importance of exploring facets of relational communication and development, which could provide a more intelligible insight into the study and understanding of Protestant–Catholic, and other race relations.

ACKNOWLEDGEMENTS

We are grateful for the financial support received from the Central Community Relations Unit and the Physical and Social Environment Programme of the European Regional Development Fund, which enabled us to undertake the study described in this chapter.

NOTES

[1] Students residing with relatives or who were allocated accommodation by the university were less able to choose the religious make-up of cohabitants, therefore they were asked if they would be *willing* to share accommodation with out-group members. Figures are the summation of these students and those who had chosen their term-time housing.

[2] P or C refers to the religion of the group members (Protestant or Catholic respectively). G refers to the focus group they participated in, where G1–3 represent groups participating in First year and G4–6 Second year. S refers to their individual subject number within their group.

5. THE ROOTS OF SECTARIANISM IN NORTHERN IRELAND

Gareth I. Higgins and John D. Brewer

INTRODUCTION

The project funded by the Central Community Relations Unit under the title, 'The Roots of Sectarianism', on which we both worked, was a small and modestly funded affair, lasting six months, to examine some of the taproots to sectarianism in Northern Ireland, specifically to explore the role theology played in social division. Given the small scale of the project, we restricted ourselves to one dimension, the belief that there is a scriptural basis to anti-Catholicism. This focus was chosen because it forms part of the self-defining identity of certain Protestants and inhibits reconciliation between the two communities by suggesting that divisions are immutable as a result of being upheld by theology. As sociologists we wanted to explore the social dynamics to this claim and to show how biblical hermeneutics amongst certain Protestants formed part of a sociological project to develop, sustain and rationalise social inequality. In this view, scripture was appropriated to justify social divisions at a particular historical context in Protestant–Catholic relations and can be located sociologically by the socio-economic and political processes that led to theology being used in this way (the results are discussed in Brewer, 1998; and Brewer and Higgins, 1999). This research was later augmented by a study of one form of anti-Catholicism, the papal antichrist myth (Higgins, 2000). We believed that an analysis of the roots of anti-Catholicism could inform public debate about the nature and causes of some features of the Northern Irish conflict, as well as assist in overcoming commonsense myths that inhibit reconciliation.

Our ambition in this chapter is to summarise the results and incorporate the role played by the papal antichrist myth. We close by speculating on the future of these beliefs and the impact that broader social changes are having on Northern Irish Protestants. While anti-Catholicism and belief in the papal antichrist myth are part of the separatist tendencies found in fundamentalist Protestants, globalisation and other social processes threaten this separatism. First it is necessary to define what we mean by sectarianism.

WHAT IS SECTARIANISM?

It is a common complaint that sectarianism is an under-theorised concept, although there have been attempts to define its features (*see* Brewer, 1992; McVeigh, 1995). It can be considered as 'the determination of actions, attitudes and practices by practices about religious difference, which results in them invoked as the boundary marker to represent social stratification and conflict' (Brewer, 1992: 359). It thus refers to a whole cluster of ideas, beliefs, myths and demonology about religious difference which are used to make religion a social marker, to assign different attributes to various religious groups and to make derogatory remarks about others. It is more than a set of prejudiced attitudes but refers to behaviours, policies and types of treatment that are informed by religious difference. It occurs at three levels (Brewer, 1992: 360): the levels of ideas, individual action, and the social structure. At the level of ideas it is expressed in negative stereotypes and pejorative beliefs and language about members of another religion. At the level of individual action it shows itself in direct discrimination and various types of intimidation and harassment against members of another religion because of their group membership. At the social structural level it expresses itself in patterns of indirect and institutional discrimination and disadvantage.

It is obvious that anti-Catholicism is a form of sectarianism and, as we have argued in previous work, it also occurs at the same three levels. Thus we defined anti-Catholicism as the determination of actions, attitudes and practices by negative beliefs about individual Catholics, the Catholic Church as an institution, or Catholic doctrine. These negative beliefs become invoked as an ethnic boundary marker, which can be used in some settings to represent social stratification and conflict. In terms of its three levels, anti-Catholicism is expressed at the level of ideas in negative stereotypes and pejorative beliefs, notions and language about Catholics and the Catholic Church. At the level of individual action, it shows itself in various forms of direct discrimination, intimidation and harassment against Catholics or the Catholic Church because of their Catholicism. At the level of the social structure, anti-Catholicism expresses itself in patterns of indirect and institutional discrimination and social disadvantage experienced by Catholics because they are Catholics. There is nothing inevitable about the progression through these levels, for anti-Catholicism can remain as a set of ideas without them affecting behaviour or having implications at the social structural level. In its worst manifestations, however, it occurs at all three levels, although the number of these case is becoming fewer and fewer. Great Britain was once a good example.[1] Northern Ireland still is.

WHAT ABOUT ANTI-PROTESTANTISM?

While the research did not address the issue of anti-Protestantism our conceptualisation of sectarianism can accommodate it as a sociological process. It can exist at the same three levels and result in systematic and structured inequality, as historical examples illustrate, from the treatment of Huguenots in France to the Spanish Inquisition. Allegations of anti-Protestantism are a feature of Unionist political discourse in Northern Ireland but it is clear from our conceptualisation that there are differences with anti-Catholicism. At the level of ideas, anti-Protestantism exists in the same way in that there are negative stereotypes, beliefs and language used against Protestants. At the level of action it exists as acts of harassment, intimidation and hostility toward Protestants. Ireland's history is as replete with these examples as with the contrary process. However, the major difference is with respect to the level of the social structure. Protestants in Northern Ireland have never experienced social disadvantage as a group in terms of access to social structural resources. In material terms the Protestant working class were mostly in the same position as their Catholic neighbours, but in terms of cultural and political resources they had a sense of belonging to the State that poor Catholics lacked. It is often alleged that, if not in the North, the South evidenced anti-Protestantism at the social structural level. But the evidence is quite contrary, for Protestants in general are a privileged economic minority in the Irish Republic, despite their sense of cultural distance from the State.

The problem for Protestants in Northern Ireland is not theologically derived but political in that they experience anti-Britishness – an objection by association with the State rather than direct opposition to their religion. However, this is a distinction difficult to absorb when Ulster Protestant identity is so wrapped up with the cultural and political link to Britain. IRA violence against so-called 'legitimate' targets of the State has been experienced by ordinary Protestants as ethnic cleansing and an attempt to remove Protestant witness from the island. So interconnected is Protestant identity with Britishness, that anti-Britishness easily blends into anti-Protestantism as Protestants perceive it. That Republicanism believes it can make this fine distinction is irrelevant to Protestants.

THEOLOGY, SECTARIANISM AND ANTI-CATHOLICISM IN NORTHERN IRELAND

The aims of the CCRU-funded research were to explore the deterministic belief system that underpins some aspects of Northern Ireland's conflict, namely anti-Catholicism and its assumed scriptural basis, and to locate the emergence of this belief system in the context of wider Protestant–Catholic relations in Northern Ireland. We were not interested as researchers in the question of whether the Catholic faith really is non-scriptural, but rather to understand the sociological dynamics that lead to *claims* that it is and the use to which these claims are put outside theology. Lying behind this approach was the assumption that sociological dynamics at times cause theology to be appropriated to justify social divisions. We intended thereby to critically confront some of the beliefs that self-define the identity of a key section of the Protestant community and hoped to reinforce the wider process of reconciliation by challenging the claim that some divisions are immutable because they are determined by God. Our findings can be briefly summarised as follows (for greater detail, see Brewer, 1998; Brewer and Higgins, 1999).

Anti-Catholicism is awkward to pronounce, but easy to perpetuate and obvious to see in Northern Ireland. This phenomenon has unique manifestations in Northern Ireland,[2] and although its proponents believe themselves to be doing God's will, engaged in simple obedience to the transcendent, there are clearly identifiable social characteristics to the way in which they express anti-Catholicism. Anti-Catholic discourse thus combines theological, mythical and social factors to produce a cultural template that has sociological resonance wherever social cleavage depends on Protestant–Catholic difference. While anti-Catholicism is constituted as a debate about scripture and Christian faith, in Northern Ireland it is much more than that. The conviction held by some Protestants that anti-Catholicism is a fundamental tenet of their faith fits seamlessly with, and even helps to reinforce and maintain the lines of social cleavage in the North, which themselves are a cornerstone of the conflict. Anti-Catholicism thus needs to be approached sociologically, for anti-Catholicism was given a scriptural underpinning in the history of Protestant–Catholic relations in Northern Ireland in order to reinforce divisions between the religious communities and to offer a deterministic belief system to justify them. It has been mobilised in this way at particular historical junctures in Protestant–Catholic relations in Ireland and as a result of specific socio-economic and political processes. Anti-Catholicism in some settings is therefore mobilised as a resource for critical socio-economic and political reasons, using processes that are recognisably sociological rather than theological. But it operates for this purpose in a restricted social setting. In Northern Ireland's case, this setting is distinguished by two kinds of social relationships – an endogenous one between Protestant and Catholic, and an exogenous one between Ireland and Britain generally. The colonial relationship between Britain and Ireland ensured that the social structure of Irish society was dominated by the endogenous relationship between Catholics (natives) and Protestants (settlers), which persisted in Northern Ireland after partition. This explains its continued resonance. Anti-Catholicism survives in Northern Ireland when it has declined elsewhere, notably in Britain and the Irish Republic, nearest neighbours to Northern Ireland in the British Isles, because it helps to define group boundaries and plays a major sociological role in producing and rationalising political and economic inequality. Yet this is only part of the sociological explanation for its saliency. There is a sociological dynamic which explains why it is 'received' so readily amongst its primary constituency.

Historically, theological differences in Ireland obtained their saliency because they corresponded to all the major patterns of structural differentiation in plantation society, such as ethnic and cultural status, social class, ownership of property and land, economic wealth, employment, education, and political power (*see* Ruane and Todd, 1996). Anti-Catholicism has remained important down the centuries because the patterns of differentiation in Northern Irish society have stayed essentially the same. Alternative lines of division are relatively weak in Northern Ireland (*see* Bruce, 1994: 28), with ethnicity, marked by religious difference, remaining as the only salient social cleavage, at least until very recently. Modern industrial society in the North has not produced secularisation on a grand scale, and religious difference remains critical to many Protestants. As Bruce (1986: 244–45) argued in relation to Free Presbyterians, 'being possessed of a strongly religious worldview, many Ulster Protestants explain a great deal of what happens to them in religious terms. They see the conflict in Ireland as a religious conflict. Their culture and their circumstances are mutually reinforcing.' However, the continued saliency of religion is only partly to be explained by the slow progress of secularisation, with the commensurate high levels of religiosity in Northern Ireland. It also continues because religion stands in place for ethnic identity and thus represents the patterns of differentiation in an ethnically structured society. In the former respect anti-Catholicism continues as a throwback to Reformation debates about theology in a society still wedded to doctrinal conflicts because of its high religiosity. In the latter, anti-Catholicism helps to define the boundaries of the groups involved in competition over power, wealth and status, it is mobilised to regulate and control that competition, and is used in social closure to defend the monopoly of the Protestant ethnic group.

Anti-Catholicism has been employed as a resource for ethnic mobilisation amongst Protestants in specific historical circumstances and events. While some of these have been theological (such as when Catholicism seemed to progress as a faith through church expansion), anti-Catholicism has also been mobilised in political events – especially when there is a need for political unity – throughout Irish history, such as when the political interests of Protestants had to be defended during Catholic emancipation, Home Rule, the 1974 Loyalist Workers' Strike, and Drumcree and the issue of contentious parades by Protestant loyal orders. Durkheim's theory of religion, formulated at the beginning of the twentieth century from an analysis of pre-Christian religions, stresses the socially integrative functions of religious belief and this fits Ulster Protestant politics well. In times of political threat and instability, conservative evangelicalism acted as the sacred canopy, lending itself readily to anti-Catholicism because of the deep antipathy within conservative evangelicalism to the doctrine of the Catholic Church. Historians recognise this sociological truth (*see*, for example, Hempton, 1996; Hyndman, 1996; Loughlin, 1985).

Economic circumstances have also provoked the mobilisation of Protestants by means of anti-Catholicism, especially when social closure was necessary to protect access to scarce resources, as occurred, for example, during Catholic threats to Protestant domination of the linen industry in the eighteenth century (which witnessed the formation of the Orange Order) and shipbuilding in the nineteenth century. This also occurred when high levels of Protestant unemployment, notably during the 1930s, threatened their position as a labour aristocracy, and when non-sectarian forms of class mobilisation seemed to be successful in advancing the position of the Catholic working class, such as during the Catholic Civil Rights marches in the late 1960s.

Mobilisation on the basis of anti-Catholicism during these events made reference to various features about Catholicism and Catholics, which illustrate the different dimensions of anti-Catholicism as a sociological process. As we shall demonstrate shortly, there is a theological dimension, going back to the Reformation, with references to Catholic doctrine, but there is also a cultural dimension, involving everyday discourse, imagery and values within Protestant popular culture. This anti-Catholic language can be called a 'discursive formation' and it permeates deep within Northern Irish popular culture. Other dimensions to anti-Catholicism exist as well. There is a political dimension that involves defence of the Union, which Catholicism supposedly threatens, and an attack on Republicanism, which Catholicism is supposed to advance, even, in some cases, to the point of supporting the use of violence against Catholics. There is an economic dimension also, with the need for Protestant ascendancy and privilege to be protected, which involves references to Catholicism as allegedly endangering Ulster's wealth and prosperity because of its encouragement of sloth and laziness, and to Catholics as threatening jobs, housing and 'social capital'.

It is not surprising that in a society where religious labels are used to define group boundaries, anti-Catholicism becomes readily available and easily recognisable culturally as a resource for the purpose of social stratification and social closure because it fits seamlessly with society and its patterns of cleavage and conflicts. Anti-Catholicism fits neatly with Northern Irish society for the following reasons:

- it has long historical roots in ethno-national traditions in Ireland, going back to the original conflict between planters and Gaels and forming part of their ethnic myths;
- it has a legacy of efficacy and effectiveness in the past, providing many lessons of its effectiveness as a resource across time;
- it is very consistent with the rendering of the Northern Irish society into the simple zero-sum game between two competing groups, which is the way the groups like to see the conflict;
- it fits the self-identities of the groups involved in this zero-sum conflict as religious groups, since religious labels are appropriated commonsensically to define the competition for power and privilege and group boundaries;
- the deployment of anti-Catholicism as a resource in structuring group relations fits with the high levels of religiosity in Northern Ireland and the value people place on religious belief in their sense of personal and national identity;

- anti-Catholicism comes with its own immutable and in-built legitimation (the perceived scriptural injunction to oppose doctrinal error), which has a special cultural sanction in Northern Ireland because of the society's high religiosity.

This congruity becomes a constraint for those people and groups that seek to move beyond sectarian politics. As David Ervine, a leading member of the Progressive Unionist Party, commented in an interview:

> Sectarianism is a flower that's cultivated, nurtured, and owes its origins to historical circumstances and socio-political causes. I dislike use of the term because it suggests the conflict is about religion, when it's about politics. I prefer the term 'tribalism': religion is used to keep people in tribes. Tribalism is like piss down the leg, it initially gives a warm glow but it quickly goes cold. Some people use fear of the Pope and papal conspiracies in order to keep the problem as a two-party zero-sum conflict. Certain Unionists create tribalism, through creating fear, in order to keep people in their entrenched positions.

In short, anti-Catholicism is part of the ideological apparatus that constructs two mutually exclusive groups with opposed sets of interests and identities, and it forms part of the symbolic myths, rituals and language which reproduce and represent polarised and sectarian experiences and behaviour.

FOUR MODES OF ANTI-CATHOLICISM

Our analysis of contemporary articulations of anti-Catholicism demonstrated that it has distinct modes or types in the way it operates. The first is what we called 'passive anti-Catholicism', the kind that remains unsystematic at the level of ideas and not reflected in behaviour. It is the kind that some Protestants have transmitted to them as part of their socialisation, but which remains as a cultural context, rarely articulated or enacted. 'Active anti-Catholicism' is something different and represents a fully formulated structure of ideas, language and behaviour. Three types of active anti-Catholicism can be identified, called the covenantal, secular and Pharisaic modes. We plotted these on two axes or continuums – theological content (high to low) and political content (high to low), as represented in Figure 5.1. This illustrates the paradox of anti-Catholicism, in that it may be based on scriptural interpretation (covenantal and Pharisaic modes), which may (covenantal mode) or may not (Pharisaic mode) find political articulation, and also make little reference to theology and be highly political (secular mode), emphasising an approach to politics which is very similar to one of the more theological modes (the covenantal). The modes are therefore

Figure 5.1: Plotting the Modes of Anti-Catholicism Along Two Axes

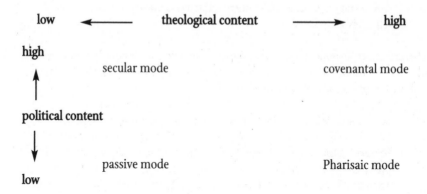

Figure 5.2: The Three Modes of Active Anti-Catholicism

COVENANTAL MODE	SECULAR MODE	PHARISAIC MODE
based on conventional ideas about God, land and a chosen people	based on defence of the Union and attack on Republicanism	based on biblical truth and Catholic doctinal error
prophetic language based on the Old Testament	political language based around Unionism and Loyalism	irenic language based on the New Testament
Roman Catholics as threat to Ulster and Protestantism; RC Church as biblical evil and enemy; Catholicism and Millenninal conspiracies and threats; Roman Catholicism is unChristian; theology and politics interwoven	negative role of RC Church in the Irish Republic and political violence in Ulster; Catholicism as a threat to political and civil liberty and economic success; absence of theology	critical of Catholic doctrine and practice; Roman Catholicism is Christian but in error; evangelism of Catholics to bring them to truth; absence of politics
appeals to the 'holy remnant', such as 'Bible Protestants' and other fundamentalists	appeals to 'political Protestants', secular Unionists and militant Loyalists	wide appeal to evangelicals and other Protestants
no relationship with Catholics	politically expedient relationshps	dialogue with Catholics in order to evangelise them

best understood as ideal types, in that they do not exist in pure form in people's language and behaviour: there is overlap in the concerns of each mode, and this cross-over is expressed in people's own versions of anti-Catholicism. Each of the ideal types has a common structure, with its own set of foundational ideas, using a characteristic form of rhetoric, emphasising different things in the articulation of anti-Catholicism, appealing to a different primary constituency, and having different implications for relationships with Catholics, as summarised in Figure 5.2.

The covenantal mode is perhaps that type which is most recognised as anti-Catholicism, and admitted by its proponents to be.[3] Its ideological premises are linked to Old Testament notions of covenant, wherein God promises untold blessings, including land, to a chosen people so long as they remain faithful to Him. These scriptural ideas have been employed in Protestant discourse since the sixteenth century when some reformers reinterpreted the notion of covenant as a political contract between government and citizens, supposedly upheld by God (Miller, 1978). In this mode, Ulster (and its union with Britain) may be seen as a promised land to Protestants, or at least one highly blessed by God. Covenantal anti-Catholicism in this mode thus emphasises the divine mission of 'the Protestant people' to oppose Roman Catholicism, which is a threat to Ulster and to Protestantism. This is a threat manifested in many alleged conspiracies orchestrated by the 'forces of Catholicism', including civil unrest in the North of Ireland. In this mode, Irish Republicanism is sometimes seen simply as Catholicism at war. Catholicism seeks to destroy Ulster's God-ordained political, constitutional and social arrangements and impose a United Ireland, which would simply be an extension of Rome Rule. Politics and theology are thus cross-pollinated, with scripture being used to support Union with Britain. Advocates of this mode may see themselves as a 'holy remnant', part of the faithful few left in an unrighteous, sinful and secular world.[4] This is a constituency found in conservative and fundamentalist Protestants, who identify themselves in contrast to those whom they see as using the 'Protestant' label inaccurately, either because they are 'liberals', or because they employ it solely as a political identity. Clearly, since Catholicism is un-Christian and seeks to annihilate Protestantism, no meaningful relationship with the Catholic Church can ever be considered, and any relationship with ordinary Catholics is viewed as an evangelistic opportunity, if not discouraged out of hand.[5]

The secular mode, meanwhile, may not appear to be a type of anti-Catholicism at all, since its ideological premises are thoroughly political, based on a defence of the Union and an attack on Republicanism. Gone is the covenantal association between land, God and Ulster. However, this mode alleges an umbilical link between Catholicism and Republicanism, and its political, economic and social objections to a United Ireland have been replete with negative stereotypes of Catholics and the alleged disproportionate influence of the Church in all aspects of the Irish Republic's politics and culture.

Theology, however, is virtually absent. Catholicism threatens civil and political liberties rather than Protestantism per se, and is criticised for its political manifestations rather than its heresy, although there is an implicit ecclesiology behind the claim that Catholicism threatens liberties and freedoms. In the secular mode, anti-Catholicism is articulated using conventionally political rhetoric, centring on typical Unionist and Loyalist arguments in defence of the Union. Its constituency is 'political Protestants', secular Unionists and that majority of militant Loyalists whose paramilitary activities were not underscored by a theological conviction. In as much as the objection is to what it sees as Catholicism's political manifestations, which are contingent, rather than to its theological ones, which are immutable, certain relationships with Catholics are permissible if they are politically expedient.

These are the main two types and their use in drawing ethnic and moral boundaries to exclude Catholics politically, economically and socially should be evident. The third type does not function in social closure but it nonetheless helps to mark boundaries. The Pharisaic mode is so called because it has ideological premises reminiscent of a popular impression of the biblical Pharisees. Its advocates are convinced that they know biblical truth and right doctrine, although this is through adherence to mainstream Reformed, not covenantal, theology, particularly as Reformed theology interprets the doctrine of justification by faith. Catholic doctrine is rejected because it is believed to argue for salvation through works and by means of Church tradition rather than grace alone. However, the rhetoric is conciliatory and open, rather than denunciatory and impolite. The emphasis of the Pharisaic mode is theological, entirely devoid of political rhetoric, and Catholicism is even acknowledged to be 'Christian but in error'. Evangelism of Catholics is stressed, which is partly why relationship and dialogue are encouraged with Catholics. This mode appeals extensively to non-fundamentalist evangelicals and what Boal et al. (1991) called the more conservative liberal Protestants.

THE PAPAL ANTICHRIST MYTH

An important part of some forms of anti-Catholicism is the belief that the papacy is the antichrist. This section briefly examines the sociological features of this myth, summarised from a much more extensive study (Higgins, 2000). Myths can feature in many kinds of sociological discourse – as myths of territory, redemption, injustice, divine appointment, bravery, regeneration, the axis of change, origin and ethnicity. Myths are a method of ordering experience, of defining social and moral boundaries, or concealing unpalatable truths; they are, indeed, a form of communication, and tell of the past, present and future. They are often explicitly related to the sacred, they can be ritually expressed, and they are closely related with the development and maintenance of culture.

The papal antichrist myth envisages a role for the Catholic papacy in the end-times and a final battle between God and Satan. In Northern Ireland these end-times ideas function in the context of anti-Catholicism at the level of ideas and individual behaviour. This belief is found among certain kinds of fundamentalist Protestants only, who consider a defence of the faith to be paramount. That their faith is conflated with ethnicity and national identity reinforces the myth's saliency as a socio-political phenomenon in Northern Ireland. Of course, separatism and 'chosen nation' sentiment have significant purchase in Northern Ireland, and the papal antichrist myth is pervasive amongst certain kinds of Protestants. It is clear that anti-Catholicism and the papal antichrist myth are significant parts of the cultural 'air' breathed by fundamentalist Protestants in Northern Ireland. The key social resonances of this myth are in terms of furthering the cultural interests of believers, which in practice relates to Protestant socio-political hegemony, reaffirming individual and group identity, and encouraging the conversion of Catholics. The believers' world-view includes reference to a number of conspiracy theories, which link perceived socio-political crises to theology and constructing Ulster Protestant identity as a target of massive threat. Contemporary conspiracy theories include tacit or explicit reference to the peace process – there is an elective affinity between belief in the papal antichrist myth and anti-Agreement sentiment. The network of relationships that reinforce belief in the myth include traditional foci of religious legitimation (the family, congregation, denomination, and so on). What might be termed 'religious xenophobia', within the fundamentalist 'closed set', acts as a form of social control to discourage believers from changing their beliefs or leaving the sect. The narrowing base of social acceptability for fundamentalism arising from its unpopularity reinforces the separatist fear of threats from without.

The myth has many uses, from the construction of social and moral boundaries to its role in the denial of a Protestant role in responsibility for the conflict or for sectarianism in Northern Ireland. Simply put, in Northern Ireland the myth connects with the overarching line of social cleavage and has influence at the level of the social structure. In contrast with America, for example, the only other Western society with significant levels of belief in the papal antichrist myth particularly within the Southern 'Bible Belt', the existence of pluralist lines of social cleavage means that the myth has saliency for a relatively insignificant number of people. If pluralist lines of social cleavage were to develop in Northern Ireland, the religious marketplace, already well established elsewhere, would be open for vigorous business, with anti-Catholicism and the papal antichrist myth as merely one of many paradigmatic choices and identity markers. Meanwhile, there is evidence of former believers who have changed their minds and become involved in proactive peace, reconciliation, and ecumenical initiatives. Global social phenomena have set the context for such change in the form of globalisation, civil and human rights discourse, the development of a panoply of alternative identity markers, ecumenism and the Northern Irish peace process. All have begun to 'squeeze out' the space for public acceptability of anti-Catholicism and the papal antichrist myth. At a local level, there has been some mainline Protestant alienation from conservative evangelicals and a breakdown of barriers between Protestants and Catholics in reaction to the conflict. There has also been a broadening of Protestant experience in terms of education, travel and occupation, as well as the development of anti-sectarian initiatives and modernising economic changes. It appears that as the space for papal antichrist myth and other anti-Catholic belief is eroded, opportunities for other identity markers and change among some believers will increase.

Despite its universalistic tenets across the world, the local distinctiveness of Protestantism is greater where secularisation is less developed; this is partly why it has retained its distinctiveness in Northern Ireland, although this is currently being challenged, as secularisation processes and post-modern norms assert themselves. The role of power and tradition within Protestantism is illuminated by analysis of anti-Catholicism and the papal antichrist myth. The individualistic emphasis on doctrine and the lack of hierarchical authority and tradition within Protestantism means that believers can rewrite their own traditions and doctrines, and do so often in situations of religious conflict. The preoccupation with ideology over pragmatism within conservative Protestantism lends itself to schism, as Bruce (1990: 40, 43) suggested:

> [Such] movements have no source of authority superior to the ideology from which legitimacy is derived. Hence any factional leader can claim to have the correct interpretation of the ideology. In the absence of any superior power to arbitrate . . . disputes, schism becomes common . . . Propensity to schism increases with the availability of means of legitimation.

This is reflected by the case of the papal antichrist myth. As a method of conflict management, some Protestants in Northern Ireland reassess their beliefs and become involved in ecumenism with Catholics and in the development of 'civic unionism', while others interpret the conflict as *resulting from* this very ecumenism and so-called 'liberalism' within Protestantism, reinforcing their anti-Catholicism. The location of authority in the individual conscience, as contrasted with hierarchical authority vested in the Catholic Church, means that both anti-Catholics and ecumenists can assert that they are being true to Protestantism. The tendency toward schism within Protestantism often manifests itself in separatism; the separatist mindset naturally defines an outside enemy and 'closes ranks' to protect itself from this enemy. This tendency is ideally suited to Northern Ireland, where it is reinforced because the ethnic identity of some Protestants depends on defining enemies 'outside the camp': Republicans and Nationalists (and ecumenists) are the temporal and political enemy, and the papacy the ubiquitous spiritual enemy. Theology and politics combine with cultural assertions to produce the specific local expressions of the anti-Catholicism and the papal antichrist myth.

Protestants in Northern Ireland who assert generalised anti-Catholicism or believe that the pope is the antichrist do not, on the whole, do so for cynical reasons. They assert that their anti-Catholicism is rooted in a sincere and correct interpretation of scripture, Protestant culture and tradition. The nature of Protestant religion permits this variation and allows both believers in the myth and those who reject it the comfort that they are being true to Protestantism in doing so. Tony Blair once made a statement to the effect that anti-Agreement Unionists had no place in the future of Northern Ireland unless they changed their minds about what was important to them. He referred to these people as 'men of the past', and appeared to consider their concerns to be cynical and irrational. However, while an identity that depends on myths may indeed be irrational, they are held sincerely by committed adherents. Any attempt at transforming the conflict in Northern Ireland must take account of the seriousness with which some people hold their anti-Catholicism and it is necessary to locate such beliefs in sociological processes rather than in terms of relativistic notions of irrationality. The process of globalisation proffers a better location for understanding these beliefs.

Supporters of the globalisation thesis suggest that identities are now developed by exposure to mass media rather than inculcation in local traditions. In other words, as Brewer (1999: 4) satirised them: 'People are no longer what their position in the [local] social structure makes them; they are what they shop.' As Featherstone (1995: 86) said, 'in effect, we are all in each other's backyard'. Local traditions come under pressure as the de-routinisation of social life increases, leading to what Giddens (1996) called 'ontological insecurity'. For the 'ultra-globalisationist', globalisation will eventually lead to the erosion of all local traditions, as what Brewer (1999:6) called 'the onward march of the cultural glob' tramples everything distinctive in its wake. However, critics of this view (for instance, Hall, 1991; Robertson, 1992; Featherstone, 1995) contend that globalisation and the fragmentation of cultures are part of the same process. To put it simply, the more globalisation proceeds, the more it will be challenged by the reassertion of tradition in the face of perceived threat. As Hall (1991: 34–35) said:

> The return to the local is often a response to globalisation . . . Face to face with a culture, an economy and a set of histories which seem to be written or inscribed elsewhere, and which are so immense, transmitted from one continent to another with such extraordinary speed, the subjects of the local . . . can only come into representation by . . . recovering their own hidden histories. *They have to tell the story from the bottom up, instead of from the top down.* [emphasis ours]

From this perspective, contemporary forms of Protestant fundamentalism may be actually a *part* of globalisation, as people assert their traditions ever more strongly in order to maintain at least a vestige of their identity, either as a form of resistance to the globalisation 'steamroller', or as part of the re-emergence of local conflicts.

Northern Ireland could almost be an 'ideal type' crucible for such processes (called 'glocalisation' by Sklair, 1999), as traditional identities are reasserted as a challenge to global and post-modern pressure.

CONCLUSIONS

Anti-Catholicism and the papal antichrist myth cannot be dismissed as sociologically uninteresting, as claimed by Jenkins (1997). While doctrinal and theological disputes are in themselves not sociologically fecund, sociology has an input into explaining why, in some restricted social settings, four-century-old theological conflicts remain pertinent. As stressed here, ancient theological disputes can resonate because of high levels of religiosity, but the absence of secularisation is only part of a sociological account. In some settings, ancient religious differences are functional equivalents of other lines of differentiation. In this kind of social milieu, anti-Catholicism does important interactional work. It is one of the major resources which define group boundaries, and it helps to create and rationalise social closure, because it constitutes a significant part of the 'cultural stuff', as Jenkins (1997) put it, which comprises ethnicity in Northern Ireland. Although this argument is restricted to the Northern Irish case, it is possible to speculate about anti-Catholicism having wider applicability to other ethnic conflicts that have a religious dimension.

The future survival of the papal antichrist myth, and anti-Catholicism generally in Northern Ireland, depends on the capacity of separatists to *be separate*. Sections of the Protestant community in Northern Ireland who hold strongly to these beliefs will seek to maintain their identity as separatist fundamentalists but this is likely to be periodically redefined according to circumstances as they confront the wider social world they are forced to inhabit. This redefinition will occur in two ways, what Hall (1991: 36) calls 'an expansive [or] a defensive way'. The abandonment of a ban on inter-racial dating by the fundamentalist Bob Jones University in South Carolina is an example of the former, while the use of scripture by dissident Loyalists to justify burning Catholic churches is an example of the latter. The mediation Northern Irish Protestants make between local circumstances and identity concerns with wider global processes will shape whether the future is a pluralist or separatist one.

It must be reiterated that anti-Catholicism is not the sum of what Protestantism 'means' in Northern Ireland nor does our analysis deny the existence of anti-Protestantism. Those people whose identity is predicated even partly on anti-Catholicism do so because they believe it to be true, and they comprise an important group whose influence on the peace process is disproportionately high. They cannot be ignored by those whose zeal for 'peace' may blind them to the stark fact that Northern Ireland's sectarian division is understood theologically by some people and is for them immutable. To put it another way, threatening those people whose identity is itself partly based on a sense of threat will not help the conflict transformation process in Northern Ireland, but merely serve to reinforce their separatism and embed further the roots of conflict.

NOTES

[1] Great Britain generally was once a good case, although anti-Catholicism has now lost its saliency. We know a great deal about anti-Catholicism in Great Britain, covering twentieth-century Scotland (Bruce, 1985a, 1985b; Hickman, 1995), and England for the seventeenth (Hill, 1971; Millar, 1973), eighteenth (Colley, 1992; Haydon, 1993), nineteenth (Arnstein, 1982; Norman, 1968; Paz, 1992; Wolffe, 1991), and twentieth centuries (Hickman, 1995).

[2] There are small pockets of similar social cleavage in parts of the United States, but due to the pluralistic nature of that society, anti-Catholicism finds no succour at the level of the social structure.

[3] Paisleyism is the best example of the covenantal mode, and Bruce's (1986; 1994) analysis of Paisleyism is the most comprehensive.

[4] Hence the paradox, the 'holy remnant' want to keep Union with Britain, despite its secularism but only because the reverse is worse as they see it, unification with a Catholic Ireland.

[5] Paisley makes a distinction between the system of Catholicism and individual believers, claiming that he reserves his hatred for the system (Bruce, 1986: 232). While there are examples of tireless work for those Catholics in his constituency, the distinction breaks down in his rhetoric and is hardly maintained by others, such as in paramilitary violence against Catholics and the boycott of Catholic businesses.

6. CONTACT AND CONFLICT IN NORTHERN IRELAND

Ulrike Niens, Ed Cairns and Miles Hewstone

INTRODUCTION

Psychological research into inter-group conflict and conflict resolution dates back almost 100 years and interest in theory and research about inter-group conflict increased especially after World War II and the Holocaust in Germany. Today, ethno-political conflict may be considered as one of the most important threats to global security (Seligman, 1998), which may further increase the need for and importance of research about conflict and conflict reduction. Ethno-political conflict is often regarded as identity-based (Smith, 1999), meaning the individual's identification with ethnic, religious or national groups, which may be promoted by political leadership.

This chapter will examine the conflict in Northern Ireland in relation to the effect of cross-community contact on inter-group attitudes. Starting with psychological perspectives on the conflict in Northern Ireland, in particular social identity theory and the contact hypothesis, the chapter goes on to report research about the relationship between cross-community contact and inter-group attitudes. Limitations of this research are pointed out, and a study is reported which attempts to overcome some of these limitations by investigating relevant key constructs in the general population.

SOCIAL IDENTITY THEORY

One theory that has attracted a vast amount of attention in social psychological research, particularly in the context of ethno-political conflict, is social identity theory, developed by Tajfel (1978, 1981; Tajfel and Turner, 1979). The following paragraphs outline the basic assumptions of Social Identity Theory (SIT) and its application to the Northern Irish context (see also Chapter 7 for further discussion of this theory). This is followed by a brief review of the contact hypothesis, the relevance of contact in the context of countries experiencing inter-group conflict and issues for the measurement of inter-group contact.

According to SIT, individuals identify with social groups in order to increase their self-esteem by comparing their in-group with out-groups along comparison dimensions. SIT proposes an interpersonal-inter-group continuum (Tajfel and Turner, 1979), along which an individual may move in different contexts. In personal contexts, the individual is supposed to be closer to the interpersonal end of the continuum; in contexts where group identity is at stake, the individual is supposed to move closer to the interpersonal end of the continuum. The degree of group identification determines the individual's inclination to apply a specific social category to a specific social context. This means that the more an individual identifies with a social group, the more likely it is that this specific group identity will be 'switched on' when a situation requires it. Social categorisation theory (e.g. Turner, 1982, 1984; Turner et al., 1987) was proposed as an extension to SIT. According to social categorisation theory, the self-concept comprises an individual and collective self, which reflect different categories of identity. In social situations, the individual's self-categorisation depends on identity salience. Hence, interpersonal and inter-group behaviour is inherent to the personal or social categories the individual has switched on. SIT and social categorisation theory further propose that social categorisation and identification with a specific social group lead to the need to differentiate the in-group from comparable out-groups, which in turn may lead to in-group favouritism and out-group hostility (Tajfel, 1978; Turner and Onarato, 1999).

In this way SIT has also come to play a role in understanding the psychological dimensions of ethnic conflict, especially in Northern Ireland (Cairns, 1982; Cairns et al., 1995; Trew and Benson, 1996; Whyte, 1990). This research established that social categorisation plays a key part in the maintenance of the conflict. It has been shown that people in Northern Ireland categorise others according to religion using names, place of origin, or school one attended as cues for categorisation (Cairns, 1980). The majority of people in Northern Ireland identify with being Catholic or Protestant (Cairns and Mercer, 1984). Cairns and Mercer (1984) also suggested that the two communities were divided, with no social categories cross-cutting the religious division. In in-group experiments, involving Catholics and Protestants, in-group identification was found to be related to in-group favouritism (Gallagher, 1982) and out-group discrimination (Gallagher, 1983). In their research about stereotypes in young Catholics and Protestants, Stringer and Cairns (1983: 245) found that while 'in-group attitudes for Protestants are as one would expect from a majority group and reveal clear-cut positive in-group evaluation', Catholics evaluated their in-group negatively on specific dimensions, but, overall, they rated their in-group as positively as the out-group. In sum, previous research has shown that SIT helps to explain certain aspects of the conflict in Northern Ireland in relation to the minority group (Catholics) as well as the majority group (Protestants).

WHY IS CONTACT IMPORTANT?

There are two main perspectives here. Contact as 'cure' for conflict and lack of contact as cause of conflict. We will examine each in turn.

CONTACT HYPOTHESIS: CONTACT AS 'CURE' FOR CONFLICT

One of the most frequently applied approaches to conflict resolution is the contact hypothesis (Allport, 1954; Hewstone and Brown, 1986; Pettigrew, 1986). In its most simple form, the contact hypothesis proposes that inter-group conflict can be reduced by bringing together individuals from opposing groups under optimal conditions (Pettigrew and Tropp, 2000). One of the underlying assumptions is that conflict arises from lack of information about the other group and from lack of opportunities to obtain information about members of the other group (Amir and Ben-Ari, 1988). However, Allport (1954) suggested four conditions to bring about contact, which may reduce inter-group conflict. Firstly, there should be equal status among the groups who meet or at least among the individuals from groups who meet. Secondly, the situation in which inter-group contact occurs should require co-operation between groups or offer common goals to both groups. Thirdly, social competition among the groups involved should be avoided. And lastly, the contact situation should be legitimised through institutional support (Pettigrew, 1971).

Inspired by SIT and social categorisation theory, the contact hypothesis has been further developed in the last 20 years. Three contrasting models can be identified encompassing the contact hypothesis (Pettigrew, 1998). The 'decategorisation model' (Brewer and Miller, 1984) called for contact between *individuals* of two opposing groups, hence encouraging individuals to 'switch off' their social identity and so to distance themselves from the in-group in order to promote personalised contact between in-group and out-group members. Gaertner et al. (1993) focused on 'recategorisation into broader social categories' and the establishment of a common in-group identity for social groups in inter-group conflict, again a process that requires a salient social identity to be 'switched off'. Hewstone, Rubin and Willis (2002) pointed out two major limitations to the common group identity model:

> First a common group identity may only be short-lived, or unrealistic in the face of powerful ethnic and racial categorizations . . . Second, for groups with a history of antagonism, and for minorities who are likely to resist assimilation into a superordinate category . . . the prospect of superordinate group identity may constitute a threat, which actually increases bias. (Brewer, 2000; Hornsey and Hogg, 1999: 26)

Hewstone and Brown (1986) proposed *inter-group* contact (that is contact with one's social identity 'switched on') as the most effective means to achieve a reduction of inter-group conflict. Recently, Pettigrew (1998) attempted to combine these theoretical approaches by suggesting that all three are important, although the order in which they are introduced would decide the effectiveness of contact interventions. According to Pettigrew (1998), contact should first be introduced between individuals from different groups, then inter-group contact should be emphasised and finally a superordinate category of identification established. However, these assumptions still have to be tested systematically. The main limitation of the contact hypothesis is that often contact is not generalised from one member of the out-group to the out-group as a whole (Hewstone and Brown, 1986; Hewstone and Cairns, 2001; Pettigrew, 1998). On a more practical note, as Hewstone and Cairns (2001) point out, it is often difficult to bring about inter-group contact on a large scale in real-life contexts. Aron and co-workers (Aron et al., 1991; Wright et al., 1997) tried to overcome this limitation by proposing that 'extended contact' (the individual experiencing his or her friends having close out-group friends) may also lead to more positive out-group attitudes.

CONTACT AND CONFLICT: LACK OF CONTACT AS CAUSE OF CONFLICT

The question could be asked why contact between members of opposing groups should be so important that it could be a catalyst for the reduction of inter-group hostility. In many countries experiencing ethno-political conflict, inter-group contact is reduced to a minimum as social and environmental barriers limit opportunities to meet people from opposing groups. In South Africa during the years of apartheid, racial categorisation was introduced with the Population Registration Act in 1950. Following that was a 'formidable battery of laws, regulations, proclamations and judicial interpretations that prescribe behaviour in a vast array of potentially interracial situations, such as wedding, bedding, dining, entertaining, learning . . .' (Foster and Finchilescu, 1986: 122). In Northern Ireland, too, Catholics and Protestants often live segregated lives. Segregation here affects residential areas, education, marriage, work and leisure (Whyte, 1990).

'Barriers to inter-group contact, then, may arise from the situation itself. They may also be caused by a number of other factors, including tendencies to associate primarily with members of one's group, perception of out-group members as "invaders" (Wolf, 1957, 1960), and actual differences between groups in language, religion and perceived status.' (Amir, 1976: 253).

The lack of inter-group contact that is often presented as a consequence of ethno-political conflict is believed to be a catalyst for conflict, too. A dearth of knowledge and misperception about the out-group may lead to inter-group anxiety and, hence, foster negative out-group attitudes and increase out-group derogation (Stephan and Stephan, 1985). However, Hewstone and Brown (1986) emphasise that conflict itself is caused by other factors rather than only lack of knowledge and misperception about the out-group.

MEASUREMENT ISSUES

There are a number of issues relating to measurement and these will now be examined.

MEASURING CONTACT

For the measurement of inter-group contact in quantitative or qualitative research, different levels of contact may be looked at. On the one hand, contact can be investigated in the light of quantity of contact, meaning how frequently individuals meet members of the out-group. On the other hand, contact can be measured in its quality, meaning how positive or negative individuals' experience contact with out-group members is and how meaningful this is to them.

Quantity of contact. This refers to the frequency with which an individual meets members of the out-group. This contact may occur through meeting neighbours, work colleagues, leisure activities, or friends etc. Quantity of contact may be measured by asking how frequently a person meets with members of the other community. What it does not address, however, is how positive or negative an individual perceives it to be. This question is targeted when measuring quality of contact.

Quality of contact. In terms of quality of contact, there are two basic dimensions. Firstly, positive versus negative experiences of contact may affect the outcome of inter-group contact. Secondly, casual versus intimate contact may also affect the outcome of the contact experience. Generally speaking, positive inter-group contact is believed to improve out-group attitudes (Amir, 1976; Hewstone and Brown, 1986). However, if contact with out-group members is experienced as negative, out-group attitudes may actually deteriorate. Therefore, it is important to measure the individual perception of the contact situation. Similarly, intimate, rather than casual contact is believed to improve out-group attitudes. Amir (1976: 276) even warns: 'Casual contact typically has little or no effect on basic attitude change. When such contact is frequent, it may even reinforce negative attitudes, especially when it occurs between non-equal status groups.'

VARIABLES RELATED TO INTER-GROUP CONTACT

Several different factors are believed to influence inter-group contact or the relationship between inter-group contact and attitude change. These variables range from background factors such as social class and age, to opportunities for contact and attitudes, social identity and inter-group anxiety.

Demographic variables. Age and social class. Age might be related to contact, as with increasing age the likelihood of having experienced contact with out-group members should also increase. Furthermore, the impact of other variables such as opportunity for contact, out-group attitudes, and in-group identification may have established itself only in later years, while young people might be more subjected to their parents' and the environment's influence without further possibilities to

127

affect these. Studying inter-group contact in Northern Ireland, Craig and Cairns (1999) found that 50% of their interviewees did not have any out-group friends before the age of 15, and if they had out-group friends from an early age, it was usually a neighbour.

Social class might be another demographic variable associated with inter-group contact and out-group attitudes. Education may positively influence attitudes towards inter-group contact, as university education in Northern Ireland is mixed (Cairns et al., 1993) whereas primary and secondary education is almost completely segregated. Also, segregated housing often concerns relatively deprived social areas in Northern Ireland, concerning people from lower social class backgrounds (Whyte, 1990). Middle-class and upper-class residential areas are often more mixed, which again may affect people's attitudes towards inter-group contact and opportunities for contact.

Opportunity for contact. Opportunity for contact is a main factor affecting inter-group contact. In countries experiencing ethno-political conflict, opportunities for contact may be limited through legislation (as in South Africa during the years of apartheid where, for example, inter-racial marriages were prohibited) or through segregation (as in Northern Ireland or Israel where, for example, residential areas and education are mostly segregated; Knox and Hughes, 1994). Opportunity for contact may be one determining factor for inter-group contact to occur at all.

Attitudes towards contact and inter-group attitudes. Amir (1976) emphasised attitudes towards inter-group contact as an important factor in the analyses of contact, as negative attitudes towards inter-group contact may reduce actual contact and, hence, be associated with negative out-group attitudes. Hence, out-group attitudes as well as group identification are further variables believed to be related to inter-group contact (Amir, 1976). On the one hand, negative out-group attitudes might prevent people from taking up opportunities for contact. On the other hand, individuals holding negative attitudes and experiencing situations of inter-group contact may interpret the contact situation more negatively.

Social identity. Social identity may be another important factor affecting inter-group contact. In countries experiencing ethno-political conflict, inter-group contact may be inhibited through social norms, which may be enforced by social exclusion or even violent means and could proscribe meeting or being friendly with out-group members. The more a person identifies with the in-group, the more inclined he or she will be to follow the group norms (Abrams et al., 1998; Hinkle et al., 1996). Hence, people identifying strongly with their in-group may be more inclined to follow the group norms and to avoid contact with out-group members.

Inter-group anxiety. Inter-group anxiety theory suggests that anxiety interferes with the ability to intake new information and, consequently, it hinders the assimilation of information about positive characteristics of negatively stereotyped out-group members (Stephan and Stephan, 1985). Thus, it is believed that a reduction in anxiety will lead to less prejudiced perceptions of out groups. Stephan and Stephan (1985) propose inter-group interaction as a way to reduce inter-group anxiety. Inter-group contact should involve positive interaction with out-group members who are at best partly typical of their group in order for inter-group interaction to be successful in reducing inter-group anxiety and for improved attitudes to be generalised towards the out-group as a whole (Johnston and Hewstone, 1992).

INTER-GROUP CONTACT IN NORTHERN IRELAND

The conflict in Northern Ireland has been shown to be not only a religious one, but to be based on the interrelation of multiple social, economic, and political aspects (Cairns and Darby, 1998). As a psychological factor, identification with one of the two religious communities has been shown to play an important role in the maintenance of the conflict (Cairns, 1982; Trew and Benson, 1996). Northern Ireland is often described as a divided society where members of the Catholic and the Protestant communities have limited opportunities for inter-group contact because of segregation in different areas of social life. Even though segregation is not thought to be the cause of inter-group conflict, it is believed to play a major role in establishing and maintaining conflict between two communities.

Hamilton (1995: 1) suggested a 'cyclical and interdependent' effect between segregation and violence. As the problem of segregation and its relevance for the Northern Ireland conflict has been recognised for quite some time, policies and methods to reduce the level of segregation and to increase opportunities for inter-group contact have been introduced. The types of segregation that have received most attention in Northern Ireland are personal and matrimonial (Moxon-Browne, 1983; Rose, 1971), residential segregation (Poole, 1982), and educational segregation (Darby et al., 1977; Gallagher, 1989; McClenaghan et al., 1996). We will now examine these, while recognising that other types of segregation (e.g. at work, sport and leisure) have been identified as well (Smyth, 1995).

PERSONAL SEGREGATION
On an individual level, cross-community friendships exist, even though a majority of respondents in surveys from 1968 to 1998 report that all or most of their friends are from their own community (see Table 6.1).

An even more important way to measure intimacy across community lines might be to look at cross-community marriages. In terms of endogamy, Rose (1971) found 5% of marriages were inter-community. Moxon-Browne (1983) reported 5% of marriages across community lines, and Gallagher and Dunn (1991) found 4% cross-community marriages. More recently, data from the Northern Ireland Life and Times Survey (NILT) (1988, 1999, 2000) indicated 8.3%–10.6% cross-community marriages (see Table 6.2). Whyte (1990: 40) noted that the 'proportion of mixed marriages is higher in younger age groups', suggesting a

Table 6.1: Proportion of Respondents Reporting that 'All or Most' of
their FRIENDS were of the Same Religion as Themselves
(after Cairns & Hewstone, in press)

YEAR	CATHOLIC (%)	PROTESTANT (%)	SOURCE
1968	57	78	Rose (1971)
1978	56	75	Moxon-Browne (1983)
1989	63	72	Gallagher & Dunn (1991)
1998	55*	68*	Cairns & Hewstone (1999)

*Original item: 'All or most of your FRIENDS are of a different religion from you'; response
scores reversed

Table 6.2: Proportion of Respondents Reporting that their
Partner was of a Different Religion

YEAR	ALL (%)	SOURCE
1968	5	Rose (1971)
1978	5	Moxon-Browne (1983)
1989	4	Gallagher & Dunn (1991)
1998	9	NILT (1998)
1999	11	NILT (1999)
2000	8	NILT (2000)

careful optimism about mixed marriages possibly being a more frequent
phenomenon in the future. However, more recently Cairns and Hewstone (in press)
cautioned 'attitudes towards mixed marriages are not improving, at least not
among those not directly involved in them' (p. 7).

RESIDENTIAL SEGREGATION
Smyth (1995: 1) noted that 'the history of segregation in Ireland pre-dates the
Troubles. In urban centres as well as in the country the Catholic and the Protestant
community often led segregated lives. However, as Cairns and Hewstone (in press:
3) pointed out: 'Total segregation does not exist.' Whyte (1990: 34) estimated that
'about 35% to 40% of the population live in segregated neighbourhoods', which
means that more than 50% of the population live in mixed neighbourhoods. In
general, segregated living appears to have slightly increased over the past 30 years
(see Table 6.3).

Table 6.3: Proportion of Respondents Reporting that 'All or Most' of their
NEIGHBOURS are of the Same Religion as Themselves
(from Cairns & Hewstone, in press)

YEAR	CATHOLIC (%)	PROTESTANT (%)	SOURCE
1968	57	68	Rose (1971)
1978	61	75	Moxon-Browne (1983)
1989	62	67	Gallagher & Dunn (1991)
1998	64*	75*	Cairns & Hewstone (1999)

*Original item: 'All or Most' of your NEIGHBOURS are of a different religion from you';
responses scored reversed

EDUCATIONAL SEGREGATION
In Northern Ireland, primary as well as secondary education is mostly segregated, with most Protestants going to government schools and most Catholics going to so-called 'Maintained Schools', which are partly funded by the Catholic Church. Support for this school system comes from both communities, even though in surveys the majority of the population claims it would support integrated education (Hughes and Carmichael, 1998). Because segregation in education in Northern Ireland was 'almost total, particularly at the primary or elementary level' (Cairns, 1987: 119), the government introduced Education for Mutual Understanding (EMU) in 1987, which promotes cross-community school activities. At about the same time, Integrated schools were established, which involve pupils from both sides of the community. In 1989 about 1,400 pupils went to ten Integrated schools. In contrast, there are currently 46 Integrated schools comprising 17 Integrated Second Level Colleges, and 29 Integrated primary schools. In addition there are 13 Integrated nursery schools, most of which are linked to primary schools. However, the Integrated sector still educates only a small minority of the total pupil population.

LIMITATIONS OF EXISTING RESEARCH
The contact hypothesis has provided the basis for many projects and organisations aimed at reducing conflict in Northern Ireland. Formal policies promoting contact[1] were introduced in Northern Ireland by the Central Community Relations Unit in 1987 and additionally through EMU in the educational sector. Other less formal schemes involved short-term cross-community holidays and trips abroad. Looking at short-term to long-term interventions, Trew (1986: 104–105) summarised her evaluation of these projects:

> . . . the evidence from small-scale studies, including direct intervention, suggests that on 'neutral' ground, or in appropriate institutional settings, even Protestants and Catholics who previously mixed only with their co-

religionists will develop close personal friendships. The contact may also contribute to the moderation of gross misperceptions about the 'other' group and an appreciation of a shared cultural background. At the same time, there is no empirical evidence or theoretical rationale to suggest that contact per se will either influence salient political beliefs or have any impact on sectarianism in the society.

Cairns and Dunn (1995) carried out a secondary analysis of Northern Ireland Social Attitude data sets for 1989 and 1991 proposing, firstly, a positive correlation between cross-community contact and attitudes towards cross-community contact and, secondly, a positive correlation between cross-community contact and attitudes towards the other community. The data sets included variables addressing 'contact with people you are not related to' and 'contact with people you are related to'; 'attitudes favouring mixing' and 'preference for mixing' and 'attitudes towards government intervention in mixing'; and 'attitudes towards out-group'. Cairns and Dunn (1995) reported Catholics showing more positive out-group attitudes than Protestants and people with higher social status showing more positive attitudes than people with lower socio-economic status. Overall, the results of these analyses confirmed the hypothesis that greater experience of contact was positively associated with more favourable attitudes to cross-community contact. However, it also indicated that '. . . increased contact does not necessarily lead to improved attitudes towards the out-group' (p. 1). Furthermore, results revealed two independent components to contact, namely contact with strangers and contact with relatives. The former of these components appeared to be more important in relation to attitude change than the latter.

Cairns, Hamberger and Hewstone (in preparation) analysed data provided by the Northern Ireland Social Attitude Surveys from 1989, 1991 and 1993. The objective was to develop a theoretical model of inter-group contact in the Northern Irish context. Using path analyses, the criterion variable was attitudes towards contact (are you in favour of more mixing or more separation in primary schools/secondary schools/residential areas/work/leisure?), which was interpreted as out-group attitudes. Predictor variables were education, social class, attendance at Integrated schools, and quantity of contact. Results indicated contact to be positively related to education, class and integrated schooling. Contact was a significant predictor of attitudes towards out-groups. In comparison to education, the predictor variable social class was a stronger predictor of quantity of contact. Cairns et al. (in preparation) concluded that the positive association between social class and out-group attitudes reflected the fact that the conflict is more potent in predominantly poor areas in Northern Ireland. However, the measurement of some of the key variables in this study was limited (e.g. out-group attitudes measured by attitudes towards contact).

Reviewing social psychological literature about the effects of inter-group contact in Northern Ireland, Cairns and Hewstone (2000) concluded: 'Previous studies of cross-community contact in Northern Ireland have confirmed the limited extent of contact between Catholics and Protestants in the province, but suggest that there is a positive association between contact and attitudes towards the religious out-group.' (p. 4). However, they also pointed out that previous research was often hampered by unreliable measures of key constructs and missing administration of others, in particular the variables 'quality of contact', and 'inter-group anxiety'. In other words, much research in this area has been content with noting simply that inter-group contact took place without assessing if this was seen as positive or negative. In particular, as research in other societies has suggested that inter-group contact can be anxiety producing, a major weakness in research in Northern Ireland is that this variable has been largely ignored.

INVESTIGATING 'INTER-GROUP ANXIETY' AND 'QUALITY OF CONTACT' AS KEY CONSTRUCTS FOR THE EFFECTIVENESS OF INTER-GROUP CONTACT

In the following part of this chapter, a study is presented addressing the contact hypothesis and related variables. In particular, this study tried to overcome limitations noted above by measuring key concepts, such as quality of contact and inter-group anxiety. Before reporting this study in more detail, this chapter outlines several preliminary studies conducted at Northern Irish universities in 1993 and 1998.

PRELIMINARY STUDIES
Cairns et al. (1993) investigated students at the University of Ulster in Coleraine and Jordanstown in relation to the effect of inter-group contact on students' attitudes. The sample consisted of 84 students in their first and third years, with approximately equal numbers of Catholics and Protestants. Using semi-structured interviews and analysing the data qualitatively, results indicated that the campuses were 'functionally segregated' (p. 2) and that contact was more an option for individual students. Furthermore, in terms of quality of contact, contact with members of the out-group was found to be superficial and off-campus contact was more likely in less sectarian environments. This result was confirmed by Hargie et al. (1999) who looked at out-group contact among first-year university students in Northern Ireland and also found it to be at a more superficial level while close friendships mostly remained co-religious. Attitudes appeared to change as a result of contact, but also as a result of readings in the course of studies. Results from this research also showed a negative association between inter-group anxiety and inter-group contact as proposed by Stephan and Stephan (1985) as well as Wright et al. (1997).

The second study was designed to investigate the salience of group membership, quantity and quality of inter-group contact and the relationship between salience, contact and stereotypical views of out-groups. It also aimed to examine the degree of anxiety caused by actual or projected inter-group interactions and to explore the antecedents of such anxiety (Craig and Cairns, 1999). The study was conducted in 1998 and employed two main methods: firstly, a questionnaire survey carried out at Further and Higher Education Colleges in Northern Ireland; and, secondly, in-depth interviews conducted with a similar sample from the University of Ulster in Coleraine. The survey involved 648 students of whom 60% were female and 42% Catholic. Participants' ages ranged from 16 to 20 years. Results were summarised in terms of church attendance, out-group contact, out-group attitudes, inter-group anxiety, denominational differences and identity.

Although students in this survey evaluated religion as important to them, church attendance was less frequent than could have been expected. In contrast to Protestant students, Catholics attended church more frequently and they regarded their own as well as other people's religion as more important. The level of inter-group contact was high with 80% of the students having visited friends from the other community at their home. Catholics and Protestants did not differ in terms of inter-group interaction before the age of five, but Catholics were twice as likely to have had no out-group friends before they were 16 years old.

Overall, the out-group was rated positively although out-group friends were not believed to be typical out-group members. There were no religious differences in the ratings of out-group friends but Protestants were more negative than Catholics about the other community as a whole. However, Catholics were more likely to think that Protestants supported paramilitary groups. In general, reported levels of inter-group anxiety were relatively low. At the same time, in situations where individuals found themselves in the minority, anxiety levels were higher, while students were less anxious about balanced interactions. Results from independent sample t-tests revealed that, in contrast to Catholic students, Protestant students showed higher levels of anxiety in balanced interactions (*see* Table 6.4).

Table 6.4: Independent Sample t-test with Religion as
Independent and Anxiety as Dependent Variable

VARIABLE	GROUP	N	MEAN	SD	T	Df	P
Anxiety in balanced situations (scale from 1 to 5, with 5 indicating high anxiety levels)	Catholic	268	1.43	0.59	2.498	640	0.015
	Protestant	374	1.57	0.75			
Anxiety in minority situations (scale from 1 to 5, with 5 indicating high anxiety levels)	Catholic	271	2.62	1.16	0.132	646	0.895
	Protestant	377	2.63	1.13			

SD = Standard Deviation   DF = Degrees of Freedom   P = Probability   T = T-Value

Church attendance and religiosity were significantly related to out-group ratings and inter-group anxiety. Respondents who did not attend church and who did not think religion was important were less anxious and more positive towards out-groups than respondents who did regard religion as important. Having friends, especially intimate friends, who were out-group members, was negatively related to inter-group anxiety. The Ulster identity was associated with lower levels of inter-group contact, more negative out-group ratings and higher levels of inter-group anxiety. Feeling Northern Irish was significantly related to higher levels of inter-group contact, lower levels of inter-group anxiety and more positive out-group ratings.

The survey was supplemented by semi-structured interviews carried out with 80 students at the University of Ulster at Coleraine. Results generally confirmed the findings from the questionnaire survey. Most of the respondents went to church although that was often to 'please their parents' or to 'keep the peace'. While for Catholics identity was linked to cultural traditions, Protestants' sense of identity was rather abstract. Inter-group contact was common for the majority of respondents although half of them did not have any out-group friends before the age of 15. Interviewees gave credit to Education for Mutual Understanding and cross-community projects as offering opportunities for meeting members of the other community. In contrast, parents often played a role that discouraged respondents from having out-group friends. Almost none of the respondents perceived the other community to be against their community, although most students believed that individual members of the out-group might be against their in-group. To sum up, the hypotheses of this study could be supported. The degree of stereotyping was related to levels of contact and inter-group anxiety. The level of contact was also associated with inter-group anxiety.

While the results of these studies confirmed the importance of the investigation of the key constructs of 'quality of contact' and 'inter-group anxiety' in Northern Ireland, their scope was limited: both studies were conducted with student samples only and, hence, the generalisability of the results was potentially limited. To address this deficit a random sample survey of the Northern Irish population was carried out in 1998 (Cairns and Hewstone, 2000), and this study is described in more detail below. Similar to the two studies reported above, results confirmed the relationship between quantity and quality of contact, inter-group anxiety, group identification and out-group attitudes.

RANDOM SURVEY INVESTIGATING 'QUALITY OF CONTACT' AND 'INTER-GROUP ANXIETY'

The random sample survey of the Northern Irish population conducted in 1998 involved 928 participants of whom 36% were Catholics and 18% were female (Cairns and Hewstone, 2000). Respondents' ages ranged from 19 to 94 years. It was the aim of this study to investigate possible antecedents of out-group attitudes. Basing the analyses on Islam and Hewstone's (1993) study of Hindu–Muslim contact in Bangladesh, a model was proposed linking contact, inter-group anxiety and out-group perceptions. It was hypothesised that contact was negatively associated with inter-group anxiety and positively with out-group attitudes. Furthermore, inter-group anxiety was suggested to be negatively related to out-group attitudes, mediating the relationship between the contact variables and out-group attitudes.

The variables that were measured included contact (opportunity for contact, quantitative, qualitative and interpersonal versus inter-group contact), inter-group anxiety (adapted from Stephan and Stephan, 1985) as well as out-group attitudes (adapted from Pettigrew and Mertens 1995; and Wright et al., 1997). In general, the majority of participants reported having had the opportunity for contact in their neighbourhood while reporting that actual contact with out-group members was relatively infrequent. In terms of quality of contact, contact with out-group members was generally considered as pleasant and not competitive (*see* Table 6.5).

Inter-group anxiety levels were at a medium level. In general, attitudes towards the out-group were rather positive. Participants rated their own attitude towards the out-group as more positive than most people's attitudes (*see* Table 6.6).

Table 6.5: Descriptive Statistics for
Inter-group Contact Variables

VARIABLES	SCALE	MEAN CATHOLIC/ PROTESTANT	SD CATHOLIC/ PROTESTANT
Opportunity for inter-group contact			
Often see out-group in area	Never, 1; Very often, 5	3.82/3.50	1.36/1.33
% of in-group members in the area	0–100%	32.62/48.64	55.03/45.77
Examples of questions tapping quantity of inter-group contact			
Has out-group members as family	None, 1; Most, 3	1.61/1.48	0.53/0.56
Has out-group friends	None, 0; All, 5	2.54/2.31	0.85/0.81
Quality of inter-group contact			
Contact pleasant?	Unpleasant, 1; Definitely pleasant, 4	3.38/3.38	0.83/0.81
Contact competitive?	Always competitive, 1; Not competitive, 4	3.89/3.77	1.13/1.12

Table 6.6: Examples for Questions Tapping Intergroup
Anxiety and Out-group Attitudes

VARIABLES	SCALE	MEAN CATHOLIC/ PROTESTANT	SD CATHOLIC/ PROTESTANT
Anxiety			
In a room full of out-group members would you feel awkward?	Not at all, 1; Very much so, 5	2.82/2.89	1.51/1.45
In a room full of out-group members would you feel happy?	Not at all, 1; Very much so, 5	2.65/2.61	1.16/1.16
Out-group attitudes			
Would most people mind if they had a boss of a different religion?	Mind a lot, 1; Not mind, 3	2.47/2.35	0.65/0.63
		2.54/2.31	0.85/0.81
Do you think that out-group members get jobs that in-group members should have?	Mind a lot, 1; Not mind, 3	2.98/2.94	0.12/0.27
Do you think that out-group members get jobs that in-group members should have?	Strongly agree, 1; Strongly disagree, 5	3.27/3.56	1.05/0.97
How do you feel about the out-group – friendly?	Very much so, 0; Not at all, 10	7.86/7.35	2.26/2.35

Using path analyses, results reported a direct effect of inter-group anxiety on out-group attitudes. Cairns and Hewstone (2000: 2) concluded: '. . . while contact had a small direct influence on out-group attitudes the main impact from contact comes via its influence on inter-group anxiety.' Generally speaking, opportunity for contact was positively related to quality of contact and even more so to quantity of contact. Quantity and quality of contact were negatively associated with inter-group anxiety. A higher degree of all three types of contact correlated with more positive attitudes towards the out-group and inter-group anxiety was negatively related to out-group attitudes.

For all dependent measures, large percentages of variance could be explained by the investigated variables. The additional inclusion of the demographic variables age and social class in the analyses increased the explained variance only marginally. Cairns and Hewstone (2000) summarised their results by writing that '. . . interrelations between contact, inter-group anxiety and out-group attitudes are fundamental to relations between groups, just as Islam and Hewstone (1993) concluded from their research on Hindus and Muslims in Bangladesh' (p. 17). In general, inter-group relationships were similar for Catholic and Protestant respondents even though minor differences were found and, overall, similarities in terms of relationships between variables appeared more significant than differences between the two religious communities.

To sum up, the studies described in this part of the chapter support the hypothesised relationship between quantity and quality of contact, inter-group anxiety and out-group attitudes, with inter-group anxiety serving as a mediating variable. This model seems to hold for a student sample just as well as for the normal population. Reduction of inter-group anxiety appears to be an important factor for the implementation of effective inter-group contact programmes. Results also emphasise that it is not just cross-community contact per se that fosters attitude change, but it is the quality of contact that is important to counteract inter-group anxiety and to affect attitude change.

CONCLUSIONS

Northern Ireland has a long-standing tradition in governmental and non-governmental schemes of promoting cross-community contact and of research on the contact hypothesis (Cairns and Hewstone, in press; Trew, 1986). In this chapter, we have examined in some detail variables relevant to research on inter-group contact and attitude change in Northern Ireland, of which inter-group anxiety appears to be the most relevant. For future research, it may be important to look at causal relationships between quality and quantity of contact, inter-group anxiety and attitude change by employing longitudinal research designs in order to establish a model of the effects of inter-group contact on attitudes (Cairns and Hewstone, 2000). Furthermore, systematic research could be carried out in existing cross-community programmes where the contact hypothesis is implicitly or explicitly employed to promote attitude change (Cairns and Hewstone, in press). In this way, research and practice could complement each other, promoting further knowledge into inter-group conflict and contact and enabling ways to reduce conflict. This might also be an important step forward in reaching the aim of introducing projects at the individual level in order to meet macro community relations objectives (Hughes and Knox, 1997).

NOTES

[1] The assumption has been that the type of contact promoted has been *inter-group* contact although empirical evidence to support this claim is weak.

ACKNOWLEDGEMENTS

We are grateful to the Central Community Relations Unit and the Templeton Foundation for financial support for research reported here.

7. CROSS-COMMUNITY RELATIONS PROJECTS AND INTERDEPENDENT IDENTITIES

Fiona Bloomer and Peter Weinreich

INTRODUCTION

This study is concerned with assessing the impact of projects operating in Northern Ireland whose aim is to deal directly with problems of ethnic conflict. The projects, commonly referred to as community relations projects, or reconciliation projects, aim to address the problems associated with ethnic conflict by bringing together members of the two main communities and facilitating a process of reconciliation. The primary ideology which informs community relations work states that to bring conflicting groups together, facilitating them to get to know each other, will lead to each group seeing the other in a more positive manner and as a result the conflict between the groups will diminish. The theoretical background of this ideology is referred to as contact theory or the contact hypothesis (Allport 1954; Amir 1969, 1976; Cook 1970; Hewstone and Brown, 1986; Pettigrew, 1971, 1979, 1986, 1997).

Wilson and Tyrrell (1995) described how the first contact projects in Northern Ireland were primarily concerned with bringing Protestant and Catholic children together, but not with attempting to achieve reconciliation between the two communities as a whole. During the 1980s, however, the holiday contact schemes began to focus on the reconciliation agenda (Smith and Murray, 1993). The adoption of a proactive approach to reconciliation was mirrored by government policy, in particular the introduction of Education for Mutual Understanding and Cultural Heritage initiatives which were aimed at promoting good relations between Protestant and Catholic school children (Gallagher 1995; Richardson, 1997; Smith and Robinson 1992; 1996). In addition to adopting strategies of conflict resolution, community relations projects also began to adopt follow-up activities to their work. This included using ex-participants as peer educators and volunteers within projects. The volunteers were drawn from the same areas as the children, and this was seen as adding to the validity of the programmes in the eyes of the communities (Wilson and Tyrrell, 1995).

Following on from the demand for contact schemes, and in response to government policies, the increase of contact schemes at community and school level grew from a handful during the 1960s to over 100 in 1997 (Hinds, 1998). As well as having a specific community relations dimension, to reduce hostility, projects were also encouraged to increase appreciation of cultural diversity between the Protestant and Catholic communities. Funding for such projects was provided via a range of sources, including central and local government.

CONTEMPORARY CONTEXT

Despite the fact that in recent years political progress has been made in Northern Ireland, the underlying sectarian and socio-economic conflict has remained. The increase in sectarian assaults and arson attacks in the marching seasons during the mid- to late 1990s reflected the continuing high levels of tension between both communities. In 1995 there were a total of 65 shootings/bombs/incendiary devices reported to the RUC, by 1998 this figure had risen to 474 (Royal Ulster Constabulary, 2001). Certain areas of social and political life, those that emphasise the continuing division between the communities, have grown in symbolic importance. This is particularly so in relation to contentious parades. Since the ceasefires in 1994 and 1997 that effectively ended the Troubles, these parades have become the stage on which sectarian division is now played out. They provide a ritual timetable of events that allow the public rehearsal and reiteration of each side's viewpoint and opposition to the other, and consequently, they have become of great symbolic importance. They reflect how each community perceives it would be treated in a new political arrangement or the transitional phase that would usher it in. Fear and uncertainty in both communities, as well as a sense of triumphalism, have ensured that resolving the sectarian problems at community level will not occur in a short time scale.

In terms of the social divisions between Protestants and Catholics both 'have to face the permanent necessity of having to deal with an "other" whose existence is a threat to one's own' (Eyben et al., 1997a: 323). Eyben et al., (1997a) commented that the main impact of this threat is seen through segregated living, segregated schools, attendance at different churches and social clubs, and the celebration of different traditions. Whilst interface areas do exist they are mainly centred around public places and the workplace.

As the main theme of this research is concerned with changes in identification patterns of participants in community relations work, we review two specific aspects of literature on these matters, firstly research on identity, secondly research on assessing the impact of community relations work.

PREVIOUS RESEARCH

In reviewing the research evidence in relation to identity in Northern Ireland it is immediately apparent that one theory dominates the academic literature – Social Identity Theory (SIT) (Cairns, 1982, 1983, 1987, 1989, 1992; Cairns et al., 1978, 1980; Ferguson and Cairns, 1996, Hewstone et al., 2001a, 2001b; Hunter and Stringer, 1999). SIT aims to link together the concepts of social categorisation, social identity, and social comparisons. The theory was developed initially by Henry Tajfel (Tajfel, 1978, 1982) and, in collaboration with John Turner and others, became a popular theoretical basis for the study of group relations, group processes and the social self (Tajfel and Turner, 1978; Turner et al., 1987).

The basis of SIT begins with the concept of social categorisation. According to SIT an individual is defined in terms of his/her sense of belonging to a series of available categories, such as religion, nationality and political affiliation. Individuals have a series of discrete categories to choose from, each of which may vary in their relative importance in the self-concept. The theory proposes that the individual defines him/herself in terms of the characteristics that the category possesses, and thus membership of the categories both describes and prescribes their perceived social identity. As well as being descriptive and prescriptive, social identities are held to be evaluative. SIT contends that comparisons of in-group membership and out-group memberships lead the individual to achieve or maintain the favoured in-group concept of the group and thus the self.

The process of categorisation has been operationalised by SIT theorists for empirical studies. Indeed, in the Northern Ireland context, research has indicated that children as young as ten have acquired the necessary skills to use the cues required for categorisation purposes (Cairns, 1980; Stringer and McLaughlin-Cook, 1985; Houston et al., 1990). However, operationalisation of the remaining key components of SIT has yet to take place, ensuring that empirical studies of the remaining processes have proved difficult. Those SIT researchers who have focused their work on the concept of social categorisation have been criticised for an over-reliance on the emphasis of the current context within which social identities are construed (Bloomer, 2002; Rougier, 2000; Weinreich, 1992, 2002a). Whilst SIT provides a view of the self in relation to the dynamic between self and society at large, it fails to address the historical context of the society in question or the biographical experiences of individuals within society.

SIT fails to operationalise all of the basic concepts associated with it into easily understood measurements of identity development and change. Indeed while the theory has been applied extensively in the Northern Ireland situation, most commonly with children and young people, it lacks consummate procedures for application across a variety of studies, each researcher seemingly using a range of ad hoc instruments and methods of assessment. This leads to problems when attempting to draw comparisons across these projects.

The most important point in respect of these problems is the theoretical background to such limitations, namely the theoretical conceptualisation of the person, who makes new identifications and attempts to resolve conflicted identifications, as part of the self's life experiences and continuing biography. Weinreich (1992: 345) explained that one of the shortfalls of SIT is that it fails to acknowledge the role of developmental processes in respect of a person's ethnic identity in Northern Ireland:

> ... the fundamental fact of ethnicity is generally not explicit in the research as a conceptual tool for unravelling the complex socio-psychological processes of ethnic conflict ... it does not conceptualise, nor operationalise, the integral place that long-standing membership of societal groupings has in the individual's identity development.

Weinreich (1992: 345) also commented that SIT fails to acknowledge how, at a societal level, the history of a community affects the identity of its members, or how the individual's personal biography also influences their concept of self:

> It does not locate the actual value and belief systems with which different people operate, nor the affect accompanying the folklore and symbols of ethnicity as internal to their ethnic identifications ... A major deficiency in the SIT conceptualisation is its deliberate separation of the individual from the social, since the social has no meaning to a person except as interpreted through the individual's biography.

Although SIT provides an analysis of the self in terms of structure and function as a dynamic construct in the relationship between self and society, its reliance on the 'here and now' neglects the role of past experience. At a more generic level the research to date in relation to identity and the Northern Ireland conflict has tended to be purely descriptive in nature. It offers little analysis of why identities develop in certain manners. The influence of factors at community and society level is not adequately assessed. The context of the Northern Ireland situation is largely ignored, or removed from the studies under question. Indeed Brown (2000: 760) commented that SIT needs to: 'give greater recognition to the enormous diversity of groups that can serve as the basis of people's social identity. At present SIT acknowledgement of this issue is limited to the incorporation of certain structural variables in its analysis.'Brown (2000: 761) further pointed out that SIT does not differentiate between different kinds of groups: 'all groups are thought to be psychologically equivalent to their members. Some research has suggested that different groups might have different identity functions but there has been no widespread acknowledgement of this in SIT.'

In summary, whilst SIT provides a means of measuring the values and attitudes that children apply to the social categorisations that they make, it fails to provide a framework for studying the development of these attitudes or their significance to the individual's sense of identity. Instead, SIT has imposed a rigid and static perception of identity and its approach has engendered an over-rigid and decontextualised understanding of identity development and redefinition.

Turning now to evaluations of government-based initiatives, it is interesting to note that despite the fact that the Department of Education has been funding community relations projects in schools since the 1980s no direct assessment has yet been made of individual pupils participating in initiatives such as Education for Mutual Understanding and Cultural Heritage, although evaluations of the policy have been carried out (Smith and Robinson, 1992, 1996; DENI, 1999). On a broader level despite the significant number of community relations organisations operating in Northern Ireland (over 100: Hinds, 1998) empirical evidence on their impact is limited. A small number of academic studies of such organisations have been conducted, but the contents of these hold little comfort for the researcher. In her review of the field, Trew (1989) found that researchers employed a wide range of data collection methods to measure change in participants, ranging from interviews with project leaders or teachers to observation accompanied by questionnaires completed by the participants, making comparisons between projects difficult.

As Smith and Robinson (1996: 77) noted: 'despite the inherent attraction of the notion that increased contact and interaction between groups is likely to lead to a reduction in conflict, the empirical evidence to support this assertion is limited'. Smith and Robinson suggested a number of reasons for the difficulty in establishing a direct causal link between inter-group attraction and attitudinal change. These include the research instrument being unable to detect small changes in participants' attitude to the other community; and that changes may only emerge after a much longer period of time. They also criticised the approaches adopted by academics, which typically 'do not necessarily take account of the influence of biographical experience and the way people learn "new understandings" in the context of inter-group relations' (Smith and Robinson, 1996: 78).

In a review of 22 evaluations of cross-community and single identity projects in Northern Ireland, Hughes and Knox (1997) found that, as a result of non-prescriptive objectives from the funding organisation (the CCRU), a wide variety of projects were in operation:

> Most can claim to promote contact between Protestants and Catholics, though not all enhance community relations or engender mutual understanding amongst participants. Indeed, the review lends support to the argument that contact can be ineffectual or, more worryingly, counterproductive, if it is not augmented by conditions which accommodate inter-group as opposed to interpersonal relations. (Hughes and Knox 1997: 1)

Few of the evaluations of community relations projects included in the Hughes and Knox study, or any conducted since then by the CCRU (and as it is now known the CR branch of the Office of the First Minister/Deputy First Minister), have incorporated a before/after measurement to their methodology. To date, aside from the current study, the CCRU has no empirical evidence to demonstrate that the funds it provides for community relations work in Northern Ireland are having positive and lasting effects upon the participants of such projects. Indeed, the independent working group on the strategic promotion of Education for Mutual Understanding echoed the calls from previous reviews stating 'there is a need for evidence based assessment of the impact and value of inter-school contacts, so as to identify the most effective approaches' (Department of Education Northern Ireland, 1999: 14).

THEORETICAL BACKGROUND TO THE CURRENT STUDY

In contrast to the methodologies typically involved in studying identity and in evaluating community relations projects, Identity Structure Analysis (ISA) offers a highly sensitive and fully operationalised framework which allows for the analysis of the variety of identity processes utilised by the individual in their appraisal of their world and the people around them. The current study and previous ISA studies demonstrate clearly ISA's ability to detect change and to place salience upon the individual's value and belief system (Weinreich et al., 1988, 1996; Kelly, 1989; Northover, 1988a, 1988b; Weinreich and Saunderson, 2002).

A meaningful study of identity redefinition through a transition period needs to consider the nature and importance of the range of identifications that individuals have with significant others in their social world. It is essential that such an approach should consider how the individual construes his/her identity, and how this construal is affected by the changing world around them. ISA provides the opportunity to discover the kinds of processes people use in their attempts to resolve conflicted identifications, which processes are brought into effect when new identifications are formed, and how individuals cope with a period of change in their social world.

ISA is used within this context to challenge the 'classic' empirically based approaches of studying identity in Northern Ireland, which have relied heavily on categorisation and stereotyping, and have failed to give due attention to the complex processes involved in identity development and redefinition. The ISA framework occasions the means for the integration of the various features of identity development and provides an empirical basis for testing theoretical postulates concerned with identity redefinition of both individual and groups whilst acknowledging the role of the socio-historical context within which the study operates.

The study reported here took place at a time in Northern Ireland (October 1997

– March 1998) when political progress was being made, but also at a time when crude sectarianism was evident amongst members of both communities. Whilst the Catholic population in Northern Ireland was seen as making substantial gains from the peace process in terms of the emphasis on the equality agenda, early release of prisoners and disbandment of the RUC, Protestants were left feeling alienated and victimised. The peace process had entailed them having to acknowledge the legitimate rights of Catholics to play an equal role in the government of Northern Ireland, and in doing so they had to relinquish their status as the dominant force in Northern Ireland (Elliot, 2000; Morrow, 2000; Murray, 2000).

METHODOLOGY

The current study explores the identity redefinition of young Catholics and Protestants in Northern Ireland, as a result of their participation in a reconciliation programme. Identity Structure Analysis (ISA) is used in this study to conceptualise and empirically investigate the identity processes of the respondents (Weinreich, 1986, 1989; Weinreich and Saunderson, 2002). ISA is an open-ended theoretical framework that draws upon several theoretical orientations from psychology, sociology, and social anthropology, hence its approach to identity development is interdisciplinary by nature. It is primarily concerned with detailed analyses of individual identity structures, which provide the groundwork for assessing commonalities in identity processes across individuals as members of a group. Analysis of the data from this study is carried out using Identity Exploration (IDEX: Weinreich and Ewart, 1998) and SPSS software.

The study investigates, using a before/after or follow-up design, how reconciliation programmes in Northern Ireland influence the identity development of young Catholics and Protestants. In particular the study examines respondents' identifications with groupings such as Catholics, Protestants, Nationalists and Unionists, as well as their views on a range of reconciliation issues. A control group of young people not involved in a reconciliation programme also took part in the study to provide comparative results.

Respondents completed customised identity instruments (Bloomer, 2002) at the early stages of a programme of community relations (phase 1), at the end of the programme (phase 2) and three months after the programme had finished (phase 3) – these respondents from the community relations group are hereafter referred to as 'the project group'. In addition, a control group matching the profile of the project group also completed identity instruments over the same time periods.

The ISA approach to identity is concerned with how individuals develop notions of their identities and characteristic ways of thinking about themselves through a complex of social and developmental processes:

> Such processes include those of forming identifications with others, internalising ascriptions of self by others, comparing self with others in relation to various skills and competencies, and assessing self in terms of one's desires and aspirations. It follows therefore that one's concept of oneself is situated within the social context of one's family and the broader community within which one experiences the trials and tribulations of everyday life. In other words, one's identity is located within a specific socio-historical context. (Weinreich, 1996: 2)

Weinreich's definition of identity holds the key to how identity formation can be assessed:

> One's identity is defined as the totality of one's self-construal, in which how one construes oneself in the present expresses the continuity between how one construes oneself as one was in the past and how one construes oneself as one aspires to be in the future. (Weinreich, 1983a: 151)

An identity instrument is based on a format consisting of a series of paired statements or discourses ('constructs') and a list of significant others ('entities'). The respondent appraises each entity in respect of each of the paired statements by way of one or the other statement (the left or the right pole) giving the degree to which it applies in terms of a simple bipolar scale. The mid-point of each scale (zero) is used to denote that for the entity concerned the respondent is unable to make a differentiation in respect of a particular construct. The choice of the zero point may occur for a variety of reasons, perhaps both poles of the construct apply to that entity in equal degree, or perhaps for that construct the respondent has no knowledge of the entity in that respect. In line with the non-judgemental aspect of the opposing poles neither pole is labelled as positive or negative, thus the scale reads 3, 2, 1, 0, 1, 2, 3. A typical example of the layout of an identity instrument is given below (mandatory features and computational procedures are given in Weinreich, 1980, 1986, 1988, and Weinreich, 2002b):

	... is/are trustworthy				... cannot be trusted		
	3	2	1	0	1	2	3
My best friend ...				0			
Someone I dislike ...				0			
My parents ...				0			

Identity parameters in accordance with ISA definitions of psychological concepts pertaining to identity are computed using the IDEX computer software (Weinreich and Ewart, 1998). For this study the majority of the constructs and entities making up the identity instrument were derived from pilot discussions about topical community relations issues. For instance the constructs represented discourses about issues such as parades, the Irish language etc., and the entities consisted of groups such as Catholics, Protestants, Nationalists, Unionists, etc. The customised identity instruments incorporated constructs and entities that were representative of detailed discussions with community relations practitioners and academics, focus group research, and reviews of previous research, subject to refinement following a pilot study (for details, see Bloomer, 2002).

Statistical analyses of ISA parameters across selected groups, collated using IDEX from the results of individual identity structure analyses, were carried out using SPSS for Windows. These analyses were directed to ascertaining whether, as a result of taking part in a community relations project, respondents had reformulated aspects of their identity in relation to either community relations issues generally or their views of the other community. The respondents' identity structures were analysed comparing phase 1 and 2 of the study for immediate effects, and then phase 1 and 3 for longer-term changes. Comparisons with the control group occurred at both stages of the analyses to assess the impact of the community relations project in the context of the impact of wider societal events upon participants.

Using a database of projects funded by the CCRU, four projects were selected for inclusion in the study. Two of these (*Jigtime, Speak Your Piece*) conducted their work within schools throughout Northern Ireland. The *Jigtime* Project operated around half of its time in the primary school sector, and the remaining half in the secondary/grammar school sector: two secondary level schools agreed to take part in the study. For the *Speak Your Piece* project, which operated solely in the secondary level sector, four schools took part. The third venture, the Prince's Trust Volunteer Project, operated in ten different locations throughout Northern Ireland and for the purposes of this study four of these locations were selected for inclusion. The fourth was the YMCA community relations project, which from a Belfast base operated throughout Northern Ireland, from which participants were selected across the province.

RESPONDENT DETAILS

As detailed in Table 7.1, respondents were drawn from rural and urban areas throughout Northern Ireland. The socio-economic profile encompassed lower and middle socio-economic groupings. Control group respondents were selected from the same geographic areas as the participants' group and from institutions whose socio-economic grouping matched that of the project group.

The respondents were drawn from projects, schools, and FE colleges during the autumn of 1998. In total 234 individuals took part in the study. Of these, 121 (52%) formed the project group and 113 (48%) the control group. Follow-up rates for the project group were 76% at phase 2 and 64% at phase 3, and for the control group 85% at phase 2 and 58% at phase 3. Only those respondents who had completed all three phases of the study were included in the analyses: 77 from the project group and 66 from the control group. Table 7.2 profiles the religion, age and gender of these respondents.

Table 7.1: Geographical Location of Data Collection Sites

PROJECT	LOCATION
Jigtime	Coleraine
Speak Your Piece	Ballymena, Belfast, Magherafelt, Newtownards
Prince's Trust Volunteer	Ballymena, Derry/Londonderry, Newry, Omagh
YMCA Peer project	Belfast based but participants drawn from across NI
Control group	Antrim, Bangor, Ballymena, Belfast, Coleraine, Derry/Londonderry, Newry, Omagh

Table 7.2: Biographical Profiles of Respondents

		PROJECT	CONTROL
Number of respondents		77	66
Religion	Catholic	55%	60%
	Protestant	45%	40%
Age	13–14	10%	30%
	15–16	48%	27%
	17–18	17%	28%
	>19	25%	15%
Gender	Male	37%	43%
	Female	63%	57%
Peer group contact with other community	In-group predominant	63%	65%
	Gross group mixing	27%	35%

IDENTITY STRUCTURE ANALYSES

ISA generates a number of identity indices. The indices are based in key psychological concepts pertaining to processes of identity development and change. Two theoretical postulates central to ISA are explicitly concerned with the processes by means of which people attempt to resynthesise their existing identifications and synthesise further ones with those already existing. The first of these two postulates relates to the resolution of conflicted identifications: 'When one's identifications with others are conflicted, one attempts to resolve the conflicts, thereby inducing re-evaluations of self in relation to the others within the limitations of one's currently existing value system.' (Weinreich, 1989: 53). The second postulate focuses on formations of new identifications: 'When one forms further identifications with newly encountered individuals, one broadens one's value system and establishes a new context for one's self-definition, thereby initiating a reappraisal of self and others which is dependent on fundamental changes in one's value system.' (Weinreich 1989a: 53).

In this chapter three key sections are presented, concerning:

- core values and beliefs – in terms of respondents' views on general community relations issues;
- 'role model' identification – in terms of respondents views' of their own and the other community;
- overall patterns of identification – to illustrate the extent of respondents' cross-ethnic identification with the other community (Weinreich, 1979), and alienation from the entire society.

FINDINGS

CORE VALUES AND BELIEFS

The core values and beliefs of participants are assessed in terms of how consistently respondents have used each statement to assess self and others, including the key communities. Essentially the higher the 'structural pressure'[1] for each statement, the more consistently the respondent has used this issue to judge the social world and thus the more centrally evaluative this issue is in that person's value system.

Previous research conducted by the Northern Ireland Social Attitudes Surveys (Breen et al., 1996; Stringer and Robinson, 1993) indicated that the teaching of British history in schools is an issue which commands differing responses between the Catholic and Protestant communities, with the Catholic community being less supportive of British history being taught in Catholic schools. When appraising their social world using the construct consisting of the paired statements 'all school children should be taught British history/British history is not relevant to Catholic school children', the majority of respondents favoured the first statement relating to all schoolchildren being taught the subject. As illustrated in Figure 7.1, Catholic respondents from the project group assessed self and others in terms of the statement 'all school children should be taught British history' on average as a secondary dimension[2] at phase 1, and more consistently used this statement over time until it became generally a core dimension of their value system at phase 3. Whilst the Catholic controls also increased their consistent use of this judgement, this was not to the same extent as for the project group. Statistical analysis of the increase was significant at both phase 2 and phase 3 (project/control by phase interaction: phase 1,2:F=5.045 df=1,99 p<0.05; phase 1,3: F=6.146, df=1,99 p<0.05). In overall terms Protestants from the project group become more consistent in their use of the construct, whilst Protestants from the control group exhibited a slight increase in their use of the statement between phase 1 and 2, viewing it as a core issue and then reducing it to a secondary evaluative dimension of their belief system at phase 3. The reason for this decrease is unclear, a redefinition phase in respondents' identity may have contributed to these changes, coupled with the impact of external events, such as the peace process.

A similar pattern of results was found in relation to issues such as parading and Irish language, indicating that *over the period of the study both project and control*

Figure 7.1: All Schoolchildren Should be Taught British History

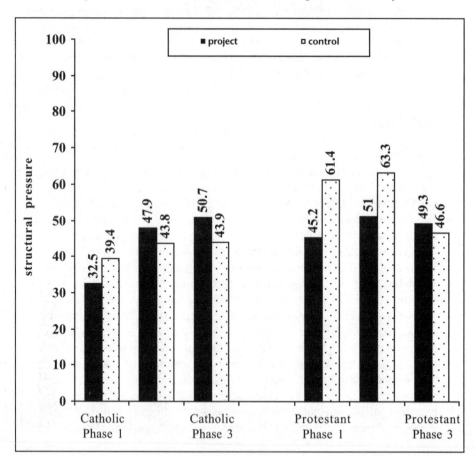

respondents adopted more liberal views of community relations issues, but with the project group tending to more consistently appraise self and others in terms of community relations issues. [3]

'ROLE MODEL' IDENTIFICATION

This section reports results in terms of participants' degrees of positive 'role model' identification (idealistic-identification) with the other religious (Catholic/Protestant) community (Figure 7.2), and the other political (Nationalist/Unionist) community (Figure 7.3) at phases 1, 2 and 3. The respondents are here classified according to whether they stated that amongst their peer group most or all were of the same religious background as themselves (in-group predominant) or that around half or more of their friends were from the other community (cross-group mixing). Using this categorisation the data was analysed to determine whether previously established contact with the other community had led respondents to view that community in a more positive manner than those who had little or no previous contact. The greater the magnitude of idealistic-identification the more the other community is seen as a positive reference group.[4]

Figure 7.2: Idealistic-Identification with Other Religion

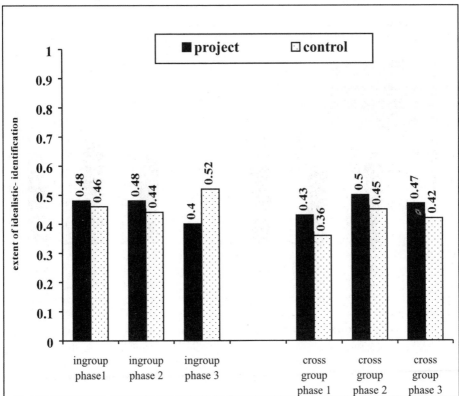

Figure 7.2 indicates that respondents moderately idealistically-identified with the other religion, while Figure 7.3 reveals their low respect for the other political grouping. Idealistic-identification with the other religion and the other political group did not differ between those who had peers of both religions (cross-group mixing) and those who had few peers of the other religion (in-group predominant). In addition, while as indicated above there were some changes in respect of beliefs at phase 2 and phase 3 in both the project and control group, *there were no significant changes in a positive direction in relation to how respondents viewed the other community* (project/control by phase interaction: other religion phase 1,2 $F=0.384$ $df=1,142$ $p=ns$; phase 1,3 $F=0.565$ $df=1,142$ $p=ns$; other political grouping phase 1,2 $F=0.049$ $df=1,142$ $p=ns$; phase 1,3 $F=0.081$ $df=1,142$ $p=ns$).

Figure 7.3: Idealistic-Identification with other politcal group

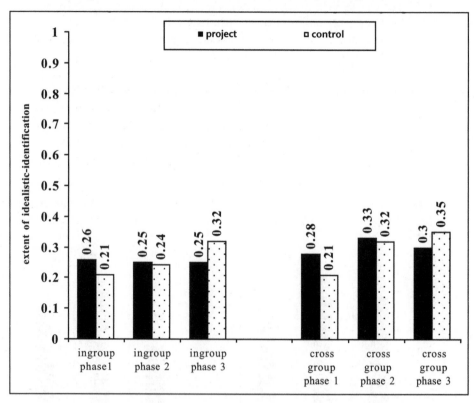

As demonstrated here, respondents viewed the other religious community in a reasonably positive manner, but the other political grouping quite negatively. The fact that the participants differentiated clearly between each community and its associated political grouping indicated that they did not simply stereotype

Catholics and Protestants in terms of the views held by their political representatives, indicating that stereotyping of the Catholic and Protestant communities in terms of their political preferences is not commonplace.

OVERALL PATTERNS OF IDENTIFICATION

As detailed above, participants in this study taken at large were found to have neither strong positive nor negative identification with the other community, although individual case studies demonstrated great variability (Bloomer, 2002). This section reports on individual variability in respect of the relative extent to which respondents identified with their own community, the other community, or were alienated from both. Identification patterns of individuals from both project and control groups according to religious affiliation at phase 1 were examined. As the previous results indicated that few changes had occurred over the three phases of the study in relation to how participants from each community identified with the other, the findings presented here focus on a snapshot at phase 1.

The procedure adopted to ascertain the overall identification profile of participants involved comparing the extent of their identification with their own and the other religious community in relation to the following identity indices: idealistic-identification, contra-identification, empathetic identification and identification conflict.[5] These indices provided evidence of the extent to which respondents associated with each community, whether this association was in positive or negative terms, and whether identification conflict with the communities was apparent. Table 7.3 outlines the rationale used to categorise respondents into one of five overall identification profiles.

These categories are *in-group identified* (prejudicial against the other community), *mixed identified* (identifying with both own and other community), *conflicted* (having conflicted identifications with both communities), *alienated* (having low identification with both communities), and *cross-ethnically identified* (having greater identification with the other than with own community). With respect to the last category, instances of cross-ethnic identification in respect of race have been earlier reported (Weinreich, 1979), but not to date in respect of ethnicity in the Northern Ireland context.

Figure 7.4 indicates that only a third of Protestant respondents(33.3%) and just over half of Catholic respondents (57.1%) identified more closely with their own community than with the other community (in-group identified). Instead, 19.7% of Protestants cross-ethnically identified with Catholics and 10.4% of Catholics did so with Protestants. In other words, 19.7% of Protestants identified more with the Catholic community than the Protestant community, and 10.4% of Catholics identified more with the Protestant community that the Catholic community.

These findings provide a fascinating insight into the identity profiles of the respondents in this study, particularly in relation to the sizeable number of respondents who identified more with the other community than their own, and

Table 7.3: Rationale for Categorisation of
Respondents' Overall Identification Profile

CATEGORY	RATIONALE
In-group identified	Respondent identified more with their own community (in-group) as opposed to the other community (regarded as out-group). Typically this was a respondent who has high levels of idealistic and empathetic identification with their own group, moderate levels of contra-identification with the other group, and low levels of empathetic identification and moderate identification conflict with the other group
Mixed identified	Respondent identified with both communities in the same manner or in highly similar manner. This was a respondent who had moderate levels of idealistic, empathetic identification and identification conflict with both their own group and the other group
Conflicted	Respondents identified in conflicted manner with both communities and exhibited moderate empathetic and moderate contra-identification with both communities
Alienated	Respondent alienated from both their own community and the other community, exhibiting very low levels of empathetic identification and high levels of contra-identification with both communities
Cross-ethnically identified	Respondent identified more closely with other community rather than with their own community, and had moderate idealistic identification with the other group, low idealistic identification with their own group, high empathic identification with the other group, low empathetic identification with their own group, high levels identification conflict with their own group.

who thereby demonstrated some alienation from their own community. The high proportion of participants (36.4% in total) from the Protestant community who were alienated from their own (cross-ethnically identified 19.7%) or from *both* communities (alienated 16.7%) is not entirely surprising. Alienation within the Protestant community has existed in Northern Ireland for some time and has received attention from a range of sources from academia to journalism (Dunn and Morgan, 1994; McKay, 2000). Catholic alienation from the Catholic community (20.8%, of whichcross-ethnically identified 10.4% and alienated 10.4%) though less has, however, not received substantive

Figure 7.4: Overall Identification Profile

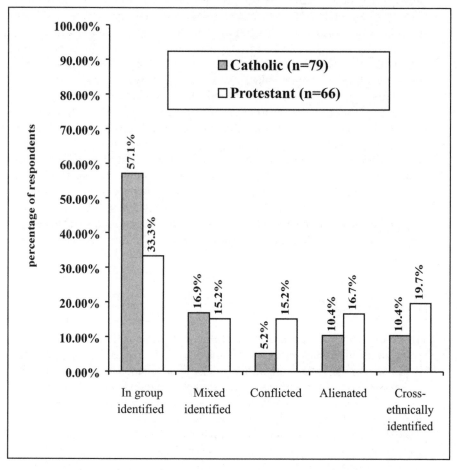

attention. The fact that the current study has been able to quantify the levels of alienation amongst the study participants, albeit in a selected sample, places it in a unique position. Whilst the most recent *Northern Ireland Life and Times Survey* (Hughes and Donnelly, 2001) provides evidence of the high levels of Protestant alienation amongst the adult population, the current study has been able to quantify alienation amongst young people and adolescents using a coherent research methodology, namely ISA. More generally, cross-ethnic identification (identifying more with the other community than one's own) is a phenomenon that has largely been ignored by researchers. Apart from Weinreich's (1979) case study, few studies have been undertaken which have investigated this phenomenon in detail.

Instances of 'non-prejudicial' perspectives towards the other community comprised those participants categorised as *mixed identified* in a non-problematic manner and those as *conflicted* for whom identification with both communities were to an extent equally problematic. Among Protestant participants the 'non-prejudicial' proportion was 30.4% (mixed 15.2%, conflicted 15.2%) and among Catholic respondents it was 22.1% (mixed 16.9%, conflicted 5.2%). Adding those who cross-ethnically identified (prejudicial in favour of the other community), instances of being non-prejudicial in a negative manner towards the other community rose to 50.1% of Protestant and 30.5% of Catholic respondents.

The results presented here provide a unique insight into the identity preferences of Catholic and Protestant adolescents and young people within Northern Ireland. It is possible that because of the age profile of respondents (mainly under 18) many were experiencing an adolescent transition phase of identity redefinition at the time of the study. These overall patterns of identification would therefore not be expected to hold in similar proportions in the adult population of Northern Ireland. However, recognising the significance of such differing patterns, whatever the proportions, in the population at large would profoundly enhance our appreciation of the differing psychological dynamics in individuals that underpin the identity politics of Northern Ireland.

CONCLUSIONS

The study clearly has some limitations. The characteristics of the sample have to be borne in mind. Participants were all voluntary: this invariably excluded those individuals whose outlook would not ordinarily accommodate cross-community enterprises. They were young and not representative of the adult population at large, though as voluntary participants they were deemed to be reasonably representative in respect of geographic region and socio-economic status. A substantially greater research exercise needs to be undertaken to elucidate such diversities of identification patterns in the general population by region and age across Northern Ireland. In terms of the principal purpose of the study, namely the impact of the CR projects, the controls were as well matched as could be expected, so that the effectiveness of these projects with volunteer participants could be reliably ascertained.

The results indicated the following:

The projects were partially successful in generating greater tolerance towards issues of central concern to members of the other community, though individual case studies indicated that other more powerful societal and developmental psychological processes would eclipse the aims of the projects (*see* selected case studies in Bloomer, 2002). The young participants were members of families partaking of everyday activities in the community, witnessing violence and intransigent political expression, and were of an age when peer group developmental identity concerns of adolescents predominate.

The interdependence of the sense of identity between the two communities in Northern Ireland was confirmed. These results, in line with earlier ones (Weinreich, 1983a, 1983b, 1986), clearly demonstrated the place of the other community, as well as one's own, in one's sense of identity as a member of one's community.

A diversity of outlooks on the Catholic and Protestant communities was demonstrated both from members within each community and from members of the other community. No single image of the other community prevailed. Instead, several images contended, whereby an individual might latch upon one or another. Although in broad terms people were seen to have membership of one or the other community, the meaning of such membership depended on the individual as was demonstrated by the range of participants' differing identification with both communities in terms of those attributes of both uppermost in their minds.

A greater diversity of perspectives characterised the Protestant young people compared with their Catholic counterparts, which included alienation from recalcitrant imageries of the Protestant community or of both communities. Other evidence has indicated that the 'Irish Catholic' ethos is imbued with notions of ethnic primordialism to a greater extent than is the 'British Protestant' ethos, the latter being perceived to be more situationalist orientated (Weinreich, Bacova and Rougier, 2002) and in line with the greater diversity of perspectives typifying the Protestant youth of the current study.

An inference from these findings was that multiple stereotypical images, rather than a single stereotype, typified Protestant participants' views of the Catholic community, this being somewhat less the case for Catholic participants' views of the Protestant community.

The community relations projects included in this study managed only partially to achieve their intended outcome. However, given the overall socio-historical context of the communities in Northern Ireland this may well be the best that could be expected, until such time that community-wide commitment to reciprocal accommodation between the communities becomes the societal norm. *Though participants generally exhibited more tolerance in terms of community relations issues, their views on the continuing intolerance of the other community were thereby reinforced, so that their overall orientation towards the other remained largely the same.*

The implications of these findings for policy makers and practitioners must be considered:

Are projects to some extent preaching to the converted? By relying on individuals to volunteer for community relations work the projects are targeted at those who are already open-minded on issues related to respect for diversity and tolerance of difference. Thus 'conversion' from an intolerant viewpoint to a tolerant viewpoint is unlikely.

Is the content of the work promoted by practitioners suitable? As we have discovered through this investigation the high levels of alienation and cross-ethnic identification counteract the myth that surrounds community relations work, i.e. that each community regards the other in an unfavourable manner. If community relations work fails to recognise this phenomenon then the content of its work will fail to have the desired impact.

Are the expectations of what can be achieved in an eight- to twelve-week community relations programme realistic? Typically a reconciliation programme is delivered to adolescents/young people during one-hour slots over a period of eight weeks. If this is the only community relations intervention which adolescents/ young people receive its impact upon them is likely to be limited if the remainder of the social world is focused upon issues which counteract respect for diversity and increasing tolerance towards the other community.

Community relations work in Northern Ireland is governed by reliance on grants from various sources to conduct its work. As the policy makers are primarily responsible for devising the grant systems, they have a responsibility to ensure that the work that they fund is having its desired impact. If research indicates that this is not the case, as in the current investigation, then policy makers in consultation with all stakeholders should be seeking to determine what is good practice in community relations work. Attention must also be focused on how effective reconciliation programmes can be devised and implemented to ensure that community relations work in Northern Ireland is having the desired effect.

In terms of the current study perhaps the most significant theme to emerge from the research was the overall patterns of identification between each community. The levels of alienation and cross-ethnic identification were the first to *be quantified* in any research project in Northern Ireland. The results indicated that, while the imagery of two communities predominated, the identity orientations of their members were far from being homogeneous. Protestant identities were more heterogeneous than Catholic ones. Though these findings cannot be generalised across the entirety of Northern Ireland they should alert policy makers and practitioners to take into consideration the diversity of identity orientations making up the two communities. Of the study's young Catholics, 21% were alienated from their Catholic community and 36% of young Protestants were alienated from their Protestant community.

Community relations work in Northern Ireland is largely based upon the application of contact theory. As was discussed in depth in Chapter 6, contact theory sets out a number of conditions under which contact between conflicting groups should take place if improvements in relations are to be achieved. The basic assumption is that conflicting groups have quite separate identities and view each other in a negative manner (Brown, 2000; Pettigrew, 1998). In recent years in Northern Ireland the influence of the work of Weinreich (1983a, 1983b, 1986; Rougier, 2000), Wilson and colleagues (Eyben et al., 1997) has seen the introduction of concepts such as interdependence between the two communities. However, whilst some research has pointed to the complexity of identity and the interdependence between communities (Weinreich, 1983a, 1983b, 1986; Rougier,

2000) most academic attention in this field still focuses on the monolithic blocks of Catholic/Protestant or Nationalist/Unionist (*see* Trew, 1992; Rougier, 2000; Bloomer, 2002, for full debate on this issue) and thus fails to deal with the core characteristics of the identity profiles of inhabitants of Northern Ireland.

To some extent, alienation from one's own community is dealt with through community relations work in the format of single identity work. Single identity work is offered in Northern Ireland as a vehicle through which single identity communities take part in various exercises to increase their self-confidence in preparation for engagement with the other community (Hughes and Knox, 1997; Hughes, 1998). However, cross-ethnic identification and the interdependence of identification across communities are largely not recognised by any of the key stakeholders. The current study thus provides evidence of identity phenomena that will have to be addressed by policy makers, academics, and practitioners. Recognition that the phenomena exist, along with significant alienation in both communities, would ensure that all stakeholders in the community relations field could assess strategically the developments needed to ensure that their projects adopt effective approaches to key issues of participants' identity.

NOTES

[1] High structural pressures denote processes ensuring stability in the individual's use of a construct, whereas low or negative pressures represent incompatibilities and instabilities in its use (Weinreich, 2002a).

[2] Secondary dimension <50.00, core dimension >50.00.

[3] Details available in Bloomer (2002).

[4] The figure 0.70 indicates the group being viewed as a positive reference group, >0.50 as having little such presence.

[5] These psychological concepts are defined within the ISA conceptual framework (Weinreich, 1989; Weinreich, 2002a). Whereas idealistic-identification and contra-identification refer to the person's identity aspirations, empathetic identification refers to de facto actuality. Identification conflict refers to the extent to which the person empathetically identifies and simultaneously contra-identifies with the other. These indices are calculated from the data elicited by the identity instrument using the IDEX computer software.

8. FROM THE MARGIN TO THE MIDDLE: TAKING EQUITY, DIVERSITY AND INTERDEPENDENCE SERIOUSLY

Duncan Morrow, Karin Eyben and Derick Wilson

INTRODUCTION

Over the last 30 years or more, the range of problems and opportunities resulting from the shifting, and often hostile, quality of relationships between Nationalists and Unionists in Northern Ireland has commonly been referred to as 'community relations'. The crisis at the core of these relationships has been the dominant political fact in Northern Ireland since its inception, determining the form and course of partition on the island of Ireland in the 1920s and dominating the political identity of the vast majority of the Northern population thereafter (Wright, 1987).

For much of the first 50 years of Northern Ireland's existence, the only public acknowledgement that sectarianism impacted on social and economic choices was made through the megaphones of politics and occasional outbreaks of violence. Very few of those concerned with public affairs were under any illusion that political and sectarian division remained the core political fact defining social, political and economic choices. The public display of Irish flags and emblems was outlawed and patrolled. Yet both republicanism and the Irish constitution talked about the inalienable right of the Irish people to national self-determination. Implicitly, the Northern Ireland system required the long-term political marginalisation of 'the minority'. Unionists measured progress according to the degree to which the Catholic population opted for assimilation within a functioning Northern Ireland in preference to the aspiration of an all-Ireland republic. At one and the same time, Unionism's close, if informal, identification with militant Protestantism made the assimilation of Catholics difficult or even impossible. The continued existence, however shadowy, of an Irish Republican Army kept Protestant suspicions intact (Wichert, 1991).

The insecurity of the political environment paradoxically increased the pressure to avoid all reference to political difference outside organised political groups. The discussion of politics in personal or uncertain settings carried a risk that the relationship in question would be overwhelmed by the dynamic violence of the political dispute. In the formal documentation of the period, there was little acknowledgement by the public authorities of the nature and scope of hostility and resentment. Public policy was structured as if Northern Ireland was simply another part of the United Kingdom, albeit with its own devolved institutions. The weakness of political legitimacy and the absence of anything resembling a complete social contract were simply ignored and no concessions were made to the permanent cleft that divided Northern Ireland into clearly identifiable camps of 'them' and 'us'.

The practical result of these contradictory elements was a culture where resentment and suspicion lingered. The outbreak of serious inter-communal violence in the 1960s forced an end to the culture of public denial. The emergence of community relations as an explicit theme in the public realm was part of a belated recognition that the fragility of inter-community relationships represented a potentially fatal threat to sustainable development. The campaign for Civil Rights in the late 1960s degenerated into rioting and mutual recrimination along sectarian lines. Importantly, demands for political and socio-economic reform triggered resistance along ethno-national lines (Purdie, 1990). The core political debates at the heart of any democratic society – social and economic justice, diversity, interdependence and social cohesion – were understood in terms of the threat posed by one community to the survival of the other. On the ground, attempts to generate sustainable interdependence were being abandoned in favour of inter-communal warfare in the name of justice.

A Minister for Community Relations sat in the last Stormont cabinet after 1970, albeit from outside the Unionist Party and a Community Relations Commission was established. Community relations policy was still understood as a means to resolve a problem limited to specific groups (Hayes, 1998). Community relations policy was intended to mend limited problems rather than engage underlying socio-economic and political issues. As most of the visible violence took place within and between working-class districts, much of the early community relations emphasis was on creating an infrastructure that would enable growth in local leadership and confidence, the coherent articulation of demands and ordered dialogue.

Within a short period of time, however, it was clear that the crisis in community relationships was not limited to those neighbourhoods where it was physically visible. Indeed by 1972, the crisis of confidence and legitimacy had infected the whole political system of Northern Ireland and the human, economic and social costs of violence, and of its containment, were grimly evident. Relationships between the communities had deteriorated to such an extent that they could not now be improved without clear understandings about the political and socio-economic future. Northern Ireland became internationally synonymous with violence in pursuit of the enforcement of mutually exclusive national goals.

Unsurprisingly, respite from the ongoing injury and trauma remained the continuing focus of much of what passed for community relations work. But real change demanded engagement with real differences, not retreat from them. Ultimately, community relations implied nothing less than the engagement of the whole community or communities in long, difficult and complex consideration of the problems between them, with a view to finding new, practical and sustainable ways of living together into the future. Given that the difficulties in inter-community relationships were primarily experienced as matters of politics, law, economics and social development, community relations work meant devising new approaches to accommodate engagement on precisely those themes which people were most loath to confront. The search was for a means whereby both practical issues and trust building could be dealt with in a single context. Trying to deal with them consecutively effectively meant failure on both counts.

By 1972, at the latest, it was clear that the inherited social and political rituals of Northern Irish life no longer contained violence: rather they tended to unleash it. The really difficult task of community relations work was to establish ways to generate new patterns, structures and presuppositions in Northern Ireland in the midst of violence and fear. This could not be accomplished by avoidance and respite alone. Community relations work could only be meaningful if it allowed people to explore their experience of threat and the dilemmas of change and, from there, to explore and develop new arrangements and institutions whose sustainable existence would establish confidence. While this could never enforce a commitment to a particular political outcome, it had to be rooted in the fundamental principles of Western liberal democracy, which alone provided a transcendent theme among all the political parties of Northern Ireland.

All of this may have been credible in theory. In the midst of violent turmoil, real engagement on these matters continued to risk turning all meetings between people and groups in Northern Ireland into miniature reproductions of the political conflict raging outside. Unless it is arrested, the logic of violent conflict on a recurrent inter-group pattern leads inexorably to parallel institutions, developed largely in opposition to one other. Friendship, marriage, housing, schooling, employment, policing, religion and politics all divide along the same fault line. Worryingly, each of these contexts creates new sites for generating the same underlying pattern of offence, antagonism and hostility. By the early 1970s, this pattern was re-emerging in the expulsions and mass-movements of population taking place in Belfast and Derry/Londonderry (Darby, 1976).

An approach to community relations work which takes seriously the range of experiences of the past, while working towards something more sustainable in the future is inevitably akin to opening Pandora's box. The initial commonsense response is always the same – don't open the box. This informal convention has long been the first line of defence in Northern Ireland against an immeasurable threat of violence. As the singer Colm Sands put it: 'Whatever you say, say nothing.' In a context of actual violence, the potential threat grows and the incentive to silence grows with it.

The intuition that conflict should not be stoked unnecessarily has the beneficial outcome that social and interpersonal interchange can be maintained in contexts where community conflict has no direct connection to the specific matter at hand. Mixed town centres, places of employment and even areas of residence can be maintained. But by ruthlessly driving all reference to pivotal experiences of fear, exclusion and threat at each other's hands out of the interpersonal domain and restricting them to competitive megaphone politics, relationships across the political division are confined to the netherworld of inference, rumour and presumption. In a context where killing, exclusion and threat are within the direct experience of the communities in contact, it is easy to generate a level of wariness and tension which renders relationships formed by a preference for silence superficial and artificial.

Even where there is no personal hostility, the potential for violence arising from politics justifies defensiveness, evasiveness, diversion, avoidance and caution in public relationships. Alone the threat of violence generates discomfort and unease and a new idea of what is 'sensible', creating a common sense for distance and separation. Moreover, all change is read within a paradigm that measures advancement for one group as defeat for another. Without relationship building, all work for 'justice', from whatever angle it appears, threatens to deepen the cycle of resentment by always carrying a cost for the other community. By turning avoidance into politeness, the primary mechanism for dealing with social conflict in democracies – dialogue and exchange – is rendered impolite and taboo. The only remaining outlet for the exchange of experiences is the arena of formal politics, which is overwhelmed by the need of each group for self-assertion and self-defence in the midst of violence.

It is thus all too easy for community relations work to continue to find itself restricted to providing contexts of polite interaction and respite in the midst of conflict, especially if it is held to be effective to the degree that it takes people away from the social conflicts which obsess and constrict them. The threat that Pandora's box might be opened continues to haunt the community. Meaningful community relations work must aim to empty the box rather than to lock it up more tightly. In practice this means building a capacity to face and express fear while designing and learning new ways of working and dealing with one another so as to allow trust to emerge over the long run. Community relations succeeds to the extent that it generates and sustains opportunities for people, whether on their own or in groups and organisations, to experience that they no longer need to fear what might come out of Pandora's box. Given the number of monsters to be slain, it is unrealistic to suggest that such efforts will achieve harmony in the medium run (Whyte, 1990). While the long-run goal is a sustainable society, the interim measures of success can only be found in the realms of increased capacity to deal with fear and a reduction in the level of taboo attaching to matters of inter-community controversy.

Engagement with issues of inter-community relationships is therefore simultaneously both a necessity and a risk. Caught between the irrelevance of avoidance and the apparent impossibility of real engagement, community relations has had to fight for its place in the public policy sun since 1969. While events on the street gave daily evidence of the urgency of finding new approaches to inter-community relationships, serious engagement with community relations would imply a willingness on behalf of all participants, including the politicians and civil servants who decided on it, to examine long-held views and habits and to contemplate change in deeply ingrained and sometimes cherished ways of behaving and believing.

THE LANGUAGE OF COMMUNITY RELATIONS

By the 1990s, the strains between the need for real inter-community dialogue and the reality of avoidance of the risks involved were beginning to show. Community relations developed as the Cinderella of public policy and private activity: the most desirable goal of all policy and yet too subversive to be actually invited to the ball.

Northern Ireland's politicians were, by virtue of their public visibility, the embodiment of this ambivalence: always supportive in theory, but anxious to confine and define it in such a way that change remained the prerogative of others. Inevitably, any decision to change in the future implies some acknowledgement of past failure or inadequacy. By associating acknowledgement with weakness (the cardinal sin for political leadership) it predictably remained taboo. In 1974, the SDLP Minister for Community Relations abolished the Community Relations Commission, leaving no formal policy institution in place until the establishment by the Conservative direct rule administration of the Central Community Relations Unit (CCRU) in 1987 and the Community Relations Council (CRC) in 1989.

This underlying ambivalence about policy was reflected in confusion about conceptual frameworks. Policy has been characterised by serious ambiguity about what community relations might mean in practical terms, an ambiguity which no-one has seemed anxious or able to resolve. While the term did gain a general currency as shorthand for the visible problems of violence and disharmony between local communities, which both stem from and cause the lack of political rapprochement in Northern Ireland, the formal goals of community relations were seldom defined beyond an aim to create harmony where there was division. The result, unsurprisingly, was that community relations became a term used simultaneously to describe a vague general vision, to which everyone subscribed, and a variety of haphazard practices aimed at 'harmony' that allowed everyone to remain publicly detached and knowingly cynical.

Problematically, the term itself gave no hint as to how the vision might be made operational. While 'community relations' as a term might conceivably give coherence to a raft of policies geared at engineering social change among others, it is not at all clear what this implies in practice for people, organisations or communities at local level. What exactly does it mean for a person 'to community relate' or 'to relate communally'. What kind of activity 'improves' community relations and what kind of activity works to weaken it?

SHARPENING THE FOCUS

In 1996, the Future Ways Project of the University of Ulster (Eyben, Morrow and Wilson) was engaged by CCRU to research the scope and scale of community relations education for adults in Northern Ireland. As soon as the decision was made to examine inter-community relationships in a wide variety of contexts and settings, the poverty and superficiality of the language of community relations emerged (Eyben et al., 1997). Early research found that popular conceptions of the term included:

- a public relations exercise by the security forces;
- a quick and easy way to access funding;
- work which focuses on 'niceness' and avoids the issues of justice and deprivation;
- middle-class guilt trips;
- 'tea and cucumber sandwiches';
- a softening-up plot aimed at undermining nationalism/the Union;
- *not* community development, social engineering;
- something you do to others, something to do with ghettos;
- the slippery slope to a United Ireland;
- a nice holiday.

Lacking any rigorous core, public understanding of community relations work was de facto dependent on what was experienced or heard of within its rubric, rather than on any overarching intellectual framework. Since this was overwhelmingly within the fields of community development, education and youth work, community relations were widely restricted within the popular mind to the possibilities and limits that such settings offered.

Most worryingly, the very association of community relations with the generation of warmth and harmony destroyed the possibilities which inter-community settings offered to create better arenas for facing and addressing conflict and difference. While community relations work was widely associated with inter-community contact, it was intellectually separated from attempts to express difference and uniqueness in a pluralist and antagonistic context and from the issues of social distribution and justice which had motivated the civil rights campaign in the 1960s.

Far too often, the first step in creating cross-community harmony was to promote a depoliticised environment. Left in this ghetto, community relations work had nothing to say about the desirable socio-economic, political or cultural basis for good relationships nor could it accommodate difficult discussions about ill treatment, injustice or identity. Stripped of these elements, it is unsurprising that community relations became associated with superficial engagement which acted to disguise underlying tensions rather than to heal them. The paradoxical consequence of insisting on fixed harmonic outcomes in community relations was that the programmes became empty of content. Public debates about identity and diversity were overwhelmingly shaped as parallel claims for separate self-assertion, without reference to a common framework that could accommodate all. At the same time, debates on equality focused on narrowly quantitative measures, which took no account of the costs of social apartheid.

The result of this confusion was that measures aimed at fostering social relationships that were both desirable and sustainable in Northern Ireland often ran at cross purposes to one another. Furthermore, the absence of a single framework within which the dilemmas of equality and justice, difference and cohesion could be named and resolved had significant social and economic costs.

Eyben, Morrow and Wilson identified a need to refocus community relations work on its underlying intentions within the framework of liberal democracy. This implied a desire to reach beyond the experienced perception of community relations work, to an articulation of the principles which all such work sought to embody. In theory at least, the articulation of first principles could then release community relations work from the caricature of perceived practice and challenge all elements of society to consider their contribution to real common goals.

The goal of a sustainable interdependence is clearly at the heart of all inter-community work. Yet unless people working for interdependence can successfully engage with the need to ensure real social justice while recognising difference, the work is doomed to appear as naïve and tangential to core practical concerns. At the same time, as Eyben, Morrow and Wilson underlined, public debates on equality and cultural diversity seem to proceed without reference to each other or to the need to generate a sustainable community which could deliver them.

Real sustainability demands that interdependence, equity and diversity be taken into consideration together. This has the further advantage of locating community relations work in the middle of the search for a democratic society, an aspiration theoretically shared by *all* political parties in Northern Ireland. Within a framework of equity, diversity and interdependence, legislative efforts to enforce minimum conditions of fair employment can be understood and measured alongside seemingly unrelated tools such as education for mutual understanding in schools, local community development initiatives, and the engagement of culturally important organisations such as the churches, sports and the arts. In a framework of sustainable development, trust and the distribution of social goods and power can at last be dealt with in parallel.

RESEARCHING EQUITY, DIVERSITY AND INTERDEPENDENCE: A WORTHWHILE VENTURE?

Having defined the scope of what could be understood as community relations work, Eyben, Morrow and Wilson's research had three further aims:

- to assess the quantity and quality of formal training activity being undertaken in Northern Ireland in pursuit of better community relations;
- to sharpen the conceptual framework of such work;
- to suggest new practical approaches and emphases which might improve the quality of community relations activity.

In order to achieve these aims, three broad methodological approaches to the research were adopted:

- quantitative measurement of formal training programmes for equity, diversity and interdependence being undertaken across many areas of Northern Irish society;
- qualitative research into projects chosen to represent the broad range of contexts in which the core principles of community relations might apply;
- two case studies of very different local communities designed to illustrate the ways in which a geographical area comes into contact with this sort of activity and training.

By combining these research methods, the team sought to capture a flavour of both the range and depth of community relations training activity and to gain an insight into the real limitations and opportunities of this kind of work. From the beginning it was clear that 'training' in the activity of trust building was a deeply flawed concept.Training presupposes a fixed body of knowledge and overwhelmingly relies on the capacity of didactic education (teaching what is) to a context of uncertainty and discovery (exploring what is and what might be). The underlying aim of the project was to explore the degree to which organisations at the heart of Northern Irish society, a society where conflict has been endemic, were formally investing in better relationships in their areas of activity.

THE SCALE AND SCOPE OF COMMUNITY RELATIONS TRAINING IN NORTHERN IRELAND

To establish whether education and training providers dealt explicitly with the social and political divisions that shape its public life, a postal questionnaire was sent to 2,006 people formally or informally responsible for the training or education of adults aged 17 or over in a wide variety of organisations throughout Northern Ireland (Eyben et al., 1997). The emphasis on *explicit* training was not intended to detract from much deeper implicit or informal learning, but rather to identify the level of formal and structural support for breaking the normative social convention of *not* talking about the conflict. Explicit approaches demand considerable courage as they involve dealing with at least three fears:

- the fear of acknowledging the impact of one's own experiences on one's capacity to be 'objective';
- the fear of damaging functioning relationships by raising divisive issues;
- the fear of the potentially violent reactions of others.

Our interest was to identify the extent to which Northern Irish society had developed mainstream educational and training provision, which formally supports people working together in a context of fear.

Consistent with the assumption that equity, diversity and interdependence are universal responsibilities in a democracy, respondents were drawn from the whole of public life in Northern Ireland, including businesses, training organisations, central and local government and those working in education, law and order, schools and community groups. In all, 15 different sectors were identified. Different methods were applied in each sector to identify appropriate respondents. The overall return rate of 54.6% varied across different sectors. Whereas educational institutes (79%) and local government agencies (78%) recorded relatively high rates of return, less than 50% of identified respondents among trade unionists (30%), those working in the sphere of housing (35%), and churches (42%) replied. There were also cultural variations. Among churches, for example, 68% of Presbyterian ministers contacted replied, whereas only 24% of Roman Catholic clergy and 10% of Free Presbyterians contributed. Likewise, among businesses, those with larger and medium size businesses were considerably more likely to respond than those with fewer than 25 employees.

Within these limitations, the survey revealed some clear consistencies. More than 60% of organisations across all sectors in Northern Ireland could identify no formal training or learning opportunities within their organisation aimed at dealing with the political divisions or its impact. This figure can be taken as a minimal reflection of the situation, given the broad definitions of equity, diversity and interdependence which were adopted and was the case in spite of widespread agreement with the proposition that 'it is the responsibility of *all* sectors of public life in Northern Ireland to provide in-house opportunities for greater community understanding'.

This gap between a general affirmation of the principle that inter-community dialogue was a critical responsibility and the reality that it was largely undeveloped in many settings was consistent across all sectors. The broad agreement on the need to address real issues has not translated into the development of expertise. Only 10% disagreed with the proposition that free discussion of all issues would improve relationships in the workplace while a mere 11.5% agreed with the proposition that training which explicitly deals with social and political divisions in

Northern Ireland creates more problems than it solves for an organisation. On the other hand, many agreed that such work was low priority for training needs and complained of a lack of expertise as well as of human and financial resources. The ambiguity between aspiration and activity, visible at the level of general public policy, extends through the body of Northern Irish society. While practical obstacles rather than principled objections were the main reasons cited for the absence of training, it is hard to escape the conclusion that the practical obstacles to movement are a symptom of a deep-seated difficulty.

Three further points emerged strongly from the survey. First, while issues of conflict around social differences clearly impact directly on the activities of a considerable number of organisations and bodies, the point of contact with equity, diversity and interdependence varies across different sectors of the economy and society. As a result, different sectors have developed different emphases in their training provision. The different contact points represent different stages at which arguments based on values (or 'should do') merge with arguments based on business ('must do') and become issues which groups or organisations take on voluntarily.

Whereas 83% of those working directly with law and order issues, 61% of Trade Union trainers and 45% of health sector trainers provided training in foundational legislation (Fair Employment, Equal Opportunities, Emergency Powers) only 2% of church groups and 3% of cultural groups did likewise. On the other hand, 42% of central policy makers and 48% of local government workers provided help in understanding policies (such as anti-sectarianism, PAFT, anti-harassment policies) while only 2% of sports bodies did likewise. Only the Youth sector (53%) has developed systematic training in anti-sectarianism, equality, mutual understanding or community relations.

Community relations work has become associated with voluntary areas of social life (youth work and community work) and with activities relating to education. As a result there is a strong 'brand' emphasis on relationship-building work appropriate to these activities. The variety of needs and points of contact with poor relationships across lines of social division in other areas of life and its connection with the improvement of community relations has often gone unrecognised. By failing to take differences of organisational culture and social location into account, community relations work has often seemed irrelevant in many fields of endeavour and has been relegated to a specific marginal niche. Many organisations, on the other hand, have relied almost exclusively on legislative and coercive instruments to achieve internal harmony and have failed to connect with innovative approaches to relationship-building which can foster learning.

Secondly, the survey suggests that a great deal of community relations work does not address core issues. At the centre of good community relations work is a search for practical ways of working in a society where there are fundamental disagreements about the nature of the state, its laws and what constitutes equity and justice. Only 37% of those surveyed indicated any training in these issues, falling as low as 20% in the private sector. What training exists is usually short in length and relatively infrequent. There were far more seminars than courses, and far more events of one day or less than those of longer duration. Only among young people were long training and learning events popular. Furthermore, the numbers participating in training events tended to involve fewer than 100 people per year in each organisation. This implies both that community relations events need to match organisational training culture and that the culture of short events make training in this area very difficult.

Thirdly, the majority of activity in this area is new and untested. Almost all training programmes in equity, diversity or interdependence have emerged since the 1980s. Until this point, most institutions seemed to presume that Northern Ireland would return to 'normality' and the known, rather than require any specific transformation. Small numbers of training initiatives can therefore be understood both as representing lack of substantive interest and as representing significant growth from an almost non-existent base. Here lies both the problem and hope of work in this field: there is a growing interest in devising practical solutions to identified problems and at the same time such work contrasts sharply with received organisational norms and expectations.

ASSESSING QUALITY: LEARNING FROM INITIATIVES IN COMMUNITY RELATIONS WORK

Practical inter-community work in Northern Ireland is overwhelmingly the result of decisions by a series of entrepreneurial individuals and small groups. Many practitioners could be described as *bricoleurs* in the sense used by Levi-Strauss: people who are able to use whatever is at hand without being able to explain how or why it works (Levi-Strauss, 1962). Qualitative research in this field has two primary objectives: to identify and make explicit core learning themes for more general use and to capture the variety of initiatives and attention to difference which allows general principles to be applied appropriately in a series of ultimately unique contexts. In a context where all learning is new learning, the task of capturing and categorising is a central element in the development of new rituals and norms.

Through 30 case studies undertaken to reflect practice in 12 distinct 'sectors' identified across public life in Northern Ireland, a more three-dimensional picture of the state of current community relations practice was possible (Eyben et al., 1997a). Consistent with the findings of the quantitative research, there was significant variation in approaches to these issues across different organisations and sectors. Many focused on legally driven compliance, although others had developed new procedures and practices. Still others had instituted formal learning programmes intended to enhance levels of awareness, skills and knowledge.

Within the community and voluntary sector, there has been a strong emphasis on relationship-building. Relationships with people who inspire fear are inevitably more difficult than those with people who do not. Many organisations operate in a context where working with or towards 'the other community' is a counter-intuitive process. This manifests itself in an inherent tendency to find ways around serious engagement with issues raising powerful, and sometimes uncontrollable, emotion, or the development of euphemistic language which allows a noble intention to deteriorate into an empty vehicle in practice (McVeigh, 1995). Community relations practice in community and voluntary groups is often part of a multi-dimensional strategy to develop greater ownership and reflective practice by socially marginal groups. It is therefore intimately linked with both community development and community education. Problematically, when the precise boundaries between these categories have become blurred, the more difficult areas of inter-community activity are often those that fade first.

Real change only happens if community relations work is aligned with and explicitly integrated into the key values and objectives of the group. Community and voluntary organisations often rely on a strong value statement, which both expresses a vision and ensures a long-term commitment. Such statements have often acted as the vital trigger to return to work which is difficult to sustain in a hostile or indifferent climate. Many regard themselves as dedicated to the pursuit of equity, diversity and interdependence, but do not necessarily connect this into all organisational programmes. While voluntary groups recognise the value of offering community relations seeding activity, this work often withers if it is not part of a wider organisational commitment supported by repeated opportunities for learning and training. Without persistence, community relations work appears as an additional add-on activity, done to appease funders or evaluators but without much prospect of development.

These problems are reflected in the important debate about the location of community relations work within the structures of community and voluntary groups. Should community relations be dealt with as a 'stand-alone' issue, thereby ensuring its visibility but risking marginalising community relations work as the responsibility of one person or area of work? Or, should it be located across all departments as the responsibility of all staff and structures, thereby ensuring organisational commitment but risking the practical disappearance of all but a token commitment? While the precise outcome of this debate sometimes hinges on resources, there is a widespread recognition of the need for both elements to be present within a single organisation if inter-community work is to remain a recurrent theme. Here again, a consistent attention to principles and values may allow greater linkages to emerge, rather than a simple demand that organisations pursue community relations programmes.

The emphasis on relationship-building in youth work is, if anything, greater. Youth work invites young people to explore the depth of their own formation and ambiguities and provides 'safe space' in which to explore options, possibilities and obstacles. Community relations work in this context is rooted in personal experience and surrounding influences. The need to model good behaviour before preaching to young people was a constant theme among youth workers indicating a need for serious staff support and development. We found considerable resentment among youth workers that community relations work was devalued as something for children and young people, as if the behaviour of the supporting adult community was not the primary source of knowledge about what was or was not legitimate in terms of behaviour and attitudes. Youth workers indicated a strong need for community leaders and middle managers to explore their own formation and development in parallel to the demands being placed on them and their young people.

Our studies indicate a high level of nervousness and anxiety among adults tasked with this work. Even where appeals to a founding vision can be linked with the need to address community relations, some organisations are unable to grasp this theme firmly. This may be because the work is new or threatening to existing boundaries and practice or contrary to the perceived wishes of the people among whom workers work. What is clear is that real change cannot be left to vulnerable or relatively powerless people or focused on areas where the young people are caught up in endless turmoil. There is too much at stake for both workers and young people in these contexts as they balance maintaining their jobs, retaining credibility in the community and developing issues inimical to an area or organisational culture, especially if they believe that they are acting in isolation from the rest of society (Wilson, 1996).

The theme of uncertainty and anxiety was repeated among groups with cultural groups, groups with an explicit theological or religious dimension and sports groups. Sports groups appeared resistant to admit any direct involvement in community relations work. Community relations are widely perceived as weakening the sports development objective and as opening a door to issues best left outside the sports ethos. Many organisations have coped with the implications of sectarianism by denying any relationship to wider social relationships. By sticking strictly to their narrowly defined niche, civic life can continue. On the other hand, organisational activity takes place within the sectarianism that shapes their scope, structure and reach rather than impacting on it.

While many people from church backgrounds recognise the importance of placing their faith and its structures in the context of real historical responsibilities, a significant number were exercised by the absence of safeguards and limits for 'legitimate diversity'. The ecumenical movement's espousal of the goal of full Christian unity is a serious obstacle for groups whose identity is established as the protection of truth from erosion by compromise. The association of community relations with ecumenism in these circles has sometimes acted to make both anathema. For many, the theological differences between Catholicism and Protestantism make it almost impossible for them to relate directly on theological matters. Many prefer to accept the undesirable results of protecting difference to the potential costs of engaging with others. The coherence of denominational identity has been shaken by different answers to these questions within single structures. The result of this ambivalence is usually ad hoc engagement, dependent on individuals or congregations and often without comment from any central body (Morrow, 1994). This raises a significant question for community relations: how can people be allowed to engage with one another, without feeling that they have to betray their core identity to do so? Put in other words: how can diversity be reconciled with interdependence?

While churches, youth groups and community organisations seek to engage with their members on a holistic level, large organisations have more restricted goals. While the public sector seeks efficiency, objectivity and best value, private business has a clear 'bottom line' emphasis on profitability and shareholder value. The development of community relations work within the informal committed activity of voluntary groups paradoxically acted to distance more formal institutions from any direct connection with the underlying themes by generating a series of presumptions about what community relations activity 'is'. Yet companies and larger organisations act and react to changes in wider society. The language of community relations has failed to connect these core dimensions of peacebuilding into a single discourse.

Once employment differentials, workplace security and social injustice were recognised as critical issues within the political debate between Nationalists and Unionists, legislation became inevitable. Although both community relations work and fair employment initiatives are clearly aimed at eliminating violence and discrimination in relationships in Northern Ireland, they have been kept conceptually separate. Without doubt, however, fair employment legislation forced companies to face two important questions: what is the impact of violent division on private companies; and its reverse, what is the role of the private sector in a contested society?

The legislation forced changes in informal recruitment practices, workplace culture and rights of redress. Forced to monitor employment practice along lines of perceived religious background and to shift from 'partisan' to 'neutral' working environments, companies found themselves confronting emotive triggers such as identity, religion and politics which they had traditionally avoided. The development of a 'good and harmonious working environment' was universally interpreted as entailing the removal of any signs of political or religious identity that could be viewed as belonging to one community or the other.

 Fair employment roots companies within a framework which asserts that private enterprise has social responsibilities as corporate citizens (Marsden, 1996). Only after the implementation of fair employment legislation, however, did many companies act directly on any moral conviction that 'this was the right thing to do'. But legislation is insufficient to address the emotional and human consequences which implementing such change brings. Good practice in this area requires the possibility of airing and acknowledging emotional issues in a safe and contained context as well as ongoing support and development opportunities. Not only does this reduce the potential for conflict, but it also allows a sense of commitment and ownership to grow among the workforce.

These questions chime with the concerns of companies across the globe, seeking sustainability across a variety of cultural and historical settings. Our study found little evidence of clear analysis regarding the role of business in promoting and sustaining good community relationships in Northern Ireland. Companies with high staff turnover have little opportunity to invest in relationships at work. Others are caught between the need to contain violence and the requirement to build trust. What is clear is that change has highlighted new learning requirements within companies including an acknowledgement of the importance of relationships and the impact of social issues on workplace capacity and even viability. While this is immediately true of those responsible for maintaining workplace harmony, it is clear that long-term sustainability in this area requires the emergence of new organisational cultures in which issues previously thought 'external' can be acknowledged within the sphere of private business.

These issues are mirrored in the public sector where many agencies have focused on delivering quantitatively equitable services to the whole community and removing themselves as far as possible from the wider social and political situation (NICS, 1994). Usually this has involved adopting internal cultural practices which avoid or forbid open communication regarding community divisions. In local government, the advent of community relations officers gave formal recognition to the task of building community relations, but usually without requiring any significant change in organisational culture.

Against the thrust of modern managerial practice, the rigorous promotion of neutrality over diversity tends to deny the value of difference in maximising personal and organisational performance. Not only is there no context in which to challenge prevailing organisational norms, but the absence of a culture of trust distorts the public service's capacity to be sensitive to the changing needs of its stakeholders. By emphasising quantitative equity, the public sector plays no role in modelling interdependence or valuing diversity. Ambivalence over diversity in the area of sectarianism also complicates otherwise more widely supported initiatives in equal opportunities in other areas such as gender, age, disability and even race. By sticking rigorously to the letter of the law, legislation functions as a ceiling to good practice rather than as a baseline beyond which innovation is both welcome and possible. In effect, the public sector relies on the (unproven) assertion that quantitative equity alone will generate social sustainability.

At the same time, individual workers and managers deal with the problems of division on a case-by-case basis, usually without formal organisational support or training. Agencies working in the field of law and order come into daily contact with controversial decisions and contexts. Higher education institutions have faced increasing public scrutiny over their employment records. Health and Social Services Trust managers identified numerous direct experiences of intimidation of staff and patients, contradicting the notion of strict separation between personal life and the workplace. Where there is any management support, this tends to occur within small units and fails to challenge the culture of public service in

Northern Ireland as a whole. This is directly traceable to the absence of official recognition of the relevance of social and political context to professional capacity.

Of course, attempts to generate new approaches to community relations still exist in a climate which tolerates hostility and separation. Two local studies confirmed that there was strong pressure to maintain public tranquillity, and strong public disapproval of anything which would rock the boat. In general, the majority get on with life as if there were no potential problem. Only when major events, such as local shootings or events around the 'marching season', have shaken the tranquillity is there any acknowledgement of the potential weakness of relationships and the risks these contain for wider social sustainability. There is a strong preference for dealing with 'hard' issues such as economic development, which are the subject of uniform goals, over matters of trust-building, and very little willingness to address the inter-relationships between the two elements. The implicit presumption appears to be that economic prosperity will produce sufficient diversion to generate social stability, with little consideration that the reverse may also be true; economic prosperity is unlikely to be sustainable unless social relationships are built on trust.

This preference for avoiding relationship-building is embodied in the willingness of public bodies to deliver 'equity' along traditional sectarian lines, inevitably resulting in the embedding of these same divisions into the future through the actions of bureaucracy. In this context, community relations are easily perceived of as 'forced' or 'contrived'. The separation of Community Relations Officers from the peace and reconciliation partnerships further isolates community relations from the mainstream of community consciousness, even around peace-building.

CONCLUSIONS

Until now, equity, diversity and interdependence have developed largely separately without any coherent strategy linking the strands. Unless the three are consciously inter-related, the practical result is to create competing arenas, in which the learning and challenges compete and diverge. An emphasis on one is seen to undermine policies in another. For example, equity policy can be used to support a concept of balanced separation which ignores cultural differences and the necessary engagement with building real trust and interdependence. Diversity arguments can be and have been used to hide real inequalities. An over-emphasis on inter-community harmony can be used to cover up necessary arguments and change. In reality, many business and government decisions in Northern Ireland taken without reference to all three elements have unplanned and occasionally disastrous implications.

Community relations, understood as the pursuit of equity, diversity and interdependence in Northern Ireland is a common purpose not a minority concern. Nonetheless, the persistent policy preference for addressing community relations at its most visible points – urban ghettos, victims work, work with paramilitaries – or among constituencies accepted as visibly important for the future – children and young people – ensnares this work within a centre-periphery paradigm. This presumes a broadly healthy core of society with marginal manifestations of sectarian violence. Such a paradigm suggests that the politically weakest groups in Northern Ireland should be the focus of policy concern.

This research confirms that mistrust and violence are not seen as proper areas of active concern in many areas of Northern Irish society. Indeed, the very 'bracketing off' of large areas of activity is held up as success, and has become habitual. Outside the points of greatest stress, tensions are largely contained by silence and legislative exclusion from the public domain.

The search for respite is not the preserve of a narrow 'community relations' industry: it is the core adaptive pattern of learning in Northern Ireland. Indeed it is most successful where it is least visible; in the protected central core of socio-economic life. The fact that community relations work became the province of school children, community groups and youth clubs further underlined the association of community relations with informal education and encounter, where relationship-building is already a central theme.

The failure to engage large elements in active pursuit of common goals is partly attributable to a consistent vagueness within the field about the purpose and underlying goals of community relations work. In part, too, it is the result of the lack of any culture within the public, private or even voluntary sectors of open-ended innovation in this area. In general, the culture of avoidance of open-ended, voluntary commitment by formal organisations in relation to conflict remains intact. However, the result of this recognition must be a move away from the centre-periphery paradigm towards a model which expects change to be led by those with the greatest capacity to model change – i.e. those at the heart of political, social and economic life. While the immediate needs of areas and groups which have suffered disproportionately must continue to receive the lion's share of public *financial support*, the possibilities for real change depend at least as much on the active *engagement and learning* of core public, voluntary and private activity across the whole of Northern Irish society.

In order to detach community relations from this over-close identification with a single form of practice, it needs to be more sharply defined in terms of underlying organisational values and goals. This entails linking or reformulating ethical or social objectives in a way that conforms to the more limited business objectives of a wide variety of groups and organisations. Practitioners must learn to be innovative and adaptable in their practice in pursuit of a clear central vision.

Unless this happens, the yawning gap between the expressed wish in many organisations to contribute to better relationships and the development of practical programmes to address this concern will continue. It is clear that very little progress has been made in devising appropriate models of engagement for a wide range of organisations and sub-cultures. The notion of community relations 'training' is inadequate to the task facing organisations in Northern Ireland. Instruction is inappropriate when exploring open-ended questions and issues. Instead of looking to 'training' to deliver good relations, the focus must shift to cultures which encourage learning and allow capacity to grow. In a context where there are no fixed models of practice, an invitation to explore the hard, practical implications of equity, diversity and interdependence in an organisation is an invitation into unmapped territory. Capacity building will require dialogue, open inquiry, problem solving, design, implementation and reflection.

All slogans tend to go the way of all flesh. While 'equity, diversity and interdependence' can allow for a wider debate on the relevance of inter-community relations issues, they can easily descend into empty words unless they are translated actively into the lived culture of each group or organisation. The task is not to impose 'equity, diversity and interdependence' but to work towards them, by aligning the culture of groups and organisations towards them. Persisting with 'one size fits all' approaches simply cements the cultural gulf which currently exists between community relations practice and the mainstream of Northern Ireland's public life.

Change in relationships cannot be enforced. While legislation provides an essential floor, below which rights to equitable treatment and recognition of difference cannot slip without damage to civilisation itself, the future of inter-community relations depends on the generation of active engagement in change. While the underlying ethical principles of democratic societies or religions can provide an overarching framework for such work, this will remain largely theoretical unless it can be shown that improved relationships have a direct bearing on improved quality of life and capacity to achieve key organisational goals. This is especially true for the private and public sectors. Rather than new coercive legislation, which enforces conformity with pre-ordained legislative outcomes, the requirement is for measures which support the development of a culture of learning and development which encourages innovation and commitment in pursuit of an agreed vision and values. The key measure of success in such policy is in the growth of new capacity to deal with difficult but real problems rather than the absence of surface difficulties which leaves underlying issues untouched.

Moving from a received partisan culture and beyond a culture which polices neutrality to one which fosters and protects diversity will require considerable growth in this kind of learning in Northern Ireland. Generating a society where everybody is at ease rather than patrolled is an extremely delicate and difficult process, usually involving organisations learning to do what they have no previous experience of doing and therefore often have every inclination to avoid. What is important is the active development of settings within which people and organisations can learn to face these difficult issues, consciously developing new practice over time. The protection and promotion of these questions requires the active participation of many people holding leadership positions with the experiences and concern of others who have a stake in their groups or organisations.

9. CROSS-COMMUNITY COMMUNICATION AND RELATIONSHIPS IN THE WORKPLACE: A CASE STUDY OF A LARGE NORTHERN IRELAND ORGANISATION[1]

David Dickson, Owen Hargie and Seanenne Nelson

INTRODUCTION

Work is one of the many institutions in Northern Ireland affected by the deep fault line of cross-community division that pervades much of social life. For example, Shirlow et al. (2001) reported that almost half of those sampled had experienced intimidation within the workplace due to their religious affiliation and that fear was a major factor that influenced job seeking. Likewise, while Sheehan and Tomlinson (1998) found a willingness amongst both Protestants and Catholics to work in sites where they were in a minority, much less satisfaction was expressed with this arrangement when the work site was in an area perceived to be the 'territory' of the other religious community.

That said, the workplace represents an environment where members of both groups *do* come together and associate to at least some degree. In many instances this may stand in stark contrast to arrangements in the broader community. In certain areas of Belfast, communities are physically divided by so-called 'peacelines' to protect those living on each side from the threat of violence by the other. These barriers in turn affect many aspects of life where they are erected (*see* Jarman, Chapter 11). In other sectors, of course, Catholics and Protestants live side-by-side in mixed communities. However, these are often functionally desegregated rather than integrated (*see* Murtagh, Chapter 10). In other words, some Protestants and Catholics may live close to one another, use the same shops, walk in the same park, and so on, but each 'side' still follows separate social, sporting and cultural lives with members from their own community.

When workplace contact is typified by tension, disharmony and mutual recrimination, the organisation can suffer. Good internal working relationships and quality communication, on the other hand, have the potential to profit the organisation (Winstead et al., 1995). There now exists a considerable body of research to link improved communication practices in organisations with a range of advantageous outcomes including enhanced productivity, higher quality of services and products, lower rates of absenteeism, fewer strikes, less industrial unease and reduced costs (Clampitt and Downs, 1993). Positive associations between employee perceptions of communication, job satisfaction, commitment and overall organisational functioning and effectiveness have also been reported (Snyder and Morris, 1984; Meyer and Allen, 1997). Companies that pay attention to the health of their internal communications also seem to create conditions favouring innovation and creativity (Kanter, 1988).

Certainly workers, when asked, value the workplace as more than a location where a living can be made. In many cases it provides an important outlet for social contact and the forging of friendships: co-workers often become work-*mates*. Furthermore, job satisfaction has been found to be higher for those accepted by fellow workers and who belong to what are regarded as cohesive groups (Argyle, 1994). That said, work can seldom be entirely a conflict-free zone, nor, it has been argued, should there be attempts to make it so (Van Slyke, 1999). An element of conflict can be creative, and indeed hone the overall competitive edge of companies. Nevertheless, when allowed to go unmanaged it becomes dysfunctional. This is especially the case when it takes the form of factionalised prejudice and rampant discrimination based upon religion, ethnicity etc. The pathology of such festering internal relationships can compromise the overall health of the company, including the haemorrhaging of finances to meet law suits brought by victimised members (Garrison and Bly, 1997).

No organisation can exist in a totally detached manner, hermetically sealed from events in the broader community within which it is embedded. Workers, for example, reported increased tension at work during times of heightened emotion in society at large over events like Drumcree (Dickson et al., 1999). Taking active steps to improve inter-group relations at work, it could be argued, can have effects over and above those narrowly accruing to the organisation and its workforce. Just as reports of sectarian trouble in organisations may contribute to a generalised sense of division and enmity, so good working relationships have the potential to ripple out through the wider community. It is therefore surprising that little research has been conducted into cross-community relations in the Northern Ireland workplace. Indeed, here institutions generally have been criticised for failing to play a more prominent role in promoting inter-group rapprochement. As put by Robinson and Nolan (1999: 1670):

> Addressing differences has long been regarded as the responsibility of community groups, the churches, or the voluntary sector, and within these sectors the promotion of community relations has often been the task of individuals ... As a result, peace-building has remained dependent on the vision and motivation of a small number of people, with institutions at best adopting a neutral approach to these issues.

More generally, while considerable comparative research has been conducted into organisational behaviour across cultures (Tayeb, 1994), little has been devoted to the impact of cultural diversity within a single work site. Issues pertaining to relational communication between traditionally disparate sub-cultural groups co-existing in a work environment have been largely ignored, as has the impact of these on corporate functioning. Yet such issues are of paramount importance for the reasons already mentioned.

This chapter presents the findings of an in-depth study of cross-community relations, carried out by the authors, within a large private sector employer in Northern Ireland (to be referred to as OrgX to protect its anonymity). In particular, we were interested in:

- benchmarking staff satisfaction with inter-group relations within the organisation;
- highlighting the primary causes of poor community relations in the workplace to illuminate recurring instances of ineffective practice;
- assessing the effectiveness of organisational attempts to produce a harmonious working environment;
- charting staff suggestions for improving the handling of socio-politically sensitive or contentious issues;
- examining employees' familiarity and satisfaction with formal organisational policies designed to deal with contentious issues at work;
- exploring the adequacy of existing decision-making and dissemination processes designed to deal with the display of signs, symbols etc. at work, and ascertaining how these can be improved;
- determining the manner in which contentious situations of a sectarian nature can best be managed;
- drawing implications for policy making in this field.

METHODOLOGY

The in-depth case study approach focused upon OrgX, one of Northern Ireland's largest private sector employers and involved in production. It had a workforce comprised of 85% Protestant, 15% Catholic. Questionnaires, focus groups and in-depth interviews were the data-gathering techniques utilised.

SAMPLING
A stratified random sampling procedure was used, representing occupational status and gender as well as religious affiliation, to identify a sample for inclusion in the questionnaire and focus group parts of the study. A 6% sample of the workforce was taken for questionnaire distribution. In-depth interviews were also conducted with managers and trade union officials selected on a purposive sampling basis.

From a total sample of 400 (240 Protestants [P]; 160 Catholics [C]), representing each of the sites within the organisation, 203 participants (115 P [56.66%]; 88C [43.34%]) completed the Communication Audit Questionnaire, a response rate of 50.75%. The respondent sample comprised 177 (87%) males and 26 (13%) females.

Sixty-six participants took part in twelve focus groups. Six groups were comprised of Catholic and six of Protestant participants selected using a stratified sampling procedure from amongst non-supervisory/managerial staff not included in the questionnaire study.

Six in-depth interviews were carried out with trade union representatives, managers and senior managers who had experience in resolving incidents of a sectarian nature in OrgX. Interviewees were selected using a snowballing technique where networks of other employees who had been involved in resolving issues were identified by interviewees.

DATA-GATHERING TECHNIQUES

As mentioned, data-gathering in the project embraced a range of techniques including: a Communication Audit Questionnaire incorporating an ECCO (Episodic Channels of Communication in Organisations) analysis; focus group discussions; and in-depth interviews.

The Communication Audit Questionnaire

The Communication Audit has been defined as a 'comprehensive and thorough study of communication philosophy, concepts, structure, flow and practice within an organisation' (Emmanuel, 1985: 50). It provides a detailed account of the success of organisational communication according to staff views, exploring gaps between real and imagined practice, and evaluating organisational life. According to Hargie and Tourish (2000), Communication Audits provide an assessment of: who is communicating with whom; which issues receive most attention and which cause the greatest anxiety; the extent of information received and sent on important topics; and the level of trust amongst employees. The instrument employed in this study was an adaptation of the ICA Questionnaire, which has been shown to have validity, reliability and utility (Clampitt, 2000). It was a composite instrument comprising four main elements:

- Section 1 – biographical information on participants;
- Sections 2–6 – audit of general communication within the organisation;
- Sections 7–8 – audit of cross-community contact and relationships within the organisation;
- Sections 9–13 – ECCO analysis.

Sections 2–7 of the overall questionnaire were responded to using a five-point Likert Scale with a score of 1 representing 'Very Little' and a score of 5 'Very Much' of the activity or quality specified. These sections indexed aspects of present levels of internal communication in the workplace, corresponding preferred levels, and the degree of satisfaction with each. Sections 2–6 concerned general levels of communication and were included to provide a backdrop of the functioning of the organisation against which cross-community issues and the dissemination of associated policy information could be assessed. Sections 7–8 concentrated upon cross-community contact and relationships in the workplace using the same Likert Scale procedures. Items had to do with the extent of inter-group association, together with the amount of trust, enjoyment, friendship, support and tension experienced. Items within these scales have been shown to have very acceptable levels of internal consistency (Hargie and Tourish, 2000). Additionally, in Section 8, respondents were invited, in an open-format section, to offer three suggestions for improving inter-group relationships within OrgX.

Sections 9–13 were devoted to ECCO analysis. An ECCO analysis (Davis, 1953) evaluates the flow of communication in an organisation, testing staff understanding of key internal messages, assessing the efficiency of channels of dissemination and identifying the most effective media for delivering information. Three ECCOs were included, focusing upon:

- staff knowledge of their organisation's *informal* procedures for raising grievances of a sectarian nature;
- staff knowledge of their organisation's *formal* procedures for raising grievances of a sectarian nature;
- staff interpretation of in-house policies relating to the organisation's Flags and Emblems Policy.

These three key pieces of information were selected due to their level of importance and the expected high accessibility of such information on the part of staff.

All questionnaires were completed at work locations with participants being given time off to do this. The questionnaires contained a total of 91 items across all sections, and took approximately one hour to complete. Responses remained anonymous.

Focus Groups

The focus group has been defined as 'a group of individuals selected and assembled by researchers to discuss and comment on, from personal experience, the topic that is the subject of the research' (Powell and Single, 1996: 499). This technique was selected to encourage discussion and to generate from staff themselves what they perceived to be the key issues, from their personal experiences and interpretations, in cross-community communication in OrgX.

In keeping with the principle of creating homogeneity within, and heterogeneity between, groups (Morgan, 1997), Protestant and Catholic workers took part in separate focus group meetings each led by a co-religionist facilitator. This serves to encourage honesty, prevent social desirability responses, and facilitate interaction in a non-threatening environment. Both facilitators were trained and experienced in using the focus group method. Broad issues discussed were: communication at work; cross-community communication within the organisation; and knowledge, efficacy, and dissemination of in-house policies to deal with grievances.

Participants were assured of anonymity, and consent forms were signed by staff, confirming their understanding that participation was voluntary and that discussion would be audio-recorded. Discussions were then transcribed, and submitted to thematic content analysis (Boyatzis, 1998). A sample of 50% of transcriptions was independently scrutinised to test the robustness of the established themes and associated analysis. No major restructuring was found to be necessary.

In-depth Interviews
In-depth probe interviews provide detailed accounts of actual experiences described by participants (Downs et al., 2000). This method is more likely to elicit unanticipated information as well as documenting in detail the personal meaning attached to experiences (Millar and Gallagher, 2000). The six interviewees in this part of the project were managers and trade union representatives. Interviews were structured around critical incidents concerning sectarian harassment in the organisation. Each participant was asked to describe in detail two incidents where harassment had occurred. It was further requested that, of their two chosen examples, one be selected that had a perceived unsuccessful outcome, and the other a successful outcome. Examples should have occurred in OrgX and the individual should have been involved in some capacity in attempting a resolution. Participants were also asked about the operational effectiveness of current organisational systems on grievance procedures, and how well policies worked in practice. Implications for improving practice were also garnered.

Interviews were carried out in the interviewees' offices or at alternative locations in the organisation. Each interview lasted from forty-five minutes to one hour and was audio-recorded. Transcripts were subjected to a similar system of thematic analysis as applied to the focus group material, with steps taken to ensure consistency of interpretation and application.

RESULTS

The results that emerged will be structured around: questionnaire findings relating to general internal communication in OrgX, cross-community contact and relationships, and knowledge of in-house policies and procedures covering sectarianism in the workplace; focus group outcomes; and findings from the in-depth interviews.

GENERAL INTERNAL COMMUNICATION

With regard to overall levels of communication, staff identified a significant deficit between the amounts of information currently received, and those that they would like, in relation to the organisation and their position in it. The main areas where staff needed most information related to major management decisions taken, how decisions that affected their job were reached, and performance appraisal systems. These findings may have reflected organisational structural changes occurring at the time of this project.

When asked to reflect upon the various *sources* from which information was received, a pattern consistent with the above findings emerged. More information from all sources was requested, with the exception of that from the media and the grapevine. In the case of the latter, participants wanted significantly fewer messages from this source. Whilst greater communication was requested in both cases, present levels of communication from supervisors and immediate managers were amongst the highest. However, staff generally wished to see an increase in communication received from all managerial levels. Team briefings comprised a major form of dissemination in OrgX, but here again respondents felt that they operated with only limited success. This aspect was also highlighted further during focus group discussions.

Turning attention to the *channels* of communication employed, respondents requested greater information through all those available, with all but three mentioned being thought to provide little or very little information. These three were face-to-face contact amongst colleagues; internal publications; and noticeboards. Channels that were most noticeably under-utilised included face-to-face contact with managers, communication included with pay-slips, policy statements, and written communications from managers.

Employees remained positive regarding the extent to which they *sent* information, being content to raise problems, report mistakes about their jobs and express opinions. This suggests positive upward communication. Whilst they recognised that in all cases significantly greater information could be imparted, only one item raised particular concern. This had to do with giving an opinion on the performance of a manager where the least upward feedback was provided.

Finally, the reasonably positive levels of *trust* documented by employees with regard to other colleagues, immediate line managers, and middle managers, is indicative of a good working environment. Less trust was expressed with regard to senior managers. This is likely to be related to the lack of communication received from this group.

CROSS-COMMUNITY CONTACT AND RELATIONSHIPS

The profile of results for all respondents is presented in Table 9.1. Correlated t-tests were used to test for significant differences between present and preferred scores in relation to each of the items. Results are indicative of broadly positive levels of inter-group contact and relationships in this organisation. Moreover, and with the exception of 'Tension between staff from the two religious groups', employees recorded an increase in their preferred score for each, indicating a willingness to create an even more harmonious workplace. In each case, and again with the exception of 'Tension between staff from the two religious groups', differences between scores for present and preferred circumstances were significant (p<.001). There would appear to be considerable contact between employees from the two sections of the community during the course of everyday work (mean score = 4.07). Nor is this contact restricted to mere functional matters, since socialising during work breaks, for example, also took place (mean score = 3.78). Relationships were reported to be largely friendly, supportive and trusting. Participants also enjoyed working with colleagues from 'the other religious group' (mean score = 3.92).

Much less socialising took place with members of the other religion outside work (mean score = 2.53), certainly less than preferred (mean score = 3.26). This could be improved to further enhance inter-group relations, and suggestions generated (described later) could be considered by OrgX which would serve to further improve morale and working relations.

A mean score of 2.16 suggests low levels of tension in the workplace. The organisation was seen to take some action to deal with that which did occur (mean score = 2.68), but it was felt that a great deal more could be done in this regard. The mean difference score (−1.44; p<.001) for this item, between what existed and what was preferred, is the largest reported in the table.

A further breakdown of communication into Protestant and Catholic sub-groups (see Tables 9.2 and 9.3) similarly indicates a largely positive picture of inter-group working relations. Perhaps the most noticeable difference between the results for the two groups lies in the fewer number of significant differences for Protestants between present and preferred circumstances in respect of the various items. It would appear that the majority group in the organisation was somewhat more satisfied with present relationships and less committed to closer contacts than was the minority. Likewise, Protestants seemed to experience less tension amongst staff (mean score = 2.01) than did their Catholic counterparts (mean score = 2.36). However, Catholics reported slightly fewer steps taken by the organisation to dissipate tension that did exist (mean score = 2.61), than did Protestants (mean score = 2.74).

Whilst the picture of inter-group relations is successful, it seems marginally less satisfying for the minority than the majority group with the former reporting greater differences between current and preferred amounts of contact and levels of relationships.

As part of the questionnaire, staff were asked to make suggestions for improving inter-group relations at OrgX. Some 290 comments were generated, and these were content-analysed and categorised. The results are displayed in Table 9.4. For the entire sample, organising social events where staff could associate was the most popular suggestion to enhance working relations (24.5%). It also enjoyed cross-

Table 9.1: Cross-Community Relationships at Work

TOPIC	PRESENT CROSS-COMMUNITY WORKING RELATIONSHIPS	PREFERRED CROSS-COMMUNITY WORKING RELATIONSHIPS	DIFFERENCE OF MEANS
Day-to-day communication with colleagues from 'the other religious group'	4.07	4.33	-0.26*
Frequency of work breaks shared with colleagues from 'the other religious group'	3.78	4.13	-0.35*
Degree of socialising outside work with colleagues from 'the other religious group'	2.53	3.26	-0.73*
Extent of close friendships developed with colleagues from 'the other religious group'	3.28	3.72	-0.44*
Enjoyment of working with colleagues from 'the other religious group'	3.92	4.14	-0.22*
Friendliness of colleagues from 'the other religious group'	3.88	4.23	-0.35*
Supportiveness of colleagues from 'the other religious group'	3.65	4.17	-0.52*
Trust and respect of colleagues from 'the other religious group'	3.54	4.18	-0.64*
Friendliness towards colleagues from 'the other religious group'	4.14	4.34	-0.20*
Supportiveness towards colleagues from 'the other religious group'	3.96	4.22	-0.26*
Trust and respect towards colleagues from 'the other religious group'	3.72	4.15	-0.43*
Tension between staff from the two religious groups°	2.16	2.07	0.09
Steps taken by your organisation to reduce tension between the two religious groups	2.68	4.12	-1.44*
Total Mean Score	3.48	3.95	-0.47*

*Paired t-test revealed significance p<.001

KEY FOR SCORING ITEMS: 1=VERY LITTLE; 2=LITTLE; 3=SOME; 4=MUCH; 5=VERY MUCH

° Note: For the purposes of analysis this item was reverse scored

Table 9.2: Protestant Perceptions of Cross-Community Relationships at Work

TOPIC	PRESENT CROSS-COMMUNITY WORKING RELATIONSHIPS	PREFERRED CROSS-COMMUNITY WORKING RELATIONSHIPS	DIFFERENCE OF MEANS
Day-to-day communication with colleagues from 'the other religious group'	4.12	4.23	-0.11
Frequency of work breaks shared with colleagues from 'the other religious group'	3.69	4.00	-0.31*
Degree of socialising outside work with colleagues from 'the other religious group'	2.59	3.18	-0.59*
Extent of close friendships developed with colleagues from 'the other religious group'	3.24	3.63	-0.39*
Enjoyment of working with colleagues from 'the other religious group'	3.88	3.99	-0.11
Friendliness of colleagues from 'the other religious group'	3.93	4.07	-0.14
Supportiveness of colleagues from 'the other religious group'	3.73	4.03	-0.30*
Trust and respect of colleagues from 'the other religious group'	3.61	4.07	-0.46*
Friendliness towards colleagues from 'the other religious group'	4.15	4.26	-0.11
Supportiveness towards colleagues from 'the other religious group'	3.95	4.12	-0.17
Trust and respect towards colleagues from 'the other religious group'	3.78	4.06	-0.28*
Tension between staff from the two religious groups°	2.01	1.88	0.13
Steps taken by your organisation to reduce tension between the two religious groups	2.74	4.05	-1.31*
Total Mean Score	3.51	3.85	-0.35*

*Paired t-test revealed significance p<.001

KEY FOR SCORING ITEMS: 1=VERY LITTLE; 2=LITTLE; 3=SOME; 4=MUCH; 5=VERY MUCH

° Note: For the purposes of analysis this item was reverse scored

Table 9.3: Catholic Perceptions of Cross-Community Relationships at Work

TOPIC	PRESENT CROSS-COMMUNITY WORKING RELATIONSHIPS	PREFERRED CROSS-COMMUNITY WORKING RELATIONSHIPS	DIFFERENCE OF MEANS
Day-to-day communication with colleagues from 'the other religious group'	3.99	4.47	-0.48*
Frequency of work breaks shared with colleagues from 'the other religious group'	3.89	4.31	-0.42*
Degree of socialising outside work with colleagues from 'the other religious group'	2.45	3.36	-0.91*
Extent of close friendships developed with colleagues from 'the other religious group'	3.32	3.85	-0.53*
Enjoyment of working with colleagues from 'the other religious group'	3.96	4.33	-0.37*
Friendliness of colleagues from 'the other religious group'	3.81	4.44	-0.63*
Supportiveness of colleagues from 'the other religious group'	3.54	4.35	-0.81*
Trust and respect of colleagues from 'the other religious group'	3.45	4.32	-0.87*
Friendliness towards colleagues from 'the other religious group'	4.12	4.45	-0.33*
Supportiveness towards colleagues from 'the other religious group'	3.98	4.35	-0.37*
Trust and respect towards colleagues from 'the other religious group'	3.65	4.27	-0.62*
Tension between staff from the two religious groups°	2.36	2.31	0.05
Steps taken by your organisation to reduce tension between the two religious groups.	2.61	4.23	-1.62*
Total Mean Score	3.45	4.09	-0.64*

*Paired t-test revealed significance p<.001

KEY FOR SCORING ITEMS: 1=VERY LITTLE; 2=LITTLE; 3=SOME; 4=MUCH; 5=VERY MUCH

° Note: For the purposes of analysis this item was reverse scored

Table 9.4: Suggestions to Improve Inter-Group Relations at Work

SUGGESTIONS	CATHOLIC EMPLOYEES (%)	PROTESTANT EMPLOYEES (%)	TOTAL (%)
Organise social events	20.6 (33)	29.2 (38)	24.5 (71)
Neutralise the work environment	23.8 (38)	1.5 (2)	14 (40)
Structural stoppage to bigotry	9.4 (15)	8.5 (11)	9 (26)
No cross-community problems exist at work	6.2 (10)	12.3 (16)	9 (26)
Team-building exercises	8 (13)	9.2 (12)	8.6 (25)
Affirmative action	8.1 (13)	0.8 (1)	4.8 (14)
Promote a more neutral organisation	1.3 (2)	6.1 (8)	3.4 (10)
Increase tolerance	3.8 (6)	2.3 (3)	3.1 (9)
Improve communication	2.5 (4)	3.9 (5)	3.1 (9)
Increase training	2.5 (4)	2.3 (3)	2.4 (7)
Management neutrality	0.6 (1)	4.6 (6)	2.4 (7)
Community level problem	1.3 (2)	3.9 (5)	2.4 (7)
Selection by ability	1.3 (2)	3 (4)	2.1 (6)
St Patrick's day closure	3.1 (5)	0.8 (1)	2.1 (6)
Discuss cross-community relations	0	3.9 (5)	1.7 (5)
Remain open 12th July	1.9 (3)	1.5 (2)	1.7 (5)
Remove name badges	1.9 (3)	0.8 (1)	1.4 (4)
Workload and supervision	0.6 (1)	1.5 (2)	1 (3)
Exploring cross-community relations causes problems	0.6 (1)	1.5 (2)	1 (3)
Encourage diversity	1.3 (2)	0	0.7 (2)
Promote minority-group activities	0.6 (1)	0.8 (1)	0.7 (2)
Increase the number of females	0.6 (1)	0	0.3 (1)
Equality principles	0	0.8 (1)	0.3 (1)
Reduce religious gatherings	0	0.8 (1)	0.3 (1)
Total	100% (160)	100% (130)	100% (290)

community support, comprising some 21% of Catholic comments and 29% of those from Protestants. Suggestions related to both formally and informally arranged activities such as charity fundraising, more frequent social events (than that arranged once a year), and day trips.

The second most popular suggestion was to 'neutralise the environment' where suggestions related to tattoos being covered, and football tops, rings, scarves, badges, and other paraphernalia associated with division, being banned. Of significance is the fact that all but two of these proposals came from Catholics, indicating that this is a greater concern for them than for Protestants. Neutralising the environment was also seen to involve removing graffiti, as this was described as problematic for cross-community relations.

Implementing a structural stoppage to bigotry was ranked as the third most common proposal (9%). Descriptions of this category related to 'stamping out groups and cliques', 'exchanging staff across working groups annually', 'prohibiting discussion of politics and religion at work', 'stiff penalties for harassers' and 'zero tolerance to bigotry'.

Of comments, 9% were to the effect that cross-community problems did not exist at work, highlighting that for some this was an important issue while for others it was largely irrelevant. Protestants were twice as likely as Catholics to be numbered amongst the latter. This could reflect differences in how well the situation is monitored by individual managers, highlighted later in results. Team-building exercises were next on the ranked list of comments made by staff, which could be integrated with the first suggestion for effective practice

KNOWLEDGE OF IN-HOUSE POLICIES AND PROCEDURES
The results of the ECCO analysis in respect of (1) knowledge of *informal* procedures for dealing with grievances, (2) knowledge of *formal* procedures for dealing with grievances, and (3) knowledge of policies covering symbols and the wearing of contentious emblems, will now be discussed.

Participants' knowledge of *informal* grievance procedures revealed that, for each question raised, approximately one-quarter of respondents were incorrect with regard to procedures while a further 35% of responses indicated that staff were 'unsure' of available options to take. Only two participants were able to correctly identify all parts of the policy (i.e. that three of the four stated options were specified in in-house regulations). Trade union policies were not included in this definition and employees may, however, have considered these relevant.

For the entire sample, the most common sources of communication about informal procedures for dealing with harassment were through: informal conversations such as with colleagues (43.7%), supervisors/managers (32.3%), and the trade union (13.3%). Some 4.4% commented, in relation to policy, that 'they had never heard of one', while others learned via policy information such as circulars (3%). Human resources provided a small amount of information (2.5%) and noticeboards highlighted information to only 0.2% of the sample. This is a concerning figure given that for many staff, noticeboards comprise a main access point to information.

Information on *informal grievances* was delivered predominantly through informal conversations as highlighted by 40.7% of respondents. Some 30.6% received communication through training (including induction [13.3%], staff meetings [12%], managers [2%] and organisational videos [1.3%]). A further 27.4% reported having received information by written communication, with a remaining 1.3% indicating they used the intranet to access this detail. The high level of informal conversations through which information on policy was disseminated indicates a good working network. However, a formal communication method might be more effective in ensuring higher levels of accuracy on policy matters and greater understanding amongst staff.

When asked about the length of time since the information had been received, approximately one-third (36.6%) received this information one to three years ago, and a further third (35.6%) stated that they heard policy detail over three years ago. Over one-tenth (13.1%) reported acquiring the information in the last seven to eleven months, a further tenth (9.7%) heard two to six months ago and a remaining 5% had only received information in the last six weeks. There was clearly a need to update staff through retraining.

Employees were also tested on their understanding of grievance procedures at the *formal* stage. They were presented with time-scales by which the organisation should respond to acknowledge a complaint/interview regarding a sectarian incident, according to in-house policies. Slightly over 18% of participants identified two days as the correct response; 5.4% were incorrect, while 76.5% were unsure.

The most common sources of communication about formal procedures were through: colleagues (35%), supervisors/managers (33.3%), trade union (19.7%) and policy documents (4.5%). A further 4.5% stated they 'had never heard of one', while 3% received the information through 'Personnel'.

Information on formal grievances was received mainly through written communication (31.1%) with a further 26.2% finding out through policies. Some 16.4% were apprised via training; 14.8% in the course of informal conversations and a final 11.5% read the detail via email.

As far as time since being informed was concerned, the majority of participants (41.6%) stated having received this information over three years ago, whilst a further 37.2% were informed one to three years ago. Some 7.9% found out in the last seven to eleven months, with 7.1% and 6.2% reporting that they found out in the last two to six months and previous three weeks, respectively.

Respondents' knowledge of OrgX's policies relating to flags and emblems was also tested to establish the clarity of these policies in practice, as well as evaluating knowledge of regulations surrounding potentially provocative items in the workplace. While the vast majority (95%) recognised that flags associated with community conflict were banned, greater uncertainty surrounded certain other items. For example, only 45% knew that it was acceptable to wear a shamrock, and

58% religious badges such as 'Jesus Saves'. Nevertheless, OrgX had ensured the successful transfer of their flags and emblems policy into understandable and well-communicated documentation with which staff were largely au fait.

FOCUS GROUP STUDY OUTCOMES

Here, two broad themes emerged: the nature of internal communication within the organisation and cross-community relations at work. We will concentrate upon the latter. Within each of these themes, a range of sub-issues was identified. Excerpts from transcripts will be identified by work site and religion of the participant.

Sub-themes teased out included: addressing decreased levels of sectarianism in the organisation; management handling of sectarian issues that did emerge; tolerance amongst the workforce; and dealing with grievances.

Decreased Levels of Sectarianism

Staff felt there had been a significant decrease in sectarian tension in OrgX over the years. Almost all participants indicated that during their time there they had never witnessed harassment of this type. Sectarianism was frequently described as 'not an issue anymore'. However, it must also be mentioned that *following* a focus group involving the minority community, the facilitator was approached by one individual and informed that there were difficulties which the participant felt could not be aired openly and indicated that the working environment remained highly sectarian and difficult. This viewpoint was, however, in sharp contrast to a strong pattern across groups on how the organisation had changed over time:

> It used to be, come certain times of the year, there would be parades up in work . . . you know there would be flags and bunting up throughout . . . t-shirts . . . there would be noticeboards, there would be posters and 'please turn up in full regalia' you know. If you don't happen to be of that community that can be a bit daunting . . . but it doesn't happen anymore. (C, Site B)

> Everybody has wised up now, everybody has family, you don't want to be coming out of an area where you live and see all that, you don't want to come into work and have those problems, you come in and earn a living and you go home. This is your place of work. (P, Site A)

Some staff highlighted tension in the workplace at certain times of the year when community conflict was heightened, but almost all reported how this remained largely outside the work environment:

> Sometimes there's a bit of tension you know around Drumcree. The last couple of years it's OK,but a few years back there was tension . . . there

wasn't confrontation or anything, bother or, you just feel sort of . . . but there's no actual problem. (P, site A)

From my point of view whether they leave their problems at home, but they are rarely talked about, they are rarely discussed. Like this thing going on with the Assembly at the minute, nobody to my knowledge has discussed it to this day, in my area, you know what I mean. Things like that rarely come up . . . they're left at the gate, maybe. (C, Site A)

Some members of the minority group felt that improvements had occurred since OrgX had been taken over in recent years. However, greater emphasis from both Protestant and Catholic staff was attributed to the enhancement of working relations resulting from the instigation of legislation to provide a neutral environment. This was reported to have brought about changes in the organisation:

I have been here 23 years and things has improved over the 23 years, like. Basically in line with changes outside, you know. You know, things that were acceptable became unacceptable and then had to be dealt with, you know. It has just changed over the years. (C, Site A)

Both Protestant and Catholic staff reported an avoidance of sensitive topics:

The only discussion is 'did you have any trouble getting in here this morning'. (P, Site A)

No there's no ugly meanings taken out of it . . . if there was somebody that wouldn't take it well, then I wouldn't mention it, you know. If I thought I was offending anyone, you know, it works both ways. I mean, I think in this type of environment you need a thick skin to work here anyway no matter what it is. (C, Site A)

Use of 'banter' was an established way of addressing differences and facilitating good working relations between groups:

Well, I've never seen anything, no. I mean I'm here 11 years now and I've been [employed on various sites], it's just the relationship you have with people, with the people that you work with. I mean, I had a bit of a slagging match with . . . a bit of banter with some of the people I work with, you know, it may involve Celtic and Rangers or something like there when it happens. (C, Site A)

There was evidence of some sectarian difficulties on only one of the sites sampled.

Minority group staff described how if an allegation was made it then divided staff into their respective categories and one side 'played off against the other'. Here again, however, it was noted that the situation in general had improved in comparison to a decade ago. As one Catholic employee stated:

> They [OrgX] don't tolerate an awful lot now, so they don't. But there definitely is [some cross-community division]. (C, Site C)

Management Handling of Sectarian Issues

Problems relating to sectarian graffiti on toilet walls, which was particularly offensive and actually named specific individuals, was mentioned in this regard. Employees wished to see this area kept clean and felt that graffiti should be erased immediately. This group discussed how, if graffiti was not reported, it was not removed, or its removal depended on the manager responsible. Criticism was levied at management for not intervening sufficiently when this occurred in order to prevent further tension. The pretext that intervention could enflame the situation and worsen an atmosphere which would otherwise 'blow over', was not accepted.

> . . . a couple of times things have been wrote in the toilets about fellas, it's been reported and they've went in and they've taken the door off, or something. But there's other writing that's been left there. Unless it's really outlined, a pure sectarian thing about, somebody's named about it, or something, it'll not, something will not be done about it. But if it's just, there's other things, they can get offended over as well . . . and it's let lie there. (C, Site C)

It was acknowledged that once a complaint was registered action would often be taken. However, managers were required to be more proactive. Legislation in place was also felt to be beneficial in ensuring appropriate action when complaints were registered.

> . . . ifyou seen them [managers] to be picking on you because you report something like that, maybe they're scared of it going further. It's really looked upon very seriously, it definitely is. But if people let it go then the manager will let it go. But if it's brought to their attention they'll not let it go. Which is a good thing too. I would have no problems with that there . . . only the fact of the writing on the toilets. (P, Site C)

> Unless they're told about it then they let it go. They're not going to stir it up. So unless somebody actually goes and says 'listen I'm offended by that there' then they'll do something about it. (P, Site E)

Asked to forward suggestions to improve inter-groups relations in the workplace, staff on one site suggested that the best course of action was still to remain quiet about difficulties – a rather disconcerting admission:

> If you have views on it [improving working relations between groups], you just keep it to yourself. But that's what happens, someone says something and then it starts escalating so I don't say anything, I just keep it to myself. There's other people may not and then it gets other people's hump up. (C, Site C)

There was recognition of the progress OrgX had made in terms of improving cross-community relations by attempting to maintain a neutral environment free from harassment or victimisation of any kind. It was clearly acknowledged that policies were taken very seriously by the organisation:

> I think we've worked well at it, you know. I mean to say they've an Equal Opportunities manager, they've most things in place you know. If you're feeling harassed or victimised or anything there's outlets for all that, you know what I mean . . . you can go and see about any of those things . . . if you really feel you need to. (C, Site A)

Despite acceptance that OrgX was strict with regard to maintaining a neutral environment, some slippage was recognised with regard to football tops. Staff reported how managers would approach employees who were not abiding by rules regarding the wearing of football tops. However, the policy was not fully adhered to:

> I've only ever seen one brand of football jersey. To be as you say, blunt, I've never seen anybody turn up at [this organisation] in Celtic kit. (C, Site B)

> It's probably nearly impossible for them to implement it like [the flags and emblems act]. You know. Because I think that you would probably end up with a strike on your hands, if they did, you know. (C, Site B)

Tolerance

Polite avoidance of topics, use of humour amongst cross-community sections of the workforce, incidents of items prohibited in the workplace being displayed in practice, and lack of complaints from employees when this does occur, is indicative of a 'culture of tolerance' existing in the workplace. This also seems to stretch to a certain level of 'permissible' rule-breaking:

> I started in 1977 – it's tolerated – the changes are brought in and people tolerate it and get on with it. Information is passed down the line, this is how it's going to be, this is now policy, and people adhere to it as if it's health and safety issues. (P, Site F)

You never really hear much bother about it. There was an issue a while ago where you weren't allowed to wear certain football tops but it doesn't really bother that many I think. It doesn't appear to. (C, Site A)

Sectarianism is banned – it's not allowed. There's a tolerated level both in terms of humour and who you have it with, and also when policies come in, it's do this, do that – it's tolerated. (P, Site B)

In another excerpt, the use of humour and tolerance were emphasised:

Maybe it's because they [Rangers] haven't really been doing so well this season, that's why you're not seeing so many [jerseys] being worn [laughter]. It's different when they're winning ten in a row, they were never off. But that's not so bad you know, if you think about it. That's a pure reflection on the sporting excellence of the team, whereas if you found [community] tensions it's strange if people start to wear Linfield jerseys or Celtic . . . highly unlikely Celtic jerseys . . . that's a dangerous reflection rather than the other way round. You know if they're winning the football season . . . to me that's not so bad . . . I find it banter if anything. (C, Site B)

Dealing with Grievances

Groups were divided on their understanding of in-house policies and practices relating to resolving sectarian grievances at work. In a similar manner their feelings towards approaching a manager in this regard remained disparate. Staff discussed the merits of following commonsense action such as discussing problems with a shop steward before making an official complaint. Regardless of whether employees were completely au fait with policies, they generally reported how they would refer their problem to either the union or a manager, and if they were not satisfied with the response, they would take the problem to the EO manager. Should that avenue fail to provide a satisfactory result, they recognised that procedures were available to go further with a grievance, highlighting a clear chain of command which staff understood to exist. Furthermore, even if employees did have personal difficulties with their line managers, they stated that they would not be afraid to raise a grievance of a sectarian nature above his/her head, confident that the organisation would take the matter seriously:

If it's political or sexual, it would be taken seriously immediately . . . any sensitive topics which get a lot of publicity. Other issues, personality clashes or bullying, might not be taken so seriously. (P, Site F)

Especially now I think they do take . . . they're very conscious of their place in the community and that their image and they would act quickly you know to deal with anything that they thought was untoward. (C, Site A)

Employees were also asked if they would feel safe and secure in raising a problem of a sectarian nature if it arose. This question was responded to affirmatively by the vast majority of those who took part. A small dissenting voice was heard, however, representing a few of the minority community who felt that there could be repercussions from other colleagues if they were to make a complaint of this type.

OUTCOMES OF IN-DEPTH INTERVIEWS

The six interviewees provided twelve incidents along the lines already explained. Here, broad findings will be extracted.

In general, it was felt that the policies that OrgX had in place to deal with sectarianism were admirable, that the organisation was committed to them, but that their implementation by immediate line managers sometimes let them down.

One TU representative praised OrgX's approach to sectarianism in the workplace and the seriousness with which policies were upheld. The procedure whereby the manager interviewed both the complainant and the alleged harasser was credited for completing the process by listening to both sides fairly and ensuring the interviews were conducted in a thorough and professional way. It was believed that policies were widely available to staff and access would not prove a point of difficulty for individuals who were suffering harassment. Furthermore, the TU representative believed that the policies had had an impact:

> That was years ago, but that has ceased and finished and has just remained in the past, you know. It's a, if you like, a neutral environment for everybody. I think . . . society has maybe changed away from, you know, it's sort of . . . There is tribalism obviously, you know, outside here but I think people would rather just come into work.

A particularly commendable feature commented upon by several interviewees had to do with the flexibility of the procedures for dealing with grievance. One manager was particularly impressed with the informal option to tackling sectarian incidents, pointing out that not all in-house policies had this as a possibility. Another manager concurred that problems of this nature were best resolved informally to ensure the credibility and cohesiveness of the working team. The interviewee considered that when formal procedures were enacted the problem was highlighted and this could cause disruption and increased difficulties:

> If you can informally resolve something and it goes away never to return again then you keep the credibility of the team, you keep the team working together and if you can't nip it in the bud . . . you have to go down the formal lines . . . [the disadvantages are that] you are highlighting it, truth is within their own grapevine they'll stir it up you know within, whereas if you can come to some sort of agreement . . . I think the lower level that you can close it out at the better it is for all concerned.

Being able to move from a formal stage of grievance back to an informal stage as necessary was a further example of flexibility cited:

> The fact that the system itself had the ability to let it go informal after it was very formal I think I suppose it did have a good positive affect on it because, as I say, it allowed local relationships, where they could be potentially working for the good, to kick in.

The clear structure of support from higher authorities in OrgX was very useful for all staff involved in resolving inter-group difficulties and the EO manger was praised for support, advice and the quick manner through which issues were resolved, in one incident. Having TU backing was also mentioned as a strength. The system also seemed to work smoothly with individuals aware of their respective roles and responsibilities. A manager who had been caught up in an incident where a threatening hand-written note had been left in a worker's toolbox reported:

> ... the fact that there is a system is a strength ... I think the other thing that struck me was you know certainly there was a lot of role clarity in it and there was a lot of specific actions that different people did that they knew they had to do, without you know ... it wasn't a case of, you know, who's going to do this and it was like I'm doing this, I'm doing this, I'm doing this. So, that seemed to work well.

That said, criticisms were also mooted, both of policies but more so of their outworkings. Several managers experienced a lack of support from the organisation when handling complaints during which they had come under threat from the alleged harasser. In one such case, the manager disciplining a worker for inappropriately aggressive sectarian behaviour was accused of discriminating against that individual on religious grounds. He commented:

> [The organisation needs to] protect the manager's reputation and integrity ... from unsubstantiated [claims] ... I feel that is very unfair you know because you happen to be the manager that is trying to resolve the difficulty and you're not involved in it in any shape, form or fashion ... but you end up getting all this abuse based on your sex or your religion, it's just not the right basis ... it's different if they tell you ... you are completely incompetent.

The need for greater levels of training in the policies and the skills necessary for their effective implementation, was also voiced. But perhaps the greatest concern lay in the inconsistency with which policy was actioned by individual line managers on the shop floor. As one EO manager commented:

> Procedures rarely let individuals down, it's usually people who let procedures down by failing to implement them.

This seemed in part due to a feeling by some that policies to do with, for example, flags and emblems were impractical in that, were they to be carried out to the letter of the law, they could provoke greater difficulties. This mindset was summed up by a TU representative:

> I think if you were to go in and get really heavy-handed about that you would have problems because and I'm not really sure if it's to do with sectarianism . . . But people seem to wear football tops as fashion items and certainly football teams if you are a track fanatic you will support. So to actually go and attack that I think might cause problems . . .

Some believed that such policies had to be implemented with discretion and accepted a tolerable level of infringement:

> The thing is that nobody is complaining about it . . . I think there is [a tolerable level of sectarian behaviour]. I think this is where the jewellery and the football shirts is within that tolerance level, and I think that the fact of both sides . . . kind of get off with that, it's seen as 'well we both can do it'.

However, the greater the degree of discretion exercised by individual managers, the greater the lack of consistency, an issue also identified as problematic at a more general level during focus groups. As one interviewee put it:

> . . . but there also has to be a happy medium that says 'well, OK, you know if it's not broke let's not fix it.

This stands in marked contrast to the stance of an EO manager who stressed:

> . . . managers shouldn't sit back, companies shouldn't sit back . . . and wait for a complaint, they should actually be creating the [appropriate neutral] environment.

Furthermore, it would seem that HR and non-HR managers may see their roles in enforcing policy, especially flags and emblems policy, somewhat differently. According to a TU official:

> You see the company is divided into HR Corporate and Operations. The impression I get is that they can trust each other, but the [way] Operations people see it they are the wealth creators and they want to get the parts out, and the HR people are probably a series of people who can be [obstructive] to that, whereas if they are bringing these policies in that's maybe going to disrupt . . .

CONCLUSIONS

There are many optimistic features of inter-group relations within OrgX. Staff from the two community groups did come into daily contact and this was not restricted to mere functionality. Relationships were described, on the whole, as friendly, trusting, supportive and enjoyable. Again there was a consistently expressed aspiration for these to become even better. Certainly a marked improvement in inter-group relations at OrgX over the past few years was widely commented upon. Outside the workplace, however, little evidence emerged of Catholic and Protestant sections of the workforce socialising together. Of course, a broad range of reasons could be suggested to account for this, but it is consistent with a more general lack of integration between the communities in many areas (see Murtagh, Chapter 10).

There was some indication that relations were less satisfactory for minority group members (Catholics in this organisation). Catholics reported inter-group tensions to be slightly higher than those reported by Protestants. Catholics also seemed less satisfied with frequency and quality of contact with members of the other religion, based upon the differences between current levels experienced and those desired. However, this was mainly a reflection of higher levels of aspiration of this group. In focus groups, some Catholics also reported that they avoided raising formal complaints and expressed a fear of reprisals if they were to complain. This expression evidently requires attention by management.

Both Protestants and Catholics thought that OrgX could do more to dissipate tension that did emerge. The policy of neutralising the environment was described as working well, in the main, in this regard. Inconsistencies emerged, however, in its implementation. Some line managers were much more lax about intervening to deal with sectarian graffiti and violations of flags and emblems policy than others. Nevertheless, participants were agreed that senior management was committed to creating a workplace where all sections of the community could feel comfortable. If grievances were raised, workers were confident that they would be taken seriously.

The ECCO revealed that policy information relating to grievance procedures should be updated. Information needed to be more readily displayed and notice-boards should be checked more frequently for communication on main organisation issues. Staff were not as au fait with procedures on formal and informal grievance procedures as might have been hoped, and revision of policy is recommended. OrgX had, however, successfully ensured that staff had a firm appreciation of the flags and emblems policy. Further work with managers in ensuring that this remains so would be beneficial, as well as training with employees to promote sensitivities towards other groups. A more rigorous system for consistently implementing and enforcing policy could also be considered.

While the situation at OrgX had improved, and while the workforce had confidence that the upper echelons of the organisation are firmly wedded to still greater change, it should not be thought that sectarianism had been eradicated. One interesting theme that emerged from the focus group analysis had to do with perceptions of tolerance. For some this meant recognising informal boundaries within which displays of politico-religious group identity could take place, and be accepted, in violation of a strict interpretation of policy. This also stretched to the use of banter that touched upon group differences and had to do, for example, with the changing fortunes of Glasgow Celtic and Rangers. In some instances acceptance did seem to exist with neither party seemingly offended. In other cases, such practices were merely tolerated (mainly by minority members) in reluctant compliance with an informal norm. Better to grin and bear it than to speak out in protest, seemed to be the stance taken. To protest could invoke the ire of colleagues and lead to accusations of troublemaking. Obviously, further work on increasing sensitivity within the workforce is required.

The broader question of how Catholic and Protestant sections of the workforce, in general, relate in Northern Ireland, of course remains unanswered. A single case study is a limited basis for making generalisations of this nature. However, in the larger investigation upon which this chapter draws (Dickson et al., 2002), we discovered, perhaps predictably, that relations were better in some organisations than in others. In all of the organisations, though, there was evidence of considerable positive contact on a day-to-day basis between Catholics and Protestants including employees sharing tea/lunch breaks together. Additionally, there was a general feeling that definite improvements had taken place in the cross-community situation at work, together with a strong desire for this to continue. It was evident that an overwhelming groundswell of inter-group goodwill exists in organisations, and this should be fostered and developed by management. Neutralising the workplace, as a strategy for managing difference, received a very strong endorsement from the workforces. It is clear that at present there is a very definite preference for what we call the 'sanctuary of neutrality' in organisations. A situation where both sections can accept displays of group-based emblems and traditional markers of identity of the other community, without experiencing offence or threat, still seems some way off for many employees. The vast majority of employees wished to leave sectarian divisions outside the factory gate or office door. At the same time, some willingness to move further towards exploring and accepting difference emerged from one organisation.

Incidents of sectarianism were detected in the broader study, although these seemed to be isolated and more prevalent in some organisations than in others. Of some concern is the fact that in two organisations small sections of the minority expressed a reluctance to bring such matters to the attention of management lest they be branded 'troublemakers' or attract unwanted repercussions from colleagues. A common problem was the need for organisations to deal effectively with sectarian graffiti, especially when individuals were specifically named.

While employees had some appreciation of elements of the policies and procedures put in place by the organisation for dealing with sectarian harassment, overall there was no depth of understanding of these. A diversity of communication mechanisms within organisations suggested no specific strategy in place to inform staff of procedures surrounding harassment. Some organisations had much sharper flags and emblems policies than others and were more proactive in ensuring that these were clearly interpreted for the benefit of the workforce. In one organisation there was a high level of confusion about which insignia were allowed or banned, and about how reported breaches of policy should be handled. This confusion was prevalent at both managerial and shop-floor levels.

In relation to policies and their implementation, it emerged that those incidents of a sectarian nature that did occur, and that led to some sort of action by the organisation concerned, were more successfully resolved when: there were firm policies in place; an informal approach was initially adopted; the system had the flexibility to permit movement back from more formal to less formal avenues; an identified member of staff had a designated central role as contact person; and trade union representatives were involved alongside management.

Perhaps the most telling finding from OrgX, and the others, was the desire expressed by workers for cross-community relations at their work sites to improve further and for their employers to be much more proactively involved in bringing this about. A recurring theme was the need for organisations, for instance, to introduce social functions or events where staff could socialise together outside the work environment. Organisations in Northern Ireland should respond, not only for narrow, selfish reasons, but potentially for the greater good of the wider community.

[1] This chapter is based upon some of the findings of a research project entitled 'Relational Communication between Catholics and Protestants in the Workplace: A Study of Policies, Practices and Procedures', funded by The Office of First Minister and Deputy First Minister, Equality Unit, and the Physical and Social Environment Programme, from 2000 and 2002.

10. TERRITORIALITY, RESEARCH AND POLICY MAKING IN NORTHERN IRELAND

Brendan Murtagh

INTRODUCTION

Residential segregation has been one of the most enduring and brutal images of the Northern Ireland conflict. This chapter is concerned with researching its causes and effects and, in particular, with the connection between empiricism and policy making. Despite its deep impact on spatial production and consumption patterns, the issue of segregation has made little imprint on key territorial policies including land use planning, housing management and urban regeneration. The chapter explores and attempts to explain how the State can mobilise to resist the weight of research and insulate its own routines and decision-making processes from empirical critiques. During nearly 30 years of violence, major strategic and operational policy documents concerned with land management hardly mention the effects of violence on the actions of decision makers. Policy was lacking in content and context in its reference to the distinctive ethno-religious character of Northern Ireland and avoidance and denial characterised the response of policy makers to research that claimed a connection between segregation and planning.

The first part of the chapter explores the nature of segregation in Northern Ireland, its meaning in the construction of identities and the challenge it poses to the planning system in its widest sense. This section draws on a range of research studies to explore the continuum of segregation from enclaves to assimilated or mixed housing environments. The chapter then examines the dominant policy discourses around land use planning and, in particular, it identifies the research-policy deficit in the treatment of ethnic geography. More recently, global and local forces have interlocked to produce a shift in official thinking about the scope of planning to engage ethnicity, territoriality and segregation. This is evidenced in the Regional Development Strategy, 'Shaping Our Future' (Department of Regional Development, 2001), and its commitment to produce a more inclusive society. The chapter argues that research has played a limited role in creating this shift but that it has had a significant impact on detailing the content of local approaches. It concludes by arguing for a more normative focus to community relations research especially in areas such as planning where its validity is constantly questioned.

Kliot and Mansfeld (1999) reviewed the nature of segregation and desegregation in Berlin, Beirut, Belfast, Jerusalem and Nicosia and developed a paradigmatic model for analysing and researching division or partition in six stages:

- Division/Pre-Partition stage, which includes the time when the urban area functioned as one spatial entity.
- Actual Division or Partitioning, which is a stage in which inter-communal conflicts and/or total war occurred in which superpowers or other states were involved, created and maintained the divisions.
- Initial Division or Partition is marked by the mutual non-recognition and intense ideological or national-ethnic antagonism between the two divided/partitioned sides of the city.
- Middle Term Division/Partition is characterised by declining hostility between units and by implicit or explicit mutual acceptance of coexistence
- Rapprochement is characterised by close economic cooperation with respect to tourism, trade and limited joint apparatus is established.
- Unification is marked by physical eradication of the divide or partition and the unification of not only the divided/partitioned cities but also of the divided nations and the partitioned cities (Based on Kliot and Mansfeld, 1999: 171–172).

Kliot and Mansfeld saw the transition between these stages in a temporal framework and located Belfast in an uncertain central position between integration and complete (sovereign) separation where 'because of ethnic rivalry, history of conflict and social differences, the various groups are reluctant to integrate' (Kliot and Mansfeld, 1999: 221). But this is only a partial analysis and the value of the framework applied to a Northern Ireland setting is in spatially differentiating areas and processes within the region rather than seeing the movement between one category and another as time dependent. In short, the six conditions can be recognised in one region at one time and the research challenge in Northern Ireland is to unravel the web of factors that produce different spatial outcomes in different urban and rural localities. Three specific circumstances within their framework are analysed including:

- the nature of territoriality in peaceline communities where separation is reproduced by walls and rigid ethno-religious segregation;
- areas of transition in mid-rural Ulster where the processes of ethnic-religious 'sorting' are still at work;
- areas that are residentially integrated where the conditions of assimilation and mixing are recognised in lifestyle patterns and social interaction.

RESEARCHING RESIDENTIAL SEGREGATION, SORTING AND INTEGRATION

Studies on segregation in Northern Ireland have drawn on research traditions from geography, anthropology and sociology. Darby (1986) made the crucial point that segregation is both the cause and consequence of Northern Ireland's violent past and that 'it is often religious segregation, especially in towns, which converts distrust and dislike into violence' (Darby, 1986: 25). Boal (1999), Poole and Doherty (1996) and Harris (1972) all emphasised the link between spatial separation and lack of contact, understanding and knowledge of the 'out-group'. In such circumstances, conformity is reproduced, difference accentuated and spatial segregation correlated with widening social distance thus minimising opportunities for mutual learning and respect about the 'other's' identity. In times of heightened segregation, increasing violence fuels deepening cleavages making conflict resolution a difficult and unpredictable process. Boal's (1999) historical analysis of urban trends demonstrated a 'ratchet effect' whereby segregation increased rapidly in times of violence but rarely reached its pre-conflict levels at times of comparative peace. Poole and Doherty (1996) examined the processes of segregation and spatial change in 39 towns of more than 5,000 people in Northern Ireland. They showed that of the 20 towns where change was analysed between 1911 and 1981, 15 experienced an increase in the Catholic share of their total population. They concluded: 'In consequence, Protestants adjust to the threatening "Catholicisation" of their town by moving house just enough to ensure that they continue to live in the same kind of local environment as before' (Poole and Doherty, 1996: 248). The authors compared the results of their research with that of Massey and Denton (1993) on American housing where a fundamental control on the amount of desegregation which could take place was the attitude of the white community to having a black minority in its neighbourhood, suggesting that as little as 5% was a threshold.

Whilst the literature on rural segregation and conflict is not as well developed as the material on urban environments, there are some important studies on the experiences of individual communities especially where they are undergoing the transitional processes that Kliot and Mansfeld (1999) referred to as initial division and partition. Early work in this area was carried out by Rosemary Harris in the 1950s in an area she called 'Ballybeg' (Harris, 1972). Written in a period of relative peace, it is not surprising that her study highlighted the frequent and positive nature of contact between neighbours. However, she also revealed the existence of quite separate worlds where religion and social institutions dictated mutually exclusive patterns of behaviour and interaction. Leyton's (1975) study of the small Protestant rural community of 'Perrin' observed that its inhabitants 'see their village as a bastion of Protestant morality and Protestant virtue' (Leyton, 1975: 11–12) but that, in areas experiencing high levels of violence, Protestants emphasised their political rather than their religious identity. Similarly, in their analysis of the small border village 'Daviestown', Hamilton et al. (1990: 54–55) highlighted the damaging consequences for community relations of a prolonged paramilitary campaign in the area:

> In such a small and close-knit community, the resultant deaths had a traumatic effect, arousing suspicion and fear and leading to an almost total polarisation and lack of understanding between Catholics and Protestants . . . The violence had strengthened the constraints which had always existed, leading to increased social segregation and polarisation.

Unification, the eradication of physical difference or integration, is the last stage that Kliot and Mansfeld (1999) refered to in their continuum. DeMarco and Galster (1993) defined residential integration as a continuous process rather than a fixed geographic form. They coined the term 'Stable Integrative Process' (SIP) which they argued should form the basis of policy making in highly segregated areas:

> SIP should be thought of as a particular kind of market dynamic rather than a particular kind of residential outcome. SIP is a dynamic in which homeseekers representing two or more races actively seek to occupy the same vacant dwellings in a substantial proportion of a metropolitan area's neighborhood over an extended period. (DeMarco and Galster, 1993: 142)

Seitles (1996: 17) was critical of the role of public policy in producing residential segregation in American cities:

> The devastating effects of residential racial discrimination on the quality of life for minority families and for our culture at large, represent the importance of initiating policies to integrate residential neighbourhoods. Without the efforts of integration, the negative effects of decades of bigoted housing policies will be exacerbated, therefore perpetuating the existence of segregation and racial division.

Seitles recommended a radical programme that involved inclusionary zoning techniques, which would ensure that a range of low-income housing opportunities could be available within private sector developments. Mobility programmes have helped to support the relocation of people to new areas and housing opportunities. In the Chicago scheme, 5,000 families were relocated by the Chicago Housing Authority (CHA) by 1993, and 84% of those who moved to non-concentrated areas felt their quality of life had improved. In addition, the CHA was mandated to construct public housing in predominately white neighbourhoods and by 1993, 591 units had been provided. The Cincinnati Metropolitan Housing Authority also housed more than 600 families using the mobility scheme between 1984 and 1993.

As a result, black suburban residents reported a 57% employment rate, compared with a 24% rate among those still living in public housing. Families also reported that they did not experience racist behaviour from their new neighbours, they liked the schools better than those in the inner-city and worked in higher paid jobs with increased benefits (Seitles, 1996).

Seekings (2000) identified three types of integration in the post-apartheid city. Racial integration has been more rapid in towns where there are no former African areas close to the city centre or where large numbers of African people were appointed to administrative posts. A more thorough form of integration characterises some newly built residential areas especially where they have provided opportunities for people moving out of shack developments. A third kind of integration involves new settlements for predominantly African people in previously high income, predominantly white residential areas. But Christopher (2001) pointed out that the pace of racial integration remains slow, especially for blacks, largely because race and class continue to overlap and because 'affirmative actions in the economic and political fields were not converted into schemes to undo the apartheid city' (p. 454).

DATA: SEGREGATION ON BELFAST'S PEACELINES

One of the most striking features of the Northern Ireland conflict is Belfast's peacelines. In nearly 20 localities, physical barriers are used to separate Catholic and Protestant territory. This section is based on research carried out on Belfast's peacelines in 1994, before the first Republican and Loyalist ceasefires. It examines planning and housing management documents concerned with interface areas, the results of 44 semi-structured in-depth interviews with policy makers and community practitioners and statistics from a survey of 1,061 people in the three interface areas of Suffolk in West Belfast, Ardoyne in North Belfast and the Short Strand in East Belfast.

Indicators of social deprivation illustrate graphically the extent of the problem among peaceline communities. For example, if the case study areas are considered typical of peaceline zones, then 69% of the community earned less than £5,000 per annum compared to only 45% of Northern Ireland as a whole (PPRU, 1994). The unemployment rate for Northern Ireland as a whole was 11% in 1994 but at the interface it was nearly three times that rate (31%). High benefit dependency underscored the nature of poverty at the peaceline. Some 41% of households received Income Support compared with half that for the region as a whole (21%). In addition, 12% of the economically active population of Northern Ireland achieved Advanced Level standard as their highest qualification and the same proportion a university degree (12%). The comparative figures for the peaceline were 2% and 1% for Advanced Level and Degree standard, respectively.

The population mix of peaceline communities is linked to the different demographic profile of Protestants and Catholics. This has implications for policy in these areas as the Catholic community is characterised by higher waiting lists, lower dwelling void rates and a more equitable match between household size and property size. For example, only 27% of the households in Protestant Suffolk were equal to the bedroom standard measure of dwelling occupancy compared to 46% on the Catholic side of the line. In Ardoyne and Short Strand nearly half (43% and 44% respectively) of Protestant households were classified as elderly compared to 26% of Catholic households in each area. The two communities, however, share a common position in the social hierarchy as low head of household income was a feature of all areas with almost identical statistics for each locality whether it was Protestant or Catholic. Similarly, when employment data was considered, they showed a degree of variation between peaceline communities but relatively even profiles within each zone. In the Short Strand, 17% of household heads on the Protestant side of the line were in full-time work compared to 16% on the Catholic side.

It has already been shown that peaceline areas experience multi-dimensional problems. While many affect local people directly, they also have indirect impacts, particularly on the way in which people move and interact. The survey showed that communities that were in a minority in one area experienced significant problems in daily activities such as going to work, seeing friends and relatives, getting access to health services or recreation facilities. For example, 28% of Catholics in the Short Strand said that accessing monthly shopping was a problem and 11% of residents in Protestant Suffolk had a problem getting to a leisure centre.

The research also explored the attitudes of the communities to their own identity and that of the community on the opposite side of the peace fence. Most of those living in Protestant communities described themselves as 'British' (Suffolk 60%, Ardoyne 58%, Short Strand 39%). The next most common description for all three communities was 'Protestant'. Similarly, Catholics were more likely to call themselves 'Irish' and secondly, 'Catholic'. There was a high degree of acceptance of both communities of the out-group. For example, 81% of the total sample would allow a member of the out-group to join their clubs and societies. This figure rose when entry into neighbourhood (90%), country (94%) and visiting rights to area (94%), were considered.

DATA: SORTING PROCESSES IN RURAL ULSTER

The processes that produced physical peacelines in Belfast clearly do not stop at the greenbelt but are acted out in a range of spatial settings and with different environmental effects. The research upon which this analysis is based was carried out in 1997 and it explored the nature of territoriality and ethno-religious sorting in mid-County Armagh where tensions between the rural Catholic south of the county, and growing Protestant urban centres in North Armagh, were being worked out in an increasingly narrow territorial band. Part of the research examined conditions and activity patterns in two villages in the centre of the study area that were one kilometre apart, approximately seven kilometres north-west of Newry and nine kilometres south-east of Armagh city. Glenanne is predominantly Protestant and has a population of 140 persons, whilst Whitecross is predominately Catholic and has a population of 170 persons. The research used a household survey of residents in both villages as a context for more semi-structured in-depth interviews with community leaders. A total of 33 interviews were completed in Whitecross out of 65 households in the village (or 51%) and 22 interviews in Glenanne out of 45 households (or 47%).

According to the survey data, Whitecross was 96% Catholic whereas Glenanne was 92% Protestant. Moreover, respondents in Whitecross were most likely to describe the village as Catholic (96%) while respondents in Glenanne perceived their village to be Protestant (86%). The survey highlighted the long-established attachment to place in both villages. Nearly two-thirds (64%) of respondents in Whitecross and half (50%) of those in Glenanne had lived there all their lives. Despite this, there were comparatively few close friendship or kinship ties across the religious divide. More than three-quarters (77%) of people in Whitecross had most or all of their friends and relatives of the same religion, compared to 86% of people in Glenanne. There was also a sharp contrast in the perceptions of respondents when attitudes to community relations within and between the villages were examined. In Whitecross, 84% described relations within the two communities as either 'very good' or 'quite good'. The figure for Glenanne was 93%. However, only 45% of people in Whitecross and 29% in Glenanne felt that community relations between the two villages could be described in that way. Indeed, more respondents in Glenanne (38%) described community relations with Whitecross as 'poor' rather than 'good'.

The lack of contact is borne out by the statistics, as almost two-thirds (64%) of people in Whitecross said they never visit Glenanne and 29% of respondents in Glenanne said they never visit Whitecross. Attitudes to the future religious composition of the villages also revealed interesting contrasts. Around half (50%) of the respondents in Glenanne wanted the area to remain all or mostly comprised of people of the same religion as themselves whilst 30% stated that they would prefer to see the village religiously integrated. In Whitecross, however, 62% of respondents said they would like to see the village mixed although a sizeable proportion (29%) wanted the dominance of the Catholic community maintained. The literature has already emphasised that territorial behaviour in the use of services, shops and community facilities has always been a feature of community life in highly segregated parts of Northern Ireland (Boal, 1999). As Figures 10.1 and 10.2 illustrate, this part of rural Armagh is no exception. The diagrams show that the residents of Glenanne mainly look north to largely Protestant towns such as Armagh, Markethill and Portadown for comparison goods, convenience goods and services. It is interesting that more people go to Markethill for these goods than

Newry despite the latter's more dominant settlement status offering a wider number, range and quality of services than Markethill. When the activity profile for Whitecross is examined an almost mirror image emerges. Here, the population is drawn south to the mainly Catholic towns of Newry, Keady and even across the border to Dundalk.

Figure 10.1: Activity Analysis for Glenanne

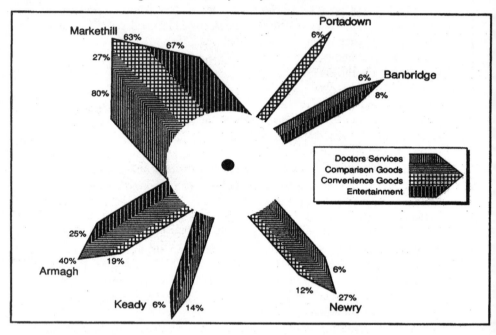

The recent past of Glenanne represents a catalogue of incidents that has created collective uncertainty, fear and, at times, hostility among local people. A number of incidents highlighted in discussions with local people revealed the extent to which the basic economic, commercial, cultural and security 'institutions', that any community relies upon for survival and development, have been progressively eroded in a short period of time. When these events are placed in the context of wider demographic shifts, the northward orientation of the community is hardly surprising. The first major incident happened in 1976 during a period of sectarian murders, high paramilitary activity and a strengthening of security force presence with the development of an Army base in the village. The main employment in Glenanne was a small textile factory and after a period of tit-for-tat sectarian murders in the area, ten employees (all male and Protestant) were taken from the factory bus and shot dead three miles outside the village. Another violent attack came in 1983 when Ireland's largest bomb destroyed the Army base and killed three soldiers. The base was not reopened. As the population declined this

Figure 10.2: Activity Analysis for Whitecross

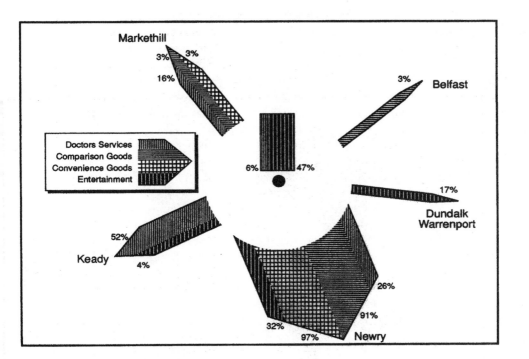

had a negative impact on local commerce and in the early 1990s, the post office and local grocery shop both closed and what passed for the commercial core of the village fell into physical neglect.

Census data from 1991 showed that the Protestant population in the area was declining, aging and, with fewer numbers in the younger age cohorts, it had less opportunity for self-renewal. In contrast the local Catholic population was characterised by higher than average household sizes (3.7 for Catholics compared to 3.0 for Protestant households in the area), more people in the younger age cohorts (21% for Catholics compared to 7% for Protestants) and equal proportions in the age range 65-plus (6% compared to 5% for Protestants). These demographic trends have had an impact on the local primary school which closed in 1995 leaving the remaining pupils to be transported by bus to a school five miles away. Finally, the local Orange hall was destroyed by fire in the same year. Indeed four out of five Orange halls in the area were attacked from mid-1994 to the end of 1995. As 'Protestant' community infrastructure and institutions were dismantled, exit became a more attractive option for those who could, leaving a residualised population with disproportionate numbers of elderly, benefit dependent and unemployed people.

217

DATA: MIXED LIVING ENVIRONMENTS

This section describes the empirical analysis of integration in public sector housing carried out in 2000 in Northern Ireland as an illustration of the opposite end of the Kliot and Mansfeld (1999) continuum. The research consisted of two stages:

Stage one involved a statistical analysis of integration and segregation at the level of the Housing Executive's Housing Management District, of which there are 39 in Northern Ireland. This helped to identify seven Housing Management Districts, in three sub-market clusters, where integrated housing had a significant presence and had some prospects for development.

The second stage consisted of a deeper analysis of conditions in these seven Districts using semi-structured in-depth interviews with key actors in the local housing and community relations policy systems. A total of 66 interviews were carried out during this phase of the work.

The Housing Executive's public attitudes survey showed that 32% of the population stated that they lived in a mixed area, 29% thought that it was easier now to live in a mixed environment than before the 1994 ceasefires and 61% felt that integration should be a specific policy objective of the agency (NIHE, 2000). However, ethno-religious cleavages must also be understood in the context of social restratification in Northern Ireland. Tenure is becoming an increasingly important discriminatory variable between social position locally as well as globally (Saunders, 1990). A gap in wealth is opening between those who can satisfy their own consumption needs, especially in housing but also in transport, education and health, and those who must rely on dwindling welfare support. The poor are being increasingly marginalised in a residual housing stock and owner occupation is providing new wealth-making opportunities for those who can afford it. Figure 10.3 examines changes in tenure by religion between 1983 and 1998, using data from the Continuous Household Survey in Northern Ireland (Murtagh, 2001). Owner occupation has increased for both Protestants but especially for Catholics. The close relationship between Catholic proportions in the public and private sectors at the start of the 1980s widened dramatically throughout the late 1980s and early 1990s as fair employment policies, new job opportunities in the public and service sectors, and rising third level education produced an expanding professional middle class (Shirlow, 1997). Smaller proportions of both Catholics and Protestants are now living in the social housing sector, which has become more socially, spatially and religiously differentiated. Whilst a higher proportion of Catholics live in the public rented sector, numerically more Protestants are living in the tenure. The Social Component of the 1996 House Condition Survey showed that 75,100 Protestant households were in the public sector compared with 57,820 Catholic households and that there were 3,660 mixed religion households in this tenure group. Protestants were still numerically and proportionately dominant in the owner occupied tenure group (NIHE, 1998).

Figure 10.3: Religion and Tenure in Northern Ireland

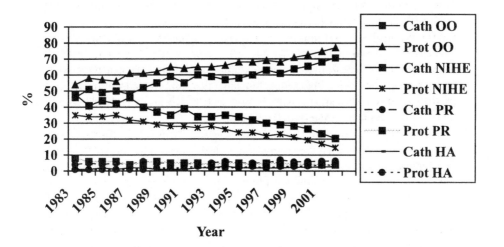

The identification of the case study clusters involved an analysis of indicators of segregation across Northern Ireland's 37 Housing Management Districts. This included the number and percentage of estates that were either integrated, mainly Protestant or mainly Catholic, and the religious composition of the tenant household. Data was also included on the reported incidents of intimidation in each district and the death rate per 1,000, as a result of the Troubles. The Housing Executive classifies integrated estates as having populations of more than 10% Protestant or Catholic, and, using this estimate, the total number of units located in integrated housing estates was 37,691, or 29% of the stock. A total of 55,054 units (42%) were in Protestant only estates and a further 39,400 units (30%) were in all Catholic estates. Districts that were most religiously stable and had low rates of intimidation and low death rates during 30 years of violence were those where integrated housing was most prevalent. They include three main clusters:

The first is in the mid north-west of the region. In Cookstown, Magherafelt and Limavady both estate distribution and tenant data suggests a balance between Catholic, Protestant and mixed estates. For example, 94% of all tenants in Limavady lived on mixed housing estates, there were no recorded cases of intimidation and the area had a comparatively low death rate during the Troubles (0.91 per 1,000 people).

The appearance of high rates of integrated estates in County Antrim disguises more sectarian trends in the local housing market. For example, in Antrim District there were six reported cases of intimidation in 1999, twenty-two in Carrickfergus, twenty-two in Ballymoney and six in Larne. Moreover, in Ballymena District, more than three-quarters of tenants (76%) were Protestant. But the data shows that there were high rates of mixing in both Coleraine and Ballycastle in North Antrim. A total of 68% of estates were categorised as mixed in Coleraine and 48% in Ballycastle.

The mid-Down cluster is centred on Downpatrick and Banbridge where 88% and 90% respectively of the estate population were categorised as mixed. The death rate per thousand people over the period of the Troubles in Downpatrick was low at 0.78. Newry also had a high proportion of mixing but was affected by a process of change that has seen border areas become increasingly Catholic and where 92% of the tenant population was of that religion.

This section reviews the north-west cluster as the area where integrated housing was most prevalent and the district that displayed the most appropriate conditions for mixing was Limavady. The Social Component of the 1996 House Conditions Survey showed that the household composition of the district was 48% Catholic, 43% Protestant and 5% mixed religion (NIHE, 1998). The historical geography of the area in part explains the comparative stability of community relations. Limavady was home to a major RAF base, which produced a high rate of British–Irish as well as Protestant–Catholic links, especially during the Second World War. The Housing Trust, the forerunner to the Housing Executive, made an active attempt to avoid segregation on estates and to deliberately create and maintain integration in the social rented sector. There was very little evidence of sectarian graffiti, a traditional territorial marker, apart from on one road in one estate around the July parading season. Another factor in the development of integrated living was the presence of cross-community infrastructure especially in the field of local development. The organisation GEL brought together tenants' associations, voluntary sector organisations and local groups within the district to campaign on problems such as the needs of young people, drug misuse and poverty and was successful at drawing down funding from EU regeneration and reconciliation programmes.

Magherafelt also had a good network of crosscutting community infrastructure. Much of the secondary level schooling system was mixed, local sporting facilities including the rugby, soccer and golf clubs were well integrated and town centre shops, clubs and pubs provided a neutral environment that traditionally enjoyed mixed clientele. The importance of school integration for residential mixing was also recognised by DeMarco and Galster (1993: 150) who concluded that:

> Because schools tend to resegregate before neighbourhood housing markets, the paramount challenge is defined in terms of avoiding the resegregation of school districts and neighbourhoods where racial change has occurred.

But the town's strategic location on the regional road network places it within commuting distance of both Derry/ Londonderry and Belfast which has produced distinctive housing pressures, especially from a growing professional Catholic middle class. The town's leading estate agent noted that: 'Most of the new demand for housing at the top end of the market is from Catholics working outside this area.'

Cookstown also exhibits some important features of community integration including comparatively centrist politics on the local authority, an active cross-community sector and successful initiatives in school exchanges and neighbourhood policing. But this case study also demonstrated the fragility of mixing and the impact of external 'shocks' on a delicately balanced housing market. In the early part of the Troubles, Cookstown avoided the worst effects of sectarianism and violence, but in the 1981 Republican Hunger Strikes a number of local people were among the ten men who died. Tension, violence and mistrust increased, producing new patterns of segregation between the Protestant north end of the town and the Catholic southern sector. This created problems for some communities reaching services and facilities safely and underscored the importance of accessibility to the development and maintenance of mixed housing spaces. Although intimidation and violence eased off considerably before the 1994 ceasefires, segregation has been reproduced over the last 20 years, with high rates of graffiti, flags and wall murals in some peripheral housing estates in the town.

POLICY IMPLICATIONS OF THE RESEARCH

Each of the three circumstances examined in this analysis suggests a distinctive policy response. In peaceline areas, imaginative initiatives to address community division and build trust and reciprocity could be combined with initiatives to connect people trapped in ethnic space to jobs, training opportunities and services. All of this implies a planning response sensitised to the way in which land is produced and consumed in contemporary Belfast. Similarly, supporting the institutional infrastructure upon which vulnerable communities rely for survival and sustainability could form the core of a strategy in areas undergoing ethno-spatial change. Early intervention to regenerate Glenanne, by maintaining the services and facilities that any community needs to maintain a sense of confidence and place, may have helped to stop the village's creeping and seemingly inexorable decline. Finally, the need to maintain the depleted stock of integrated housing highlights the importance of intensive demand management in order to support delicately balanced communities. Initiatives that maintain tenurial and religious mix and that remove the chill factors, especially in the form of graffiti and other territorial markers, could be interlinked to produce a broadly based strategy to build integrated housing options in Northern Ireland.

All of this implies that planners can read land use processes through a distinctive set of ethnic lenses and interpret the type of research evidence presented here within the formal planning processes and routines. However, in nearly 30 years of conflict this connection has been resisted and the empirical claims for an explicit engagement of territoriality in local planning have gone, until recently, largely unmet. Moreover, recent shifts in the stance of the planning system to engage issues of segregated and shared places have come about, not from the weight of empirical argument, but from a range of global and local forces that have produced a strong political imperative for action. Post-industrialisation has set urban change on a much less predicable trajectory and planners have sought new partners and embraced new issues to deal with the sheer uncertainty of spatial management. Race and social exclusion have become important in the vocabulary of planners in a range of late capitalist cities and Belfast is certainly not insulated from these increasingly global trends and forces. But, at a local scale, Ellis (2000) highlighted the growing importance of the equality agenda and the inescapability of planners from its mandatory requirements to analyse the effects of planning outcomes on people of different religions, political identities and races. It would be wrong to assume that the planning system has embraced this agenda fully. The Physical Development Strategy for Northern Ireland (Department of Regional Development, 2001) makes a commitment to producing a more cohesive society and recognises the preferred choice of people to live in segregated areas whilst at the same time developing the spatial opportunities for mixing. However, few of these sentiments have found their way into local development plans that have been prepared recently, development control criteria or the sort of proactive 'ethnic' strategies that may help to address highly sensitive or contentious spatial problems. The key questions for this chapter are why the weight of research has had only a marginal impact on planning and what its role might be in the emerging equality context in Northern Ireland.

Part of the explanation can be sought in the distinctive policy history of Northern Ireland and in particular the priority attached to professional planning values in the dominant techno-rational discourse within decision-making in the Direct Rule state. The pre-1972 Stormont administration was traditionally resistant to economic and physical planning and inefficiency and lack of professionalism characterised early state management in public policy (Murtagh, 1998). The whole modernist project brought the Unionist government into resource planning in a range of social areas including housing and new town development. The inequity with which these services were planned and delivered satisfied the Cameron Commission, at least, that land and territorial management was being abused for narrow sectarian advantage (Murtagh, 1998). The violence of the late 1960s and the imposition of Direct Rule in 1972 brought a range of new political and economic crises that involved a complete reinvention of the local state. Saunders (1990) argued that advanced capitalist states responded to the crises of the early 1970s by centralising and corporatising contentious, expensive or strategic policy areas and the shape of the new Northern Ireland state can be read within that context. Areas of previously contested policy such as housing and land management were located in new, highly centralised bureaucracies, removed from local political control and insulated from sectarian pressures.

A key instrument in reinventing the state as fair and objective was the development of professional values in land use planning and housing management and the promotion of technical and rational systems in the way in which policies were constructed and implemented. Success would be guaranteed by avoidance or denial of any ethnic content to local policy and this produced, what Bollens (1999) called, a 'colour-blind' approach to town and country planning. This helped to protect the profession from accusations of discrimination and bias and rescued a state whose very legitimacy had been violently questioned. But it left little scope for an interrogation of the sharper realities of locational planning in a deeply divided region. Ethnic boundaries were sharpened, people were cut off from services and facilities, communities withered as new religious geographies were formed and the opportunities for integrated living declined to narrower spatial and social strata. In short, the policy of avoidance, denial and do-nothing has had real and significant costs, as identified in the research, which have been felt beyond the localities under analysis. The dominant techno-rational policy style meant that we were in a sense, 'Planning for Anywhere' (Murtagh, 1998) and empiricism with a local colour held little sway in the key effort of the State which involved moving as far away as possible from the grim nadir of pre-1969 discrimination and inefficiencies. Research in different areas, presenting different problems and suggesting different remedies had little punch in a state that has determined to stick to the formula for decision-making that had worked to achieve important advantages without compromising the core professional integrity of planners or the administration. But professional values in organisations such as the Royal Town Planning Institute and the Chartered Institute of Housing are shaped by very different urban influences from those in contemporary Belfast or South Armagh. The defined competencies for both professions fail to mention an understanding of race, ethnicity and place as required skills. For planners, the claim to technical superiority is fashioned around knowledge of methodology for projecting populations, effective organisation of competing functions and the procedural systems needed to make efficient land use decisions. The inefficiencies produced by segregation and the research that makes explicit the waste involved in dual provision of services and facilities has had little imprint on these core professional values, the substantive content of strategies and the methods and systems for local plan making. The value of the research is that it defined the costs associated with residential segregation in Northern Ireland, underscored the need for a comprehensive policy response and challenged planners and housing managers to critically reflect on their role in reproducing these patterns or even redressing their more brutal effects. Moreover, it drew attention to the detailed planning problems in each context and the importance of a spatial approach to Northern Ireland's ethnic, as well as economic, geography.

CONCLUSIONS

Kliot and Mansfeld (1999) suggested that we can understand the transition of ethnic territory from initial partition to segregation and ultimately back to mixing. The research presented in this chapter shows that these conditions can be recognised spatially within Northern Ireland rather than temporally as they have suggested. The individual studies highlighted the connection between structural ethno-religious forces and area change from the stark division of Belfast's peacelines to the transitional character of mid-Armagh and finally to integrated living patterns in Limavady. The research combined quantitative and qualitative analysis to produce valid and reliable data on the community, ethnic, economic and physical costs and opportunities in each scenario. Policy makers have largely avoided and denied the significance of this empiricism for the content and context of local plan making and have produced approaches based on technical processes and professional values shaped by very different environmental circumstances. But neo-liberal planning policies suited to urban Britain have only partial relevance to the complex spatial issues described in this chapter.

The peace process, Belfast Peace Agreement and the equality agenda have caused planners to engage this discourse, albeit in a very tentative and partial way. There is an urgent priority to equip them with the skills, practice and models to develop a locally sensitive planning agenda that responds to the issues raised in the research presented here and elsewhere. Research needs to take a more normative stance and action, and test and critically reflect on the community relations practice that educators and practitioners can use to develop an ethnic dimension to planning and land management. Just as planners have resisted the connection between community relations and the discipline, the community relations sector has provided little in the way of evidence-based policy or practical tools to develop such a prescriptive agenda. The gulf between community relations and policy has been broadened in a two-way process in which community relations organisations have failed to engage professionals with the practical knowledge and models around prejudice reduction, conflict mediation and dispute resolution that are directly applicable to the management of interface, transitional or mixed ethno-religious communities. The implication is that research needs to take on a more applied and practical focus if planners and housing managers are to have the competencies to respond effectively to spatial problems and build on the positive direction of the equality agenda within mainstream policy.

But research also needs to equip the consumers as well as the producers of planning policy. In emerging from societal conflict, fair and equal access to decision-making will become a vital instrument in community empowerment and participatory planning. Research that equips people with knowledge, negotiating skills and data to identify local priorities and make claims for policy attention could help to articulate different local agendas from those shaped by the technical imperatives of the formal planning system. Here the connection between community relations and community development could be more effectively made. Deepening the technical capacity of both planners and the planned around the management and recovery of contested ethnic-religious territory could provide an urgent priority for the development of community relations research in Northern Ireland's uncertain emergence from conflict to unpredictable stability.

11. MANAGING DISORDER: RESPONSES TO INTERFACE VIOLENCE IN NORTH BELFAST

Neil Jarman

INTRODUCTION

Over the summer of 2001, scenes of street protests, public disorder and rioting in North Belfast dominated the news about Northern Ireland and at a time of uncertainty over the peace process provided uncomfortable reminders of the communal violence of the early days of the Troubles. There were recurrent and persistent scenes of violent protests towards children and parents walking from the Ardoyne to Holy Cross primary school, regular riots at sectarian interfaces on the Limestone Road, the Whitewell Road and Duncairn Gardens, protests against Loyal Order parades in a number of areas and numerous clashes between the police and local youth and men with paramilitary affiliations. The disturbances continued into 2002.

In fact, the Troubles have had a significant impact on North Belfast, and the area has suffered a disproportionate number of deaths and injuries between 1969 and 1994 (see Chapter 1, and also Fay et al., 1997, 1999). However, there is also a longer history of low-level public disorder, inter-communal clashes and rioting which, though clearly remembered among local people, is largely undocumented. The current protests and public disorder can therefore be seen, in part, as a continuation of long-standing problems of antagonism and antipathy both between local working-class communities and between some communities and the State. But they are also a product of the contemporary political process and the attempts to move Northern Ireland away from militarised conflict and to ground it in a consolidated democratic political system.

This paper briefly reviews the scale, nature, impact and causes of the current cycle of violence and disorder in North Belfast before describing in more detail some of the local attempts that have been made to respond to and manage the trouble. These attempts include community-based projects, developing partnerships between the statutory and community sectors and projects that involve working in some way with the police. The paper concludes by suggesting a number of reasons why it has proved difficult to respond more effectively to the recurrent cycles of communal and sectarian public disorder.

PUBLIC DISORDER IN NORTH BELFAST

The current cycle of disorder and violence can be traced to 22 June 1996 when rioting followed the Orange Order's 'Tour of the North' parade after it was permitted to pass along Clifton Park Avenue in spite of the opposition of many local residents. Although the violence did not last long, tension remained high in the complex geographical patchwork of tightly defined communities. Further protests, violence and rioting broke out when the police stopped the Drumcree parade early the next month. There were nightly protests and riots around all the major interfaces and lesser disturbances occurred elsewhere. Roads were blocked, vehicles hijacked and communities placed under siege; members of the 'other' community who lived in the wrong area were threatened and sometimes physically attacked in their homes; private houses were attacked and burnt; people were forced to abandon homes and belongings, taking only what they could carry; schools and business premises were attacked and burnt; the police were stretched to the limit and officers were attacked on numerous occasions; petrol bombs were used in large numbers and at a number of locations the police fired plastic bullets in response (Jarman, 1997). The violence and disorder continued throughout the autumn and winter months and the mistrust and hostility that had been generated has meant that disturbances have continued to break out with regularity, particularly during subsequent marching seasons.

Anecdotal evidence from people living in North Belfast suggests that the persistence of localised low-level disruption and violence is as great now as at any time in the recent past. As shown in Table 11.1, police data on the ongoing public disorder indicates that they recorded 1,445 cases of criminal damage, 409 cases of assault and 316 cases of riot, an astonishing total of 2,170 incidents in just seven tightly defined interface areas across North Belfast in the four-year period between 1996 and 1999.

Table 11.1: Gross Figures for Public Order Incidents
in Key Areas of North Belfast 1996–99

	CRIMINAL DAMAGE	ASSAULT	RIOT	TOTAL
1996	267	67	90	424
1997	444	113	73	630
1998	416	105	67	588
1999	318	124	86	528
Total	1445	409	316	2170

ROOTS OF DISORDER

There is no single cause that can be used to explain the persistence of ongoing sectarian disturbances across North Belfast but rather there are a number of interlocking and layered factors that have to be taken into account if one is to try to understand the problem. Some of these factors are localised issues; others are related to the broader political debate and even to the deeper social and historical basis of Northern Irish society. It is in fact the complex interplay between local and national, between contemporary activities and historical events, between social processes and political practices, which makes the problem of sectarian violence in interface areas so persistent and difficult to address.

Parades. These have been a prominent source of hostility and antagonism between the two dominant communities across Northern Ireland in recent years. Where the Unionist community argue that they are celebrating their culture and traditions and commemorating their history, the Nationalist community see provocation, bigotry and coat trailing. There is no common understanding of the issue, no acceptance of the other's point of view, no desire to compromise and no willingness to give ground. Disputes over parades in North Belfast have increased in recent years (notably in the Ardoyne and Glenbryn area) while the Drumcree Church parade continues to raise tension, provoke street protests and generate disorder in North Belfast each year.

Territory. The parades create problems because they often breach, or threaten to breach, perceived territorial boundaries. North Belfast is divided into a large number of distinctive geographically based working-class communities, which are regarded either as exclusively Protestant/Unionist or Catholic/Nationalist territory. The boundaries or interfaces are the fracture zones where the hostility and antipathy is sustained and renewed through violence and disorder (Jarman and O'Halloran, 2000). There are few mixed working-class areas in North Belfast and such areas are largely seen as transient places. With a young and growing Catholic community and an ageing and declining Protestant community the shift in territorial identity is seen as unidirectional: Nationalists are thus perceived to be gaining while Unionists are losing ground. It is thus increasingly important to defend the boundaries of one's area and ensure that the land does not pass into the hands of the 'other'.

Segregation. The hardening of territorial boundaries and conflict between communities has increased the scale and the depth of segregation (Murtagh, 1994, 2002; Shirlow, 1999). Residential areas, social environments, sporting and cultural activities, education and worship are all primarily carried on among and within one's own community. The level of understanding of, sympathy for, and acceptance of, the 'other' community can only have suffered as a result. In particular the younger generation, those who have been born since the 1970s, have had less interaction with and understanding of, the 'other' community than their parental generation and recent, as yet unpublished, research by Peter Shirlow suggests that they are often more sectarian in their attitudes than their elders. In general people are prepared to tolerate the presence of the 'other' as long as they do not cause any problems, but there is little desire to engage with them.

Power. Control of territory is linked to power, both political and paramilitary. The changing demographic geography has implications for the power and status of political representatives. The capacity to fight for or defend territorial and political interests is being fought out both between and within each of the two communities. Within the Unionist community the increasing fragmentation of political representation is compounded by the presence of rival paramilitary groups who are claiming the right to defend existing interests, while at the same time aiming to extend their power and authority over other working-class territories. In such a context launching attacks upon the 'other' (whether rhetorical or otherwise) is a well-established political strategy that continues to be pursued across the area.

Young People. These are seen as one of the most prominent and visible elements in the persistence of low-level sectarian violence and disorder that plagues interface areas. For many young people 'recreational rioting' is a relief from boredom and is considered as routine fun and excitement (Jarman and O'Halloran, 2001). In many cases the traditional structures of parental, familial, communal or political authority offer little or no significant restraint on young males when compared to a culture that celebrates paramilitarism and has widely demonised the neighbouring 'other'.

Policing. The hostility of many in the Nationalist community to the police is well documented, but since the signing of the Anglo-Irish Agreement in 1985 relations between the police and the Loyalist community have also been less amicable. In the early stages of the disputes over parade routes the police were often the target of abuse and violence by protesters, while people in both communities have in turn accused the police of unnecessary aggression and use of force. More recently the police have generally taken a softer approach to many street protests, have reduced their use of plastic bullets and have engaged in wider ranging forms of dialogue with community activists and political representatives. However, policing still remains a critical and unresolved issue for many people.

The Agreement. There was an attempt to address many of these concerns (territory, power, representation, sense of identity, culture, policing) in the

Belfast/Good Friday Agreement. However the fear, suspicion and mistrust felt variously towards the British and Irish governments, towards Republican or Loyalist paramilitary groupings, the continued resistance to any idea of compromise or reciprocal understanding and the lack of any public expression of reconciliation among opposing political leadership has fuelled antagonisms and uncertainties and hardened attitudes among members of both communities. Furthermore, there is no history of a win-win scenario in local political history and if one side believes they are gaining in some way, then the other side must be losing. In North Belfast the Protestant/Unionist community feels that they have been losing more than anyone else: local territory, their rights to cultural expression and potentially their political influence. Aggression has thus become one prominent aspect of their defensive strategy.

Ambiguity. One final factor is the ambivalent and ambiguous attitude of many of the relevant players to the persistence of violence. Although all politicians, community activists, community representatives and paramilitary spokespeople would claim to be against such violence, too many people wear more than one hat and assert different things to different constituencies at different times. At times it suits some interests to have the violence persist and, while others might not actively encourage the disorder, they do not necessarily do all they can to stop it. On those occasions when everyone has pulled together to calm the situation down, things have been quickly brought under control. Unfortunately such occasions have been all too rare.

One prominent impact that these factors have had on members of the local residential, geographical, territorial, persuasional and political communities of North Belfast has been to reduce the level of dialogue and discussion about how problems of sectarian violence can be addressed. In fact, there is no general agreement on the cause of the disorder, each side blames the other while excusing the actions of its members as justifiable or understandable retaliation. No one has been prepared, or has the political or moral authority, to initiate a process of dialogue that will lead to a solution to the persistence of sectarianism in the area. The general lack of political leadership has meant that members of local community groups have been reluctant to engage in discussion with their neighbouring communities about local violence and disorder. Those who have been willing to meet people from the 'other' side have often been castigated, undermined or intimidated by people from within their own community. Too often meetings and proposals have led nowhere, except to more meetings and other proposals. Too often people have found excuses why they should not talk rather than argued for the importance of dialogue. Too often people and communities have preferred to blame the other and play the victim rather than seek a solution.

As with the wider problem of resolving the disputes over contentious parade routes, one side or the other has raised obstacles to a process rather than attempt to find ways around difficult issues. And in a similar fashion to the disputes over parades, once the summer marching season has ended and the worst of the trouble has stopped then the impetus for dialogue has also dissolved. People have preferred to hope that somehow the same problems will not re-emerge the following year rather than engage in a process of dialogue and debate. These types of factors have meant that the only sustained responses to the cyclical sectarian violence and disorder have been attempts to contain and restrain the trouble rather than to stop it completely or to divert people's attention and interest away from the flashpoint areas into more benign activities.

POLICING DISORDER

The primary responsibility for dealing with disorder and violence in interface areas rests with the police. They have a range of standard responses to such problems: they can increase mobile patrols to try to reduce opportunities for clashes, they can establish static patrols to monitor a flashpoint, or they can respond to disturbances by deploying mobile support units (MSUs). However, none of these responses is ideal. Mobile patrols are often not effective in acting as deterrents, static patrols may themselves become a target for hostility and violence and the appearance of MSUs often provokes anger and hostility within local communities. Furthermore, each of these options is expensive in terms of police resources and means that less attention can be given to day-to-day crime and other police activities.

Local residents, members of community groups and political activists also often take an interest in outbreaks of disorder, and over recent years residents across North Belfast have spent considerable time during the summer monitoring activity at interfaces and even organising patrols around their home area through the night. For some people, community-based activity to counter disorder, crime or anti-social behaviour has been viewed with suspicion, and is seen as part of a strategy for excluding the police from local communities or for legitimising the role of members of paramilitary groups as a local community-based police body (for example in relation to some of the restorative justice programmes). However, from another perspective this can be seen as a means of developing a broader problem-solving approach to local difficulties and acknowledging that different agencies and actors might be more effective in different situations.

One example of this type of approach would be the reform of the public order legislation which removed the police from their primary role in deciding whether a parade should take place or whether it should be rerouted, and reducing their part to one of managing the proceedings on the ground. Senior police officers were initially not particularly happy at the prospect of losing many of their powers over such events to the Parades Commission, but three years later senior officers have acknowledged that the new regime has made policing work on the ground easier and few, if any, such officers would prefer to return to the old system.

The creation of police–community partnerships has been highlighted in both the Patten Report (1999) and the Criminal Justice Review (2000) as the way forward in developing more effective responses to problems of rising crime and disorder. But these have yet to be developed to any extent because of the often difficult relationships between the police and working-class communities and in particular the unwillingness of the nationalist community to engage with the police until the police reform programme has been fully implemented. Community-based activity is therefore often organised without the involvement of the police, because of the poor relationships and feelings of mutual suspicion and mistrust.

The responses to localised violence and disorder have occurred at a number of different levels in what can be described as strategies of containment, intervention, prevention and development. These approaches can variously be seen as short-term, medium-term and long-term responses to the problem of interface violence:

- strategies for *containment* involve attempting to reduce the opportunities for the eruption of disorder or conflict;
- strategies for *intervention* involve rapid responses to emerging violent situations;
- strategies of *prevention* involve providing activities that will divert people from violent situations;
- *development* programmes aim to build the overall capacity of the community to address local community relations and other issues.

The following sections focus primarily on the approaches that have been developed or supported through the work of the Community Development Centre in North Belfast in response to persistent interface violence across that area. However, similar work has been carried out by a range of community-based groups in other interface areas across Belfast and in other towns in the north (Belfast Interface Project 1998, 1999; Hamilton, 2001; SICDP, 1999).

BUILDING BARRIERS

Building barriers, or peacelines, to separate communities and reduce the opportunities for violent attacks, has been one of the more prominent and distinctive approaches to conflict management throughout the Troubles. They have been erected in areas where there has been persistent and widespread violence and disorder and where the demands on the security forces have become too great. The hope has been that the barriers will reduce the ease with which members of one community are able to attack their neighbours. In some cases they do appear to have helped to reduce the severity of the violence and the opportunity for face-to-face conflict. However, while the erection of a barrier may help to reduce tension on residents in the immediate area, it has also been argued that they displace the violence to neighbouring or adjacent streets. Furthermore, the presence of such barriers also becomes a visible indicator of the territory of the 'other' and at times of tension these interfaces may still become the sites of conflict.

In spite of the paramilitary ceasefires and the ongoing peace process, barrier building is still seen as an appropriate response to persistent, localised conflict. Seven new barriers have been built since 1993 and six of these are located in North Belfast: between Ligoniel and Squires Hill/Ballysillan; between Longlands and Rathcoole; across Alexandra Park; between Mountcollyer and Parkside; between Mountainview and Twaddell Avenue; and between White City and Whitewell. Furthermore, a number of existing barriers in the area have been extended in some way.

Many people see the presence of a barrier as a blight on the landscape, but people living in interface areas often regard them as the most effective solution to the problems of ongoing violence. In areas where sectarian violence has remained persistent, demands have often been made by local people to have new barriers erected or to have roads or entries closed off entirely and permanently. These demands illustrate one of the distinctive features of the ongoing round of barrier building: the demand for a barrier comes from within the community, from people who see a permanent structure as one way of resolving the problem of violence in their area, rather than being erected because of the concerns of the security forces. However, the need for a barrier is not always accepted by people in adjacent or neighbouring areas. While one community sees a barrier as a way to reduce ongoing violence, people on the other side claim the violence is being orchestrated in order to justify a barrier. The suspicion is that the barriers are being used to more clearly stake out territorial boundaries or to limit access to social resources, such as shops or schools.

In the past the decision to erect a barrier has been taken on the basis of security considerations and on the recommendation of the local RUC commander. There is no formal requirement to consult with, or sound out, opinion among local residents. However, in a number of recent cases the police have responded to the concerns of community groups and representatives and have delayed their decision in order to canvas opinion. Such a process allows time for more considered discussion within local areas about the implications of having a barrier erected and also creates the space for attempts to address the cause of the violence and thereby reduce the need for physical barriers. Three examples can illustrate the varying value and effectiveness of this approach:

After extensive disorder and violence between the White City and Whitewell areas, residents in White City demanded a barrier across Navarre Place and between Serpentine Gardens and Gunnell Hill. In contrast, community groups in the Whitewell area opposed the plans and argued for attempts to address the causes of the violence, which they believed was being orchestrated by local paramilitary groups. Over the winter of 1997–98 the police surveyed residents in the area while community groups canvassed a broader range of opinion and a number of meetings were held with relevant individuals and groups. However, no agreement could be reached and as the violence continued the decision was taken to erect a barrier in early 1998. The violence subsequently declined in the area of the barrier but has continued in adjacent areas.

Over the same period there was persistent trouble in the Alliance area involving clashes between young people from the Ardoyne and Glenbryn estates. Demands were made both for an extension of the Alliance Avenue barrier and for a new barrier across Ardoyne Road. Extensive consultation within both communities produced an agreement that the barrier should be extended, but no agreement was reached over proposals for the barrier across Ardoyne Road. At the same time, attempts were made to reduce the level of violence and when this proved to be largely successful and the marching season passed relatively peacefully, the question of extending the barriers was quietly dropped. However, this did not mean the tensions had completely disappeared and three years later in June 2001 serious trouble once again broke out on the Ardoyne Road interface. This time, the problems were related both to ongoing disorder and to problems relating to access to a Catholic primary school which had been built when Glenbryn was conceived of as a mixed area.

After persistent trouble from groups of young people using a footpath between Whitewell Road and Graymount Crescent through the summer and autumn of 1998 there were calls to have the entry closed off. Graymount Community Association organised a survey of local residents to canvas opinion. Approximately one-third of households replied and this revealed that, while opinion was divided, 73% of local people wanted some form of access through the entry, while only 27% wanted the access permanently closed off. The results encouraged local groups to renew their attempts to deal with the source of the trouble and although disturbances still occasionally take place, the entry has remained open.

There are still calls for barriers whenever there is persistent trouble or disorder in interface areas, but most people living in such areas would prefer to have the violence brought under control, rather than have a barrier erected, as the violence is never as permanent as the numerous barriers have so far proved to be. The examples from North Belfast suggest that there are advantages in involving a broad section of the local community (rather than just those residents who are immediately affected by the trouble) in any decision to erect or extend a barrier and it is quite possible that the process of debate and discussion can encourage renewed attempts to address the causes of disorder.

MAINTAINING COMMUNICATION

The violence in North Belfast in 1996 was underpinned by rumour, mistrust and suspicion, and fuelled by a breakdown in the existing levels of communication – within communities, between communities, and between communities and statutory agencies. Subsequent meetings between organisations such as the Community Development Centre (CDC) and key statutory agencies concluded that there was need both for an overhaul of contingency plans and working arrangements, and for a more flexible and imaginative response to major public disorder.

The issue of contingency planning was addressed by the formation of the Interagency Working Group on Displaced Families (see below), while staff at CDC proposed creating a network of community groups linked by mobile phone. This network would allow lines of communication to be maintained within communities, between neighbouring communities, and with the police and other statutory bodies. 'Making Belfast Work' (now Belfast Regeneration Office) agreed to fund the project for a two-month period through the 1997 marching season. Key groups and individuals were identified from existing community networks that were prepared to participate in the phone network. Each phone holder was given the numbers of the other phones in the network and contact numbers of key people in the statutory sector. They agreed to keep the phones switched on 20 hours a day, 7 days a week, throughout the marching season, from mid-June to late August, and to contact other members of the network in response to rumours or concerns, to crowds gathering or minor incidents, and to respond to all such calls coming to them. Over the summer many of the phone holders spent long hours on the streets trying to keep young people and adults away from interfaces, stopping instances of stone throwing, calming tensions and defusing rumours. The phones were also used to contact members of the 'other' community to try to synchronise attempts to reduce the violence while in some areas contacts were maintained with the RUC so that community workers were given time and space to stop trouble before police in riot uniforms arrived on the scene.

The mobile phone network has functioned each summer since 1997 and increased from having phones in ten interface areas of North Belfast in 1997 to twenty-five areas in 2000 (Jarman, 1999). Similar networks have been set up in other parts of the city so that each summer up to sixty phones have been used by networks across Belfast. The idea has also been adopted by interface communities in Derry/Londonderry and has also been adopted as part of a wider community safety strategy in Antrim and Carrickfergus (Cunningham, 2001; Hamilton, 2001). Acts of violence and disorder continue to occur in North Belfast, but the participation of local community activists in responding to disorder has become an important component in helping to keep the peace.

A recent evaluation of the mobile phone networks in North Belfast and elsewhere (Hamilton, 2001) indicates that they are highly regarded by a diverse range of statutory agencies as an effective and efficient form of communication which facilitates localised conflict management. In some areas, networks have proved to be a useful way of consolidating or extending working relationships between different interface communities and building trust between the community and statutory sectors. The networks have also proved to be a relatively cheap option, although it is expensive in human resources and in terms of the time commitment of volunteers. It has cost between £3,000 and £6,000 to run the phone network in North Belfast each summer (depending on the number of phones and the length of time they are available for use) but this should be considered money well spent if even one car is saved from being hijacked or one household is saved from being forced to abandon their home.

However, there are problems in maintaining the networks:

- many of those participating feel drained at the end of the summer because of the time and energy spent responding to calls and monitoring activity on the streets;
- a number of phone holders have been challenged (and on occasion assaulted) about what they were doing by people within their own community;
- there have been numerous complaints that the 'other' side has not been as responsive as might have been hoped;
- a number of people have complained that the police have come to expect too much of members of the phone networks and put them under pressure to take a more interventionist role.

Furthermore, a willingness to participate as a phone holder and the ability of people to intervene effectively in emerging conflicts is often dependent on the wider political context. The North Belfast network was probably most effective in 1998 when the feel-good factor following the signing of the Belfast Agreement and the Assembly elections was most apparent. In contrast, it proved more difficult to mobilise people to participate in 2001, in part because of the factors noted above, but also compounded by a reluctance to take phones by some individuals or groups within the Protestant/Unionist community because of residual tensions following the Loyalist paramilitary feud. It is also worth noting that when the network was set up in 1997 mobile phones were still something of a novelty, while by 2001 they have become much more widely available. In some cases people have created their own smaller networks, which run in conjunction with and thus extend the wider community networks, but in other areas people feel that they can use their existing phone links with relevant people in statutory or community groups without being part of a more formal network.

One of the major difficulties each year has been the uncertainty as to whether the networks will continue to be run because of a lack of commitment to fund the projects on an ongoing basis by any single statutory body. This lack of assured funding has meant that networks have often been set up later than they might have been and with less effective preparation. Ironically, the very success and effectiveness of these community-based networks can contribute to the uncertainty over future funding. If the network is successful and little or nothing happens on the interfaces, this can create the response: 'There was very little trouble last year –

so why do we need the phones this year?' However, the phone network is about *spending money* to try to ensure that *nothing* does happen.

DISTRACTING THE CHILDREN

The phone network was designed as a response to emerging problems of violence and disorder, but many community groups have also been keen to do what they could to reduce opportunities for children and young people to hang around interface areas, and get drawn into clashes whether as perpetrators or as victims (Jarman and O'Halloran, 2001). The marching season coincides with the school holidays and with the closure of many youth facilities to facilitate staff holidays. The restrictions on movement and access to leisure resources that affect people in interface areas means that many youngsters have little to do but hang about the streets. The interfaces, therefore, become attractive places to play and to meet friends during the summer weeks.

As a result, many groups have sought funding to provide summer schemes and activities for their children, both to complement and to extend similar programmes run by statutory bodies. Many groups use the money to take children out of their own area to places of safety or for diversionary purposes over times of anticipated tension and conflict. Trips to the coast, to camps or other leisure pursuits are frequent favourites. The majority of such schemes last for only a week or two, but, if they are organised at key times, they can be useful in providing activities which divert young people from interface areas and violent activities.

Most of the summer schemes are necessarily small scale, localised and single identity programmes, but groups in the Little America and Westland areas have used the opportunity to develop an imaginative cross-community programme. There had been few obvious problems between the two communities before 1996, but trouble occurred in July of that year, and again in 1997 and 1998. In the following two years members of the community groups agreed to try to ease local tensions while ensuring that each side was able to celebrate their own culture and key anniversaries. They organised a joint summer scheme for two weeks in July to bring together children from both communities for a range of outings, street events, sporting activities and similar events. The scheme was a success in terms of attracting participation from large numbers of children and parents, and the interface remained quiet in comparison with the previous year. After the first joint summer scheme, young people from the two areas began to develop a programme of activities for themselves to run outside the framework of the marching season. Over a series of meetings the two groups developed plans for a cross-community team-building residential course and a 12-week Community Leadership training programme.

Such work is time consuming and often seems to progress very slowly. However, the experience suggests that community groups and young people are willing and effective in addressing some of the problems and issues that they face if they are given some support. Groups in many interface areas have recognised the value of locally run and organised summer schemes for their young people and many in relevant statutory agencies have acknowledged the effectiveness of this work. One problem is that, while the overall level of funding has increased in recent years, it has too often only been made available at a late stage. For example, in 1999, groups were given only a few days' notice of the availability of one source of funding. Furthermore, the bureaucracy that is sometimes involved and the paperwork demanded of small community groups meant that some groups would not apply for available funds. However, it was clear that, with better planning and co-ordination, more effective use could have been made of the money and greater numbers of children could have been offered more enjoyable things to do than hanging around the peacelines.

PARTNERSHIPS AND PLANNING

The extensive disorder and violence of 1996 revealed a clear lack of planning and preparation within the statutory sector to deal with such situations. As a result, an Inter-Agency Working Group on Displaced Families was convened to bring together representatives of all the relevant agencies with the aim of ensuring that responses would be better prepared and more co-ordinated in the future. The working group initially included representatives from North and West Health and Social Services Trust, South and East Health and Social Services Trust, the Northern Ireland Housing Executive, 'Making Belfast Work' and the RUC; it was subsequently extended to include the Social Security Agency, Belfast City Council, Belfast Education and Library Board, the NIO Civil Representative, the Community Development Centre, Belfast Interface Project and Springfield Inter-Community Development Project.

The working group meets on an occasional basis, mainly in the run-up to the summer, to ensure that operational arrangements for temporary rehousing, furniture removal and storage, childcare arrangements, homelessness assessments and other support activities are in place and co-ordinated and that the information is available to all relevant agencies and to people in the community sector. In June 1999 when the working group met to review the contingency plans for the marching season they agreed to set up a further working group to look at the problem of ongoing and persistent violence in interface areas. The group decided to focus on the communities on the Whitewell Road axis and became the Outer North Interface Working Group (ONIWG). The group has included representatives of Belfast Regeneration Office, North and West Health and Social Services Trust, BELB Youth Services, Newtownabbey Borough Council, North Eastern Education and Library Board Youth Services, Save the Children, Belfast City Council Community and Leisure Services, Housing Executive, RUC, Belfast Interface Project and the Community Development Centre.

The original remit for ONIWG was to look at ways of responding to the ongoing problems between the numerous local communities. However, research among local people revealed that they were concerned about a much more varied range of issues. These concerns included problems related to young people and the apparent lack of resources and facilities for them, traffic and environmental issues, access to wider resources, and conflict with neighbouring communities. Many of the key problems were related to young people, as it was often felt that they caused as many problems for their own community as they did for the neighbouring communities. Residents cited the apprehension and fear they felt when seeing a group of young men gathered on a street corner. They complained of the noise caused by young people standing in the streets and playing music, the litter, the graffiti, the damage caused by footballs and the abuse that was often received if they complained. But there was also a general acknowledgement that many of the problems were due to the scarcity of resources and facilities available locally and the consequent boredom, rather than any inherent malice on the part of the young people.

Finding a way to address these sorts of issues should be a challenge for multi-agency partnerships, much vaunted at the moment but yet to prove themselves in practice. Building effective partnerships asks questions of both statutory and community organisations in terms of service delivery, transparency and the relevance of their work to local people. The challenge of such community development work is to build the capacity within local communities so that local people can work more effectively to respond to local problems, within their own community, between neighbouring communities and in partnership with statutory agencies. One of the supposed advantages of working in partnership is the ability to focus a diverse range of bodies on a single 'problem' and thereby improve co-ordination of resource provision and reduce inefficiencies. Working in partnership should also be a means of bringing statutory agencies closer to the ground and improving relationships with people dealing with difficult social problems. However, such a strategy demands a real commitment of time, staff and resources, if it is to be successful.

At the outset, ONIWG was envisaged as a pilot project for dealing with problems in interface areas. It was felt that it would take at least three years before an evaluation of the working group's effectiveness would show significant positive results 'on the ground'. However, finding a way to respond effectively to problems in the Outer North area proved beyond the capacity of the working group and after little more than a year some members felt that it was acting as little more than a talking shop; there had been little engagement with local communities and the working group had no clear idea of what practical action it should take. An evaluation commissioned by BRO (Gillespie,2001) revealed a number of problems with ONIWG:

- some of the agencies involved in the working group did show a consistent commitment to building a working partnership, but the majority were less actively committed;

- attendance at meetings was frequently poor and the representatives often changed;
- few people who attended had the authority to commit their organisation's time, money or resources without approval from a senior member of staff.

These problems all served to undermine continuity within the working group, meant that there was often a lack of participative knowledge or institutional memory, and ensured that decision-making was very slow.

In the end, the working group did little more than exchange information between different agencies rather than create the type of joint working strategies that had been envisaged at the outset. The evaluation suggested a number of possible ways forward for the working group, ranging from a minimal continuation as a loose network to a more formalised structure employing a worker to develop contacts with the local communities and work more actively on local problems. Although no final decision has been taken, it is most probable that ONIWG will continue as an informal network and not develop a more interventionist strategy, which would require a more serious commitment of time and resources from member agencies.

It was clear from the experiences of ONIWG that if such partnerships are to work they need strong support from within the management of each member agency and representative members need sufficient authority to commit themselves to act or to resource any agreed work. Less than wholehearted participation in such partnerships does no more than feed the apathy and mistrust felt by many local communities towards the bureaucracies which are supposed to serve local people.

CONCLUSIONS

This overview of some recent projects which have attempted to respond to interface violence in North Belfast illustrates the prominent role that residents from the local communities and members of community groups can and do play in dealing with actual or threatened public disorder. It is also, necessarily, only a sample of the overall range of activity in such areas. As well as the cross-community activities discussed here, there is also a diversity of single identity community development work under way, which aims to build the capacity of communities to address issues and problems; a number of youth projects are attempting to work with young people to address their concerns on their own terms; and several restorative justice programmes have been established in Belfast and elsewhere in response to problems of anti-social behaviour and to try to rebuild relations between victims and perpetrators of crime (Hall, 2000). Further afield, several towns and areas have set up more formal community safety projects to begin to address wider issues of crime prevention, anti-social activity and levels of fear and intimidation (ACSC, 2000; CSC, 2000).

Some of this activity has been initiated in response to the specific problems that have emerged in Northern Ireland as a result of the violence of the past 30 years. But such local problems also resonate with examples of rioting and public disorder in Britain and elsewhere (Campbell, 1993; Power and Tunstall, 1997). Many of the approaches being developed to deal with the problems in Belfast also have similarities to those tried in other places (Crawford and Matassa, 2000; Feenan, 2000; Kitchin, 2000) and it is important to recognise the lessons that can be learnt in attempting to deal with similar problems in different locations.

The discussion of some of the strategies that have been developed in Belfast throws into relief some of the problems and difficulties that have arisen in attempting to sustain and develop such community-based activities. The main difficulties that have emerged relate to the following:

- *Uncertainty of Financial Support.* Projects like the mobile phone network have been organised for several years but they continue on a very insecure financial footing. Although all relevant statutory agencies support and value the project, no one has been willing to take overall responsibility for this activity. Longer-term planning and development of these schemes has proved difficult because decisions about funding availability are too often 'last minute'.

- *Resourcing Community-based Activity.* The mobile phone networks and local summer schemes rely on local goodwill and volunteers to function, which places considerable demands on community groups and their members. Many groups feel forced to become involved in youth work or conflict management activity because of a lack of support or resources from specialist agencies, rather than because they have chosen this role. Again, such activity is often taken for granted, and little thought is given to building the sustainability of such bodies through focused support and training.

- *Sustaining Community Development Work.* Much of the capacity within local communities has come about because of support from the wider community development sector. However, much of this work is also maintained on a fragile basis. Few, if any, groups have any secure medium-term or long-term core funding and most projects are only guaranteed funding for two or at best three years at a time. Therefore, most such bodies are unable to plan and implement a longer-term strategy to respond to the type of problems under discussion. Furthermore, many groups are forced to respond to priorities set at national level rather than respond to priorities determined by the problems they confront at a local level.

- *Building Effective Partnerships.* Although partnerships are held up as the way forward and as the way to develop more effective and efficient responses to social problems, experience in North Belfast suggests that they are most effective at reacting to a crisis or activities such as information sharing. Partnerships have proved less effective in developing strategies and programmes that require a commitment of time and resources over a longer period of time. This may be a general problem related to competition and self-interest among agencies, but may also be a problem related to the blurred responsibilities between the local and Westminster administrations for matters which fall within the broader policing, security and crime portfolios. In that case, it may well prove more difficult to develop effective long-term partnerships.

● *Community-Statutory Relationships.* These relationships have been plagued by similar difficulties to those raised in the previous paragraph, but they are compounded by such matters as differentials in power, responsibility, resources and permanence, as well as issues of trust, reliability and openness (which in turn are linked to the issues in Point 3). Building and sustaining institutional (rather than personalised) relationships between the statutory and community sectors remains an important issue to address. Probably the most important and most sensitive of these relationships – the one between the community and the police – has proved to be the most difficult to create and sustain.

● *Lack of an Overall Strategy.* Perhaps the main problem, and the one issue that links all of the above points, is that there is no overarching strategy, either to deal with specific problems such as the persistent and recurrent sectarian interface violence or to attempt to address the uniquely complex problems of North Belfast. Each of the approaches discussed above has been developed, organised and funded independently of the others. There is no formal or structured link between the planning of the various summer schemes or of the phone networks, no forum for developing or extending the range of activities and no overall evaluation of whether such projects are the most appropriate or effective responses to the ongoing threat of summer disorder. Part of the reason for the lack of an overall strategy is the tenuous or non-existent relationships between many of the key local players, but in many ways these problems transcend the local experience and thus point to the need for a broader body to take a lead in developing an effective and sustained response to the annual disruption and the ongoing problems of disorder in violence areas and sectarian violence more generally.

To develop an effective strategy would require the involvement of as wide a range of stakeholders and interested parties as possible and would include: political and community representatives; statutory agencies; voluntary bodies; commercial and business interests; representatives of schools and youth groups; representatives of minority ethnic communities; and religious communities. Furthermore, any such overall strategy should not be limited to attempting to reduce outbreaks of violence and disorder but should also seek to address the root causes of the ongoing hostility and antipathy between the two major communities in North Belfast, and this would mean acknowledging problems such as geographical fragmentation, claims to territory, lack of appropriate housing, economic development and social resources, as well as the almost complete lack of respect for each other's customs, traditions, cultures and aspirations.

Creating some form of forum or commission which had both the authority and the capacity to address the specific problems of North Belfast and the ability to design and begin to implement an appropriate, realistic development programme, would require significant funding, resources and political support from the highest levels. However, a continued failure to acknowledge, and to begin to address, the problems of North Belfast will incur considerable costs in terms of policing and security, damage to housing and property, resistance to economic development, and persistent and recurring cycles of public violence and disorder.

EPILOGUE

Shortly after this paper was completed and in response to persistent ongoing disorder on the interface between Ardoyne and Glenbryn (the Holy Cross dispute) and elsewhere the government appointed the Reverend John Dunlop to chair the North Belfast Community Action Project. The project team was asked to review the situation in North Belfast and to recommend 'short, medium and long-term actions to address social and community issues in North Belfast'.

The report was published in May 2002. It recommended that the government:

- set up a dedicated unit to develop a long-term strategy for North Belfast;
- create a community capacity building programme with adequate staff and resources;
- make available an extra £3 million per year for five years for a community capacity building programme;
- develop a major site for mix-usage as symbol of hope and economic regeneration;
- develop a Centre for Citizenship;
- support the development of two Health and Well-being centres;
- make additional resources available to schools to boost links between school and home;
- develop the local capacity for e-technology to facilitate inter and intra community communication via the internet;
- establish a Music Action Zone and a School of Percussion as a means of cross community contact.

At the time of writing (August 2002) the government was still considering its response to these proposals.

12. THE ROLE OF WOMEN IN COMMUNITY DEVELOPMENT IN NORTHERN IRELAND

Valerie Morgan

INTRODUCTION

Any brief attempt to examine and evaluate the ways in which women have contributed to community development in Northern Ireland over the last 30 years faces formidable problems. On the one hand, the underlying questions, relating both to the position of women in Irish society and to the definition of community development, are vast and largely unresolved and, on the other hand, the range and impact of women's actual work 'on the ground' is extremely difficult to summarise and quantify.

Whilst this chapter does not seek to provide a historical analysis, women's recent contributions to community development cannot be understood without some reference to the factors which have shaped women's current roles in Northern Irish society. In spite of the enormous changes which have affected the whole island in recent years, Ireland was, and in some respects remains, a very conservative society. Whilst this has affected many facets of the religious, social, cultural and economic life of all citizens it has also impacted specifically on women in a number of ways (Morgan and Fraser, 1995). The strong religious basis of society, in both the Catholic and Protestant traditions, has cast women as simultaneously 'saint' and 'sinner' (Condren, 1989). Whilst women were cast as revered mothers, basic supporters of the Christian family and its values, and first educators of their children, they were at the same time suspect as a potential source of weakness and sexual temptation, and hence disruption of the very values they were entrusted to uphold. Within the private sphere of the home and the family, their influence could be channelled into positive and productive areas but the public world of politics, commerce and employment was an unsuitable, even dangerous, stage for women (MacCurtain, 1985). Such models, which became particularly entrenched during the nineteenth century, informed the campaigns mounted against higher education for women, access to the professions and female suffrage (Ward, 1993; Luddy, 1997). They also continued to influence thinking throughout most of the twentieth century and indeed were reinforced by elements in the ideology and imagery of late nineteenth-century and twentieth-century Nationalism, both Republican and Unionist. Additionally, particularly in Northern Ireland, the emphasis on the continuing contest over the constitutional status of the province has meant that there has been pressure to postpone consideration of other social issues, including many affecting the status of women, until 'the national question' is finally resolved (Gardiner, 1993; Mahon and Morgan, 1999).

However, whilst women's practical needs and concerns may have been relegated to the sidelines, female imagery has been used extensively to project the political messages of all sides. Thus, for example, Ireland itself has frequently been portrayed in music, literature and visual media, designed to promote the ideology of nationalism, as poor old woman, suffering mother or helpless maiden. When an active role has been available in such representations it has often been the mythical Celtic warrior maiden rather than the contemporary decision-maker. Thus women have been both idealised and marginalised in public and political life across the communities (Edge, 1998). Of course the reality 'on the ground' has usually borne little relation to the rhetoric. Throughout the nineteenth and twentieth centuries women played a vital role in the economy, working on family farms, in small businesses and in factories and later in schools, hospital and offices. They have also been active in many aspects of cultural activity and in a range of statutory and voluntary organisations, especially in such areas as church-related groups and charities. Perhaps, in the light of this background, their central role in community development, since the 1970s, should not come as a major surprise

THE EMERGENCE OF COMMUNITY DEVELOPMENT

Maybe indeed, it is the emergence of a community development sector, rather than the role women have played in its growth, which should be seen as the more unexpected change in Northern Ireland during the late twentieth century. The expansion of activities and organisations which can be categorised under the 'community development' and 'community relations' labels, and indeed the connections between the two designations, is complex and beyond the scope of this discussion (Knox, 1994; Knox, 1995). One significant factor was almost certainly the political frustration which characterised the 1970s. Levels of violence were high with almost daily bombings and shootings but neither the efforts of established political parties and individual politicians nor the activities of the security forces and the paramilitaries seemed to offer much hope of either a negotiated solution or a clear military victory (Rowthorne and Wayne, 1988; Fay et al., 1999; Smyth, 2000). A number of political initiatives were tried but each collapsed, usually amid recriminations from one or both sides. Indeed such experiences often served only to deepen suspicion and distrust. Similarly, attempts to defeat paramilitary activity by force had limited success and it was clear that increased army and police activity and the deployment of tactics such as 'undercover operations' in themselves generated tensions but did not eradicate violence. For many 'ordinary people' the response was despair, but others began to look for areas 'on the edges', outside the formal political arena, where there might be a possibility of fostering better understanding and positive change, even in limited areas. Inter-church groups and the Integrated school movement can be interpreted as manifestations of this desire to 'do something', a desire which can be seen as basic to community development and community relations work (Morrow et al., 1994).

Since much of this initial community development activity was focused on issues which affected families and local communities, such as the education of children, leisure provision for young people and the quality of the local environment, it clearly had direct relevance to women's lives and thus was likely to attract their interest and participation. From the outset, women were active in organisations such as ACT (All Children Together) which campaigned for Integrated schooling and PACE (Protestant and Catholic Encounter) which sought to improve inter-denominational understanding at a local level. Indeed, they often took leadership roles in such groups, gaining valuable experience and increasing the public profile of women. Whilst some women worked alongside men in organisations focused on particular issues, others were attracted to forming groups which would aim specifically to help women cope with the effects of violence and disruption, for example Women for Peace, or groups based in their own local neighbourhood and targeting the particular social and economic needs of people in the area. What these diverse initiatives had in common was that they developed initially outside official structures and almost always without public finance. Thus another of the characteristics they shared was that in the early stages they were either disregarded by official bodies and government departments or, in some cases, were the object of suspicion and even opposition. As a result, many of the initiatives began on a small scale and were initially viewed as low status, marginal or unlikely to make much impact. Many established male public figures saw little benefit in participating, or even having their name associated, with such activities and this left many openings for enthusiastic and energetic, but unknown, women (Morgan and Fraser, 1994).

THE RANGE OF WOMEN'S INVOLVEMENT

Whilst such developments were significant, any general analysis or attempted explanation of women's involvement in the growth of the community development sector is likely to give an oversimplified, even misleading, picture. For example, in relation to the scale of participation, whilst women did become prominent in many aspects of community activity, the overall number of activists was, and remains, relatively small. For a variety of reasons the great majority of women in Northern Ireland do not belong to community organisations. Some of these women have principled objections to the whole concept of community development and especially to its perceived association with community relations. For example, some see it as undermining the possibility of revolutionary change by attempting to make living within the current constitutional framework acceptable. Another critical perspective characterises community development as a device to promote acceptance of the community relations agenda, which will in turn be used to undermine the distinct culture and identity of different sections of the community. The main factors inhibiting participation are, however, more pragmatic. For a large number of women, across all sections of the community, there are practical constraints of time, resources, family circumstances and geographical location which limit their involvement in any organisations outside those directly linked to family and employment commitments (Morgan and Fraser, 1994).

It has also been argued that there have been differences in the extent of involvement of women from the Unionist/Protestant and Catholic/Nationalist communities. A number of Unionist women were active during the late nineteenth and early twentieth centuries, in organisations which opposed Home Rule, and later in groups affiliated to the Unionist Party. More radical Protestant women were also active in the suffrage movement and took part in the militant campaign which involved attacks on leading political figures and even arson (Urquhart, 2000). In addition, many Protestant women gained organisational and administrative experience in church-based groups such as the PWA (Presbyterian Women's Association) and the Mothers' Union (the main Church of Ireland women's organisation). But it has been argued that their traditional identification with the Northern Ireland state and concern for its preservation made them, initially at least, less attracted to activities which were based outside official structures and indeed often sought to criticise or change them. On the other hand, whilst women in the Nationalist/Catholic communities had less history of formal involvement, particularly with organisations associated with the Northern Ireland State, the tradition of protest within their communities has been seen as providing a more receptive base for the growth of community groups. Such differences may have been reinforced by the perceived link between women's involvement in community development and feminism, an ideology which has been regarded with particular suspicion by many Unionists. Whilst these differences have diminished over time, a recent study of the women's sector across Northern Ireland has suggested that there are fewer women's centres, groups and organisations in areas with a large Protestant/Unionist majority, such as parts of North Antrim and North Down (NIVT, 2001).

Another significant distinction, which has to be considered, is the distinction between organisations which are anxious to confine the remit of their activities to 'community development' and those which are willing to accept the additional designation of being involved in 'community relations' work (Hinds, 1999). This is a long-standing and complex area of debate, which concerns groups and individuals across the voluntary sector. Many community-based women's organisations and groups see their work as being focused on the practical needs of women and families in relation to such questions as education, employment, health care and access to welfare benefits. There may or may not be a cross-community dimension to their work but where it does exist it is secondary or even incidental to the central concern. Some groups emphasise that 'community relations' is not part of their overt agenda since they believe that to be labelled in this way might hinder their work and their acceptability in their own local area. On the other hand, some groups include an intention to address elements of the community divisions in Northern Ireland in their remit and so are comfortable to have the term 'community relations' applied to their activities. This question has become more problematic with the growth of funding opportunities for voluntary groups. Many women's organisations carry out activities in areas such as education, training and the stimulation of employment opportunities, which they define as community development work, but these would qualify for funding under community relations programmes if a cross-community element was emphasised in the make-up of the initiating team or the recipient group. This means that, quite often, there is pressure to include reference to a community relations dimension in the design and implementation of projects in order to fit the grant giving criteria of a designated programme and thus to take advantage of an opportunity to secure vital funding (NIVT, 2001).

The map of women's activities in community development is further complicated by variations across the range of organisations, groups and activities which can be linked to social class, geographical location and demographic profile. For example, women in working-class urban areas have been particularly active in setting up multi-purpose Women's Centres which provide education courses, child care facilities, advice on legal, health and benefit issues and a focal 'drop-in' point for the local area. In some rural areas a different structure has been seen as appropriate: for instance, a greater emphasis on networking, the provision of easily accessible information and mechanisms which allow small groups, operating across a wide geographical area, to keep in touch and share facilities. In addition, there has been specialisation in activities and target groups, with some organisations focusing on the needs of specific groups such as older women or young mothers. These variations in structure mean that the umbrella terms 'women's groups' or 'women's organisations' now cover a very wide range and the whole field of women and community development has become a complex mesh of interconnecting groups and activities which is extremely difficult to map accurately (NIVT, 2001).

CHANGES OVER TIME

If the existing pattern of groups, organisations and activities is characterised by variety and even, in some areas, by controversy, as, for example, over terminology and descriptors, the history of its development over the last quarter of a century shares similar features. Whilst 'traditional' women's organisations linked to the various religious denominations, to some political groups and to charitable fundraising have existed from the late nineteenth century, and changes in educational provision and employment opportunities began to affect women's roles and expectations from the early 1960s, the antecedents of much modern community-based activity were heavily influenced by the Troubles. Women from a variety of sections of the community played significant roles as grass-roots activists, in support of their own communities, during the early years of violence: for example, the Catholic/Nationalist women who brought food supplies into the Falls area of Belfast in protest at the impact of the 1971 curfew; the Nationalist women who banged dustbin lids to warn neighbours of army house searches; and the Unionist women who took part in direct action during the Ulster Workers' Strike and the protests over the signing of the Anglo–Irish Agreement. At the same time, other women were joining the pioneer peace groups and inter-church organisations. It could be argued, however, that the campaign of the Peace People during 1976 and 1978 had a particularly significant impact on the future direction of women's involvement (Fraser and Morgan, 2000). The dramatic rise of the Peace People, the hopes their demonstrations inspired and the subsequent acrimonious collapse of the mass movement shattered many ideals and images. The whole experience suggested simultaneously that women could have a significant role in addressing Northern Ireland's problems and pointed up the obstacles they faced in effecting actual change. Women were able to mobilise mass demonstrations and gain worldwide media attention but they found it very difficult to translate emotional commitment and sympathy into a direct input into the formulation of policies which would influence the established power structures and decision-making processes in Northern Ireland.

The lessons learnt provided one of the factors which marked the 1980s as a transitional decade, during which women increasingly rejected traditional labels and images and shifted their primary concerns away from attempting to promote general solutions to Northern Ireland's problems (Rooney, 1995; Rooney and Woods, 1995). The emphasis moved to more attainable and practical local level initiatives and to the adoption of lower-key, more specifically focused objectives. These changes had a number of effects. The increasing number of locally based schemes and projects meant that many more women became directly involved in the organisation and management of community development work. In this way, a considerable number of women gained leadership experience and skills in fundraising, financial management of projects, team leadership and negotiation with disparate interest groups. Whilst the initial scale of many of the initiatives was small, during the 1990s they began to cover an increasing range of issues and areas. A survey carried out for the Northern Ireland Voluntary Trust indicated that in 1999–00 there were almost 1,500 women's organisations in Northern Ireland (NIVT, 2001). Over two-thirds of these organisations could be described as 'traditional' organisations, for example, branches of church-based women's organisations. These organisations may have an interest in community development work and links with other groups, which are more clearly in the development sector, but their prime focus is in areas such as spiritual development and support of missionary work. The remaining groups, about 425 in number, could be described as 'activist' community development groups. Amongst these, the range in size and scale of activities is enormous. There are a small number of major regional organisations, such as the 'Women's Resource and Development Agency' (WRDA), which although based in Belfast, operate across Northern Ireland providing education and training for women and supporting the development of an infrastructure for women's groups, and a much larger number of local groups focusing on specific needs in particular areas or neighbourhoods. An attempt to classify organisations (NIVT, 2001) suggests that over 90% (about 383) of the women's community development organisations are locally based groups or projects. In addition, at the time of the survey, there were 14 Women's Centres (single-site facilities usually in urban areas which provide a range of education and support services) and 26 organisations which provide a network service either for a particular part of Northern Ireland or, in the case of the four largest groups, a service for the whole province.

THE GROWING SCALE OF WOMEN'S INVOLVEMENT

The actual number of women involved in community development is difficult to estimate since a distinction has to be made between the number of women who actively participate in the running of organisations, and the provision of services, and those who make use of the range of facilities they provide. A figure of about 6,000 for 'activist' membership has been suggested, but this is only an estimate (NIVT, 2001). Attempting to calculate the number of people using the services is even more difficult since full records of all types of usage are not always kept. Thus, although details of those attending specific courses may be available, there may be no records of those seeking help or advice on a 'one-off' basis or of people using 'drop-in' facilities. Some of the larger Women's Centres do have detailed records of usage. Figures for Ballybeen Women's Centre, which had a paid staff of about 17 full-time and part-time employees and a management committee of eight volunteers in 1999, indicate that, during that year, about 400 people used the Centre each week. Clearly, smaller groups would not have this level of activity but the implication is that levels of usage are probably between ten and 20 times higher than the figures for 'activists'. The majority of the 6,000 active members provide their inputs on a voluntary basis, often part-time, but almost 400 people are employed, either full time or part time. Further examination of the membership indicates that the age distribution is quite wide, although there is a concentration in the 25–40-year age range, and that there is strong representation of minority groups and the economically and socially deprived. Similarly, the geographical distribution of groups and their activities indicates a concentration in deprived areas – 68% are located in wards which are defined as deprived on the basis of the Robson Index (Robson et al., 1994). The geographical pattern, which indicates concentrations in parts of Belfast and in the west of Northern Ireland, is probably closely linked to these same social and economic factors, although the relative lack of organisations in parts of counties Antrim and Down may also be related to the suggestion, already noted, that there has been a less developed tradition of community activity in majority Unionist/Protestant areas.

As indicated, there are considerable difficulties in examining the number and distribution of groups but attempts to quantify and evaluate the ways in which they seek to contribute to community development face even more complex problems. The underlying ethos of many organisations in the women's sector is the provision of 'support' for women, thus in many cases groups see an overarching rationale in terms of supporting or 'empowering' local women in whatever ways they themselves see as necessary. This support may include providing assistance to develop skills, seek rights or influence decision-making processes. More detailed examination, however, suggests that there are three main routes through which they seek to achieve their objectives. These are the provision of information and advice, training and educational work, and advocacy or campaigning on issues which affect women, their families and the areas in which they live.

The scope of the work which has been carried out within and across these areas is enormous. It has included both high-profile campaigns which have had a major impact on policy development, as in the area of domestic violence (McWilliams and McKernan, 1993), as well as local schemes targeted very specifically at a particular need. The provision of information and advice was one of the first fields in which community groups became active and the range of services provided is now extensive and varied. Many Women's Centres provide drop-in facilities where women can come to seek advice on health issues, legal problems, benefit queries or personal issues in an informal and impartial atmosphere (Quinn, 1998). In rural areas a number of networks, such as the Fermanagh Women's Network, provide similar services through telephone helplines and newsletters. From the outset, education has been regarded as a priority and indeed the Women's Education Project was one of the pioneer groups which provided the basis for the formation, in 1983, of the Women's Resource and Development Agency. The key principle of the educational activity is the provision of access to an appropriate level and type of educational opportunity for each individual within a supportive context. The range of courses is now enormous and runs from basic skills, often provided in-house by Women's Centres, to accredited vocational and academic qualifications delivered through further education colleges. Many women whose experiences of formal education were negative, and who felt anxiety about returning to study or training, have found that the initial courses provided by women's groups have allowed them to develop confidence and establish a route back into a wide range of educational opportunities (Tracey, 1998). Of particular benefit has been the provision of child care facilities running alongside courses and the establishment of mobile or 'outreach' delivery systems in rural areas. The third major element, advocacy and campaigning, developed in relation to questions such as domestic violence and women's health concerns but now embraces a much wider field. Organisations such as the Women's Resource and Development Agency and the Northern Ireland Voluntary Trust have played an important role in bringing women's groups and organisations together to examine the impact of government initiatives in relation to policy and funding issues. Thus, amongst areas of current concern, are the possible effects of reforms in the Common Agricultural Policy on farm women and how women's organisations can contribute to the development of the Equality Agenda arising from the Good Friday Agreement.

ASSESSING THE IMPACT OF WOMEN'S INVOLVEMENT

Assessment of the impact of their inputs is as important as discussion of the actual ways in which women have contributed to community development. Again, generalisation and attempts at categorisation pose problems; for example, there is often difficulty in separating out elements of the impact of women's activities since they have been active in so many areas and each element is often multi-faceted in its effect. One way of attempting to assess impact is in terms of the effects at individual, community and policy levels. For individual women, the major impacts have probably been the result of education and training initiatives. As indicated above, the range of courses, including free standing short courses, in-house courses leading to accredited qualifications and courses offered in conjunction with other institutions, has provided opportunities for women from many different backgrounds to gain skills and confidence. The aspects which support women who find formal educational structures off-putting, those in isolated rural areas and those who need support with child care, have been particularly significant. These have meant that women's education projects have the capacity to involve groups who may be difficult to reach through other education initiatives; for example, young mothers in isolated areas and older women in deprived urban housing estates. At a practical level these initiatives have meant that a considerable number of women from disadvantaged groups have been able to re-enter the labour market or gain better-paid and more interesting work.

At the community level, women have played a major role in leading and developing voluntary activity. Individual women and the organisations through which they work have frequently been crucial in initiating wider community activity. For example, the Upper Andersonstown Women's Network was a key element in the formation of a local community development forum, whilst the Magherafelt Women's Group initiated a community business aimed at stimulating and providing support for other local enterprises (NIVT, 2001). As already indicated, much of women's community development activity is concentrated in areas of social and economic deprivation. One result of this activity has been that they have often been able to facilitate the inclusion of groups who would otherwise have been largely alienated from community development work. This capacity to create, develop and sustain links across a range of sectors and to target groups who are usually resistant to community engagement is another important strength of women's community development activities. Although, as already noted, there has often been a reluctance to embrace labels such as 'cross-community work', 'community relations' or 'reconciliation', women have made significant contributions to addressing community divisions. Frequently these have been low key and have deliberately sought to avoid publicity or grandiose claims, whilst at the same time placing emphasis on addressing relevant, practical issues. For example, a link between two women's organisations in Newtownabbey, representing different sections of the community, has sought to promote practical work improving the physical environment and addressing local concerns about crime and drugs in deprived housing areas.

Given the size of the women's sector and the range of its activities, it is hardly surprising that women's organisations have in recent years begun to have an impact on policy development and implementation. In some cases specific outcomes can be identified, as in the case of the work of women's organisations in campaigning for the recognition of the scale and seriousness of the problem of domestic violence. In this area, women's organisations have had a major impact in raising awareness, on the subsequent development of policy, and in providing services to meet the needs of victims. In other cases, the work of women's groups has provided models of 'good practice' which have influenced development in state institutions, for example, in the provision of access courses for women seeking to move back into education. As a result, women's organisations now play a considerable part in formulating, refining, supporting and implementing a number of policies in the economic, community and health fields, such as New Deal and the Equality Agenda (DHSS, 1998).

The growth in the scale and range of women's involvement in community development has, in itself, had a number of repercussions, which have begun to affect the structure and operation of the sector. Initially, most women's groups carried out their activities outside formal structures, worked on very small budgets and had limited links with funding bodies or government departments. Indeed, their independence, and the absence of formal hierarchical patterns within the groups, were seen by many activists as amongst the major strengths of women's community development work. These strengths meant the organisations could operate in areas and on issues where statutory bodies might lack credibility and that they had more flexibility to adopt radical and innovative approaches (Rooney, 1992). However, the increasing scale and cost of the projects being undertaken and the contributions in areas with legal and statutory implications, such as domestic violence, has meant that interactions with funding agencies, government departments and statutory bodies have grown significantly. One measure of this level of interaction is provided by an analysis of the income of women's community organisations. Whilst many women's groups still operate on very small budgets and rely heavily on voluntary inputs, by the end of the twentieth century the total income of women's community groups in Northern Ireland has been estimated at around £9.5m per annum (NIVT, 2001). For the majority (63%), their annual budget was below £10,000, but 23% had budgets between £10,000 and £50,000 and 14% operated with incomes over £50,000 per annum. Such figures imply an ongoing need to secure funding which means negotiating with grant-giving bodies, which, in turn, are likely to expect some influence on the activities they support.

The range of sources from which women's community organisations have sought support over recent years has been very wide and includes major national and international charitable foundations, the National Lottery Charities Board, government agencies and departments, District Councils, Education and Library Boards, and Peace and Reconciliation Funds. The largest inputs have been from bodies distributing EU Peace and Reconciliation Funds and from government departments and agencies, although it is not always easy to separate out the two since some government bodies act as intermediaries for European funding. Lottery funding has been another major source of financial support since the mid-1990s. Thus, in 1998 to 1999, funds directly traceable to EU sources accounted for 35% of the sector's income, with a further 20% coming through government departments and 18% from Lottery funding. This pattern is now causing some concern for a number of reasons. For example, Peace and Reconciliation funding is time limited and its availability is unlikely to be extended beyond the current programme. The Lotteries Charities' Board is reviewing its grant-awarding criteria along lines which could result in a reduction in their support for the types of work carried out by women's organisations. In addition, the need to produce grant applications which meet the guidelines of the various awarding bodies can raise concerns for groups themselves. Women's organisations feel that they sometimes have to adopt objectives and procedures which may not fit entirely comfortably with their organisation's ethos or organisational structure in order to have a chance of obtaining the financial support needed to retain employees or keep support services going.

A further shift has been in terms of what might be labelled 'professionalism'. Initially, the women's sector depended almost entirely on voluntary inputs. Groups were founded by enthusiastic local activists, and their programmes were organised and run by part-time volunteers who also handled administration and planning. The enormous expansion in the scale and range of work being carried out and the increasing availability of financial support has meant that the level of administration, management, financial planning and accounting needed, has also grown rapidly. This in turn has led to a significant increase in the number of paid staff. Overall, it is estimated that, by 1999, between 350 and 400 people were employed, on either a full-time or part-time basis, in organisations and projects linked to women's community activities. Women's Centres and groups, such as local branches of Women's Aid, are particularly likely to have paid staff, with over 150 people working in Women's Centres across Northern Ireland. Whilst this development has increased the level of support women can provide for their communities, for example, many Women's Centres are now able to provide high-quality child care to facilitate those attending courses or meetings, it also raises concerns about sustainability. Without ongoing external financial support the great majority of these posts cannot be sustained and many organisations are under constant pressure to balance their budgets and secure further, usually short-term, allocations of funding. (Voluntary Activity Unit, 1999; Blueprint Development Consultancy, 2000)

CONCLUSION – CHALLENGES FOR THE FUTURE

The difficulties being experienced in relation to sustainability highlight one of a number of challenges now facing women involved in community development. Women's involvement in community development has had an impact on Northern Irish society at, at least, three inter-related levels. At the social level they have contributed to social inclusion for women by combating isolation, increasing self-esteem, providing education and training, and increasing employability. This activity has also made a direct contribution to economic development since much of the work of women's groups and organisations has been carried out in areas of economic deprivation and has targeted individuals on low income. In addition, women have had a major impact on the development of the voluntary sector as a whole. Many aspects of their work have made important contributions to thinking about policy issues and have provided models of good practice. Clearly, however, there is no basis for complacency. The short-term nature of much of the sector's funding and uncertainty over future income levels are key concerns. The process of addressing them may necessitate a reassessment of priorities in terms of activities and services. There may also be a need to re-examine relationships with government departments and agencies. A number of the services, which women's community-based groups provide, complement or are directly linked with the work of statutory bodies, for example, in relation to women's health issues. Whether, or how, such relationships can be formalised and indeed the whole question of 'mainstreaming', is currently a major area of debate (European Network, 2000). Closer contacts could increase the influence of women's community organisations and also secure longer-term funding arrangements. On the other hand it might entail changes in procedures and forms of accountability, which some women would view as counter to the ethos of women's community work.

A wider issue is the relationship between the experience and skill which women have gained in community development, and their role in the future economic, social and political development of Northern Ireland. In spite of the widespread recognition of their contribution, women remain seriously under-represented in the political process. The formation of the Northern Ireland Women's Coalition in 1996 represented a major development since many of those actively involved in the Coalition had a background in community development. On the other hand, the need to establish what has inevitably been perceived as a 'women's party' underlined the problems women had had making an impact in most of the established political parties. Subsequent change has been limited. The 108-member Legislative Assembly has 14 women representatives and it was only after the June 2001 United Kingdom general election that there were women from Northern Ireland in the Westminster parliament, after a gap of over 30 years! Indeed, amidst all the debate over the peace process and the setting up of workable devolved institutions, it has been increasingly difficult for women to ensure that the issues on which they have campaigned are not lost sight of. Improvements at many levels in communities across Northern Ireland may owe much to initiatives in which women have taken the lead. The skills they have developed may be being utilised in both the voluntary and statutory sectors, but this does not mean that they will automatically be accepted as equal partners in planning for the future.

13. POLITICAL LEADERSHIP: PROTAGONISTS AND PRAGMATISTS IN NORTHERN IRELAND[1]

Cathy Gormley-Heenan and Gillian Robinson

INTRODUCTION: THE IMPORTANCE OF POLITICAL LEADERSHIP

While the main interest of this chapter is *political* leadership, one must be fully cognisant of the important role that other leaders play in divided societies and societies in transition, whether in cultural, religious, community or business settings, not least because 'they can have a moderating effect on unwise political leaders' (Carnegie Commission on Preventing Deadly Conflict [CCPDC], 1998: vii). However, political leadership is especially important for a number of reasons. Many political and peace processes are essentially elite-driven, with a relatively small number of people responsible for making final decisions and implementing policy (Darby and MacGinty, 2000). Additionally, many divided and violent societies are prone to political leaders who are willing to manipulate delicate situations, who do not necessarily behave in an altruistic fashion and who actively canvass against a peaceful settlement of conflict if such a settlement collides with their own interests. Furthermore, political leadership is one variable upon which many other variables are dependent in the transformation of a conflict. Finally, political leadership continues to be an under-researched subject area. It is only through an examination of the 'political leadership' in conflict and conflict resolution that answers may be provided to questions such as, how has 'political leadership' played its part in perpetuating the conflict and how has 'political leadership' played its part in resolving the conflict in Northern Ireland?

THE THEORY

Most literature on conflict, conflict resolution/management/regulation and peace processes has suffered from a tendency to be buried in a mass of general comparisons. Consequently, the inference can be made that it is necessary to isolate specific aspects of the process for a more comprehensive analysis. The specific aspect of the role of leadership before, during and after negotiations is one topic due for more careful analysis. While it is true that many academics do acknowledge the role that the leaders play in the process, few devote time to explaining why this is the case, and how this role has the potential to effect outcomes in real terms.

Of those who have examined the role of political leadership in broader discussions of conflict and conflict resolution/management/regulation, a number of points are elucidated. In terms of conflict regulation it is argued that any political leadership risk-taking can seriously undermine and weaken the position of a leader should such an initiative fail. This explains the common reluctance to take risks for peace in divided societies (Nordlinger, 1972). Nonetheless, the transformation of conflict is directly relational to the transformation of the actors involved. Such transformations may take the form of 'a change of character, a change of leadership, a change in the constituency of the leader or adoption of its goals, values, or beliefs' (Miall et al., 1999: 158). Societies with strong leadership on both sides are more likely to make agreement which will be sustainable (Rothstein, 1999). Societies with weak leadership on both sides are more likely to continue to maintain the status quo within their society since their own political positions continue to be assured (Rothstein, 1999). Societies with strong leadership on one side and weak leadership on the other will probably need intervention by strong outside influences, since weak leadership will not want to negotiate from a position of weakness, and strong leadership may be unwilling to make concessions (Rothstein, 1999). Internal and external elite consensus is necessary to prevent issues from becoming political footballs (Rothstein, 1999). The primary function of leaders has been to deliver to their own constituents and assisting opponents has been only secondary to this (Darby and MacGinty, 2000).

The promotion of a two-dimensional construct of leadership (strong/weak and positive/negative) is evident in much of the literature. This limited view fails, however, to address the multiplicity of leadership constructs in most conflicts. It also neglects the relationship of strong versus weak leaders on the same side of religious/ethnic divides and does not question whether changes in the political dynamic are consequential upon this. Using an illustrative example, one wonders what changes could there have been in the political dynamics of Northern Ireland during the peace process if Adams (Sinn Fein) was considered strong while Hume (SDLP) was simultaneously considered weak? If Trimble (UUP) was considered weak and Paisley (DUP) simultaneously strong? The dynamic of two strong leaders may have still existed, but not among leaders that would ordinarily feel comfortable conducting business with each other. Looking further afield, where does this dichotomy of leadership fit with the multi-dimensional nature of the South African peace negotiations, and the internal wrangling between the Inkatha Freedom Party and others?

Blondel (1987) suggests that this notion of dichotomous distinctions is something which the field of social science has suffered from for a long time and suggests that, 'what has to be done therefore is to turn away from the very idea of a dichotomy and, by recognising that the reality is vastly more complex, slowly to elaborate models, and develop methodological techniques that will make it possible to grasp more realistically the contours of leadership' (Blandel, 1987: 24). While applauding such scholars for encouraging this departure, it should be acknowledged that the continuum of methodological problems faced by leadership researchers may make the reality of grasping the contours of leadership in a divided society much more difficult. Indeed, how does one study political leadership in a divided society when most of the 'action' takes place behind closed doors? While political scientists may want to move beyond the traditional narrative, they are ill equipped for this task given the difficulties of the environment.

THE RESEARCH

The research upon which this chapter draws sets out to explore and understand the transformation of political leadership in societies in transition (Gormley-Heenan, 2001). It focused on the *development* of political leadership in societies that are moving away from a history of violence towards that of politics, and sought to analyse their adaptation to power, together with problems and perspectives for the future. Through the research, the project aimed to highlight the role that political leaders play, and the ever-changing nature of that role, as countries move from situations of intense violence to confront the pains of reconciliation and confidence building.

THE METHODS

Using political autobiography as a main research method, a total of 25 interviews were conducted with senior political leaders in Northern Ireland, South Africa, Israel, and the Palestinian Territories and these formed the primary empirical data of the study. They took place from January 2000 to December 2000. Field research was conducted in Israel/Palestine in July 2000 for a period of two weeks, and in South Africa in September 2000 for ten days.

It was agreed that all interviews given would be on a non-attributable basis to allow those interviewed to speak more freely about sensitive issues. The interviews were open-ended as opposed to structured as this allowed for the interviewees to express their ideas, thoughts, and memories in their own words rather than in someone else's (Robson, 1993). The interviews were supplemented by many other informal discussions with those involved in the political process, consistent monitoring of the media over the time period, and library-based research. The

Table 13.1: Participating Parties in Research

NORTHERN IRELAND	SOUTH AFRICA	ISRAEL/PALESTINE[2]
Ulster Unionist Party (UUP)	African National Congress (ANC)	Labour
Social Democratic and Labour Party (SDLP)	Inkatha Freedom Party (IFP)	Meretz
Democratic Unionist Party (DUP)	New National Party (NNP)	Fateh
Sinn Fein (SF)	Democratic Party (DP)	Independents
Alliance Party (ALL)	United Democratic Party (UDM)	
Progressive Unionist Party (PUP)	Freedom Front (FF)	
Women's Coalition (NIWC)		

interview material was thematically analysed and is defined in the following section. An opening conference was held in April 2000, in Parliament Buildings at Stormont in Northern Ireland, to highlight some of the issues on which the research would focus. It was attended by more than 60 delegates, which included representatives of all the major political parties within the Assembly, and was jointly sponsored by the First Minister and Deputy First Minister, David Trimble MP, MLA, and Seamus Mallon, MP, MLA. Guest speakers from Israel and South Africa provided an international perspective. A second conference was held in November 2000 in conjunction with the United Nations University's International Leadership Academy in Amman, Jordan, to explore the issues further at international level. It was attended by four young political leaders from Northern Ireland, representing the UUP, SDLP, SF and PUP. Young political leaders from South Africa, Indonesia/East Timor and Jordan were also in attendance. Political tensions in Israel/Palestine at the time prevented the Israeli and Palestinian participants from attending.

The examination of political leadership in a comparative context was seen as vital since the lessons learned from other places could provide insights into the situation in Northern Ireland, and the lessons learned from Northern Ireland could strike a chord elsewhere, although not all would agree with this premise. McGarry (1998: 854) argues that, in the case of South Africa and Northern Ireland, 'comparisons insufficiently acknowledge the many differences between the two case studies'. While acknowledging the significant contextual differences between the conflicts, peace processes and agreements in Northern Ireland, South Africa, Israel/Palestine and other case studies, recent research has demonstrated that many of the political changes and challenges facing the political leadership are indeed comparable (Gormley-Heenan, 2001). Full research results from this particular study are too extensive for the purposes of this chapter, but the findings from the Northern Ireland case study provide a valuable insight into the Northern Ireland conflict from a leadership perspective.

THE FINDINGS: NORTHERN IRELAND'S LEADERSHIP TRANSITION

An examination of the transition of political leadership from 1921 until the post-Agreement period underscores the argument that leadership was indeed a central component of the conflict, the peace process and the eventual settlement in Northern Ireland. Defining the causes of this conflict has been the subject of much research over the last 30 years. For the most part, it has been attributed to a complex construct of identity, religious, economic and social factors. An addition to this complex construct could be political leadership itself. The transition of the conflict has been attributed to a series of environmental and structural changes and it could be argued that the same political leadership, which was so central to the perpetuation of the conflict, became a driving force in creating the environmental and structural changes needed which led to the peace process and eventual agreement. Yet one can ask, how exactly did a society with many of the same political leaders in place from the 1970s and 1980s come to make a peaceful agreement in the 1990s? How did these 'political protagonists' of the 1970s and 1980s become the 'political pragmatists' of the 1990s? Furthermore, has the pragmatic behaviour espoused by the political leadership in Northern Ireland through the agreement become reflected in more permanent pragmatic principles? What are the issues and challenges which face Northern Ireland's political leadership as it comes to terms with the new political entity which now exists?

TRADITIONAL CULTURE OF LEADERSHIP

Arthur (1990, 1999) lists four primary characteristics of political leadership in Northern Ireland defining the period from 1921 to 1972 – intimidatory, underdeveloped, factional and demotic. Each contributing characteristic played its own part in the conflict. Political underdevelopment stemmed from a controlled political system with one-party rule, reliance on external guarantors during crisis and a fatalistic outlook (Arthur, 1990). The result of such underdevelopment at a leadership level led to an inability to negotiate. An inability to negotiate led to a perpetuation of the conflict. Factionalism was rife both between and within the two main communities. Broadly speaking, Nationalists were represented by political leaders who advocated a constitutional solution to the problems and those who advocated a military solution. Unionists were divided among various religious groupings and on their views on what a constitutional solution might entail. The implication of this, argued Arthur (1999) quoting Cynthia Enloe, was that each community was unable to put forward leaders that were wholly representative of their communities' viewpoints. The demotic nature of Northern Ireland, whereby power was said to emanate from bottom up rather than top down, had an additional impact on the conflict insofar as, 'political leadership has been lacking and politicians have taken their lead from their perception of how much the market will bear. This has led to an absence of risk taking and the promotion of procrastination' (Arthur, 1999: 92).

CONFLICT AND THE CULTURE OF LEADERSHIP

The more recent political period in Northern Ireland, from the late 1960s and early 1970s until the beginnings of the peace process, illustrated at least four other specific traits that have been noted about leadership. In addition to the intimidatory, underdeveloped, factional and demotic nature of leadership, a culture of leaders emerged which lacked formal power and authority, was heavily reliant on outside influences, rarely changed its leadership personnel and was a profession viewed with growing disdain.

Firstly, from 1972 until 1998, political leadership generally lacked the formal power or authority to actually do things in Northern Ireland. Of course there are notable exceptions to this generalisation in the direct rule period since 1972. In 1974, there was a period of five months when the main constitutional parties were part of a new Executive set up to rule Northern Ireland, and in 1982 another Assembly was established, on the premise that power could be devolved to it on a gradual basis. However, the SDLP would not participate in the 1982 Assembly, power was not devolved, and the Assembly was then closed in 1986. With the exception of those five months in 1974, power had essentially eluded the political leaders. Such powerlessness meant that they were not forced to consider options, make tough choices, or remain mindful of financial implications.

Secondly, this lack of power or authority outside their own party structures led the leadership to become highly dependent on external/outside influences as a way of gaining further legitimacy for their various political positions. For example, the Nationalist community courted the Irish–American constituency from the 1970s. John Hume may not have wielded much formal power in Northern Ireland but in the corridors of Washington he was seen as something of an icon. Consequently, the dependency on others allowed the leadership to further abdicate responsibility on certain issues and problems.

Thirdly, since the leadership had abdicated much of its civic and political responsibility through its reliance on outside influences, the leadership personnel did not seem to change very often, and if it did, the changes were rarely radical. Indeed, by claiming that most political events were beyond their control, the leadership further assured their own party positions since the electorate would be less likely to oust a leader that had not been perceived to be culpable of any wrongdoing.

Finally, politics in Northern Ireland became viewed with such disrespect, over the last 30 years, that many able-bodied potential leaders shunned participation in public life thus significantly diminishing the likelihood of having strong dynamic leaders in position, capable of resolving conflict (Fitzduff, 1996). The 'brain-drain' of young, educated and dynamic leader-types to England and the US further compounded this problem.

Perhaps inadvertently rather than overtly, it was a combination of these cultural leadership traits of being intimidatory, underdeveloped, factional and demotic, coupled in the latter years with a lack of power, heavy reliance on 'external influences', a stagnant leadership and widespread disdain of the political process at leadership level, that concretised the sense of protagonism which existed for much of the conflict in Northern Ireland. This sense of protagonism manifested itself in a perpetuation of the conflict from 1921 and for much of the 1970s and 1980s. A pragmatic shift of the entire leadership culture in Northern Ireland was necessary to change such sentiments, and while such a shift did eventually take place, it did not occur overnight.

CHANGES IN LEADERSHIP THROUGH THE PEACE PROCESS
A shift in leadership traits and characteristics can be traced back to the mid to late 1980s, to the point when the key actors were engaged in a reassessment of their positions, policies and preferences. Five key shifts can be noted.

Firstly, since power had eluded many of the key political players in the conflict, the concept of political power became used as a carrot with which to engage them. The Hume–Adams dialogue examined the 'efficacy of constitutional politics' (Darby and MacGinty, 2000: 64). The British and Irish governments outlined one of their objectives in the peace process as being 'to return greater power, authority and responsibility to all the Northern Ireland people' (HMSO, 1995: v). As the process developed, political leadership became redefined as a leadership with a desire to hold power.

Secondly, the external influences upon which the leadership had been so heavily reliant applied their leverage in a distinctly positive way by encouraging and facilitating training programmes and relationship-building sessions, both in Northern Ireland and abroad. The impact of a series of peer learning sessions, tailored to bring the politicians together and learn from each other's experiences, while difficult to quantify, did play its part in furthering the process (Arthur, 2000). The role of the US, and in particular Bill Clinton and George Mitchell in the latter years from 1995 to 1998, the multiple visits by the parties to South Africa, and the frequency of visits from South African counterparts and others, have been well documented. Political leadership became redefined as one that was articulate in the knowledge and experience of best and worst practice from other case studies.

Thirdly, the issue of stagnant leadership within the parties became less of a dilemma since one of the key themes to emerge from the training sessions mentioned above was that the political leader of a party should not necessarily become the key negotiator in any future processes (O'Malley, 2001). So while the political leadership in terms of the head of the political parties may have remained unchanged, the role of others within the leadership strata took on more resonance. Political leadership became more broadly defined, and more inclusive. The leadership was no longer equated with one particular party leader.

Fourthly, the previously parochial nature of politics and leadership was overturned with the emergence of a number of new actors into the process. The arrival of the Ulster Democratic Party (UDP), the Progressive Unionist Party (PUP) and the Northern Ireland Women's Coalition (NIWC) onto the political scene brought a new dimension to the process, and may have been one of the most influential catalysts for change. Political leadership was no longer seen as a 'closed shop' with select membership and selective representation. More constituents were now represented by leaders.

Finally, politics and political leadership in Northern Ireland began to be seen with less disdain. Formal recognition of some political leaders by the US, as was the case with Gerry Adams and the granting of an American visa in 1994, and at home through incidents such as the infamous handshake between Adams and the President of Ireland, Mary Robinson, were indicative of such changes. The increase in popularity of the annual St Patrick's Day event at the White House meant that more politicians, of both Unionist and Nationalist traditions, were spotted in the US than in Belfast at that time. Politics and leadership slowly became a profession which more people began to embrace.

It was a combination of these slight shifts (i.e. a leadership with a desire to hold power, a leadership articulate in the knowledge and experience of best and worst practice from other case studies, the widening of the leadership strata to include more people at the top including the voices of women and ex-political prisoners, and the internationalisation of the situation in Northern Ireland) which changed the image of politics itself and created a sense of pragmatism among the key players in the conflict. This sense of pragmatism allowed for rapidly changing policies within the parties and ultimately acceptance of the Agreement.

However, with so much influence wielded on the entire process by exogenous influences in the shape of the British and Irish governments, the US administration, and civil society, concerns were justified in wondering how the local leadership would and could conduct itself in this new era. Was it capable of facing up to the changes and challenges afoot?

POLITICAL LEADERSHIP BEYOND THE AGREEMENT
Since the signing of the Agreement in 1998, and the establishment of the Northern Ireland Assembly in 1999, much has changed in the political landscape. Political power has been devolved, suspended and again devolved from Westminster to Stormont. Previous political adversaries share regular coffee mornings (Moriarty, 2000). Sinn Fein and the DUP sit together on Assembly Committees. Informal coalitions between pro- and anti-Agreement parties have been established, as revealed during interview by a senior member of PUP (Gormley-Heenan, 2001). Transformations in behaviour by political leaders are typical, according to one

generic framework which details the transformers of conflict. However, transformations of such magnitude are not without their own problems (Miall et al., 1999).

COLLECTIVE LEADERSHIP CHANGES AND CHALLENGES

While the individual nature of the issues facing the leadership of the various political parties is important, it would seem that the main changes and challenges facing the political leadership of Northern Ireland in the post-Agreement phase have been of a more collective nature and have generally only manifested themselves since the actual establishment of the Assembly itself. Indeed, despite the turbulence surrounding the salient issues, such as police reform and decommissioning, which have stalled the process on numerous occasions, it has been a more subtle variety of issues that emerged from the research as being of concern for the leadership. These issues may provide supplementary explanations of perhaps why the process has continued to be hampered by problems in the post-Agreement phase.

The Use and Abuse of Political Power

Political power was officially devolved to Northern Ireland on 4 December 1999. Power was suspended from 11 February 2000 and then reinstated on 30 May 2000, but aside from this short interlude the Northern Ireland Assembly was to have full legislative and executive authority in respect of those matters previously within the remit of six Northern Ireland government departments. When one has a position of power in a newly elected Assembly, how does one use that power? Do others see such power as being used constructively or destructively? There are a multitude of examples from the Assembly that could be used as illustrative answers to these questions. There is no doubt that Barbara de Bruin (Sinn Fein), Minster of Health and Social Services, and Martin McGuinness (Sinn Fein), Minister of Education, who instructed that the British flag not be flown from their respective official departmental buildings on 2 May 2000 and beyond, felt that they had acted within their remit as Assembly Ministers. However, their actions caused such divisions within the Assembly itself that the Assembly Executive were unable to come to a compromise on the issue, resulting in the enactment of a new law which would regulate the flying of flags on government buildings. While Sinn Fein's argument was based on the Agreement which stated that symbols and emblems should be used in a manner which promoted mutual respect rather than division, and while the Sinn Fein Ministers' decision may have been seen as a constructive use of power within their own constituency base, it was certainly seen as a destructive use of power within the broadly Unionist constituency.

Similarly, David Trimble, in his capacity as First Minister, felt that the use of power to place a ban on the two Sinn Fein Ministers from attending North–South ministerial meetings from November 2000, may have been within his remit.

However, Sinn Fein argued that such a ban contravened the Agreement and mounted a legal challenge that resulted in a judicial review of the situation. The use of power in this case was deemed 'unlawful' in the conclusions of the judicial review. In addition to these two illustrative examples, some of the smaller parties have admitted a sense of dismay at how political power in Northern Ireland has been 'carved up' among the two largest parties in the Assembly, with accusations of patronage and an oblivious attitude to the smaller parties' needs and concerns (Gormley-Heenan, 2001).

Leading One's Own Party

Relating to one's own party has proved difficult for many of the leaders in Northern Ireland. Indicative of this is the fact that David Trimble is in the process of attempting to abolish formal ties between his party and two hard-line groups within its ruling council, the youth wing and the Orange Order, since votes against him in council meetings are said to come mostly from this bloc of voters. For the SDLP, a leaked document of an internal review in April 2000, which challenged both the party structure and the leadership, appeared to have been taken seriously by the party's leaders (Breen, 2000). Amid accusations that the leadership did not treat its party members with enough respect, it would seem that the leadership looked carefully at reorganising the party structures. One senior Unionist leader (PUP) lamented the fact that democracy can sometimes get in the way when dealing with one's party, and wished that 'executive leadership' was more of an option at party level, while still trying to encourage opinion, argument, debate and discussion through the party (Gormley-Heenan, 2001). Such 'executive leadership' is in direct contrast to the style valued by Sinn Fein – that of 'collective leadership'. A senior Sinn Fein political leader commented that it was simply a 'republican way of doing things' (Gormley-Heenan, 2001). Finding a medium between the executive and the collective continues to prove difficult.

Delivering Constituents

Since it is said that leaders are never as much in charge of the situation as they are pictured to be, and constituents are almost never as submissive as one might imagine (Gardner, 1995), delivering constituents in a Northern Ireland context has been of concern. One key player on the political scene referred to the concept of 'elastic band' leadership as the best explanation of how the leadership and its party move forward and stretch its constituents. Using the analogy again, the leadership is constantly aware that the elastic can snap if it is stretched too far or too much, according to a senior member of Sinn Fein (Gormley-Heenan, 2001).

Darby and MacGinty (2000: 256) contend that 'during negotiations the primary function of leaders is to deliver their own people'. However, a volatile constituency can make such a delivery difficult. Analysts agree that supporters/constituents have rarely been told the harsh truths about the process in Northern Ireland. This has been one method used for coping with constituents although such a method can create its own problems. The Agreement did not necessarily provide for a united Ireland or a stronger Union, despite claims to the contrary by both Adams and Trimble. By failing to manage the expectations of their constituents in relation to the changes afoot, both leaders laid the foundations for future problems. Instead of appealing to the reality of the situation many played to their constituents' best hopes, which in effect were the other communities' worst fears.

Relating to Other Leaders/Parties

For some, it would seem that relationships between leaders are as strained as they were during the initial negotiation period. A good leadership dynamic does not always exist behind closed doors, in the view of a senior member of NIWC (Gormley-Heenan, 2001). Relations between the First and Deputy First Minister (Trimble and Mallon) were reported to be strained. In contrast, the relationship between their junior counterparts was not. Overall, it would seem that the leadership has yet to come to terms with the mutual dependency aspect of the Agreement. Much like the poles of a wigwam, if one leader falls then they will probably all fall, according to a senior member of PUP (Gormley-Heenan, 2001). One significant development thus far has been the informal and voluntary coalition between the Women's Coalition, the PUP, the Alliance and the Ulster Unionist Party. This coalition, between a diverse array of political parties, was established out of necessity and a practical need to allow themselves to be represented at all committee meetings and debates. A coalition member is on each committee and feeds back to the other coalition members, on a regular basis, the information from the committees. Recognising the importance of a relationship that allowed all of the parties involved a better opportunity within the Assembly was described by a senior member of PUP as a logical and rational step forward in terms of relating to other leaders/parties (Gormley-Heenan, 2001).

Working with the Civil Service

The dynamic of the inter-relationship between the civil service and the political leaders changed dramatically with the establishment of the Assembly. It emerged from an interview with a senior member of SDLP, that the transition of power has not rested easily with the civil service, according to some political leaders (Gormley-Heenan, 2001). This was one area in which anti-Agreement Unionists were in total agreement with pro-Agreement parties. During an interview with a senior member of DUP it was claimed that, unlike the other collective challenges and issues, the challenge of working with the civil service was not a politically contentious issue, but remained a challenge nonetheless (Gormley-Heenan, 2001). Managing the relationships between the civil service and the key political players will probably continue to be tense unless steps are taken to promote an understanding between the two. Attempts were made to do this through the Northern Ireland Transition Programme, which was initiated by the then Secretary of State for Northern Ireland, Dr Marjorie Mowlam, for new Assembly members and civil servants in 1998, although the programme failed to attract sufficient numbers to make such an initiative worthwhile.

Imminent Elections

While Northern Ireland is no stranger to a constant reaffirmation of public opinion, the Agreement and the post-Agreement period has been accompanied by a series of elections. This has created certain challenges in the post-Agreement context. The May 1998 Referendum was quickly overshadowed by the Assembly Elections in June which pushed the parties towards their old adversarial and tribal positions. The death of Clifford Forsythe MP (UUP) in April 2000, and the subsequent by-election in his constituency in September 2000, resulted in the loss of a Westminster seat from the UUP to the DUP. In the case of sudden death or resignation of a member of the Assembly, a policy of co-option has been employed thereby ensuring that the electoral make-up of the Assembly itself does not shift from sitting to sitting. However, attention is now focused on the possible forthcoming general election and once again hard-line strategies will be employed in a desire to woo constituents. The 'Jekyll and Hyde' approach to politics in Northern Ireland, spurred on by election fever, is proving not only challenging for the leadership itself, but also for the electorate.

Process Management

During the suspension of the Assembly in 2000, Sinn Fein attempted to arrange a meeting to talk about the peace process between themselves and five of the other pro-Agreement parties. The UUP, SDLP, and PUP did not attend.Only the Women's Coalition and Alliance did attend. In defending their decision, the UUP claimed that they would meet anyone but that it had to be under the proper auspices. The SDLP claimed that it was a meeting of party leaders and since Trimble was not going to be there, there was no point in going. The PUP argued that the process had to be properly managed and that Gerry Adams was not the man to manage it (O'Toole, 2000). This particular incident exemplifies one of the key challenges facing leaders in the post-Agreement period in Northern Ireland. The Agreement itself did not focus on the possibility of delays, failures and suspensions, and did not detail processes for action should such problems occur. The challenge of continuing to work through the full implementation of the Agreement without any degree of process management continues to face all leaders.

Realignment of Party Politics

The realisation that the political parties are not actually implementing their party policies through the Programme for Government has begun to impact upon the parties. A senior member of SDLP commented that '. . . it's going to be like a kaleidoscope, constantly changing, from issue to issue. The realignments and the coalitions are going to change and I'm not sure how well people have thought of all of that in terms of the type of politics that there is here, and the type of politics that is going to matter to policy . . .' (Gormley-Heenan, 2001: 51). Again, another challenge to be confronted.

AN ANALYSIS OF POLITICAL LEADERSHIP IN NORTHERN IRELAND

In focusing on political leadership in Northern Ireland's transition from the period of the Agreement until the present, some key political players have been frank in detailing what they perceive to be its successes and failures. On reflection it would appear that the most significant failings to date, as revealed by a senior member of SDLP, have been: (a) failing to manage the expectations of constituents; (b) failing to recognise the referendum results; and (c) failing to recognise the changes that had taken place in themselves and others (Gormley-Heenan, 2001). Anti-Agreement unionism believes that the implementation problems encountered thus far stem from a flawed Agreement, as indicated by a senior member of DUP. On the other hand, some of the pro-Agreement leadership, including senior members of the SDLP and Sinn Fein, argues that the onus lies more with a flawed leadership (Gormley-Heenan, 2001)

Research has shown that nearly all leaders have moved far beyond their original political objectives in accepting the Agreement and working within the new political structures. This applies as much to the anti-Agreement parties as it does to those in favour of the Agreement. Recognising such changes within themselves and on the part of others did not emerge so clearly from the research. In practical terms, all appeared to have coped well with the practicality of moving from a society of 'armed revolution' to one of more mundane 'bureaucratic behaviour', taking their responsibilities with the new political arrangements very seriously. However, given the long and difficult circumstances in Northern Ireland prior to devolution, it is only natural that some relationships between party leaders have remained fraught. Less time has been given to developing such relationships with most preferring to focus on maintaining the support of 'hard-liners' than garnering support and understanding from their political adversaries. There is little speculation about how the process would be affected by a change in leadership in one/some/all of the political parties. General consensus would appear to be that the personality does not matter, rather it is the policy that is important. This is a somewhat strange perception given that changes in leadership at various junctures of the process to date have had such a profound impact in retrospect. The change in leadership in the Republic to Albert Reynolds, Trimble's election as leader of the UUP in 1995, and Blair's electoral success in 1997, are just a few cases in point.

CONCLUSIONS

Northern Ireland as a society with many of the same political leaders in place from the 1970s and 1980s came to make a peaceful agreement in the 1990s as a result of a series of shifts in their culture of leadership, made possible through a reassessment of their policies, positions and preferences. An analysis of political leadership in Northern Ireland shows that its main success during the peace process has been the 1998 Agreement. It has had numerous failings since then. A failure to manage expectations among constituents has contributed to the continuing unease with certain issues in the Agreement. A failure to recognise and acknowledge the changes that have taken place, both internally and on the part of others, has accentuated the problem of trust among the key players. Dealing with constituents and dealing with other party leaders are two key dimensions of leadership in this society as it moves from violence to politics. Attention will need to be given to these two key dimensions to ensure that previous failings are not repeated.

NOTES

[1] Material for this article has been taken from Gormley-Heenan, C. (2001) 'From Protagonist to Pragmatist: Political Leadership in Societies in Transition' (Derry/Londonderry: INCORE).

[2] The timing of the field research in Israel and the Palestinian Territories in July 2000 coincided with the impromptu Israeli–Palestinian peace summit, at Camp David in the US. Many of those, who had provisionally agreed to be interviewed, left for Camp David just as the field research began. Informal discussions were held with Israeli and Palestinian academics to supplement the formal interviews, since it was difficult to arrange alternative appointments at such short notice.

14. COMING OUT OF VIOLENCE: A COMPARATIVE STUDY OF PEACE PROCESSES

John Darby and Roger MacGinty

INTRODUCTION: THE PROJECT

This chapter describes a co-ordinated research project, involving academic partners in five places embarking on peace processes: South Africa, Israel–Palestine, Northern Ireland, the Basque Country and Sri Lanka (MacGinty and Darby, 2002; du Toit, 2001; Darby and MacGinty, 2000). Each of the five conflict settings has a different history, demographic structure and socio-economic profile. All may have embarked on a journey towards peace during the 1990s, but their progress along it was far from uniform. Each was at a different stage of the conflict resolution cycle, and had its own experience of conflict management. They also shared common features: they were all essentially internal conflicts; all have been subject to serious violence; most relevant, all had embarked on at least one attempt to reach peace within the last decade, and had encountered similar obstacles to achieving it.

The research was organised around six key themes common to peace processes: violence, external influences, economic factors, popular responses, symbolic factors and progress towards political settlement. Each theme is considered in turn, and then in relation to each other. The last theme, progress towards political settlement, is the focus of the last section of the chapter.

THE TERRAIN OF PEACE

A peace process is often compared to climbing a mountain, but a mountain range is a better metaphor, and the first peak is usually the ending of violence. All previous expeditions have failed. There are no obvious tracks to the top, nor any maps to provide guidance. The climbers, previously preoccupied with the arts of war, are unaccustomed to compromise and must pick up the skills as they go along. They must rely on each other's co-operation for survival. To make matters worse, the mountaineering team is composed of people who have previously been at each others' throats, often literally, and who must now overcome their suspicions and fears to accomplish a common task for the first time. For many, the ending of violence is more than enough.

If they succeed, a ceasefire may follow. At last the travellers are able to peer over the summit. But the view reveals new mountains, some apparently more formidable than the one just climbed. It becomes evident that the successful conquest of each new peak requires different skills and different guides. Those who negotiated a ceasefire are not necessarily the appropriate people to negotiate political agreement or to achieve economic regeneration and redistribution.

It would be easier if the mountains to be tackled were ranged in obvious sequence. Peace processes are often regarded as following three phases: first, the ending of violence; then, negotiations leading to a political/constitutional agreement; and finally, what is often referred to as post-settlement peace building. The reality is less ordered. Unexpected peaks emerge through the mists and demand the immediate attention of the climbers. Each peace process has its own distinctive terrain and its own priorities. The decommissioning of weapons became one of the most formidable obstacles in Northern Ireland, yet it was bypassed at a brisk trot in South Africa. In the Basque Country significant reforms in policing and administrative devolution were achieved before inclusive negotiations were possible. Many of Northern Ireland's fair employment grievances had been improved long before the 1998 Agreement was reached.

THE ROLE OF VIOLENCE

'It is an observable phenomenon in Northern Ireland, and elsewhere,' the Irish Taoiseach (Prime Minister), Bertie Ahern, suggested in 1998, 'that tension and violence tend to rise when compromise is in the air.' Almost three times as many people were killed in South Africa while the agreement was being negotiated between 1990 and 1994 than in the previous four years. The use of political violence also rose dramatically during the Middle East peace process.

Nor does violence disappear when a ceasefire is declared. Instead, both the forms of violence, and violence-related issues, change in ways which threaten the evolving peace process. The threats come from four main sources.

1. VIOLENCE BY THE STATE

Governments are often as divided about peace processes as their opponents. Governmental or quasi-governmental agencies may continue covert actions either to undermine the process itself or, as when the 'third force' in South Africa used violence to support the Inkatha Freedom Party (IFP), to influence the outcome of negotiations. Even if such pressure is not applied, the security apparatus built up during periods of violence is a potential danger when they end. Militants are released instead of imprisoned. The security forces augmented during the violence are abruptly reduced in number, endangering their jobs and personal security. Demands are made to reform the police force that regarded itself as the bastion against terrorism. Unless handled carefully, disaffection within the security forces has the potential to undermine the peace process itself.

2. THE PARAMILITARY FALL-OUT

Disaffection within militant organisations is a more obvious threat to progress. These are rarely the monoliths presented by their opponents. They are complex organisms performing different functions and providing umbrellas for different interests. During ceasefire periods these interests diffuse and fragment. At least four pose separate threats to peace processes:

A Return to Political Violence

Ceasefires are never unanimous, so the most obvious threat is that they will break down and political violence will return. The more disaffected members of the militants may desert to splinter groups or perform individual acts of violence. The less affected may go along with the majority view, but their agreement is conditional. Their continuing allegiance depends on measurable rewards from negotiation, including prisoner releases and the dismantling of the security apparatus. These rewards are rarely immediate. Consequently, the pendulum may swing back towards the militants. It is worth remembering that the talks broke down in both South Africa and Northern Ireland, leading to periods of renewed violence in 1992 and 1996 respectively, before the peace processes resumed.

'Tactical' Violence

A common fear among constitutional parties is that the pace of negotiation will be determined by gunmen outside the negotiating rooms, and that their political surrogates may use the threat of violence to get their way.

Acts of violence during the process are taken as confirmation of this fear. The early stages of the Oslo process were hampered by Israeli suspicion of the Palestine Liberation Organisation's (PLO) motives, and later the government regarded Hamas's atrocities as evidence that Arafat was either unable to control his own people or was colluding with Hamas for strategic advantage. During the early stages of the Northern Ireland peace process, Unionists constantly warned that Sinn Fein would use Irish Republican Army (IRA) violence to remind other negotiators of their power. As the negotiations progressed, it became increasingly clear that violence threatened Sinn Fein's interests as much as those of the Unionists. The complaints diminished, as had happened in South Africa.

Spoilers: Zealots versus Dealers

The very involvement of paramilitary interests in negotiations implies that the purity of their cause has been compromised. It imposes strains on organisations that are essentially military, and it is difficult to find any instances when such a move was not accompanied by a split between two main groups – the Zealots and the Dealers. The Zealots often comprise radical groups, like the 'Real' IRA and the Continuity IRA in Northern Ireland, who picked up the torch they believed had been surrendered by the Dealers. In Sri Lanka the result was a succession of assassinations of Tamil rivals by the Tamil Tigers; in 1998 they murdered the Tamil mayor of Jaffna, having previously killed her husband, and then killed her successor as mayor. All major attempts to start negotiations in Israel–Palestine were accompanied by Palestinian attempts to bomb them away. The killing of 28 Muslims by the Israeli settler Baruch Goldstein in 1994, and the assassination of the Israeli Prime Minister Rabin in 1995, showed that Zealots from both communities were eager to capsize the process. Both white and black dissidents threatened the South African process, although spoiler violence by blacks was relatively well controlled during the period of negotiation, perhaps a reflection of the dominance of Nelson Mandela and the African National Congress (ANC).

Family Feuding: Internal Paramilitary Violence
The determination of militants to exercise control over their own communities does not diminish when they enter a negotiation process. They are unlikely to hand over this negotiating card, even at the risk of destabilising the peace process itself. Violence between factions within the Palestinian community continued after the first transfer of land to Palestinian control in 1995. Punishment beatings persisted in Northern Ireland after the Good Friday Agreement as both Loyalists and republicans exercised what they regarded as their policing role.

3. VIOLENCE IN THE COMMUNITY
The fragmentation of paramilitary organisations is not the only violent accompaniment to peace processes. Two other forms of violence may also seriously undermine them – the revival of direct confrontations between ethnic rivals, and a rise in the conventional crime rate.

Return to the Streets
When a ceasefire is declared the discipline of the military campaign diminishes, but the underlying sectarian hatred remains, taking the form of riots and undisciplined confrontations with ethnic rivals or the police. They can become a serious threat to a peace process. The paramilitary representatives who enter negotiations are not divorced from the instincts of their communities, and may feel the need to support them. During the early months of negotiation in South Africa, sectional violence was partly orchestrated between the ANC and the IFP, but spilled over into tit-for-tat killings and more general violence. The emergence of the 'street guerrillas', mostly teenagers, in the Basque Country arose partly from Euskadi 'ta Askatasuna's (ETA) weakening authority, but was also partly a reaction to the popularity of the peace movement.

'Ordinary Decent Crime'

A rise in conventional crime may appear to present a less obvious danger. The crime rate has risen to such a degree in South Africa, however, as to seriously undermine post-settlement peace building. It is a threat to inward investment, tourism and general confidence. By the mid-1990s the high level of conventional crime had far outpaced political violence as a destabilising factor. By 1998 the daily homicide rate was 52, and still rising. More ominously, the barrier between ordinary crime and South Africa's underlying racial tensions, never sharp, became increasingly blurred. Fifteen hundred white farmers were attacked between 1994 and 1998, resulting in more than two hundred murders, and threatening to create a loop back from post-settlement civil violence to the violence familiar from the earlier struggle.

4. NEW SECURITY-RELATED ISSUES IN NEGOTIATION

During peace negotiations new substantive issues emerge, most of them security related – notably early prisoner releases, decommissioning of illegal weapons and policing. The South African peace process actually began with the release of prisoners, when Nelson Mandela and other ANC leaders were set free in February 1990. The rate of prisoner releases has been a constant source of bitter dispute in Israel–Palestine, but was implemented relatively smoothly in Northern Ireland. The decommissioning of weapons is a more complicated matter. The 1991 South African National Peace Accord did not ask the ANC to disband paramilitary units nor hand over their arms caches; it required only that firearms should not be displayed at public meetings. The stubbornness of Ulster Unionists in demanding decommissioning and of Sinn Fein in rejecting it in Northern Ireland, however irritating, arose from the need of each side to keep its primary constituency on board, and on the symbolic association between decommissioning and surrender.

Police reform is an equally emotional issue in negotiations. It is axiomatic that divided societies require a police force that reflects the divisions. Section 195 of the 1996 South African constitution, for example, insisted that the police and defence forces 'be broadly representative of the South African people' and, by 1996, 16,000 former guerrillas had been absorbed into the army. There are plenty of other examples of former combatants entering the security forces, although not all attempts at integration succeeded.

All of the forms of violence detailed above are separate threads in a single weave. The pattern that unites them is the central role of violence both before and after the declaration of a ceasefire. Each distinct form, however, demands different policy approaches, for governments, international and regional bodies, negotiators and NGOs (Non-Governmental Organisations) attempting to move towards a fair and lasting settlement.

EXTERNAL INFLUENCES

In August 1993, four Israelis, four Palestinians and four Norwegians initialled a Declaration of Principles, which were formally signed one month later on the White House lawn. The Oslo Accords were launched. The process had started in 1992 when the PLO, seeking external facilitation, approached a group of Norwegians. At that time it was illegal for Israelis and Palestinians to meet in Israel. The resulting negotiation evolved its own ground rules: a cover project was invented as camouflage; both sides agreed not to dwell on history; to ensure secrecy they met in private homes rather than hotels, and the media were not informed; the teams were kept small, and the pressure maintained; negotiations even continued during meal-times (Egelund, 1997).

The Oslo process, initially involving academics and NGOs and later politicians, was unique, but the exercise of external influence to facilitate or to apply pressure for a settlement is not. In South Africa the effect of sanctions in ending apartheid is disputed. Zartman (1997a) marks it as the 'turning point' which started the search for alternatives. The balance of evidence leans towards du Toit's view that the ending of the Cold War enabled the United States effectively to present an ultimatum to De Klerk: negotiate or face the consequences (du Toit, 2000).

No ethnic conflict is exclusively internal. All conflicts operate within a regional or international context, and are influenced by it. Similarly, all peace processes may be generally influenced by external factors. The white South African fear of communism, if exaggerated, was genuine and the ending of the Cold War eased the initiation of the peace process there. The strategic and electoral importance of the Middle East for the United States ensured that both the conflict there, and attempts to resolve it, attracted general attention. Hermann and Newman (2000: 138) argued that both depended more on external than domestic initiatives, and point out that 'all Israeli–Arab wars were brought to an end by external mediation'.

The 'armed struggles' in Sri Lanka and Northern Ireland depended heavily on financial support from diaspora populations. In Sri Lanka the proximity of massive Tamil populations in India helped to precipitate the Indian military intervention in 1987, with unfortunate consequences for both countries. Even today, although both the Sri Lankan government and the Liberation Tigers of Tamil Eelam (LTTE) claim to believe that external mediation is necessary to start a peace process, they both impose mutually unacceptable preconditions. Irish-Americans played an important role in persuading the IRA to call a ceasefire and in bringing Sinn Fein into negotiations. Both Israeli-American and Irish-American communities swung around to become more enthusiastic advocates of the peace processes than the people actually living in the Middle East and Northern Ireland.

Neither the United Nations nor any major regional organisation has had direct involvement in any of the five 'Coming out of Violence' cases, but the United States has become involved in the peace processes in South Africa, Israel–Palestine and Northern Ireland. This intervention was particularly helpful in the infant stages or to massage particular sticking points, as when the United States helped to bring the Inkatha Freedom Party into the South African process in 1992.

Internal disputes are often a proxy for larger disputes, or at least an historical echo of them – between the Irish and the British, between Israel and the Arab countries, and between Sri Lanka and India. Consequently, neighbouring countries often have a vested interest in encouraging or resolving conflicts. The roles of neighbouring Arab states in Israel (with quite different influences coming from Syria, Lebanon, Jordan and Egypt) were at times critical. Northern Ireland and Sri Lanka stand at the ends of the spectrum of external influence. All the interested external interests – the United States and the European Union, even the United Kingdom and the Irish Republic, if they can be regarded as external to the province – gave unanimous support for a negotiated settlement in Northern Ireland. Contrast this with Sri Lanka, where the Indian intervention altered the problem without improving it, and no other neighbouring state has exercised a comparable influence for peace. Of the five areas studied, external influence was greatest in Israel–Palestine and Northern Ireland, and least in the Basque Country and Sri Lanka. The best explanation is located in the United States' foreign policy and electoral politics.

ECONOMIC FACTORS

One of the arguments most often used to encourage the ending of violence is that peace will lead to new jobs, more tourism and greater investment. It was estimated that the cost of the war in Sri Lanka would reach $723,000,000 in 1999, 13.26% of the state's budget, an intolerable burden for a Third World country. The promise of a peace dividend was consciously used during the years of violence in all five areas to stimulate a peace process. The business community in Northern Ireland, predominantly Unionist, was at the fore in urging an agreement. In South Africa, the first approaches to the ANC came from the white business community.

Delivery is another matter, and the 'peace dividends' that were expected to follow the ending of violence in the Palestinian Authority and in South Africa were disappointing (INCORE, 1995). The heavy dependence of Palestinians on Israel, including the frequent barriers to their travelling to work, demonstrates the asymmetrical nature of many peace processes and the difficulty of improving structural inequalities. Indeed, the economic expectations which are routinely raised to encourage progress during a peace process are often frustrated after it has been agreed. The inability of the South African administrations to implement speedy economic improvements, and therefore to secure more equitable distribution in housing, employment and general prosperity, led to increased levels of social and political unrest. The crime rate soared and has become a major post-settlement problem. This crime was often directed against those who continued to control the economy, the whites, and the racial dimension threatens a return towards pre-settlement tensions.

By way of contrast, Northern Ireland benefited initially from substantial European Union grants to buttress the peace process from 1994, and from increased external investments; tourist revenue rose by 30% in the year following the 1994 ceasefires. Still, it is hard to find evidence that peace dividends move the process forward significantly. It might be speculated that the significant reduction in economic differentials between Catholics and Protestants in Northern Ireland before the 1998 Agreement removed a potential stimulus for Catholic disaffection after it. Certainly the Catholic community was much more enthusiastic about the Agreement than the Protestant community. The evidence across the five areas suggests that a background of economic depression is a serious obstacle to peace processes. It is more difficult to prove that economic stimuli are a significant encouragement to them.

POPULAR RESPONSES

The observation by Hermann and Newman (2000: 135) that 'mobilising for conflict is much easier than mobilising for peace, notwithstanding the initiators of the mobilisation efforts', lies close to the heart of one of the most contested current questions about peace processes. Are they essentially bottom-up or top-down exercises? Is it possible to stimulate a peace initiative by groundswell pressure, and does a strong civil and democratic infrastructure help to sustain it? Or is peace managed by leadership from the political elites, as appears to have happened in all five cases studied? Of course this is a false dichotomy. Lasting peace depends on both leadership *and* popular support.

The desire for peace expressed by the Sri Lankan government and the Tamil Tigers was undermined by their different interpretations of what constituted peace. There, and in Northern Ireland, opinion polls have consistently indicated a popular desire for peace, suggesting that ethnic politics encourages leaders to take up more intransigent positions. The Troubles in Northern Ireland were accompanied by the creation of many peace organisations, most notably the Peace People formed in August 1976, but it would be difficult to argue that any of them seriously diverted the direction of events. In Israel, Hermann and Newman (2000: 143) claimed that 'when the formal negotiations did not progress smoothly or reached a dead-end, no significant pressures from below were exerted on the decision makers to make greater concessions in order to push the process forwards'. The decision in South Africa to enter negotiations with the ANC arose from an altered view by National Party leaders rather than their followers.

The ineffectual demonstrations of the early peace movements in the Basque Country had become more organised and effective by the 1990s. The level of activity alone marked out the Basque Country from the other areas. Between 1995 and 1998 the co-ordinating peace body Gesto had held more than 15,000 silent protest meetings. Around six million people protested against the murder of the local councillor Miguel Angel Blanco in 1997, provoking counter-protests supporting ETA.

Public opinion is an amorphous concept. The generality of a population may flounder ineffectually in the face of political violence, but elements within it sometimes find it possible to make more strategic interventions. The strong civil society in Northern Ireland allowed reforms in the fair allocation of housing, employment and education to be implemented during the years of violence, prevented a bad situation from becoming worse, and reduced the roster of problems to be tackled during the peace process. Other mediators – church leaders, academics and trade unionists – helped to establish the first informal meetings between political opponents in all five countries, and at least allowed them to pursue 'what-if' scenarios within relatively risk-free settings. It is also difficult to assess the influence of community relations policies and approaches, notably in Northern Ireland, in creating an appropriate atmosphere for negotiations.

The Basque experience aside, there is little evidence that a groundswell desire for peace has pressurised leaders towards the necessary compromises. One important qualification is necessary. The effectiveness of popular opinion is enhanced after an agreement has been reached, or even when a peace process is in the air. In such circumstances it is worth paying attention to those catalytic events when an atrocity not only provokes universal condemnation but galvanises popular reaction against the perpetrators. After decades of kidnappings and murders, it took the kidnapping of Basques by ETA and Blanco's murder in 1997 to bring hundreds of thousands of Basque protesters on to the streets in opposition to ETA's violence. The murder of 28 ANC supporters in Bisho in 1992 was not followed by the same violent protests after the massacre of 48 people at Boipatong three months earlier. Instead it became a stimulus for the negotiations rather than a cause for withdrawal.

What is the nature of these atrocities, which converts them into catalysts for peace? To some degree it is war-weariness, but this condition can continue for years without stimulating compromise. The reason why certain violent events, at certain times, become catalysts for peace lies not in the nature or severity of the violence – there had often been worse atrocities in the past – but in its timing. The public demand for a renewal of negotiations after Bisho arose directly from the reminder of the alternative presented by the Boipatong massacre and from fear that the process might collapse. The point is this – courage in condemning atrocities is not enough. What converts outrage to action is condemnation within the context, or at least realistic hope, that agreement is possible, and that further violence could threaten it. It is also clear that such moments are transitory. The often mentioned 'window of opportunity' is barely ajar and soon slams shut.

SYMBOLS AND RITUALS

In May 1994, just as Nelson Mandela was sworn in as President of South Africa, there was a ceremonial flyover by the South African air force. Their exhausts released the red, green and black of the new South African flag. For some ANC supporters the planes had previously been associated with bombing their bases in the border states. 'It was the moment when I felt South African,' said one of them (Seals, 1996).

Why has South Africa been so skilled at identifying the appropriate gesture to cut across sectarian and racial barriers? A great part of the credit belongs to Mandela, who clearly manipulated symbols to encourage reconciliation. He had an unerring eye for the uniting gesture which would heal the wounds of conflict. His attendance at the final of the Rugby World Cup final, the sport of white South Africa, and donning a Springbok shirt, showed a generosity of spirit that set an example in the uneasy new state.

It is not easy to find the telling gesture which unites antagonists. Indeed rituals and symbols more often obstruct than assist reconciliation. Ritual has demonstrated its potential to disrupt the peace process in Northern Ireland. Orange processions metamorphosed into a focus for Protestant opposition to the peace process. The change was a response to the empowerment of the Catholic minority and its new determination to prohibit parades. Protestant confidence had been eroded by what they saw as concessions to their opponents; they felt an increased need to demonstrate their heritage and unity. The differences became communal rather than political, and the highly ritualistic and predictable nature of parades resulted in a serious threat to community harmony.

One of the most difficult tasks in any peace process is how to confront the sins of the past without compromising the need for reconciliation. In the early Oslo negotiations the negotiators agreed not to dwell on past grievances. Other negotiations have built into the timetable what might be described as venting time, to allow the inevitable bitterness to be expressed and then, hopefully, set aside. The South African Truth and Reconciliation Commission was established in 1995 and did not shrink from identifying atrocities from all sides, and the Northern Ireland Victims' Commissioner made a number of recommendations to identify and support victims of the Troubles. Both arose from the same root – the need to acknowledge feelings of hurt and loss and the importance of grieving – and both attempted to find ways of dissociating these feelings from guilt and acrimony, not an easy task.

What is the nature of the successful symbolic gesture? It must appear to transcend or cut across tribalism – to reach across to the other side in a way which runs counter to cultural expectations. It is the imaginative and magnanimous gesture which touches the opposite communities and erodes its suspicions. It only works if there is no suggestion of triumphalism or condescension, and if there is no obvious – or at least apparent – short-term political advantage. Only time can answer the more nagging question – do such gestures have a permanent or passing effect on stalled peace processes?

PROGRESS TOWARDS POLITICAL SETTLEMENT

This section will discuss the process of negotiations in three stages: pre-negotiation; the negotiations themselves; and post-settlement peace building. Each stage brings its own problems and requires different approaches. Pre-negotiation, for example, often includes 'Track-Two' approaches (non-governmental contact by such mediators as the business community, academics or churches), external pressure and secret talks, as well as the declaration of ceasefires. The negotiations themselves may have to tackle disputes about inclusion, violence and techniques for moving the process forward. Peace accords are not only concerned with the clauses in the agreement; equally important are their validation through elections or referenda and the schedule to deal with the remaining problems. Post-settlement arrangements often include issues such as reform of policing and the administration of justice, arms decommissioning and economic reconstruction, all of which carry different weights in different contexts.

PRE-NEGOTIATION: GETTING INTO TALKS

Zartman (1997b: 333) has argued convincingly that a 'most striking characteristic of internal conflicts is asymmetry: one party (government) is strong and the other (insurgents) is weak'. Peace processes most often occur when both these circumstances have changed, when both government and paramilitaries recognise the others' ability to frustrate their success. This circumstance has been described as a 'mutually hurting stalemate', where 'both sides perceived themselves to be in a stalemate that was painful to each of them and they saw a better alternative through negotiation' (Zartman, 1997b: 334) and may be allied to the concept of the 'ripe moment', that brief moment when the playing field is acceptably level for both sides and talks become possible (Miall et al., 1999). This point was reached in South Africa in 1989 when, du Toit (2001) argued, both sides recognised that the cost of the continuing stalemate was greater than any unlikely military gain, and De Klerk became leader of the National Party.

Sri Lanka's experience supports this argument from the opposite perspective, in that both protagonists still appear to believe that their objectives are most likely to be achieved through war. However, ripe moments and hurting stalemates are more easily identified in retrospect than in advance. It is possible to argue that, in any conflict, a number of ripe moments come and go, and hurting stalemates demonstrably continue for years – in Northern Ireland for at least 15 years before the 1994 ceasefires. The danger is that the argument is too passive and may discourage initiatives during periods of violence – reforms in the allocation of resources, informal attempts at mediation or mediation, Track-Two approaches –

which may help to prepare the ground for later negotiations. Why bother if the meal must wait for the fruit to ripen?

The peace processes in South Africa, Northern Ireland and Israel–Palestine began with secret talks. These secret talks have certain advantages over traditional diplomacy as a preliminary to substantive talks. The formal barriers imposed by protocol are dropped; the temperature of the water and the temper of one's opponents may be tested with limited risk; 'what-if' scenarios can be floated without commitment; secret talks can be a useful transition process for those who rose to leadership as security or insurgent leaders, and who often have little or no experience of the art of compromise; and working relationships are allowed to evolve between antagonists. The exclusion of the media helped to keep the talks in Oslo and Northern Ireland secret. Secret talks were attractive because, they 'held low exit costs' (du Toit, 2000: 22).

It is not uncommon for the constitutional and paramilitary opponents of the existing government to form a temporary alliance during pre-negotiation. In Northern Ireland a 'pan-nationalist front' operated between the SDLP, Sinn Fein and the Irish government following the Hume–Adams talks. These alliances help to compensate for the asymmetrical nature of negotiations, where the initial advantage leans towards the government side. They apply pressure to force a reluctant government into talks, but carry a price. The long-term cost may be increased bitterness between ethnic protagonists during negotiations and in post-settlement peace-building.

The preliminaries to peace processes are not subject to standard formulae. Chance can play a critical role. Most of the ingredients for negotiations were already in place under the Conservative administration of John Major, but talks began only after a Labour government was elected with a commanding majority in 1997. A strong argument could be made that De Klerk's election as President in 1989 started the peace process in South Africa, and that the Israeli process started with the election of Rabin in 1992 and stalled after Netanyahu's election four years later. The point is that these changes of government were not exclusively related to peace, although they profoundly affected the peace process. They were chance developments.

These changes in government did not in themselves lead to negotiations. If the ground had not been prepared in advance a breakthrough was unlikely to happen. It is the combination of preparing for, and seizing on, the moment of opportunity that makes a peace process.

NEGOTIATING THE SETTLEMENT

When talks begin, the initial need is to build confidence in the fledgling process, and to establish rules and procedures to move it forward. Israel's recognition of the PLO as legitimate representatives of the Palestinian people in the Oslo Accord, coupled with acceptance of the Palestinian right to self-determination, had immense symbolic significance. There and elsewhere the fact that negotiations are taking place at all presumes an acceptance, often implicit rather than acknowledged, that paramilitary representatives have been admitted to negotiations in return for giving up violence.

The inclusion of militants does not presume that the mechanics of their admission have been determined, and they are often required to surmount a tortuous series of tests and symbolic encounters. Peace processes are littered with 'historic' handshakes – Sadat–Begin, Rabin–Arafat, Adams–Mayhew, Netanyahu–Arafat – taken as sanctifying a break with the past. Probation periods were set before Sinn Fein was admitted to talks, and the Spanish President authorised talks with ETA six weeks after its ceasefire in 1998. It is necessary to agree to rules to deal with the resumption of violence. In Northern Ireland, the Mitchell Principles were devised, and imposed, as conditions for entry to talks and for punishing breaches by paramilitaries associated with negotiating parties.

The issue of transparency is especially critical. Hermann and Newman (2000: 148) pointed out that 'the messages which constitute part of the negotiation process with the other side of the conflict are not, and cannot be, the same as those used as a means of gaining the support of the domestic audience'. So how can a compromise be struck between the need for secrecy before agreement is reached and the obligation of public accountability? As a general rule, secrecy diminishes in importance as negotiations proceed, and the need to involve the community in the forthcoming compromises increases. An excess of publicity entrenches party differences before an agreement is reached. An excess of secrecy not only encourages conspiracy interpretations but may encourage hardline mobilisation within each negotiating community. It also fails to prepare public opinion for compromise or to mobilise the public in favour of a peace process.

Although the issues to be negotiated reflect the distinctiveness of each conflict, some themes are constant. The early release of prisoners is almost always a *sine qua non* for paramilitaries engaged in talks; it is also a highly emotive reminder to victims of violence that their sensibilities have been pushed into the background in the interests of securing peace. Reforms in policing, security and the administration of justice are also constant features if an accord is agreed. No clear pattern is discernible on decommissioning; it emerged as a major threat to the process in Northern Ireland, but hardly rated as a problem in South Africa.

The prime responsibility for preparing discussion papers on procedures for negotiation usually falls on government, especially if the talks involve a number of competing parties. This may require distance brokerage, often in two phases. Shuttle diplomacy may be needed to establish the preconditions and ground rules for participants. If these can be agreed, proximity talks are often necessary before the participants are willing to meet in plenary sessions, although ad hoc meetings on specific aspects of the negotiation process provided a useful middle way in Northern Ireland. Proximity talks were unnecessary in South Africa, but it took three years to complete what du Toit (2001) described as 'talks about substantive talks' – the conditions, ground rules and rules of engagement. Substantive negotiations actually started in 1991 before the preliminaries had been completed.

A number of innovative negotiation devices, developed to cope when the South African process stalled, were identified by du Toit (2001). Among them were the 'bush summits' designed to smooth out bilateral disagreements; the 'channel', a subcommittee of three which met daily to maintain momentum; and the creation of new institutions such as the Transitional Executive Council and the Independent Electoral Commission, to counter the asymmetrical nature of power structures in South Africa. Some of these negotiation devices were consciously imitated in other places. The concept of 'sufficient consensus', for example, designed to keep dissenters in the process if they were out-voted on a specific issue, was effectively applied in Northern Ireland. Northern Ireland itself developed distinctive procedures, notably the use of George Mitchell as an external chairman for the talks, and the development of the Mitchell Principles as a procedure to enable parties previously associated with violence to enter talks under specific conditions.

Thereafter, timetables and deadlines are essential to maintain momentum. In their absence, the 1994 ceasefires in Northern Ireland were followed by a fatal lack of urgency which eventually led to the ending of the IRA ceasefire. Contrast that with the precise deadlines established during the resumed negotiations in 1998. In Israel–Palestine the 1993 Oslo A Accord set a specific date (May 1999), five years from the start of its implementation, for the transfer of authority and land. The deadlines were not always met, but they imposed an obligation on parties which carried substantial weight.

One by-product of establishing deadlines is that negotiations sometimes advance in surges rather than by gradual increments – this encourages the emergence of a brinkmanship style of negotiation, conspicuous in Northern Ireland, when all-night sittings became *de rigueur*. Establishing a deadline focuses attention, but also has inherent risks. In addition, brinkmanship confirms to a divided community that their leaders are fighting a tough fight, thus helping to prepare them for the compromises to come.

POST-SETTLEMENT PEACE BUILDING – CEMENTING THE PEACE

As negotiations proceed, it is tempting to defer sensitive issues to post-settlement negotiation. During the Oslo negotiations, for example, five critical issues, including Jerusalem, settlements and refugee return, were 'blackboxed' to enable the two sides to move forward on other less inflexible issues. In Northern Ireland the deferred issues included some very divisive matters – cross-border structures with the Irish Republic, reforms in policing and the administration of justice, arms decommissioning and the sharing of executive power. Deadlines were set for most of these – two years in the case of decommissioning – but this runs the risk of timetabling a series of post-settlement crises in the interests of short-term gain. The South African agreement transferred potentially deadlock issues, including affirmative action and the integration of the armed forces, to the agenda of the first elected government.

The South African experience illustrates that the settlement can be seriously threatened by developments which were both unanticipated and unrelated to the conflict. The inability to deliver either economic regeneration or greater social equality led to a growing sense of disillusion with peace itself. The parallel rise in conventional crime was even more destabilising, and not unrelated to economic grievances. The transfer of ex-paramilitary activists into the police and security forces in the Palestinian Territories and South Africa was a tangible acceptance of past abuses and an effective way to convert a potentially destabilising armed threat into support for the new structures. It is also a tangible demonstration of fair employment practices by the new administrations.

Apart from having to confront these continuing disputes, post-settlement administrations are also confronted by the problems left by years of violence and confrontation. The Truth and Reconciliation Commission in South Africa and the Victims Commission in Northern Ireland were attempts to deal with victims and the injuries of the past. The controversy surrounding both bodies demonstrates the cliche that it may take as long to repair community dysfunction as it took to create it, and that means decades rather than years. In 1998, five years after the famous handshake between Rabin and Arafat, 42% of Israelis still saw Arafat as a terrorist, against 26% who saw him as a statesman.

CONCLUSIONS: THE UTILITY OF COMPARISON

Peace processes do not take place in a vacuum. There has been a high level of deliberate 'borrowing' between contemporary peace processes, inspired and stimulated by the proliferation and perceived success of other processes during the 1990s. South Africa acted as an exemplar to Northern Ireland, with cross-party visits from Northern Ireland having a significant effect on the peace process. The connection continued during the post-Accord implementation stage with, for example, Cyril Ramaphosa of the ANC acting as an independent inspector of IRA arms dumps.

Just as South Africa was an inspiration for Northern Ireland, others looked there for a model, most notably the Basque Country. In 1998 Herri Batasuna, the political party closest to ETA's aims, invited all the main Basque political parties and other movements to participate in an 'Ireland Forum' in order to explore the relevance of the Northern Ireland process to the Basque Country. The development was inspired by the 'pan-nationalist' front in Northern Ireland which brought together the main interests favouring a broad nationalist position – Sinn Fein, the SDLP, the government of the Irish Republic and Irish-American interests. The 'Ireland Forum' led directly to the Lizarra Agreement. Four days later ETA declared a ceasefire. Mees (2000: 180) argued that the Basque peace process is almost unimaginable 'without the domino effect of the Northern Irish model'. Herri Batasuna's leader Arnaldo Otegi confessed that 'Ireland was a mirror for us, and so was the republican movement' (Mees, 2000: 180).

Comparative studies do not depend on the study of borrowing to justify their efforts. The cold truth is that most peace processes fail, if success is defined as lasting for more than five years. Decisions are reached more often by stumbling from one crisis to another rather than by calculation or strategy. To make matters worse, those engaged in negotiating a peace process tend to underrate what has been accomplished, and to gaze enviously at the exaggerated accomplishments of other peace processes. In this context a comparative perspective is a cooler one, one that is likely to remind negotiators of how much the debate has moved on in a relatively short period. Even 'failed' peace processes alter the terrain for debate, often fundamentally. Even if an agreement falls well short of a constitutional settlement, much may be accomplished. Land may have been transferred, institutions removed and replaced, police and security forces subjected to new forms of scrutiny, and occasionally power shared. Even a brief opportunity to confront the enemy and hear how they express their views may begin a fresh movement towards another process in the future.

The comparative study of peace processes contributes to scholarship by identifying what is exceptional, or what distinguishes them from comparable cases: the advantages of Northern Ireland's relative prosperity in relation to other contemporary processes; its failure to forge unifying symbols, in contrast to South Africa; and the benefits in having two governments as guardians and guides. These studies of peace processes all help to establish a new basis of understanding and to identify a new research agenda. Comparative studies contextualise local studies and ultimately transform theory as well as practice.

ACKNOWLEDGEMENT

The authors would like to acknowledge, with gratitude, the support provided to the project upon which this chapter is based by grants from Northern Ireland's Central Community Relations Unit, from UNESCO's Culture of Peace programme, and the British Academy.

15. PUTTING IT ALL TOGETHER: CENTRAL THEMES FROM RESEARCHING THE TROUBLES

Owen Hargie and David Dickson

INTRODUCTION

Given the depth and diversity of material included in this book, it is almost impossible to summarise the main findings, while still doing justice to the work of the researchers. However, we feel that it is essential to provide an overview of what we regard as key recurring themes to have emanated from all of this research. The main ones to emerge are:

- Universalism/Particularism
- The Primacy of Victims and the Concept of Victimhood
- The Importance of Integrated Education
- Contact is Necessary but not Sufficient
- Community Relations Must be the Responsibility of Everyone
- Symbols, Emblems and their Management
- Learning Lessons from the Interface
- The Complexity of Identity
- External Influences on the Peace Process
- Leadership
- Sectarianism

UNIVERSALISM/PARTICULARISM

This represents a broad dimension along which chapters can be ordered in terms of their scope and inclusivity. It can also be regarded as a theme, with several contributors addressing the warrantability of deriving broad, pan-national principles underpinning conflict and conflict resolution that can be usefully applied to specific settings such as the Northern Ireland Troubles.

Returning to the idea of universalism/particularism as a dimension, some chapters such as that of Darby and MacGinty can be firmly placed towards the 'universalism' end of the continuum. These contributors sketch the results of their involvement in a multi-national piece of research on the peace processes taking place in South Africa, Israel–Palestine, the Basque Country, Sri Lanka and Northern Ireland. Likewise, the research by Gormley-Heenan and Robinson was carried out with the aim of illuminating the nature and role of political leadership in societies in transition. As part of this study they interviewed senior political leaders in South Africa, Israel and the Palestinian territories, and Northern Ireland, although the chapter mainly details findings from the latter. Moving away from the 'universalism' end of the dimension, other chapters are singularly embedded in the particular of the Northern Ireland context and indeed in sub-elements thereof. Jarman, for instance, explores the dynamics of inter-group relationships in interface areas in North Belfast, while Morgan addresses the contribution of women to community development in Northern Ireland. Moving further towards the particularist extreme, Dickson et al. and Hargie et al. take a much more in-depth, idiographic stance in their research, by opening a window on the fine detail of cross-community contact and communication within single organisations.

Universalism/particularism, derived as a theme, is touched upon by Darby and MacGinty. They argue that through comparative study they are able to tease out six major points of commonality running across the five national contexts already mentioned. These points have to do with: the nature of peace; the effects of violence; the impact of external influences; economic factors; the response of the people; and the role of symbols and rituals. That said, they are quick to acknowledge the uniqueness of historic, demographic and socio-cultural contextualisations, the idiosyncrasies of particular sets of circumstances, and the lack of uniformity of the profiles of the different peace processes. While Northern Ireland and South Africa, at the time of writing, are in various stages of post-conflict, relationships between Palestinians and Israelis have atrophied to the point where both have been dragged back into the vicious and bloody dialogue of atrocity and retaliation. Nevertheless, Darby and MacGinty are firmly wedded to the utility of a comparative perspective. Gormley-Heenan and Robinson concur, making a case in support of examining political leadership cross-culturally in different locations where movement out of conflict is taking place. In addition to issues of utility, both sets of authors point to the importance of a comparative perspective in advancing scholarship in their respective topic areas.

Thus, it is clear that to understand the Troubles we must look out as well as looking in. This book has shown how detailed, in-depth studies of particular contexts within Northern Ireland can illuminate our understanding of the processes involved. In addition, the examination of specific social dimensions (such as Niens et al.'s analysis of contact, and Morrow et al.'s evaluation of community relations) are essential if we are to build up a complete picture of the internal dynamics of the Troubles. At the same time, there is much to be learned from the experiences of conflict resolution elsewhere. There is much wisdom in the maxim followed by Otto von Bismarck: 'Only a fool learns from experience: I learn from the experience of others.' An examination of what has worked elsewhere can help to inform policy within Northern Ireland, and so prevent a return to the horrors of the bloody years of the Troubles. This leads to our next theme.

THE PRIMACY OF VICTIMS AND THE CONCEPT OF VICTIMHOOD

We deliberately decided to place the chapter on the human costs of the conflict at the start of this book. It is paramount that all debate about the Troubles should begin with, and never forget, the toll of misery and personal suffering that is an enduring legacy of the conflict. We wanted to set everything else against this dark but essential backdrop. As well as those killed and injured, psychological scars remain amongst many not 'centrally' affected. For example, the loss of a friend may not show on a statistical scoreboard of victims, but it can cause great pain and hurt for a very long period of time. For those who have had family killed or maimed the pain is enormous. No solution to the Troubles can ignore the awful waste of human lives and the sense of hurt and grievance carried by victims. Respectful remembrance must be coupled with positive steps to meet their practical and psychological needs.

Smyth and Hamilton chart the changes in attitudes to victims across the various phases of the Troubles. The history here is one of erratic and often ham-fisted reactions by government, the media and other agencies. Victims have experienced a variety of reactions from being ignored when larger atrocities occurred on the same day as the tragedy that shattered their lives, to facing intrusive attention, unfounded accusations, and even false conviction. Attention to their collective needs (e.g. the appointment of a Victims' Commissioner) emerged fairly late in the peace process, and almost as an attempt to be seen to be 'balanced' when making concessions to terrorist groups (e.g. releasing prisoners) following the Belfast Agreement. This attempt has been followed by the politicisation of victims. As a mirror to community divisions, different groups have emerged to represent Protestant and Catholic interests.

Smyth and Hamilton present a summative quantitative analysis of the 3,601 mortalities between 1969 and 2001. It is important to remember these facts:

- most fatalities occurred between 1971 and 1976 (over 50% of all deaths);
- the main perpetrators have been the paramilitary groups (80%);
- Republican groupings were responsible for 55.7% and Loyalists for 27.4% of all deaths;
- the security forces were responsible for some 10% of fatalities;
- those killed were overwhelmingly male (91%);
- the 20s and 30s age group was most affected (over 50%);
- proportionately more Catholics than Protestants have been victims;
- the IRA was responsible for some 85% of all killings by Republicans, and

as noted by Smith and Hamilton 'the IRA stands out as having made the largest contribution to the deaths' total;

• given the complex tapestry that is Northern Ireland, Republicans were responsible for a significant number of Catholic deaths and likewise with Loyalist and Protestant mortalities;

• almost all security force fatalities were caused by Republicans;

• the largest pro rata concentration of deaths has been in Belfast with a rate almost twice that of other areas;

• within Belfast the north and west sectors were most heavily affected while some parts of the east of the city remained relatively unscathed;

• there seems to be a correlation between regional deprivation indices and civilian deaths;

• one poignant and salutary finding is that for all groups responsible for deaths, the largest category of their victims was civilian.

While this detail is essential to understanding the violent topography of the Northern Irish political terrain, Smyth and Hamilton also underscore the psychology of victimhood. Both 'sides' perceive themselves to be the main victim community, and find it hard to acknowledge the suffering of the other. Given that most people know one or more victims, these become symbols so that there is at the very least a vicarious but very palpable identification with victimhood in society as a whole. The phenomenon of 'whataboutery' is pervasive (where when one side raises an issue relating to its suffering, this is met with the 'what about . . .' response in relation to an equal and opposite atrocity). Terrorists have carried out 'acts of retaliation' on the basis of avenging 'their' victims.

Government has also failed to recognise the sense of victimhood that prevails in communities as a whole. It tends to individualise this phenomenon. But needs at both individual and community levels must be identified and met. Smyth and Hamilton succinctly highlight the dangers of ignoring the latter for the entire peace process. Communities that have suffered disproportionately feel an obviously deeper sense of grievance and victimhood as a whole. This has to be recognised and dealt with if the process is to progress. Long-term strategic financial, medical and psychological planning is required. Overcoming the problem of victimhood, therefore, has to be one of the main supporting columns in the structure that will hold any stable peace process.

THE IMPORTANCE OF INTEGRATED EDUCATION

A perennial theme to emerge from social science research into the Troubles is that of the important absence of Integrated education. The media images of the sectarian dispute at Holy Cross primary school, mentioned by Jarman, focused international attention on the virulent divisions that occur from a very early age. The spectacle of parents engaging in confrontation as they marched their young children past one another to attend different schools, was viewed by many as a symptom of the social illness of educational segregation. In fact, the apartheid which prevails in education has, for some children, pre-school beginnings. While pre-school provision is limited in Northern Ireland, data provided by Gallagher shows that even at this stage, a high level of segregation exists in nursery schools and in nursery and reception classes in primary schools. Nor is it just that children are taught apart while being brought up in the one educational culture and exposed to essentially parallel sets of learning experiences. Studies carried out in Protestant and Catholic primary and post-primary schools revealed how subjects like religious education and history were treated quite differently in the two traditions with, for instance, religious education playing a more prominent part in the curriculum of Catholic pupils. History for these pupils typically concentrated much more upon Ireland, made use of source material produced in the Republic of Ireland, and had a strong focus upon battles and associated heroic figures.

More generally, Protestant pupils were more likely to go on school trips to visit community organisations and public authorities such as the police or fire brigade. In school, the two sets of pupils were exposed to contrasting sets of symbols and emblems from religious statues, on the one hand, to the flying of the Union flag on the other. Diversity of ethos even stretched to Protestant schools making more frequent contact, and having a closer affinity, with the administrative infrastructure of the education system. Initiatives introduced in the late 1980s requiring schools to introduce cross-community issues as part of Education for Mutual Understanding have received much critical attention. Meanwhile, present numbers attending Integrated schools remain low and DENI has been blamed for failing, between 1995 and 2000, to fulfil its objectives to support education provision of this type (see Dunn and Morgan, 1998).

Division and difference between our children are both emphasised and institutionalised at the formative stage in the formal education system. A pivotal opportunity is then lost to correct attitudes, beliefs and opinions that have been implanted in young children at the pre-school age. In their research, Connolly and Healy provide an illuminating insight into what is happening in the minds of children at various stages of development. Their findings confirm the fears that sectarian attitudes are taken in by children almost with mothers' milk. At the age of three to four years, they had already begun to identify with their 'own' signs and symbols (flags, soccer jerseys etc.) and were attaching positive values to these. Likewise, they were able to identify the other side's symbols and rate these negatively. Interestingly, their transcripts also reveal that these values are actively encouraged by adults, as when one young girl reveals that her grandmother had given her a Tricolour.

By the age of seven to eight years, Connolly and Healy show how these attitudes had begun to solidify. At this age children spend much of their time outside the home playing with in-group friends, and the 'them and us' socialisation process is reinforced by the peer group. This includes a matter-of-fact acceptance of, and identification with, respective paramilitary groupings (IRA, UDA, etc.). One interesting aspect to emerge from the transcripts is that at this age the children know *what* attitudes they are supposed to have but they cannot explain *why* they should hold these. Thus, they express negative views about the out-group, but when asked to proffer reasons for these the response is often 'I don't know'. By the age of ten to eleven years, the children show more understanding of the complexities of the situation, and are able to demonstrate some understanding of the need for reconciliation, and the awareness of similarities in both communities. However, they are patently aware of the dangers of showing too much support for cross-community schemes in which they are involved, and so contradictory remarks emerge in the Connolly and Healy study (e.g. two comments within a few seconds from the same girl about the cross-community scheme where each person was allocated a 'partner' from the other side: 'I never want to see them again' and 'Some partners were all right. My partner was nice.'). There is clearly a fear of being seen to be too supportive of the out-group, lest one be rejected by the in-group. Of course, the simple way to resolve this problem is to have children educated together. Children cannot be held culpable by the in-group for enjoying school, even if this involves socialising with the out-group.

Many young people reach university without having had any substantive contact with the other community. For example, Niens et al. report research to show that 50% of young people do not have any out-group friends before the age of 15, and if they do these friends are usually neighbours. In confirming this lack of cross-community contact, Hargie et al.'s study showed that when asked about this, those who had experienced integrated education rated the experience highly and indeed cherished it, while those educated in segregated schools expressed regret at having missed out on what they felt would have been an invaluable educational and social experience. It was also clear that, by this age, the strategies for handling differences of opinion about contentious issues were either to avoid raising them, when in the company of the out-group, or to hug the comfort blanket of one's in-group and avoid out-group members as much as possible. The legacy of segregated education, which for the vast majority of students was the sad reality, had resulted in an inability to handle sensitive topics with those from the other tribe. This is a tragic indictment on our education system. Yet, from the brief account by Gallagher, the movement towards integration in education certainly cannot be described as unfettered.

CONTACT IS NECESSARY BUT NOT SUFFICIENT

Given the fact of educational apartheid, there is a long history of cross-community contact initiatives, especially among school children, aimed at bringing Protestants and Catholics into face-to-face contact. Parallel to this, there has been a considerable degree of research by academics on the contact hypothesis. Basically, this hypothesis purports that a major cause of conflict is ignorance about the other group and so can be reduced by bringing people together within a conducive context. Indeed, policy makers, community leaders and academics have often seemed to operate on the basis that increased contact per se is the solution.

This has perfect face validity. Those centrally involved in the conflict in Northern Ireland live separate lives. The apartheid in schools is exacerbated by the fact that people inhabit different areas, play different sports, and so on. The violence therefore seems to be an extension of these divisions. Even if it is not a direct cause of the conflict, segregation serves to nurture and sustain it. If somehow the vicious circle of separation and conflict could be broken then a whole new shape to the geometry of communities may be formed with both sides intersecting at many angles and getting to know one another. However, while there is truth in the perspective that contact facilitates relationships and helps to break down barriers the correlation is by no means a simple linear one.

The chapters in this book clearly illustrate the complexities of contact. More is not necessarily better. Our contacts with others may be positive or negative. Indeed the more we meet others the *less* we may like them. Even if we do like people better as a result of contact, do we necessarily trust them more? The research by Hargie et al. into relationships amongst students suggests not. After a year at university, ratings of out-group attraction significantly increased, but ratings of trust significantly decreased. Trust was obviously affected by events in the wider community. It is likely that attraction is based upon *interpersonal* feelings, while trust is based upon *inter-group* attitudes. In their chapter, Niens et al. highlight this difference between attitudes to individuals as opposed to groups. Thus, the development of a relationship with one person from the out-group will not necessarily change one's attitudes to that group as a whole.

In terms of segregation, Niens et al. note that most friendships are along in-group lines. While there is an increasing trend towards mixed marriages across the religious divide, attitudes to such marriages have not really improved, at least not amongst those not involved in them. Segregated living has also increased over the period of the Troubles, with some 40% of people living in mono-community groups. In education, the number of Integrated schools has increased from 10 in 1989 to 46 today, although the Integrated sector still educates less than 3% of pupils. This is unfortunate, as Niens et al. also show that integrated education is related to extent of contact with the out-group, and contact in turn is a significant predictor of attitudes to the out-group.

There are a number of prerequisites for contact to be effective in improving inter-group relations. It should be:

- *Positive.* The contact should be designed in such a way as to be rewarding for both sides, resulting in a mutually conducive encounter. If the experience is negative, relationships may actually deteriorate.
- *Intimate.* Casual contact has little or no effect. There has to be a reasonable level of friendship or camaraderie developed.
- *Equal.* There should not be any imbalance of power between groups or individuals.

- *Co-operative.* The situation should not be one where either side is in danger of losing. Ideally it should be a context where both parties work together for a common and unthreatening goal.
- *Institutionally supported.* Key players and groups in the wider community should openly express support for the contact project. This support reduces the dangers for those involved and helps to elevate the status of participation.

It is clear that contact alone will not bring integration. A recurring feature in research studies is that for contact to produce beneficial effects it has to occur in a context of reduced inter-group anxiety. When tensions are high, people are likely to treat those from the out-group with greater suspicion and view their actions in this light. Under such circumstances, contact alone may only confirm existing biases. Indeed, in his case study of tensions in North Belfast, Jarman highlights the risks (derision, intimidation, violence etc.) facing those who engage in cross-community activities at times of heightened inter-community strife.

The other clear message is that contact will not just happen – it has to be *managed*. Thus, the Dickson et al. study found that employees wanted organisations to introduce social events after work, where both sides could interact, rather than returning home to segregated areas. Many organisations now recognise the importance of Corporate Social Responsibility, which often involves working closely with community groups or charities. The view of respondents in the Dickson et al. study was that charity should begin at home, in that the organisation should also have a corporate social responsibility for its staff, through the active promotion of good internal inter-group relations. Socialising outside work was by far the most popular suggestion made by employees in this respect. Likewise, Hargie et al. found that university students wanted the university to be proactive in promoting integration. It is difficult for individuals to bring about major change in patterns of contact, and so institutions have a key role to play. This brings us on to our next theme.

COMMUNITY RELATIONS MUST BE THE RESPONSIBILITY OF EVERYONE

The findings in relation to contact underscore another theme, as identified by Morrow et al., that the goal of improving cross-community relations must be seen to be the task of everyone. Morgan contributes a comprehensive account of the role being played by women in the broad field of community development. She estimates that some 6,000 women are actively involved, while identifying a less fully evolved tradition of engagement within Protestant areas. As emphasised by Morrow et al., if only a few people engage in this type of work then they can easily be shunted into one of a range of isolated sidings marked with labels such as 'do-gooders', 'ill-advised', or even 'traitors'. Morrow et al. have illustrated how the overarching goals of community relations have seldom been delineated, other than as a general desire to replace existing divisions with harmony. Not surprisingly, the term has become vague and woolly – a synonym for somehow 'doing good' to which everyone can subscribe. Accompanying practices are also fuzzy and lacking in co-ordination or consistency. Morrow et al. pose the pivotal question as to what precisely it means for a person 'to community relate' or 'to relate communally'. In other words, which activities improve community relations and which weaken them?

In their research they found that public attitudes to the term were often quite jaundiced. They ranged from the perspective that it was a devious way of undermining Nationalism/the Union or of achieving social engineering, to a view that is was about 'tea and cucumber sandwiches', and on to the cynical perception that it was a quick way to access funding. Morrow et al.'s contention is that the focus of community relations upon harmony has destroyed the possibility of grappling directly with the issues of division, with an emphasis upon disguising or sidelining tensions rather than trying to resolve them. They argue that this has failed, and that community relations initiatives have to be anchored to a bedrock of liberal democracy. As part of this, there is a need to re-examine first principles, such as the search for social justice, equity and acceptance of diversity. In their review of community relations activities in education, community groups, training organisations, businesses, government agencies and those working in the law and order field, they found that:

- over 60% of respondents could not identify any formal training/learning opportunities in their organisations that addressed the issue of political divisions;
- community relations emphases differed markedly across sectors;
- the centre of much of the work is in youth work, community work and education, and is largely ignored in other spheres';
- lip service is often paid to training in this field, as evidenced by the short duration of training programmes (typically one day or less, and mainly seminars rather than courses) and the numbers involved (usually fewer than 100 per organisation). This was confirmed by Bloomer and Weinreich, who found that the typical programme was delivered during one-hour slots per week over an eight- to twelve-week period;
- most of these programmes are fairly recent (post-1980) and their effectiveness largely untested. Indeed, in their research, Bloomer and Weinreich found that reconciliation programmes were only partially effective in impacting upon the perceptions of young people.

Morrow et al., in their analysis of community relations in action, found a degree of resentment amongst youth workers that this area was seen as being reserved for children and young people, and ipso facto of less value. The view of these workers was that adults in all positions needed to be involved and so act as positive role models. There was also a palpable level of anxiety associated with involvement in community relations across many sectors. Most bodies do not want to risk opening a can of worms. For example, many in the church felt a tension between deeply rooted theological beliefs and the need to embrace diversity. Likewise, sports bodies felt that involvement in this sphere might open a door best left closed, as unwanted issues might steal in.

Interestingly, when the door is prised open by others, sporting organisations can be spurred to action. The furore surrounding sectarianism at Windsor Park during Northern Ireland international football games brought this unsavoury feature to prominence and stimulated a successful anti-sectarian campaign. A further case in point is the removal of the Gaelic Athletic Association's former Rule 21. This banned members of the RUC and British military from participation in Gaelic Athletic Association (GAA) sports and in so doing alienated almost the entire Protestant population in Northern Ireland. Mounting criticisms of this discriminatory practice made retention of the rule untenable and provoked debate within the GAA about how it could become more representative of the entire community. What is needed, of course, is a more proactive approach across the board. The research by Hargie et al. has shown that sport is regarded by university students as a divisive issue. Indeed, the analogy by one student in their study, between GAA tops and orange sashes, provides an interesting insight into the depth of schism that has been caused by apartheid in sport. This leads to the issue of how visible symbols of division should be dealt with.

SYMBOLS, EMBLEMS AND THEIR MANAGEMENT

This broad theme runs through a number of chapters. It embraces three main issues: the role of symbols and emblems in perpetuating conflict; strategic choices surrounding how these can be best managed when coming out of violence and building peace; and the potential contribution in this regard of alternative sets of markers denoting a growing shared identity.

Darby and MacGinty identify symbolic factors as one of six important areas of consideration in peace processes generally. Warring factions gather about them panoplies of artefacts and rituals imbued with powerful tribal significance. These symbols serve to forge bonds of shared group identity and mark territory. At the same time, they typically alienate, antagonise and provoke the out-group. In so doing, their wilful flaunting can readily obstruct moves towards peace by marking difference, keeping memories of past grievances alive, and arousing suspicions of triumphalism and claims to victory by the other side. Established forms of symbolic expression consequently drag all back to old self-concepts and ways of relating. As Connolly and Healy have shown, the importance of these paraphernalia are assimilated by children from a very early age. In later life their importance has also been amply demonstrated. Thus, concerns over the display of flags, music, GAA regalia, and Glasgow Celtic and Rangers soccer jerseys, for instance, featured largely in the findings, by Dickson et al., of cross-community relations in the workplace and, by Hargie et al., of students in the university environment.

How best to manage these concerns is an important sub-theme from the research reported in this text. Expressed polemically, the debate is about whether to minimise divisions in organisations by banning contentious items, or to allow symbols of both communities in the workplace, so encouraging discussion and debate. Morrow et al. argue for a transformation in the current approach, away from an emphasis upon promoting harmony and introducing neutralisation policies, to one of encouraging engagement across all levels of society about how diversity can be embraced. The perspective here is that while banning emblems and debate may reduce tensions for those in that particular environment, this only treats a surface symptom while the deeper malady lingers and festers. This view holds that legislation to direct in-house policy acts as a ceiling to good practice rather than a baseline beyond which innovation is both welcome and possible. Morrow et al. suggest that once a culture of neutrality is established, the resistance to move towards diversity (learning to live with and accept one another's cultural differences and symbols) may be heightened as the risks and costs of failure are elevated.

The big question, of course, is at what point will individuals and organisations be ready to embrace diversity, and at what cost? Initial investigations certainly indicate a preference for the sanctuary of organisational neutrality. It is true that the sanctimonious attitudes of certain sectors that 'we have no problems here' is often a head-in-the-sand approach, and does little to contribute to the resolution of the problems across society as a whole. The chapters by Hargie et al. and Dickson et al. show that university students and employees in the public and private sector initially gave variants of the conditioned 'we are not bigoted and everyone gets on well' socially desirable response. However, when these bright surface views were further explored, in some instances dark areas of sectarianism were illuminated. The interesting facet of this research was an overwhelming desire by those in organisations to work in a symbol-free zone, and to leave sectarian differences outside the factory gate, office door or university entrance.

One phenomenon here is that of 'majoritarianism', in that when freedom is allowed the only symbols that tend to be shown or flown are those of the majority. The minority do not feel able to reciprocate because they lack a power base. What happens then, to take two actual quotations, is that they 'have to put up with it' or 'simmer in silence'. Being in a minority is an interesting phenomenon. It leads to very real feelings of psychological vulnerability and even physical fear. For this reason, it is vital that the rights of minorities are protected in law. Ireland, north and south, has a poor record of protecting minority rights. We must therefore listen to what the minority (and indeed the majority, in relation to symbols) in organisations are telling us. The clear message is one of ensuring an environment of neutrality.

Organisations have goals to achieve and should not be battlegrounds or hotbeds of controversial negotiation. That is not to say that the views of Morrow et al. do not have merit. Indeed they do, and they can be couched in terms of moving beyond resolution of conflict to the creation of reconciliation. If we are to progress beyond being a divided society we will have to recognise, accept and eventually embrace the differences that make us who we are. But the timing is all-important. Without seismic shifts in attitudes in the broader community, it is difficult to foresee, given the current practical realities of many organisations, how cherished symbols on both sides can easily be divested of their present powerful emotional trappings, and consequent capacity to antagonise and offend, without some transitional 'cooling-off' period during which they are put away by all. Their removal was found by Dickson et al. to usher in a more relaxed environment and help normalise relationships in the workplace. That said, Dickson et al. also identified beginnings by some employees to accept difference and a willingness to explore diversity, although this ran counter to the overall trend.

A third sub-theme has to do with the potential role of new, alternative symbols in cementing emergent, shared identities. Darby and MacGinty point to the example of the flypast by the air force as Nelson Mandela was sworn in as President of South Africa in 1994. The planes trailed red, green and black exhaust plumes, the colours of the new South African flag. Unfortunately, so far in Northern Ireland, efforts in this direction have been more transient, although still significant, and confined to such gestures as handshakes between (some) old political adversaries. More permanent symbols of togetherness to replace the old ones of division have eluded us to date.

LEARNING LESSONS FROM THE INTERFACE

Some parts of Northern Ireland experience no conflict while in others it is a fact of everyday life. Murtagh refers to the framework provided by Kliot and Mansfeld depicting the temporal stages of evolution in cities such as Beirut, Jerusalem, Nicosia and Belfast, from pre-partition, through partition and on to rapprochement and unification. He argues that in Northern Ireland the model has a valid spatial, rather than temporal, application. In other words, at the same point in time, some areas experience actual division or partition, with associated conflict, while others perhaps are better typified by rapprochement. An important line of thought here is that problems will only be resolved through a full understanding of what is happening in the former areas, why it occurs, and how it can be resolved. One such region is that of North Belfast, which has attracted enormous media attention in the past few years. However, as Jarman illustrates, it has long been at the very epicentre of the Troubles. This fact is confirmed by the high death rate in this area, as shown by Smyth and Hamilton, and by the very high rate of public disorder incidents. North Belfast therefore serves as a microcosm of the Troubles, and Jarman's work is a salutary case study of how to understand and manage conflict therein. The communities have become increasingly segregated, with the younger generation being more sectarian in their views than their parents. One reason for this is that many of them have never interacted with the out-group, whereas their parents and grandparents have had at least some experience of the 'other side', which serves to moderate their beliefs.

Young people in interface areas regularly engage in 'recreational rioting' as a form of adventure and excitement. There tends to be little control or restraint exercised by family, community or political groups. Indeed, rioting may actively be encouraged by the latter. Territories are rigidly divided along partisan lines, and there is a strong sense of needing to defend and maintain one's area for the in-group. This phenomenon is underscored by the fact that territory is directly linked to, and a sign of, political and paramilitary power. Consequently, attacks (either metaphorical or literal) on the other community as a means of reinforcing control, is a strategy adopted by both sides. This is compounded by a combined lack of faith in the police. It is an important part of the strategy, however, to carry out attacks without being caught red-handed and identified as the perpetrator, by influential third parties and particularly the watchful eye of the media. The moral high ground of victimhood must never be compromised. A media presence heightens this premium.

Jarman illustrates how some of the key players are often ambiguous in their attitude to the violence. They make different statements to different constituencies. While they may make public utterances opposing violence, it is sometimes in their vested interest to have such unrest – it literally gives them muscle. This attitude leads to the issue of negotiation, and there seems to be little evidence of a win-win approach. Gains for one side are usually viewed as losses by the other and there has been no real attempt to resolve underlying problems co-operatively. People are more inclined to give reasons as to why it is not possible to communicate with the other side rather than actively finding ways so to do. The other community is continually blamed and any aggression by one's own people is described as 'justifiable retaliation' or 'self-defence'.

One approach to preventing inter-communal conflict is to erect a physical barrier, or 'peace wall', at hot interface areas. But the psychology of barrier-building is complex. One side may see it as protection from attack, while for the other it may be viewed as a marking of territory or as a means of preventing their access to shops and facilities. Indeed, they may perceive violence as being a co-ordinated strategy to ensure the erection of a barrier. Another problem is that the barrier may stop violence in that spot, but simply move it to a neighbouring area. It is also a tangible memorial to the failure to communicate, and literally an obstruction to any future possibility of contact. Divisions become absolute. A more positive initiative described by Jarman was one in which young people took part in organised activities designed to get them away from flashpoint areas at times of tension (e.g. July). Part of this initiative involved cross-community schemes and they seem to have been very successful in reducing violent incidents.

Jarman describes another initiative in which mobile phones were issued to key players in both communities. These phones were switched on 24 hours a day and facilitated instant communication across the divide, and between community representatives and statutory bodies, proving to be very successful and relatively cheap. However, funding for this initiative petered out, reflecting the wider problem of funding tending to stop when tensions diminish. Fire fighting attracts resources but preventative measures are less appealing to funders. But this also means that the initiative that reduced the tensions can die, so that trouble again erupts. The emphasis is upon treatment rather than prevention, and as we know from the health care field, this is always a costlier option in the long run.

The haphazard and ad hoc approach to the financing of key initiatives is reflected in the dearth of any overall co-ordinated strategy by the statutory bodies to deal with cross-community tensions. Many of the programmes that have been implemented (although successful) have been short term, pitched at solving acute problems and independent of other initiatives. Jarman recommends the establishment of a broader commission, involving wide representation from all sectors and sections of the community, to formulate long-term policy, co-ordinate all activities and give direction. What is needed is more lateral thinking aimed at addressing and eventually resolving the long-standing and deeply rooted causes of the violence. This would require political will and substantial funding but the results would be well worth the effort.

THE COMPLEXITY OF IDENTITY

A further theme is that we need to be careful about concentrating upon the monochrome images of Catholic and Protestant. Anyone who has flown into Belfast International Airport will be aware that an aerial view of Northern Ireland reveals a patchwork quilt of fields of widely varying hues and shapes which serve as a metaphor for the social and political landscape. Identity is a technicolour, multi-faceted and variegated concept. It is a shifting dynamic, which is influenced by a whole panoply of personal, social, historical, local, national and international variables. In Northern Ireland the relationship between these various dimensions is often the key to understanding behaviour. To take but one example, in highly politicised interface ghettos where the conflict is endemic, political identity and its overt manifestation through signs and symbols may be of paramount importance amongst the 'underclass'– it is at the very essence of their being and a defining feature of who they are. Conversely, in leafy suburban estates, the possession and ostentatious display of a strong political identity may be regarded with a certain element of distaste among the professional classes. Here, other aspects of identity take centre stage.

The research by Bloomer and Weinreich further underscores the dangers of regarding Northern Ireland as two homogeneous communities, united together and against the other side. They found a not unsubstantial degree of alienation among Catholics and Protestants from their own communities, and a reasonable level of cross-identification with the other religious group. Perhaps not surprisingly some young people felt alienated from both sides. Furthermore, there was a diversity of views about the two communities rather than one single image, and this diversity varied greatly between individuals and was more pronounced among

Protestants than Catholics. But, as the power of the latter church continues to wane, it is very possible that the attitudes of Catholic youth may eventually mirror the more heterogeneous ones of Protestants.

Notions of majority and minority change across time and location, and their importance in terms of community religious background varies. Hargie et al. confirmed this complexity of identity among university students. For example, they found that gender was often a more salient dimension of identity than religion, in ratings of the interpersonal attractiveness of another. The authors have noted how, in university, birds of the same religious feather usually do flock together. However, if there are only two females in a class, we have also observed that they are much more likely to stay together than to form friendships with same-religion males, so that same-gender identity often predominates in this context. Thus, people have a range of in-groups as well as the politico-religious one. We identify more with those of the same age, gender or race, as well as with those who have similar interests and hobbies. These identities interact with, and in certain contexts will take precedence over, the politico-religious one.

Another aspect here is that the individual can decide whether or not to bring the politico-religious identity into play. As discussed by Niens et al. contacts with the out-group can take place with this part of one's identity 'switched on' or 'switched off'. Of course, it can also be provoked into life by the actions of others. In organisations, there is a clear preference amongst employees for it to be disengaged, and for potential triggers to be removed. The Dickson et al. and Hargie et al. studies showed that employees wanted a neutral environment that would minimise the likelihood of the politico-religious identity predominating over other important elements of identity (such as that of shared work roles).

EXTERNAL INFLUENCES ON THE PEACE PROCESS

A consistent line of thought running through many chapters relates to the impact of outside sources of influence in the perpetuation of violence, but especially on the movement towards peace. Indeed, as mentioned earlier, this is one of the six common themes identified by Darby and MacGinty in their comparative study. Few internal conflicts can be adequately understood without regard to a wider international framework. The armed struggles in both Sri Lanka and Northern Ireland, for instance, were largely financed through contributions from those living abroad with, respectively, Tamil and Irish backgrounds and senses of identity. Likewise, the demise of the Cold War and the removal of the threat of communism helped to create the circumstances for peace in South Africa. Darby and MacGinty further point to the intervention of foreign powers, and principally the United States, in acting as a catalyst for peace. Certainly the United States, and particularly the personal involvement of Bill Clinton and George Mitchell, played an invaluable role in establishing the Northern Ireland peace process and keeping it on track.

In exploring leadership in peace building, Gormley-Heenan and Robinson also make reference to intervention from outside the specific political system. They argue that this intervention is particularly likely in societies with strong leadership on one side of the internal division and weak leadership on the other. Furthermore, the general lack of power exercised by political leaders in Northern Ireland, outside the confines of their own parties, made it almost inevitable that they would have to court wider support to advance their causes. By gaining the patronage of Irish-Americans John Hume, as leader of the SDLP, achieved a significant prominence in Washington that he skilfully used to further his political agenda.

This thread of outside influences also emerges in the fabric of Higgins and Brewer's chapter. They explore the papal antichrist myth as it fuels Protestant sectarianism and speculate on the possible effects that globalisation may have. One thesis is that the mass media, rather than local traditions, is now the trellis shaping the growth of social identity. Through continuing exposure to this 'cultural glob', and the smothering of what once gave communities their distinctiveness, it could be predicted that esoteric sets of beliefs, such as the papal antichrist myth, will attenuate. Alternatively, it can be argued that globalisation and the threat to traditional identities will provoke a reaction, leading to the reaffirmation of that which people see as setting them apart from other cultural groupings and giving them a sense of who they are. Under this scenario, small fundamentalist sects would be expected to be revitalised.

LEADERSHIP

Gormley-Heenan and Robinson devote their chapter to this topic. They raise the intriguing question of how it was that peace was brought about in Northern Ireland, given that the central party leaders remained the same through this transitional period. Interestingly, Darby and MacGinty more generally point to the chance effects of changes in political leadership in moving peace processes forward. That apart, Gormley-Heenan and Robinson cite Paul Arthur in explaining that traditionally political leadership in Northern Ireland was underdeveloped, intimidatory, factional and demotic. This unhealthy combination led to the perpetuation of conflict and an inability to negotiate with conviction. Five key shifts took place that can be traced back to the 1980s, making progress possible. First, leaders rose to the lure of real political power being made available through devolution. Second, external sponsors brought traditional protagonists together, both in Northern Ireland and abroad, as part of relationship building and training initiatives. Third, party leadership became more broadly defined and less vested in a particular individual. Fourth, the emergence of a number of smaller parties such as the Progressive Unionist Party (PUP) and Northern Ireland Women's Coalition (NIWC) changed the political landscape and acted as a catalyst for change. Finally, the general image of the Northern Ireland politician began to improve.

The relationship between leaders and the led during transitions out of violence is taken up by both Gormley-Heenan and Robinson, and Darby and MacGinty. To what extent does popular opinion drive political leaders towards peace, on the one hand, or, on the other, become shaped by those representatives? Darby and MacGinty readily acknowledge that sustainable initiatives depend upon both. With the exception of the Basque Country, there has been little evidence of leaders being swept along on the crest of a huge upsurge in popular support for an end to violence. As explained by Gormley-Heenan and Robinson, power in Northern Ireland has by custom been largely 'bottom-up', placing very real limits on the extent to which party bosses can move beyond well-defined boundaries. The metaphor of an elastic band was used by a senior member of Sinn Fein to depict the interdependence between leaders and their constituents. If tensioned beyond tolerance by an overly adventurous leader, this band can snap, pitching the latter into political oblivion and constituents back into old familiar, entrenched attitudes.

The need for leadership has been more generally recognised. Thus, Morrow et al. underscore the importance of leadership at a local level in moving community relations forward, while Jarman has shown the problems caused when local leaders either implicitly or explicitly support conflict. In the organisational setting, Dickson et al. identify the role of corporate leadership as crucial in the quest to eliminate sectarianism from the workplace. Workers were confident that the upper echelons of the organisation were determined to bring about change in this regard and that grievances of a sectarian nature raised would be treated seriously at that stratum.

SECTARIANISM

This is our final theme, and it is scarcely a surprise that the concept of sectarianism should recur through any book devoted to the nature of conflict in Northern Ireland. For Liechty and Clegg (2001: 340) 'Sectarianism takes the form of destructive patterns of relating. These patterns – blaming, separating, overlooking, belittling, dehumanising, demonising, and attacking – are endemic in Northern Ireland.' Sectarianism is also a double-headed monster, as both sides of the community have mirror image structures, symbols and behaviour patterns designed to exclude or offend the other. Connolly and Healy have shown how the paraphernalia and attitudes of sectarianism are readily learned and assimilated by young children, so that by late childhood they have become ingrained into the fabric of their identities.

The topic is centrally addressed in the chapter by Higgins and Brewer who define it as 'the determination of actions, attitudes, and practices by practices about religious difference, which results in them invoked as the boundary marker to represent social stratification and conflict'. Sectarianism occurs at three levels: ideas, individual actions and social structures. In respect of the first two, parallels are drawn between Catholic and Protestant discrimination. Given the historic backdrop to the Northern Ireland conflict, it is argued that Protestant sectarianism at the institutional level, however, finds no reciprocating match on the part of

Catholics. In relation to education, for instance, Gallagher shows how more equitable treatment of the two largely community-specific systems has been mirrored in an attenuation of the difference in educational outcomes, between Protestant and Catholic children, to the point where it has virtually disappeared.

While the main thrust of the Higgins and Brewer chapter centres on the role of the papal antichrist myth in driving Protestant sectarianism, such bigotry, unfortunately, has a much wider reach. Nor is it an exclusively urban phenomenon. Murtagh details the sad demise of Glenanne, a small and almost exclusively Protestant village in Co. Armagh, following terrorist attacks on the local army base, the sectarian murder of ten workers (all Protestant males) in a single incident, the burning of the local Orange hall, and the gradual drift away of the population. A downward spiral of declining numbers took place leading to reduced amenities, creating further reductions in population. As the community withered, the local post office and grocery shop closed, young people moved away, which had the impact of forcing the local school to close etc.

Switching to the urban setting, Jarman describes how sectarianism is acted out in the interface areas of North Belfast. Segregation and the quest to gain territory, by the one side, and defend it by the other, are amongst the factors that have provided the oxygen for violence. Sectarianism was also discovered to be an unpalatable feature of the workplace in both the public and private sectors, from the research carried out by Dickson et al. (2002), although it seemed much less prevalent than was once the case. Staff were particularly keen to see further moves in this direction and were united in their view that organisations had a much more conspicuous part to play in improving cross-community relations amongst the different sections of their workforce. One intriguing issue raised by Dickson et al., in relation to the case study from their wider research, had to do with tolerance, toleration, informal norms and the tacit recognition of often soft boundaries of acceptable behaviour. What passes as largely innocent banter in some circumstances and with certain individuals, can be experienced as offensive under apparently similar sets of conditions. Sectarianism can come in subtle shades of grey.

CONCLUSIONS

While we make no claims about how comprehensive they may be to a full understanding of the Troubles, we have employed the 11 themes identified in this chapter to summarise the main findings of the social science researchers who have contributed to this text. Certainly, no analysis of the Northern Ireland conflict would be complete without taking these into consideration. It is our hope that the material presented in this book will provide valuable insights for anyone who wishes to study the Troubles seriously. The content should also make some contribution to politicians and policy makers tasked with the daunting challenge of framing decisions that count in advancing the processes of resolution and reconciliation.

REFERENCES

Abrams, D., Ando, K. and Hinkle, S. (1998) 'Psychological attachment to the group: cross-cultural differences in organizational identification and subjective norms as predictors of worker's turnover intentions', *Personality and Social Psychology Bulletin* 24: 1027–39.

ACSC (Antrim Community Safety Committee) (2000) *Community Safety Audit: Executive Summary.* Antrim, ACSC.

Afifi, W. and Guerrero, L. (2000) 'Motivations underlying topic avoidance in close relationships', in S. Petronio (ed.) *Balancing the Secrets of Private Disclosures*, Mahwah, NJ: Lawrence Erlbaum.

Akenson, D.H. (1973) *Education and Enmity: The Control of Schooling in Northern Ireland, 1920–1950.* Newton Abbot: David and Charles.

Alexander, J, Daly, P, Gallagher, A, Gray, C and Sutherland, A (1998) *An evaluation of the Craigavon two-tier system. Research Report No. 12.* Bangor: DENI.

Allport, G.W. (1954) *The Nature of Prejudice.* Reading, Mass.: Addison-Wesley.

Amir, Y. (1969) 'Contact hypothesis in ethnic relations', *Psychological Bulletin* 71: 319–42.

Amir, Y. (1976) 'The role of intergroup contact in change of prejudice and ethnic relations', in P.A. Katz (ed.) *Towards the Elimination of Racism.* Oxford: Pergamon.

Amir, Y. and Ben-Ari, R. (1988) 'Enhancing intergroup relations in Israel: A different approach in stereotyping Jewish youth in Israel: Reality and Potential', *Megamot*, 30: 306–15.

Argyle, M. (1994) *The Psychology of Social Class.* London: Routledge.

Argyle, M., and Henderson, M. (1985) *The Anatomy of Relationships.* London: Heinemann.

Arnstein, W.L. (1982) *Protestants Versus Catholics in Mid-Victorian England.* Columbia: Columbia University Press.

Aron, A., Aron, E.N., Tudor, M. and Nelson, G. (1991) 'Close relationships as including other in the self', *Journal of Personality and Social Psychology* 60: 241–53.

Arthur, P. (1990) 'Negotiating the Northern Ireland problem: track one or track two diplomacy?' *Government and Opposition,* 25, (4): 403–18

Arthur, P. (1999) 'The Anglo-Irish peace process: obstacles to reconciliation', in R. Rothstein (ed.) *After the Peace: Resistance and Reconciliation,* Boulder, CO: Lynne Rienner.

Arthur, P. (2000) 'Peer-Learning: Northern Ireland as a Case Study' (Unpublished report – see http://www.ccdpc.org/pubs/arthur/arthur.htm)

Austin, R. (1985) (ed.) *History in Schools: Essays on History Teaching in the Classroom.* Coleraine: University of Ulster.

Barritt, D.P. and Carter, C.F. (1962) *The Northern Ireland Problem: a study in group relations*. London: Oxford University Press.

Baxter, L. and Sahlstein, E. (2000) 'Some possible directions for future research', in S. Petronio (ed.) *Balancing the Secrets of Private Disclosures*, Mahwah, New Jersey: Lawrence Erlbaum.

Belfast Interface Project (1998) *Young People on the Interface*. Belfast, BIP.

Belfast Interface Project (1999) *Inner East and Outer West: Addressing Conflict in two Interface Areas*. Belfast, BIP.

Blondel, J. (1987) *Political Leadership: Towards a General Analysis*. London: Sage.

Bloomer, F (2002) *The efficacy of community reconciliation projects for identity redefinition in young people in Northern Ireland*. PhD thesis. Jordanstown: University of Ulster.

Bloomfield, K. (1998) *We Will Remember Them: Report of the Northern Ireland Victims Commissioner, Sir Kenneth Bloomfield*. Belfast: HMSO: The Stationery Office.

Bloomfield, K., Gibson, M. and Greer, D. (1999) *Criminal Injuries Compensation in Northern Ireland: A Report to the Secretary of State for Northern Ireland*. Belfast: Tactica.

Blueprint Development Consultancy (2000) Women's Centres Sustainability Conference. Belfast: Women's Support Network.

Boal, F. (1999) 'From undivided cities to undivided cities: assimilation to ethnic cleansing', *Housing Studies*, 14: 585–600.

Boal, F., Campbell, J. and Livingstone, D. (1991) '"The Protestant Mosaic": A majority of minorities', in P. Roche and B. Barton (eds.) *The Northern Ireland Question: Myth and Reality*, Aldershot: Avebury.

Bollens, S. (1999) *Urban Peace-Building in Divided Societies*. Colorado: Westview Press.

Boyatzis, R. (1998) *Transforming Qualitative Information: Thematic Analysis and Code Development*. Thousand Oaks, Cal.: Sage.

Boyle, J.F. (1976) 'Educational attainment, occupational achievement and religion in Northern Ireland', *Economic and Social Review*, 8: 79–100.

Breen, R., Devine, P. and Dowds, L. (1996) *Social Attitudes in Northern Ireland*. Belfast: Appletree.

Breen, S. (2000) 'Internal SDLP Review Cites Risk From Sinn Fein', *Irish Times*. (27/4/00)

Brewer, J. (1992) 'Sectarianism and racism, and their parallels and differences', *Ethnic and Racial Studies* 15: 352–64.

Brewer, J. (1998) *Anti-Catholicism in Northern Ireland 1600–1998: The Mote and the Beam*. London: Macmillan.

Brewer, J. (1999) *Globalisation, locality and ethnography*, paper for the American Society of Criminology Annual Conference, Toronto, 17–20 November.

Brewer, J. and Higgins, G. (1999) 'Understanding anti-Catholicism in Northern Ireland', *Sociology* 33: 235–55.

Brewer, M.B. (2000) 'Social identity theory and change in intergroup relations', in D. Capozza and R. Brown (eds) *Social Identity Processes: Trends in Theory and Research*. London: Sage Publications.

Brewer, M.B. and Miller, N. (1984) 'Beyond the contact hypothesis: theoretical perspectives on desegregation', in N. Miller and M.B. Brewer (eds) *Groups in Contact: the psychology of desegregation*. New York: Academic Press.

Brown, R. (2000) 'Social identity theory: past achievements, current problems, and future challenges', *European Journal of Social Psychology*, 30: 745–78.

Brown, R., Condor, A. M., Wade, G. and Williams, J. (1986) 'Explaining intergroup differentiation in an industrial organization', *Journal of Occupational Psychology* 59: 273–86.

Bruce, S. (1985a) *No Pope of Rome*. Edinburgh: Mainstream.

Bruce, S. (1985b) 'Authority and fission: the Protestants' divisions', *British Journal of Sociology* 36: 592–603.

Bruce, S. (1986) *God Save Ulster!* Oxford: Oxford University Press.

Bruce, S. (1990) *A House Divided: Protestantism, Schism, and Secularization*. London: Routledge.

Bruce, S. (1994) *The Edge of the Union*. Oxford: Oxford University Press.

Buckland, P. (1979) The Factory of Grievances: devolved government in Northern Ireland 1921–1939. Dublin: Gill and Macmillan.

Burns Report (2001) *Education for the 21st Century: Report of the Review Body on Post-Primary Education*. Bangor: Department of Education.

Cairns, E. (1980) 'The development of ethnic discrimination in young children', in J. Harbison and J. Harbison (eds) *Children and Young People in Northern Ireland: A Society Under Stress*. Belfast: Open Books.

Cairns, E. (1982) 'Intergroup conflict in Northern Ireland', in H. Tajfel (ed.) *Social Identity, and Intergroup Relations*. Cambridge: Cambridge University Press.

Cairns, E. (1983) 'The political socialisation of tomorrow's parents: violence, politics, and the media', in J. Harbison (ed.) *Children of the Troubles: Children in Northern Ireland*. Belfast: Stranmillis College.

Cairns, E. (1987) *Caught in the Crossfire: Children and the Northern Ireland Conflict*. Belfast: Appletree.

Cairns, E. (1989) 'Social identity, and intergroup conflict in Northern Ireland: a developmental perspective', in J. Harbison (ed.) *Growing up in Northern Ireland*. Belfast: Stranmillis College.

Cairns, E. (1992) 'Social psychological research on the conflict', *The Psychologist* 5: 342-44.

Cairns, E. (1994) 'Understanding conflict and promoting peace in Ireland: Psychology's contribution', *The Irish Journal of Psychology* 15: 480–93.

Cairns, E. and Cairns, T. (1995) 'Children and conflict: a psychological perspective', in S. Dunn (ed.) *Facets of the Conflict in Northern Ireland*. Basingstoke: Macmillan.

Cairns, E. and Darby, J. (1998) 'The conflict in Northern Ireland: Causes, consequences, and controls', *American Psychologist* 53: 754–60.

Cairns, E. and Dunn, S. (1995) *The Correlates of Adult Cross-community Contact in Northern Ireland: A Report to the Central Community Relations Unit*. Coleraine: Centre for the Study of Conflict.

Cairns, E. and Duriez, R. (1976) 'The influence of speaker's accent on recall by Catholic and Protestant school children in Northern Ireland', *British Journal of Social and Clinical Psychology* 15: 441–2.

Cairns, E. and Hewstone, M. (2000) *Qualitative Aspects of Cross-community Contact in Northern Ireland: A Multivariate Analysis. A Report to Central Community Relations Unit*. Coleraine: University of Ulster.

Cairns, E. and Hewstone, M. (in press) 'The impact of peacemaking in Northern Ireland on intergroup behaviour', in G. Salomon and B. Nevo (eds) *The Nature and Study of Peace Education*. Lawerence Erlbaum.

Cairns, E. and Mercer, G.W. (1984) 'Social identity in Northern Ireland', *Human Relations* 37: 1095–02.

Cairns, E., Gallagher, A.M. and Dunn, S. (1993) *Intergroup Contact in a Northern Irish University Setting: A Report to the Central Community Relations Unit*. Coleraine: Centre for the Study of Conflict, University of Ulster.

Cairns, E., Hamberger, J. and Hewstone, M. (in preparation) 'Cross-community contact in Northern Ireland and attitudes towards intergroup relations'.

Cairns, E., Hunter, D. and Herring, L. (1978) 'Young children's awareness of violence in Northern Ireland: the influence of Northern Irish television in Scotland and Northern Ireland'. Unpublished paper presented to the annual conference of the Northern Ireland Branch of the British Psychological Society, Virginia, Co. Cavan, Ireland.

Cairns, E., Hunter, D. and Herring, L. (1980) 'Young children's awareness of violence in Northern Ireland: the influence of television in Scotland and Northern Ireland', *British Journal of Social and Clinical Psychology* 19: 3–6.

Cairns, E., Wilson, R., Gallagher, T. and Trew, K. (1995) 'Psychology's contribution to understanding conflict in Northern Ireland', *Peace and Conflict: Journal of Peace Psychology* 1: 131–48.

Campbell, B. (1993) *Goliath: Britain's Dangerous Places*. London, Methuen.

Carlin, T. (1979) Speech at the launch of the NICTU 'Better Life for All' campaign. Belfast.

Carnegie Commission on Preventing Deadly Conflict – CCPDC (1998) *Essays on Leadership*, New York: Carnegie Corporation of New York

CCEA (1997) Mutual Understanding and Cultural Heritage: cross-curricular guidance material. Belfast: CCEA.

Christopher, A. J. (2001) 'Urban segregation in post-apartheid South Africa', *Urban Studies*, 38: 449–66.

Cialdini, R. (2001) *Influence: Science and Practice*. Boston: Allyn and Bacon.

Clampitt, P. (2000) 'The questionnaire approach'. In O. Hargie and D. Tourish (eds) *Handbook of Communication Audits for Organisations*, London: Routledge.

Clampitt, P. and Downs, C. (1993) 'Employee perceptions of the relationship between communication and productivity: A field study', *Journal of Business Communication*, 30: 5–28.

Colley, L. (1992) *Britons: Forging the Nation 1707–1837*, New Haven: Yale University Press.

Condren, M. (1989) *The Serpent and the Goddess, Women, Religion and Power in Celtic Ireland*. San Francisco: Harper Row.

Connolly, P. (1996) '"Seen but never heard": rethinking approaches to researching racism and young children', *Discourse: Studies in the Cultural Politics of Education* 17: 171–85.

Connolly, P. (1998) *Racism, Gender Identities and Young Children*. London: Routledge.

Connolly, P. (2001) 'Qualitative methods in the study of children's racial attitudes and identities', *Infant and Child Development* 10: 219–33.

Connolly, P. with Maginn, P. (1999) *Sectarianism, Children and Community Relations in Northern Ireland*. Coleraine: Centre for the Study of Conflict, University of Ulster.

Cook, S.W. (1970) 'Motives in conceptual analysis of attitude-related behaviour' in W. J. Arnold and D. Levine (eds) *Nebraska Symposium on Motivation*. Lincoln: University of Nebraska Press, vol. 17: 179–235.

Cormack, R.J. and Osborne, R.D. (1983). The Transition from School to Work (1) The Belfast Study: into work in Belfast. In Cormack, R.J. and Osborne, R.D. (eds) *Religion, Education and Employment: aspects of equal opportunity in Northern Ireland*. Belfast: Appletree Press.

Cormack, R.J., Gallagher, A.M. and Osborne, R.D. (1991) *Educational Affiliation and* educational attainment in Northern Ireland: The financing of schools in Northern Ireland, Annex E, Sixteenth Report of the Standing Advisory Commission on Human Rights, House of Commons Paper 488, London: HMSO.

Cormack, R.J., Gallagher, A.M. and Osborne,R.D. (1992a) *Access to Grammar Schools, Annex E, Seventeenth Annual Report of the Standing Advisory Commission on Human Rights, House of Commons Paper 54*, London: HMSO.

Cormack, R.J., Gallagher, A.M., Osborne, R.D. and Fisher, N. (1992b) *Secondary Analysis of the DENI Curriculum Survey, Annex F, Seventeenth Report of the Standing Advisory Commission on Human Rights, House of Commons Paper 54*, London: HMSO.

Cormack, R.J., Osborne, R.D. and Miller, R.L. (1989) 'Student loans: a Northern Ireland perspective'. *Higher Education Quarterly*, 43(3), 229–45.

Cormack, R.J., Osborne, R.D. and Thompson, W.T. (1980). *Into Work? Young School Leavers and the Structure of Opportunity in Belfast*. Belfast: Fair Employment Agency Research Paper 5.

Cormack, R.J., Osborne, R.D., Reid, N.G. and Williamson, A.P. (1984). *Participation in Higher Education: trends in the social and spatial mobility of Northern Ireland undergraduates*. Final Report SSRC Funded Project HR 6846.

Craig, J. and Cairns, E. (1999) *Intergroup Interaction: An Investigation into its Role in Reducing Intergroup Anxiety in Further Education Students in Northern Ireland: A Report to the Central Community Relations Unit*. Coleraine: University of Ulster.

Crawford, A. and Matassa, M. (2000) 'Community safety structures: An international literature review'. *Criminal Justice Review Research Report 8*. London, Stationary Office.

Criminal Justice Review Group (2000) *Review of the Criminal Justice System in Northern Ireland*. Belfast, HMSO.

CSC (Community Safety Centre) (2000) *Implementing Community Safety and Crime Reduction from Audit to Action*. Belfast, CSC.

Cunningham, J. (2001) 'Pouring oil', *Guardian Society*, 11 July 2001.

Darby, J. (1973) 'Divisiveness in education', *The Northern Teacher*, 11: 3–12.

Darby, J. (1974) 'History in the schools: a review article', *Community Forum*, 4: 37–42.

Darby, J. (1976) *Conflict in Northern Ireland*, Dublin: Gill and Macmillan.

Darby, J. (1978) 'Northern Ireland: Bonds and breaks in education'. *British Journal of Educational Studies*, 26: 215–23.

Darby, J. (1986) *Intimidation and the Control of the Conflict in Northern Ireland*, Dublin: Gill and Macmillan.

Darby, J. and Dunn, S. (1987). 'Segregated schools: The research evidence'; in Osborne, R.D., Cormack, R.J. and Miller, R.L. (eds.) *Education and Policy in Northern Ireland*. Belfast: Policy Research Institute.

Darby, J. and MacGinty, R. (eds) (2000) *The Management of Peace Processes*, London: MacMillan.

Darby, J., Murray, D., Batts, D., Dunn, S., Farren, S. and Harris, J. (1977) *Education and Community in Northern Ireland: Schools Apart?* Coleraine: the New University of Ulster.

Darby, J., Murray, D., Dunn, S., Batts, D., Farren, S. and Harris, J. (1977) *Education and Community in Northern Ireland: Schools Apart?* Coleraine: Centre for the Study of Conflict, University of Ulster.

Davis, K. (1953) 'A method of studying communication patterns in organizations', *Personnel Psychology*, 6: 301–12.

DeMarco, D. and Galster, G. (1993) 'Prointegrative policy: theory and practice', *Journal of Urban Affairs*, 15: 141–160.

DENI (1989) Unpublished survey material, Department of Education

DENI (1996a) *Transfer Procedure Test Results 1989/90 – 1995/96, Statistical Bulletin 1/96*. Bangor: Department of Education.

DENI (1996b) *Free School Meals and Low Achievement, Statistical Bulletin SB2/96*. Bangor: Department of Education.

DENI (2000) *School Performance Tables 1998/99*. Bangor: Department of Education.

Department of Education Northern Ireland (DENI) (1999) *Towards a culture of tolerance: Education for diversity. Report of the working group on the strategic promotion of Education for Mutual Understanding*. Belfast: DENI.

Department of Regional Development (DRD) (2001) *Shaping Our Future, Regional Development Strategy for Northern Ireland*. Belfast: Stationary Office.

Derlega, V. J., Metts, S., Petronio, S., and Margulis, S.T. (1993) *Self-disclosure*. Newbury Park, CA: Sage.

DHSS – Department of Health and Social Security (1998) *Building Real Partnership: Compact between Government and the Voluntary Community Sector in Northern Ireland*. Belfast: DHSS.

Dickson, D, Hargie, O. and Nelson, S. (2002) *Relational Communication Between Catholics and Protestants in the Workplace: A Study of Policies, Practices and Procedures*. Jordanstown: University of Ulster.

Dickson, D. A., Hargie, O. D. W. and Rainey, S. (1999) *Communication and Relational Development in the Workplace*. A report on research funded by The Central Community Relations Unit, Jordanstown: University of Ulster.

Dickson, D., Hargie, O. and Rainey, S. (2000) 'Communication and relational development between Catholic and Protestant students in Northern Ireland', *Australian Journal of Communication* 27: 67–82.

Dindia, K. (2000a) 'Self-disclosure, identity, and relationship development', in K. Dindia and S. Duck (eds) *Communication and Personal Relationships*, Chichester: Wiley.

Dindia, K. (2000b) 'Sex differences in self-disclosure, reciprocity of self-disclosure, and self-disclosure and liking: Three meta-analyses reviewed', in S. Petronio (ed.) *Balancing the Secrets of Private Disclosures*, Mahwah, New Jersey: Lawrence Erlbaum.

Downs, C., Hydeman, A. and Adrian, A. (2000) 'Auditing the annual business conference of a major beverage company'. In O. Hargie and D. Tourish (eds) *Handbook of Communication Audits for Organisations*. London: Routledge.

du Toit, P. (2001) *South Africa's Brittle Peace: The problem of post-settlement violence*. London: Palgrave.

Duck, S. (1999) *Relating to Others*, 2nd edition. Buckingham: Open University Press.

Dunn, S. (1993) 'A historical context to education and church-state relations in Northern Ireland'. In Osborne, RD, Cormack, RJ and Gallagher AM (eds) *After the Reforms: Education and Policy in Northern Ireland*, Avebury: Aldershot.

Dunn, S. and Morgan, V. (1988) *The social context of education in Northern Ireland*. Unpublished Paper, Centre for the Study of Conflict, University of Ulster.

Dunn, S. (1986). 'The role of education in the Northern Ireland conflict'. *Oxford Review of Education*, 12: 233–42.

Dunn, S. and Morgan, V. (1999) '"A fraught path" – education as a basis for developing improved community relations in Northern Ireland', *Oxford Review of Education*, 25: 141–53.

Dunn, S. and Smith, A. (1989) *Inter-School Links*, Coleraine: Centre for the Study of Conflict, University of Ulster.

Dunn, S. and Smith, A. (1990) *Inter-School Links*. Coleraine: Centre for the Study of Conflict.

Dunn, S., and Morgan, V. (1994) *Protestant alienation in Northern Ireland: A preliminary survey*. Coleraine: University of Ulster.

Dunn, S., Darby, J. and Mullan, K. (1984) *Schools Together?* Coleraine: Centre for the Study of Conflict.

Edge, S. (1998) 'Representing gender and National identity', in D. Miller (ed.) *Rethinking Northern Ireland*, London: Longman.

Egelund, J. (1997) *The Peace Process in the Middle East*, Presentation to the Institute of Irish Studies, Belfast, 19 November.

Elliot, M. (2000) *The Catholics of Ulster: A History*. London: Allen Lane, The Penguin Press.

Ellis, G. (2000) 'Addressing inequality: Planning in Northern Ireland', *International Planning Studies*, 5: 345–64.

Emmanuel, M. (1985) 'Auditing communication practices'. In C. Reuss and R. DiSilvas (eds) *Inside Organisational Communication* (2nd edition). New York: Longman.

European Anti-Poverty Network (2000) 'Mainstreaming social inclusion to promote social cohesion', *Network News*, No. 73: 2–4.

Eyben, K., Morrow D., and Wilson D. (1997a) *Different approaches to equity, diversity, and interdependence*. Coleraine: Future Ways, University of Ulster.

Eyben, K., Morrow, D. and Wilson, D. (1997b) *A Worthwhile Venture: Practically Investing in Equity, Diversity and Interdependence*. Coleraine and Jordanstown: University of Ulster.

Fay, M-T., Morrissey, M. and Smyth, M. (1997) *Mapping Troubles-Related Deaths in Northern Ireland 1969–1994*. Derry/Londonderry, Incore.

Fay, M.T., Morrissey, M. and Smyth, M. (1998) *Northern Ireland's Troubles: The Human Costs*. London: Pluto.

Fay, M.T., Morrissey, M., Smyth, M. and Wong, T. (1999) *The Cost of the Troubles Study: Report on the Northern Ireland Survey: the experience and impact of the Troubles*. INCORE/University of Ulster/The United Nations University.

Featherstone, M. (1995) *Undoing Culture: Globalization, Postmodernism and Identity*, London: Sage.

Feenan, D. (2000) *Community Safety: Partnerships and Local Government. Criminal Justice Review Research Report 13*. London, Stationary Office.

Ferguson, N., and Cairns, E. (1996) 'Political violence and moral maturity in Northern Ireland', *Political Psychology* 17: 713–25.

Fields, R. (1973) *A Society on the Run: A Psychology of Northern Ireland*. Harmondsworth: Penguin.

Fisher, D. (1984) 'A conceptual analysis of self-disclosure', *Journal for the Theory of Social Behavior* 14: 277–96.

Fitzduff, M. (1996) *Beyond Violence – Conflict Resolution Processes in Northern Ireland*, Tokyo: UNU Press

Foote, T. P. (1980) *The Staffing Needs of Post-Primary Schools: 1980*. Belfast: Northern Ireland Council for Educational Research.

Foster, D. and Finchilescu, G. (1986) 'Contact in a "Non-Contact" society: The case of South Africa', in M. Hewstone and R. Brown (eds) *Contact and Conflict in Intergroup Encounters*. Basil Blackstaff: Oxford.

Fraser, G. and Morgan, V. (2000) 'Miracle on the Shankill: the Peace March and rally of 28 August 1976', in T. G. Fraser (ed.) *The Irish Marching Tradition*, London: Macmillan.

Fraser, M. (1974) *Children in Conflict*, Harmondsworth: Penguin.

Fulton, J. (1982) 'Education in Northern Ireland.' In Cohen, L., Thomas, J and Manion, L. (eds) *Educational Research and Development in Britain, 1970–1980*. England: NFER-Nelson.

Gaertner, S., Dovidio, J.F., Anastasio, P.A., Bachevan, B.A. and Rust, M.C. (1993) 'The common ingroup identity model: recategorization and the reduction of intergroup bias', in W. Stroewe and M. Hewstone (eds) *European Review of Social Psychology*. Chichester: Wiley.

Gallagher, A. M. (1982) *Intergroup Relations and Political Attitudes in Northern Ireland*. Unpublished Master Thesis: Queen's University of Belfast.

Gallagher, A. M. (1983) *Criticism and self-criticism: Social Psychology and Northern Ireland*. Paper presented at the Annual Conference of the Northern Ireland Branch of the British Psychological Society, Rosapenna.

Gallagher, A.M. (1988). *Transfer Pupils at 16*. Belfast: Northern Ireland Council for Educational Research.

Gallagher, A.M. (1989a) 'Social identity and the Northern Ireland conflict', *Human Relations* 42: 917–35.

Gallagher, A.M. (1989b) 'The relationship between research and policy: an example from Northern Ireland', *The Psychologist: Bulletin of the British Psychological Society*, 2: 62–3.

Gallagher, A. M. (1992) 'Education in a divided society', *The Psychologist*, 5: 353–57.

Gallagher, A.M. (1995) 'The approach of government: Community relations and equity', in S. Dunn (Ed.) *Facets of the Conflict in Northern Ireland*. London: St Martin's Press.

Gallagher, A.M. (1995) *Majority Minority Review 1 Education in a Divided Society: A review of research and policy* (2nd ed.). Coleraine: University of Ulster.

Gallagher, A.M. (2000) 'Statistical patterns in schools', in Department of Education, *Research into the effects of the selective system of secondary schools in Northern Ireland, Research papers 1*, Bangor: Department of Education.

Gallagher, A. M. and Dunn, S. (1991) 'Community relations in Northern Ireland: Attitudes to contact and integration', in P. Stringer and G. Robinson (eds) *Social Attitudes in Northern Ireland: The First Report*. Belfast: Blackstaff Press.

Gallagher, A.M., McEwen, A. and Knipe, D. (1996) *A Levels and Science. Report to the Equal Opportunities Commission in Northern Ireland*. Belfast: EOCNI.

Gallagher, T. and Smith, A. (2000) *The effects of the selective system of secondary education in Northern Ireland: main report*. Bangor; Department of Education.

Gallagher, T., McEwen, A. and Knipe, D. (1997) 'Science education policy: a survey of the participation of sixth-form pupils in science and other subjects over a ten year period, 1985–1995', *Research Papers in Education*, 12: 121–42.

Gardiner, F. (1993) 'Political Interest and participation of Irish Women 1922–1992: The unfinished revolution', in A. Smyth (ed.) *Irish Women's Studies* Reader, Dublin: Attic Press.

Gardner, J.W. (1995) 'Leaders and followers', in J.T. Wren (ed.) *The Leaders Companion: Insights on Leadership Through The Ages*, New York: Free Press.

Garrison, M. and Bly, M. (1997) *Human relationships: Productive approaches for the workplace*, Boston: Allyn and Bacon.

Giddens, A. (1996) *In Defence of Sociology*. Cambridge: Polity Press.

Gillespie, N. (2001) *Outer North Interface Working Group: Evaluation Report*. Belfast, Community Evaluation Northern Ireland.

Gormley-Heenan, C. (2001) *From Protagonist to Pragmatist: Political Leadership in Societies in Transition*, Derry/Londonderry: INCORE.

Gough, B., Robinson, S., Kremer, J. and Mitchell, R. (1992) 'The social psychology of intergroup conflict: an appraisal of Northern Ireland research', *Canadian Psychology*, 33: 645-50.

Greer, J.E. (1972) *A Questioning Generation*. Belfast: Church of Ireland Board of Education.

Greer, J.E. (1978) Religious Education in State Primary Schools in Northern Ireland, *The Northern Teacher*, 13: 11–16.

Greer, J.E. (1979/80) *Religious Education in State Primary Schools in Northern Ireland*. The Northern Teacher, 13: 7–11.

Greer, J.E. (1983) 'The county school in Northern Ireland', *The Northern Teacher*, 14: 6–11.

Greer, J. E. (1985) 'Viewing "the other side" in Northern Ireland: Openness and attitudes to religion among Catholic and Protestant adolescents', *Journal for the Scientific Study of Religion*, 24: 275–92.

Greer, J.E. (1991) 'Education reform in Northern Ireland: the place of religious education and worship in schools', *British Journal of Religious Education*, 13: 190–98.

Greer, J.E. and Brown, W. (1981) 'The inspection of religious education in Northern Ireland schools', *The Northern Teacher*, 13: 3–7.

Gudykunst, W. B. and Hammer, M. R. (1988) 'The influence of social identity and intimacy of interethnic relationships on uncertainty reduction processes', *Human Communication Research*, 14: 569–601.

Hall, M. (2000) *Restoring Relationships: a Community Exploration of Anti-Social Behaviour, Punishment Beatings and Restorative Justice*. Newtownabbey: Island Publications.

Hall, S. (1991) 'The local and the global: Globalization and ethnicity', in King, A. (ed.), *Culture, Globalization and the World-System: Contemporary Conditions for the Representation of Identity*, London: Methuen.

Hamiliton, A., McCartney, C., Anderson, T. and Finn, A. (1990) *Violence and Communities*, Coleraine: Centre for the Study of Conflict, University of Ulster.

Hamilton, A. (1995) 'The effects of violence in Communities', *Sixth Public Discussion: The Effects of Violence*. Central Library, 15 June, 1995. University of Ulster.

Hamilton, M. (2001) *Working Relationships? An Evaluation of Community Mobile Phone Networks in Northern Ireland*. Belfast, Community Relations Council.

Harbison, J.I. (ed.) (1983) *Children of the Trouble: Children in Northern Ireland*, Belfast: Stranmillis College Learning Resources Unit.

Harbison, J.J.M. and Harbison, J.I. (eds.) (1980) *A Society Under Stress: Children and Young People in Northern Ireland*, Somerset: Open Books.

Hargie, C. and Tourish, D. (1997) Relational communication. In O. Hargie (ed.) *The Handbook of Communication Skills*. London: Routledge.

Hargie, O. and Dickson, D. (in press) *Skilled Interpersonal Communication: Research, Theory and Practice*. London: Routledge.

Hargie, O. and Tourish, D. (eds.) (2000) *Handbook of Communication Audits for Organisations*. London: Routledge.

Hargie, O., Dickson, D. and Hargie, C. (1995) 'The effects of religious affiliation in Northern Ireland upon levels of self-disclosure of undergraduates', *International Journal of Adolescence and Youth* 5: 173–87.

Hargie, O., Dickson, D. and Rainey, S. (1999) *Communication and Relational Development Among Young Adult Catholics and Protestants: A Report to the Central Community Relations Unit.* Jordanstown: University of Ulster.

Hargie, O., Dickson, D. and Rainey, S. (2002) 'Religious difference, inter-group trust, attraction, and disclosure amongst young people in Northern Ireland', *International Journal of Adolescence and Youth*, 10, 213–35.

Harris, R. (1972) *Prejudice and Tolerance in Ulster: A Study of Neighbours and Strangers in a Border Community*, Manchester: Manchester University Press.

Hastings, S. (2000a) 'Asian Indian "self-suppression" and self-disclosure: Enactment and adaptation of cultural identity', *Journal of Language and Social Psychology* 19: 85–109.

Hastings, S. (2000b) '"Egocasting" in the avoidance of dialogue: An intercultural perspective', in S. Petronio (ed.) *Balancing the Secrets of Private Disclosures*, Mahwah, New Jersey: Lawrence Erlbaum.

Haydon, C. (1993) *Anti-Catholicism in Eighteenth-Century England.* Manchester: Manchester University Press.

Hayes, M. (1998) *Minority Verdict.* Belfast: Blackstaff.

Hempton, D. (1996) *Religion and Political Culture in Britain and Ireland.* Cambridge: Cambridge University Press.

Hermann, T. and Newman, D. (2000) 'A path strewn with thorns: Along the difficult road of Israeli-Palestinian peacemaking', in J. Darby and R. MacGinty (eds.) T*he Management of Peace Processes*, London: Macmillan.

Heskin, K. (1980) *Northern Ireland. A Psychological Analysis.* Dublin: Gill and Macmillan.

Hewstone, M. and Brown, R. (1986) 'Contact is not enough: An intergroup perspective on the Contact Hypothesis', in M. Hewstone and R. Brown (eds) *Contact and Conflict in Intergroup Encounters.* Oxford: Basil Blackstaff.

Hewstone, M. and Cairns, E. (2001) 'Social psychology and intergroup conflict', in D. Chirot and M.E.P. Seligman (eds) *Ethno-Political Warfare: Causes, Consequences, and Possible Solutions.* Washington, D.C.: American Psychological Association.

Hewstone, M., Cairns, E., McClernon, F., Judd, C. M., and Voci, A. (2001a) 'Intergroup contact in a divided society: Changing group beliefs in Northern Ireland'. Paper presented at *BPS Annual Conference*, Glasgow.

Hewstone, M., Cairns, E., McClernon, F., and Paolini, S. (2001b) 'Social-psychological interventions and conflict resolution in Northern Ireland: Some lessons from recent research'. Paper presented at *BPS Annual Conference*, Glasgow.

Hewstone, M., Rubin, M. and Willis, H. (2002) 'Intergroup bias', *Annual Review of Psychology*, 53: 575–604.

Hickman, M. (1995) *Religion, Class and Identity.* Aldershot: Avebury.

Higgins, G. (2000) *Great Expectations: The Myth of Antichrist in Northern Ireland.* Unpublished Ph.D. Thesis, Queen's University, Belfast.

Hill, C. (1971) *The Anti-Christ in Seventeenth-Century England.* Oxford: Oxford University Press.

Hinds, B. (1999) 'Women working for peace in Northern Ireland', in Y. Galligan, E. Ward and R. Wilford (eds.) *Contesting Politics. Women in Ireland North and South*, Dublin: Institute for Public Administration.

Hinds, J. (1998) *Dealing with difference: A directory of peace, reconciliation, and community relations projects in Northern Ireland*, 2nd edn. Belfast: Northern Ireland Community Relations Council.

Hinkle, S., Fox-Cardamone, F., Haseleu, J.A., Brown, R. and Irwin, L.M. (1996) 'Grassroots political action as an intergroup phenomenon', *Journal of Social Issues* 52: 39–51.

HMSO (1995) *Framework for the Future*. Belfast: HMSO.

Hornsey, M.J. and Hogg, M.A. (1999) 'Subgroup differentiation as a response to an overly-inclusive Group: A test of optimal distinctiveness theory', *European Journal of Social Psychology* 29: 543–50.

Houston, J., Crozier, W. and Walker, P. (1990) 'The assessment of ethnic sensitivity among Northern Ireland schoolchildren', *British Journal of Developmental Psychology* 8: 419–22.

Hughes, J. (1998) *'Single identity' community relations in Northern Ireland: Final report*. Jordanstown: School of Public Policy, Economics and Law, University of Ulster.

Hughes, J. and Carmichael, P. (1998) 'Community relations in Northern Ireland: Attitudes to contact and segregation', In G. Robinson, D. Heenan, A.M. Gray and K. Thompson (eds) *Social Attitudes in Northern Ireland: The Seventh Report*. Aldershot: Gower.

Hughes, J. and Donnelly, C. (2001) *Community Relations in NI – Northern Ireland Life and Times Survey*. Jordanstown: School of Public Policy, Economics and Law, University of Ulster.

Hughes, J. and, Knox, C. (1997) *Ten years wasted effort? An overview of community relations in Northern Ireland*. Jordanstown: University of Ulster.

Hunter, J.A., and Stringer, M. (1999) 'Attributional bias and identity and a conflict region: The moderating effects of status' *Current Research in Social Psychology* 4: 160–65.

Hyndman, M. (1996) *Further Afield: Journeys From a Protestant Past*. Belfast: Beyond the Pale Publications.

INCORE (1995) *Coming out of Violence: Peace Dividends*, Coleraine, Northern Ireland: INCORE, University of Ulster.

Islam, M.R. and Hewstone, M. (1993) 'Dimensions of contact as predictors of intergroup anxiety, perceived out-group variability, and out-group attitude: An integrative model', *Personality and Social Psychology Bulletin* 19: 700–10.

Jahoda, G. and Harrison, S. (1975) 'Belfast children: some effects of a conflict environment', *Irish Journal of Psychology* 3: 1–19.

Jarman, N. (1997) *On the Edge: Community Perspectives on the Civil Disturbances in North Belfast, June-September 1996*. Belfast, CDC.

Jarman, N. (1999) *Drawing Back from the Edge: Community Based Responses to Violence in North Belfast*. Belfast, CDC.

Jarman, N. and O'Halloran, C. (2000) *Peacelines or Battlefields: Responding to Violence in Interface Areas*. Belfast, CDC.

Jarman, N. and O'Halloran, C. (2001) 'Recreational rioting: Young people, interface areas and violence'. *Child Care in Practice*, 7: 2–16.

Jenkins, R. (1997) *Rethinking Ethnicity*. London: Sage.

Johnston, L. and Hewstone, M. (1992) 'Cognitive models of stereotype change: III. Subtyping and the perceived typicality of disconfirming group members', *Journal of Experimental Social Psychology* 28: 360–86.

Jones, E., Gallois, C., Callan, V. and Barker, M. (1999) 'Strategies of accommodation: Development of a coding system for conversational interaction', *Journal of Language and Society* 18: 123–52.

Kanter, R. (1988) 'Three tiers for innovation research', *Communication Research*, 15: 509–23.

Kelly, A. J. D. (1989) 'Ethnic identification, association, and redefinition: Muslim Pakistanis and Greek Cypriots in Britain', in K. Liebkind (ed.) *New Identities in Europe: Immigrant Ancestry and the Ethnic Identity of Youth.* Aldershot: Gower.

Kitchin, H. (2000) *Taking Part: Promoting Children's and Young People's Participation in Safer Communities.* London: Local Government Information Unit.

Kliot, N. and Mansfeld, Y. (1999) 'Case studies of conflict and territorial organisation in divided cities', *Progress in Planning,* 52: 167–225.

Knapp, M. L., and Vangelisti, A. (1992) *Interpersonal Communication and Human Relationships.* Boston: Allyn and Bacon.

Knox C (1995) 'Concept mapping in policy evaluation: a research review of community Relations in Northern Ireland', *Evaluation,* 1: 65–79.

Knox, C. (1994) 'Conflict resolution at the micro level: Community relations in Northern Ireland', *Journal of Conflict Resolution,* 30: 595–619.

Knox, C. and Hughes, J. (1994) *Cross community contact: Northern Ireland and Israel – A Comparative Perspective.* Ulster Papers in Public Policy and Management, Number 32.

Kremer, J., Barry, R, and McNally, A. (1986) 'The Misdirected Letter and the Quasi-Questionnaire: Unobtrusive measures of prejudice in Northern Ireland', *Journal of Applied Social Psychology* 16: 303–09.

Leitch, R and Kilpatrick, R (1999) *Inside the Gates: Schools the Troubles.* Belfast: Save the Children Fund.

Levi-Strauss, C. (1962) *La Pensee Sauvage.* Paris: Plon.

Leyton, E. (1975) *The One Blood: Kinship and Class in an Irish Village.* Newfoundland: Memorial University Press.

Liechty, J. and Clegg, C. (2001) *Moving Beyond Sectarianism: Religion, Conflict, and Reconciliation in Northern Ireland.* Blackrock: The Columba Press.

Little, A. and Perett, D. (2002) 'Putting beauty back in the eye of the beholder', *The Psychologist,* 15: 28–32.

Livingstone, J. (1987) 'Equality of opportunity in education in Northern Ireland.' In Osborne,R.D., Cormack, R.J. and Miller, R.L. (eds) *Education and Policy in Northern Ireland.* Belfast: Policy Research Institute.

Loughlin, J. (1985) 'The Irish Protestant Home Rule Association and Nationalist Politics', *Irish Historical Studies* 24: 341–60.

Luddy, M. (1997) 'Women and politics in nineteenth century Ireland', in M G Valiulis and M O'Dowd (eds) *Women and Irish History,* Dublin: Wolfhound Press.

MacCurtain, M. (1985) 'The history image.' In E. NiChuilleanain (ed.) *Irish Women: Image and Achievement,* Dublin: Arlen House.

MacGinty, R. and Darby, J. (2002) *Guns and Government: The Management of the Northern Ireland Peace Process.* London: Palgrave.

Magee, J. (1970) 'The teaching of Irish history in Irish schools', *The Northern Teacher,* 10: 15–21.

Mahon, E. and Morgan, V. (1999) 'State feminism in Ireland', in E. Ward and R. Wilford (eds.) *Contesting Politics: Women in Ireland North and South,* Dublin: Institute for Public Administration.

Malone, J. (1973) 'Schools and community relations', *The Northern Teacher,* 11: 19–30.

Marsden, C. (1996) *Corporate Citizenship,* Warwick: University of Warwick.

Massey, D. and Denton, N. (1993) *American Apartheid: Segregation and the Making of the Underclass,* Cambridge, MA: Harvard University Press.

McClenahan, C., Cairns, E., Dunn, S. and Morgan, V. (1996) 'Intergroup friendships: Integrated and desegregated schools in Northern Ireland', *The Journal of Social Psychology*, 136: 549–58.

McCroskey, J. C., and Richmond, V. P. (1979) *The Reliability and Validity of Scales for the Measurement of Interpersonal Attraction and Homophily*. Paper presented at the Eastern Communication Association, Phil.

McEwen, A., Curry, C.A. and Watson, J. (1986) 'Subject preferences at A level in Northern Ireland', *European Journal of Science Education*, 8: 39–49.

McEwen, A., Knipe, D. and Gallagher, T. (1997b) 'The impact of single-sex and coeducational schooling on participation and achievement in science: a ten-year perspective', *Research in Science and Technological Education*, 15: 223–33.

McEwen, A., Knipe, D. and Gallagher, T. (1997a) 'Science and arts choices at A-Level in Northern Ireland: a ten-year perspective', *International Journal of Science Education*, 19: 761–71.

McGarry, J. (1998) 'Political settlements in Northern Ireland and South Africa', *Political Studies*, 46: 853–70.

McKay, S. (2000) *Northern Protestants: An Unsettled People*. Belfast: Blackstaff.

McKeown, M. (1973) 'Civil unrest: Secondary schools' survey', *The Northern Teacher*, 11: 39–42.

McKernan, J. (1982) 'Constraints on the handling of Controversial Issues in Northern Ireland Post-Primary Schools', *British Educational Research Journal*, 8: 57–71.

McVeigh, R. (1995) 'Cherishing the children of the nation unequally: sectarianism in Ireland', in P. Clancy, S. Drudy, K. Lynch and L. O'Dowd (eds), *Irish Society: Sociological Perspectives*, Dublin: Institute of Public Administration.

McWhirter, L. (1989) 'Longitudinal evidence on the teenage years.' In Harbison, J.I. (ed.) *Growing Up in Northern Ireland*. Belfast: Stranmillis College.

McWhirter, L. and Gamble, R. (1982) 'Development of ethnic awareness in the absence of physical cues', *Irish Journal of Psychology* 5: 109–27.

McWhirter, L., Duffy, U. Barry, R. and McGuinness, G. (1987) 'Transition from school to work: Cohort evidence' In Osborne,R.D., Cormack, R.J. and Miller, R.L. (eds) *Education and Policy in Northern Ireland*. Belfast: Policy Research Institute.

McWilliams, M. and McKernan, J. (1993) *Bringing it Out to the Open Domestic Violence in Northern Ireland,* Belfast: Department of Health and Social Security.

Mees, L. (2000) 'The Basque Peace Process, Nationalism and Political Violence', In Darby, J. and MacGinty, R. (eds.) (2000) *The Management of Peace Processes*, London: Macmillan.

Meyer, J. and Allen, N. (1997) *Commitment in the Workplace*. London: Sage.

Miall, H., Ramsbotham, O., and Woodhouse, T. (1999) *Contemporary Conflict Resolution: the Prevention, Management and Transformation of Deadly Conflict*. Oxford: Polity Press.

Millar, J. (1973) *Popery and Politics in England 1660–1688*. Cambridge: Cambridge University Press.

Millar, R. and Gallagher, M. (2000) 'The interview approach'. In O. Hargie and D. Tourish (eds) *Handbook of Communication Audits for Organisations*. London: Routledge.

Miller, D.W. (1978) *Queen's Rebels: Ulster Loyalism in Historical Perspective*. Dublin: Gill and Macmillan.

Miller, L. C., Berg, J. H., and Archer, R. L. (1983) 'Openers: Individuals who elicit intimate self-disclosure', *Journal of Personality and Social Psychology*, 44: 1234–44.

Ministry of Education (1950) *Report of the Ministry of Education*. Belfast: Ministry of Education.

Moffatt, C. (Ed) (1993) *Education together for a change: integrated education and community relations in Northern Ireland*. Belfast: Fortnight Educational Trust.

Morgan, D. (1997) *Focus Groups and Qualitative Research* (2nd ed.). Thousand Oaks, Cal.: Sage.

Morgan, V. and Fraser, G. (1994) *The Company We Keep: Women, Community and Organisations*. Coleraine: Centre for the Study of Conflict, University of Ulster.

Morgan, V. and Fraser, G. (1995) 'Women and the Northern Ireland conflict. Experiences and responses', in S. Dunn (ed.) *Facets of the Conflict in Northern Ireland*. London: Macmillan.

Moriarty, G. (2000) 'Coffee with Trimble can help to resolve differences', *Irish Times*, (30/5/00).

Morrissey, M. and Smyth, M. (2001) *Northern Ireland After the Good Friday Agreement: Victims and Victimisation*. London: Pluto.

Morrow, D. (1994) *The Churches and Inter-community Relationships*, Coleraine: Centre for the Study of Conflict.

Morrow, D. (2000) 'Nothing to fear but ...? Unionists and the Northern Ireland Peace Process', in D. Murray (ed.) *Protestant perceptions of the peace process in Northern Ireland*. Centre for Peace and Development Studies. University of Limerick.

Morrow, D. Birrell, D., Greer, J. and O'Keeffe, T. (1994) *The Churches and Inter Community Relations in Northern Ireland*, Coleraine: Centre for the Study of Conflict, University of Ulster.

Moxon-Browne, E. (1983) *Nation, Class and Creed in Northern Ireland*. Aldershot: Gower.

Murray, D. (1978) 'Education and community in Northern Ireland'. *The Northern Teacher*, 13: 3–6.

Murray, D. (1983) 'Rituals and symbols as contributors to the culture of Northern Ireland primary schools'. *Irish Educational Studies*, 3: 238–55.

Murray, D. (1985a) *Worlds Apart: segregated schools in Northern Ireland*. Belfast: Appletree Press.

Murray, D. (1985b) 'Identity: a covert pedagogy in Northern Irish schools'. *Irish Educational Studies*, 5: 182–97.

Murray, D. (2000) Protestant perceptions of the peace process in Northern Ireland. Centre for Peace and Development Studies: University of Limerick.

Murray, D. and Darby, J. (1978) The Vocational Aspirations and Expectations of School Leavers in Londonderry and Strabane. *Belfast: Fair Employment Agency Research Paper 6*.

Murray, D. and Darby, J. (1983) 'The transition from school to work (2) The Londonderry and Strabane Study: Out and down in Derry and Strabane'; in Cormack, R.J. and Osborne, R.D. (eds.) *Religion, Education and Employment: aspects of equal opportunity in Northern Ireland*. Belfast: Appletree Press.

Murtagh, B. (1994) *Ethnic Space and the Challenge to Land Use Planning: A Study of Belfast's Peacelines*. Jordanstown, Centre for Policy Research, University of Ulster.

Murtagh, B. (1998) 'Planning for anywhere: Housing policy in Northern Ireland', *Housing Studies*, 13(6): 833–9.

Murtagh, B. (2001) 'Integrated social housing in Northern Ireland', *Housing Studies*, 16: 771–89.

Murtagh, B. (2002) *The Politics of Territory: Policy and Segregation in Northern Ireland.* Basingstoke, Palgrave.

Neill, W. Fitzsimons, D. S., and Murtagh, B. (1995) *Reimaging the Pariah City. Urban Development in Belfast and Detroit.* Aldershot: Avebury Publishing Ltd.

NICS (1994) *Fifth Report of the NICS Equal Opportunities Unit.* Belfast: NICS.

NIVT – Northern Ireland Voluntary Trust (2001) *Survey of the women's sector in Northern Ireland.* Belfast: NIVT.

Nordlinger, E. (1972) *Conflict Regulation in Divided Societies.* Cambridge, Mass: Centre for International Affairs, Harvard University

Norman, E.R. (1968) *Anti-Catholicism in Victorian England,* London: Allen and Unwin.

Northern Ireland Housing Executive (1999) *Towards a Community Relations Strategy.* Belfast, NIHE.

Northern Ireland Housing Executive (NIHE) (1998) *Northern Ireland House Condition Survey 1996.* Belfast, NIHE.

Northern Ireland Housing Executive (NIHE) (2000) *NIHE Public Attitudes Survey,* Belfast: NIHE.

Northern Ireland Life and Times Survey (1998) http://www.qub.ac.uk/ss/csr/nilt

Northern Ireland Life and Times Survey (1999) http://www.qub.ac.uk/ss/csr/nilt

Northern Ireland Life and Times Survey (2000) http://www.qub.ac.uk/ss/csr/nilt

Northover, M. (1988a) 'Bilinguals and linguistic identities', in J. N. Jorgensen, E. Hansen. A. Holmen, and J. Gimbel (eds) *Bilingualism in Society and School. Copenhagen Studies.* Bilingualism Vol 5. Clevedon: Multilingual Matters.

Northover, M. (1988b) 'Bilinguals or dual linguistic identities?' in J. W. Berry and R. C. Annis (eds) *Ethnic Psychology* (International Association for Cross-Cultural Psychology). Lisse, Netherlands: Swets and Zeitlinger.

O'Connor, S. (1980) 'Reports – "Chocolate Cream Soldiers": evaluating an experiment in non-sectarian education in Northern Ireland', *Curriculum Studies,* 12: 263–70.

Office of the First Minister and Deputy First Minister (OFMDFM). (2001) Divisions in Society: Northern Ireland today. Review of Community relations Policy Working Paper. Retrieved from the World Wide Web, 30 November, 2001. http://www.ofmd fmni.gov.uk/communityrelationsunit/working_ paper/ part4.htm

O'Malley, P. (2001) 'Northern Ireland and South Africa: Hope and history at a crossroads', in J. McGarry (ed.) *Northern Ireland and the Divided World: Post Agreement Northern Ireland in Comparative Perspective,* Oxford: OUP

O'Toole, M. (2000) 'Adams anger at talks boycott', *Irish News,* (23/2/00)

Osborne, R.D. (1985) 'Religion and educational qualifications in Northern Ireland'. *Belfast: Fair Employment Agency Research Paper 8.*

Osborne, R.D. (1986) 'Segregated schools and examination results in Northern Ireland: some preliminary research', *Educational Research,* 28: 43–50.

Osborne, R.D. and Cormack, R.J. (1989) 'Gender and Religion as issues in education, training and entry to work'; in Harbison, J.I. (ed.) *Growing Up in Northern Ireland.* Belfast: Stranmillis College.

Osborne, R.D. and Murray, R.C. (1978) Educational Qualifications and Religious Affiliation in Northern Ireland: an examination of GCE 'O' and 'A' Levels. Belfast: *Fair Employment Agency Research Paper 3.*

Osborne, R.D., Gallagher, A.M. and Cormack, R.J. (1989) *Review of Aspects of Education in Northern Ireland, Annex H, Fourteenth Annual report of the Sanding Advisory Commission on Human Rights,* London: HMSO.

Patten Report (1999) *A New Beginning: Policing in Northern Ireland, the Report of the Independent Commission on Policing in Northern Ireland.* Belfast.

Paz, D.G. (1992) *Popular Anti-Catholicism in Mid-Victorian England,* Stanford: Stanford University Press.

Pettigrew, T.F. (1971) *Racially Separate or Together?* New York: McGraw-Hill.

Pettigrew, T.F. (1979) 'The ultimate attribution error: Extending Allport's cognitive analysis of prejudice', *Personality and Social Psychology Bulletin,* 5: 461–76.

Pettigrew, T.F. (1986) 'The intergroup contact hypothesis reconsidered', in M. Hewstone and R. Brown (eds) *Contact and Conflict in Intergroup Encounters.* Oxford: Blackwell.

Pettigrew, T.F. (1997) 'Generalised intergroup contact effects on prejudice' *Personality and Social Psychology Bulletin,* 23: 173–85.

Pettigrew, T.F. (1998) 'Intergroup contact theory', *Annual Review of Psychology,* 49: 65–85.

Pettigrew, T.F and Meertens, R. W. (1995) 'Subtle and blatant prejudice in western Europe', *European Journal of Social Psychology,* 25: 57–75.

Pettigrew, T.F. and Tropp, L.R. (2000) 'Does intergroup contact reduce prejudice: Recent meta-analytic findings', in S. Oskamp et al. (eds) *Reducing prejudice and discrimination. The Claremont Symposium on Applied Social Psychology.* Mahwah, NJ: Lawrence Erlbaum Associates.

Poole, M. (1982) 'Religious segregation in urban Northern Ireland', in F. W. Boal and J.N.H. Douglas (eds) *Integration and Division: Geographical Perspectives on the Northern Ireland Problem.* London: Academic Press.

Poole, M. and Doherty, P. (1996) *Ethnic Residential Segregation in Northern Ireland,* Coleraine: Centre for the Study of Conflict, University of Ulster.

Powell, R.A. and Single, H.M. (1996) 'Focus groups', *International Journal of Quality in Health Care,* 8: 199–206.

Power, A. and Tunstall, R. (1997) *Dangerous Disorder: riots and violent disturbances in thirteen areas of Britain, 1991–92.* York, Joseph Rowntree Foundation.

PPRU (1992) *Northern Ireland Annual Abstracts of Statistics No. 11,* Belfast: Department of Finance and Personnel.

PPRU (1994) *The Continuous Household Survey Bulletin,* Belfast, PPRU.

Purdie, B. (1990) *Politics in the Streets,* Belfast: Blackstaff.

Quinn, E. (1998) *From tea to tribunals – a profile of the extent, diversity and complexity of Advice and Support Services provided by community based Women's Centres in the Greater Belfast Area,* Belfast: Women's Support Network.

Rainey, S., Dickson, D. and Hargie, O. (in press) 'Learning together, living apart: The experiences of university students in Northern Ireland', *International Journal of Qualitative Studies in Education.*

Reno, R., and Kenny, D. (1992) 'Effects of self-consciousness and social anxiety on self-disclosure among unacquainted individuals: An application of the social relations model', *Journal of Personality* 60: 79–95.

Richardson, N. L. (1997) *Education for Mutual Understanding and Cultural Heritage.* CAIN Web site http://cain.ulst.ac.uk

Robertson, R. (1992) *Globalisation.* London: Sage.

Robinson, B. and Nolan, S. (1999) 'Counteract: Working for change', *Fordham International Law Journal,* 22: 1668–80.

Robson, B.T., Bradford, M. and Turnbull, B. (1994) *Relative Deprivation in Northern Ireland.* Policy Planning and Research Unit, Department of Finance, Northern Ireland.

Robson, C. (1993) *Real World Research: a resource for social scientists and practitioner-researchers.* Oxford: Blackwell

Robson. B. (1994) *Relative Deprivation in Northern Ireland.* The Department of Finance and Personnel, Belfast: PPRU.

Rooney, E. (1992) 'Women, community and politics in Northern Ireland – 'Isms' in action', *Journal of Gender Studies,* 1: 475–491.

Rooney, E. (1995) 'Political division, practical alliance, problems for women in conflict', in J. Hoff and M. Coulter (eds.) *Irish Women's Voices Past and Present,* Bloomington, University of Indiana Press.

Rooney, E. and Woods, M. (1995) *Women, Community and Politics in Northern Ireland,* Belfast: University of Ulster.

Rose, R. (1971) *Governing without Consensus.* London: Faber.

Rothstein, R. (ed.) (1999) *After The Peace: Resistance and Reconciliation.* Boulder, CO: Lynne Rienner

Rougier, N. (2000) *Ethno-religious identities: An identity structure analysis of clergy in Ireland.* DPhil thesis. Jordanstown: University of Ulster.

Rowthorne, B. and Wayne, N. (1988) *Northern Ireland – the political economy of conflict.* Cambridge: Polity Press.

Royal Ulster Constabulary (2001) *Statistics: Security Situation and Public Order.* www.ruc.police.uk

Ruane, J. and Todd, J. (1996) *The Dynamics of Conflict in Northern Ireland,* Cambridge: Cambridge University Press.

Russell, J. (1974/5) 'The sources of conflict', *The Northern Teacher,* 11: 3–11.

SACHR (Standing Advisory Commission on Human Rights) (1992) *Seventeenth Report of the Standing Advisory Commission on Human Rights, House of Commons Paper 54,* London: HMSO.

Saunders, P. (1990) *A Nation of Home Owners,* London: Unwin Hyman.

Seals, D. (1996) Personal correspondence with the authors.

Seekings, J. (2000) 'Introduction: urban studies in South Africa after Apartheid', *International Journal of Urban and Regional Research,* 24: 832–40.

Segrin, C. (1996) 'The relationship between social skills deficits and psychosocial problems. A test of vulnerability model', *Communication Research* 23: 425–50.

Seitles, M. (1996) 'The perpetualisation of residential racial segregation in America: historical discrimination, modern forms of exclusion and inclusionary remedies', *Journal of Land Use and Environmental Law,* 14: 1–30.

Seligman, M.E.P. (1998) 'Ethnopolitical warfare', *APA Monitor* 29: 3.

Sheehan, M. and Tomlinson, M. (1998) 'Government policies and employers' attitudes towards long-term unemployed people in Northern Ireland', *Journal of Social Policy,* 27: 447–70.

Sherif, M. and Sherif, C. (1953) *Groups in Harmony and Tension: An Integration of Studies on Intergroup Relations.* New York: Octagon Books.

Shirlow, P. (1997) 'Class, materialism and the fracturing of traditional alignments', in B. Graham (ed.) *In Search of Ireland,* London: Routledge.

Shirlow, P. (1999) *Fear, Mobility and Living in the Ardoyne and Upper Ardoyne Communities.* Coleraine, School of Environmental Studies, University of Ulster.

Shirlow, P., Murtagh, B. *et al.* (2001) *Spaces of Fear: Measuring and Modelling 'Chill Factors' in Belfast.* Research Report: University of Ulster.

SICDP (Springfield Inter Community Development Project) (1999) 'The Missing Peace': Development Plan. Belfast, SICDP.

Skilbeck, M. (1973) 'The school and cultural development', The Northern Teacher, 11: 13–18.

Sklair, L. (1999) 'Globalisation', in S. Taylor (ed.) Sociology: Issues and Debates, London: Macmillan.

Smith, A. (1999) Education and the Peace Process in Northern Ireland. Retrieved July 18, 2001, from CAIN on-line database on the World Wide Web: http://cain.ulst.ac.uk

Smith, A. and Dunn, S. (1990) Extending school links, Coleraine: University of Ulster.

Smith, A. and Murray, D. (1993) The chance of a lifetime: An evaluation of project children. Coleraine: University of Ulster.

Smith, A. and Robinson, A. (1992) Education for Mutual Understanding: Perceptions and policy. Coleraine: Centre for study of conflict, University of Ulster.

Smith, A. and Robinson, A. (1996) Education for Mutual Understanding: The initial statutory years. Coleraine: Centre for study of conflict, University of Ulster.

Smith, M.B. (1999) 'Political psychology and peace: A half-century perspective', Peace and Conflict: Journal of Peace Psychology 5: 1–16.

Smyth, M. (1995) Limitations on the Capacity for Citizenship in Post Cease-fires Northern Ireland. Paper presented at The Inaugural Meeting of the European Observatory on Citizenship: University College, Cork, November, 1995. Derry/Londonderry: Templegrove Action Research Ltd.

Smyth, M. (2000) 'The human consequences of armed conflict: constructing "victimhood" in the context of the Northern Ireland Troubles' in M. Cox, A. Guelke and F. Stephen (eds.) A Farewell to Arms? – from Long War to Long Peace in Northern Ireland, Manchester: University of Manchester Press.

Smyth, M. and Fay, M.T. (2000) Personal Accounts from Northern Ireland's Troubles: Public Chaos, Private Loss. London: Pluto.

Snyder, R. and Morris, J. (1984) 'Organisational communication and performance', Journal of Applied Psychology, 69: 461–65.

Spencer, AECW (1987) 'Arguments for an Integrated School System'; in Osborne,R.D., Cormack, R.J. and Miller, R.L. (eds) Education and Policy in Northern Ireland. Belfast: Policy Research Institute.

Stephan, W.G. and Stephan, C.W. (1985) 'Intergroup anxiety', Journal of Social Issues 41: 157–75.

Stringer, M. and Cairns, E. (1983) 'Catholic and Protestant young people's ratings of stereotyped Protestant and Catholic faces', British Journal of Social Psychology 22: 241–46.

Stringer, M. and McLaughlin-Cook, N. (1985) 'Effects of stereotypic and conflicting information on group categorisation in Northern Ireland', Journal of Applied Psychology 15: 399–407.

Stringer, M., and Cairns, E. (1983) 'Catholic and Protestant young people's ratings of stereotypic Protestant and Catholic faces', British Journal of Social Psychology 22: 241–46.

Stringer, M., and Hvattum, O. (1990) 'Intergroup Communication on religion and the troubles among university students in Northern Ireland', The Irish Journal of Education, xxiv, 2: 48–61.

Stringer, P. and Robinson G. (1993) Social Attitudes in Northern Ireland 1992-1993, 3rd edn. Belfast: Blackstaff Press.

Sutherland, A.E. and Gallagher, A.M. (1986). *Transfer and the Upper Primary School.* Belfast: Northern Ireland Council for Educational Research.

Sutherland, A.E. and Gallagher, A.M. (1987) *Pupils in the Border Band: a study of pupils awarded an M grade in the Transfer Procedure from primary to post-primary school, Report No. 3 from the NICER Transfer Procedure Project,* Belfast: Northern Ireland Council for Educational Research.

Tajfel, H. (1978) (ed.) *Differentiation Between Social Groups: Studies in the Social Psychology of Intergroup Relations.* London: Academic Press.

Tajfel, H. (1981) *Human groups and Social Categories.* Cambridge: Cambridge University Press.

Tajfel, H. (1982) *Social Identity and Intergroup Relations.* Cambridge: Cambridge UP.

Tajfel, H. and Turner, J. (1978) 'An integrative theory of intergroup conflict', in H. Tajfel (ed.) *Differentiation Between Social Groups: Studies in the Social Psychology of Intergroup Relations.* (European Monographs in social psychology, no. 14.) London: Academic Press.

Tajfel, H. and Turner, J.C. (1979) 'An integrative theory of intergroup conflict', in W.G. Austin and S. Worchel (eds) *The Social Psychology of Intergroup Relations.* Monterey, Cal.: Brooks/ Cole.

Tajfel, H., and Turner, C. J. (1986) 'The social identity of intergroup behavior'. In S. Worchel and W.G. Austin, (eds.) *Psychology of Intergroup Relations,* Chicago: Nelson-Hall Publishers.

Tardy, C.H. and Dindia, K. (1997) Self-disclosure. In O. Hargie (ed.) T*he Handbook of Communication Skills.* London: Routledge.

Tayeb, M. (1994) 'Japanese managers and British culture: A comparative case study', *The International Review of Human Resource Management,* 5: 145–66.

Teare, S.M. and Sutherland, A.E. (1988). *At Sixes and Sevens: a study of the curriculum in the upper primary school.* Belfast: Northern Ireland Council for Educational Research.

Toner, I.J. (1994) 'Children of "the Troubles" in Northern Ireland: perspectives and intervention', *International Journal of Behavioral Development* 17: 629–47.

Tracey, S. (1998) *Survey of Education programme and learner Support Service – Report,* Belfast: Shankill Women's Centre.

Trew, K. (1986) 'Catholic–Protestant contact in Northern Ireland', in M. Hewstone and R. Brown (eds) *Contact and Conflict in Intergroup Encounters.* Oxford: Basil Blackstaff.

Trew, K. (1989) 'Evaluating the impact of contact schemes for Catholic and Protestant children', in J. Harbison (ed.) *Growing Up in Northern Ireland.* Belfast: Stranmillis College.

Trew, K. (1992) 'Social psychological research on the conflict', *The Psychologist* 5: 342–44.

Trew, K. and Benson, D. (1996) 'Dimensions of social identity in Northern Ireland', in G.M. Breakwell and E. Lyons (eds) *Changing European Identities.* Oxford: Butterworth-Heinemann.

Turner, J. and Onarato, R. (1999) 'Social identity, personality, and the self-concept: A self-categorization perspective'. In T. Tyler, R. Kramer and O. John (eds) *The Psychology of the Social Self.* New Jersey: Lawrence Erlbaum.

Turner, J.C. (1982). 'Towards a cognitive redefinition of the social group', in H. Tajfel (ed.), *Social identity and intergroup relations.* Cambridge: Cambridge University Press.

Turner, J.C. (1984) 'Social identification and psychological group formation', in H. Tajfel (ed.) *The social dimension: European Developments in Social Psychology* (vol. 2). Cambridge: Cambridge University Press.

Turner, J.C., Hogg, M.A., Oakes, P.L., Reicher, S.D. and Wetherell, M.S. (1987) *Rediscovering the Social Group: A self-categorization Theory.* Oxford: Basil Blackwell.

Urquhart, D. (2000) *Women in Ulster politics 1890– 940.* Dublin: Irish Academic Press.

Van Slyke, E. (1999) *Listening to Conflict.* New York: AMACOM.

Voluntary Activity Unit (1999) *Community Development Working group, Mainstreaming Community Development in Heath and Personal Social Services, Report to the Targeting Health and Social Need Steering Group.* Belfast: Voluntary Activity Unit.

Waddell, N., and Cairns, E. (1986) 'Situational perspectives on social identity in Northern Ireland', *British Journal of Social Psychology,* 25: 25–31.

Ward, M. (1993) 'Suffrage first – above all else: an account of the Irish Suffrage Movement', in A. Smyth (ed.) *Irish Women's Studies Reader,* Dublin: Attic Press.

Weinreich, P. (1979) 'Cross-ethnic identification and self-rejection in a black adolescent', in G. K. Verma and C. Bagley (eds) *Race, Education and Identity.* London: Macmillan.

Weinreich, P. (1980/86/88) *Manual for Identity Exploration using Personal Constructs.* Coventry: University of Warwick, Economic and Social Research Council, Centre for Research in Ethnic Relations (2nd ed.).

Weinreich, P. (1983a) 'Psychodynamics of personal and social identity: Theoretical concepts and their measurement in adolescents from Belfast sectarian and Bristol minority groups', in A. Jacobson-Widding (ed.) *Identity: Personal and Socio-Cultural.* Uppsala: Almqvist and Wiksell and Atlantic Highlands, NJ: Humanities Press.

Weinreich, P. (1983b) 'Ulster's two interdependent identities and their sociopsychological maintenance'. Symposium: Ireland: Conflict dynamics in Ulster, Annual Meeting of the *International Society of Political Psychology,* Oxford.

Weinreich, P. (1986) 'The operationalisation of identity theory in racial and ethnic relations', in J. Rex, and D. Mason (eds) *Theories of Race and Ethnic Relations.* Cambridge: Cambridge UP.

Weinreich, P. (1989) 'Variations in ethnic identity: identity structure analysis', in K. Liebkind (ed.) *New Identities in Europe: Immigrant Ancestry and the Ethnic Identity of Youth.* Aldershot: Gower.

Weinreich, P. (1992) 'Socio-psychological maintenance of identity in Northern Ireland – a commentary' *The Psychologist,* 5: 345–46.

Weinreich, P. (1996) *ISA outline notes.* Jordanstown: University of Ulster.

Weinreich, P. (2002a) 'Identity structure analysis', in P. Weinreich and W. Saunderson (eds) *Analysing Identity: Cross-Cultural, Societal and Clinical Issues.* London: Routledge.

Weinreich, P. (2002b) 'Identity exploration: Theory into practice', in P. Weinreich and W. Saunderson (eds) *Analysing Identity: Cross-Cultural, Societal and Clinical Issues.* London: Routledge.

Weinreich, P. and Saunderson, W. (eds) (in press) *Analysing Identity: Cross-Cultural, Societal and Clinical Issues.* London: Routledge.

Weinreich, P., and Ewart, S. L. (1998) *IDEXwin (Identity Exploration for Windows). Computer Software.* Jordanstown: University of Ulster.

Weinreich, P., Bacova, V., and Rougier, N. (2002) 'Basic primordialism in ethnic and national identity', in P. Weinreich and W. Saunderson (eds) *Analysing Identity: Cross-Cultural, Societal and Clinical Issues.* London: Routledge.

Weinreich, P., Kelly, A., and Maja, C. (1988) 'Black youth on South Africa: situated identities and patterns of ethnic identifications', in D. Canter, J.C. Jesusino, L. Soczka, and G. M. Stephenson (eds) *Environmental Social Psychology.* Dordecht, Netherlands: Kluwer.

Weinreich, P., Luk C. L. and Bond, M. (1996) 'Ethnic stereotyping and identification in a multi-cultural context: "Acculturation" self esteem and identity diffusion in Hong Kong Chinese university students', *Psychology and Developing Societies* 8: 107–69.

Wells, I. and Burke, S. (1986) *Nursery Questions and Teachers' Answers*. Belfast: Northern Ireland Council for Educational Research.

Wheeless, L. R., and Grotz, J. (1977) 'The measurement of trust and its relationship to self-disclosure', *Human Communication Research*, 3, 250–57.

Whyte, J. (1990) *Interpreting Northern Ireland*. Oxford: Clarendon Press.

Wichert, S. (1991) *Northern Ireland Since 1945*. London and New York: Longman.

Wilson D. (1996) 'Adults first please... ', *CRC Journal* Spring: 6–9.

Wilson, D. and Tyrrell, J. (1995) 'Institutions for conciliation and mediation', in S. Dunn (ed.) *Facets of the Conflict in Northern Ireland*. London: St Martin.

Wilson, J.A. (1985). *Secondary School Organisation and Pupil Progress*. Belfast: Northern Ireland Council for Educational Research.

Wilson, J.A. (1986). *Transfer and the Structure of Secondary Education*. Belfast: Northern Ireland Council for Educational Research.

Wilson, J.A. (1987). 'Selection for secondary education'; in Osborne,R.D., Cormack, R.J. and Miller, R.L. (editors) E*ducation and Policy in Northern Ireland*. Belfast: Policy Research Institute.

Wilson, J.A. (1989). 'Educational Performance: a decade of evidence'; in Harbison, J.I. (ed.) *Growing Up in Northern Ireland*. Belfast: Stranmillis College.

Wilson, J.P. (1999) *A Place and a Name: Report of the Victims Commission/Áit agus Ainm: Tuarascáil an Choimisiún um Íospartaigh*. Dublin/Baile Átha Cliath: The Stationery Office/ Oifig and t-Soláthair.

Winstead, B. A., Derlega, V. J., and Montgomery, C. (1995) 'The quality of friendships at work and job satisfaction', *Journal of Social Psychology*, 12: 199–215.

Wolf, E.P. (1957) 'The invasion-succession sequence as a self-fulfilling prophecy', *Journal of Social Issues* 13: 7–20.

Wolf, E.P. (1960) 'Racial transition in a middle-class area', *Journal of Intergroup Relations* 1: 75–81.

Wolffe, J. (1991) *The Protestant Crusade in Great Britain*. Oxford: Clarendon Press.

Wright, F. (1987) *Northern Ireland: A Comparative Analysis*. Dublin: Gill and MacMillan.

Wright, S.C.; Aron, A., McLaughlin-Volpe, T. and Ropp, S.A. (1997) 'The extended contact effect: Knowledge of cross-group friendships and prejudice', *Journal of Personality and Social Psychology* 73: 73–90.

Zartman, I.W. (1997a) 'Dynamics and constraints in negotiations in internal conflicts', in I. W. Zartman and J. L. Rasmussen (eds.) *Peacemaking in International Conflict: Methods and Techniques*, Washington: D.C.: United States Institute of Peace.

Zartman, I.W. (1997b) 'Conclusions: The last mile' in I.W. Zartman and J. L. Rasmussen (eds.) *Peacemaking in International Conflict: Methods and Techniques*, Washington: D.C.: United States Institute of Peace.

INDEX